Peg Entwistle and
the Hollywood
Sign Suicide

Peg Entwistle and the Hollywood Sign Suicide

A Biography

JAMES ZERUK, JR.

Foreword by Eve Golden

McFarland & Company, Inc., Publishers
Jefferson, North Carolina, and London

Zeruk, James, Jr., 1961–
Peg Entwistle and the Hollywood sign suicide : a biography /
James Zeruk, Jr. ; foreword by Eve Golden.
p.   cm.
Includes bibliographical references and index.

ISBN 978-0-7864-7313-7
softcover : acid free paper ∞

1. Entwistle, Peg, 1908–1932.
2. Actresses—Great Britain—Biography.   I. Title.
PN2598.E49Z47 2014   792'.028'092—dc23   [B]   2013038298

British Library cataloguing data are available

© 2014 James Zeruk. All rights reserved

*No part of this book may be reproduced or transmitted in any form
or by any means, electronic or mechanical, including photocopying
or recording, or by any information storage and retrieval system,
without permission in writing from the publisher.*

On the cover: *inset* Peg Entwistle; *background* HOLLYWOODLAND
Sign (photographs courtesy Bruce Torrence Hollywood
Collection, hollywoodphotogrphs.com)

Manufactured in the United States of America

*McFarland & Company, Inc., Publishers
Box 611, Jefferson, North Carolina 28640
www.mcfarlandpub.com*

Table of Contents

Acknowledgments vii
Foreword by Eve Golden 1
Preface 3
Introduction 7
Prologue 9

ACT I
   1. The Curtain Rises 12
   2. Peg O' Peg's Heart 29
   3. Hollywoodland 43

ACT II
   4. The Stage Is Set 56
   5. The Work Begins 64
   6. As Broadway Nears 71
   7. At Last! 79
   8. Tommy 84
   9. Little White Lies on the Great White Way 92
 10. Between Curtains 104
 11. The Guild 108
 12. The Show Must Go On 120
 13. Elementary, My Dear Entwistle 127
 14. Flops, Flappers, Folly and Fun 134

ACT III
 15. Give My Regards to Broadway 146
 16. Mad Hope 151
 17. *Thirteen Women* 158

18. Cameras and Clapboards, Take One 165
19. Cameras and Clapboards, Take Two 170
20. The Love That Dared Not Speak Peg's Name 176
21. 24 Years 7 Months 12 Days 183
22. Why? 188
23. Setting Some Things Straight 196
24. The Curtain Lowers 208

Peg Entwistle Career Résumé 213
Chapter Notes 227
Bibliography 235
Index 239

Acknowledgments

Peg Entwistle's story could not have been told properly without the gracious cooperation of her family. My research into her life and work was extensive and unprecedented, but without the documents, family photographs, anecdotes, and memories provided to me by her brother Milton, his daughter Lauretta Slike, and Peg's cousin, Helen Reid, I would have had nothing more than a lengthy essay. To them, I am forever grateful.

First-time authors should all be so blessed as me to have a mentor and friend like Eve Golden, who, without a doubt, is the most talented and under-appreciated biographer the performing arts genre has ever known.

Thank you, Cheryl Strong, for putting a pen in my hand long ago. Inspectors Lou and Danny at the Santa Monica Library — thanks, guys, for supporting me even when I was a temperamental pain in your backsides. To the other staff members at Santa Monica — Vicki, Mark and the rest ... thanks for your help and patience. Alison Charie was there when I finished the final paragraphs. Thank you for your generosity, too, Ali. For all the help and advice given to me throughout this journey, a nod of deep appreciation goes to Richard Kukan, Henry Zecher, Michael Ankerich, Michelle Vogel and Mary Mallory. Thank you, Ron Erb for all the help with Peg's photos. Jenny Romero and the staff at the Margaret Herrick Library of the Academy of Motion Picture Arts and Sciences, and Lauren Buisson and Peggy Alexander at the Performing Arts Special Collections Dept. of the UCLA Charles Young Research Library were most helpful. Honorable mentions to Hope Anderson, Kate Johnson, Debbie Archainbald, Dr. Molly McClain, Chaplain Mary Katharine Allman, Suzanne Weiner, Erin DeMerchant, Chip Deffaa, Glenna Dunning, Beverly and John Deweese, Aunt Elaine, Cousin Elyse, Tom Gregory, Cheryl Rutigliano, Grant Hayter-Menzies, James Liversidge, Jeff Quinn, Jeremy Holstein, Laurie Thompson, Carol Uhrmacher, Leonard A. Coombs, Lynne Davies, Hannah Biagioni, Mark Crawford, Matthew T. Schaefer and Spencer Howard of the Herbert Hoover Presidential Library, Reeve Pierson, Matt Boylan, the Rev. Mary Katherine Allman, Richard Peterson, Robert Birchard (editor of the *AFI Catalogue of Feature Films*), Juliette Michaud, Mark Johnson, Ross Trevelyan, Carole Flynn, Ann Kautz, Jacqui Lewis Mittleman, Michael Rudas and all my other dear friends at Facebook. I would be remiss not to salute my brothers and sisters at the West Los Angeles Veterans Hospital, and to remember our Fallen. Big hug for Nunsa; coffee always tasted better when you poured. Thank you, Pastors Dave and Roche, and all the rest of the congregation at Brentwood Presbyterian Church who encouraged and supported me. To the guys in our Men's Group, Richard, Gregors, Bill, Jim, Phil, Paul, the other Paul, Dan ... you are awesome! Apologies to those I may have overlooked. Thank you, Mother, for all those late, late nights watching the Late, Late Shows and Golden Age films when TV was fun in black and white. And finally, a special thank you to my sister Debbie, who is probably at this very moment feeding a stray cat.

Foreword by Eve Golden

I have a "back-burner" list of people I want to write about. Peg Entwistle has always had a place on that list. She was—and is—a pop-culture icon, a hard-working and talented starlet on Broadway and in film of the late 1920s and early '30s. And her death fascinated me, as it has fascinated so many: the sheer brilliance of leaping from the HOLLYWOOD sign! I take my hat off to someone who can be so symbolic at her time of greatest despair.

After finishing my book about Vernon and Irene Castle, I turned my thoughts toward Peg, and thanks to the wonders of the Internet, I located her elderly brother and his daughter. "Oh, we'd love a good book to be written," they told me. "There's a fellow named James Zeruk working on one." *Curses*! I hate being beaten to a subject, and it happens all too often. This Zeruk fellow, I found out, had never written a book before. "Aha!" I thought, evilly. I will befriend him, read a few chapters, tell him sweetly that his work is unpublishable, and steal the project before he knew what hit him.

So I began e'ing with James, who turned out to be smart and funny and friendly. He sent me what he had written, and —*curses*! again — it was really, *really* good. I have been reading show-business biographies for more than 40 years, both as a fan and an editor, and I am a tough audience. But this is easily one of the ten best biographies I have ever read. There is no higher praise from an egomaniac like me than to say James did a much better job on this than I could have. I put my own hopes for a Peg book aside and helped James with his project.

He needed very little help, though —just the kind of "first draft" editing any author needs. James is that rarest of animals, a good researcher *and* a good writer. Too many books are either entertaining but crammed with dubious "facts," or dry doctoral theses. *Peg Entwistle and the Hollywood Sign Suicide* is a page-turning saga about a girl you thought you knew ("That failed starlet who jumped off a giant H," right?) but did not know at all. Almost every story you have heard about Peg Entwistle is wrong. I am astounded at the depth of information James has unearthed. I don't want to give too much away, but at least one scene gave me chills: The letters of the HOLLYWOOD sign, it turns out, were carted uphill right past Peg's house in 1923.

Settle in for a great read. I guarantee you, none of this is invented, none of it is embroidered. What you have before you is a fascinating story, told by an expert chronicler. Peg Entwistle is one of the most intriguing figures of Broadway and Hollywood, and one of the few to whom the word "tragic" can be accurately applied. And — more than 80 years after her epic death — she finally has the biographer she deserves.

Eve Golden is the author of six theater and film biographies; her articles on film history have also been collected into two anthologies. She was copy chief at More *and wrote the humor column "The Bottom Shelf" in Movieline in the 1990s. In 2013 her biography* John Gilbert: The Last of the Silent Movie Stars *was published.*

Preface

This book is the result of more than seven years of painstaking original research. Inside you will find exclusive, never-before-published information and images chronicling Peg Entwistle's career, public and private life, and shocking suicide. I have included many of her own words taken directly from letters to her family and interviews with journalists. Some of what you hear from Peg will move you, and some of it will stun and perhaps even offend you, for I have presented Peg Entwistle honestly, with all her faults and failings along with all her successes and charms. Here you will be introduced to the real Peg Entwistle, not the so-called failed actress created by tabloids and sensationalized tales passed down through the decades since her awful fall from the Hollywood Sign. Indeed, the extraordinarily talented young woman you will meet here was infinitely more interesting than the "Hollywood Sign Girl" of Tinsel Town lore.

During my years of research, I delved into every archive I could find which contained hard copies and microfilm of dozens of periodicals dating from before Peg Entwistle's birth in 1908. Thousands upon thousands of pages of newsprint, magazines, books, and images were carefully viewed, studied, and collated in order to collect the biographical information needed to present as accurate a timeline as the archives and other sources would allow. Websites such as the Internet Broadway Database (IBDb) and the Internet Movie Database (IMDb) were problematic, for their information was vague and incomplete. However, they are both included in the bibliography because of their limited use during my research.

As far as such Internet sources are concerned, I relied most heavily on databases hosted by universities and libraries. Notable among these were Proquest, Nexis, and the Access Newspaper Archives. The Google Newspaper Archives were also a fine source.

A number of Playbill Collections were helpful, including the Beinecke Playbill Collection at the University of Florida, the Theresa Helburn Theater Collection at Bryn Mawr College, and those provided by the Lakewood Theater, Skowhegan, Maine. Other playbills were purchased through auction houses, book dealers, and eBay.

Extensive use was made of the RKO archives, George Cukor Papers, and other related files containing scripts, production reports, images, inter-office memos and other correspondences and documents held by the Margaret Herrick Special Collections Department of the Academy of Motion Picture Arts and Sciences, and at the Performing Arts Special Collections Department of the Charles Young Research Library at UCLA. Other important sources I researched are listed in the bibliography.

Most of the images presented in this work have never been published. The majority of them were graciously donated by the Entwistle family. Others are from my personal collection or were obtained from various public or private collections. All credits and courtesies are noted.

Many hours of interviews (chats, really) were conducted with Milton Entwistle, Peg's brother, and Helen Reid, her cousin. They were the last two people who knew Peg intimately. Many more hundreds of hours were spent studying the Entwistle family archive, which contained a good amount of documents and images going back to the late nineteenth century.

Because of the availability of all of the above-mentioned sources, I was able to write Peg Entwistle's biography in a "traditional" manner, in a chronological order familiar to many scholarly biographies.

I have covered her childhood as far back as possible, and have included a rather detailed account of the life and acting careers of Charles and Jane Entwistle, the uncle and aunt who sacrificed so much of themselves in order to raise Peg and her brothers after they had become orphaned. You will accompany Peg across America upon her arrival from England. You will see her joys and her sorrows as she grew from an adorable young girl into a young lady with only one desire in mind: to be the most famous stage actress since Maude Adams. This book details her extraordinary apprenticeship with the Boston Repertory, where an unknown 17-year-old named Bette Davis saw Peg act and forever after cited her as the inspiration to become an actress. I have included many of Bette's own thoughts about Peg. All of Bette Davis's quotes were taken directly from her memoirs and first-person interviews.

From Boston, you will follow Peg's Broadway successes and flops including her engagements with the prestigious New York Theater Guild, her rocky marriage to actor Robert Keith, and the messy, cruel divorce which followed. You will go on cross-country tours with Peg and spend two summers with her in Skowhegan, Maine, where she first acted with Humphrey Bogart. Later, I explain in careful detail just how it was that Peg came to Los Angeles in 1932 to share the stage with Billie Burke and Bogart in what became her final appearance in theater. And you will see how her house of cards went tumbling down after she signed a film contract with David O. Selznick and RKO Studios. Several chapters have been devoted to Peg's work at RKO and her only known film, *Thirteen Women.*

You will read about Peg Entwistle's last walk, the aftermath of her suicide, and the reasons she was brought to such a low estate. I have also included a section debunking important myths and errors that have been associated with Peg's story. Another section discusses her influence in pop culture and the arts.

For the sake of convenience I have referred to Milton and Bobby Entwistle as Peg's "brothers." It was simply more agreeable to the flow of writing than to pepper the nar-

Cincinnati, Ohio, 1914 (courtesy Entwistle Family).

rative with "half-brother(s)." Because of publishing guidelines, many images and anecdotal information about Peg's family could not be included in this book. The reader is invited to visit my "Hollywood Sign Girl" website at www.hollywoodsigngirl.com to see more about Peg and her family and my interviews with notable biographers.

I believe the reader will come away with a satisfaction that the life, career, and death of Peg Entwistle has been extensively and exhaustively covered in this book.

Introduction

I first "met" Peg Entwistle in 2005 while writing a quirky (unpublished) novel called *Hollyweird*. In *Hollyweird's* climax my protagonist is on the Hollywood Sign, trying to defuse an atomic bomb as enemy agents, a mentally unstable private eye dressed as Jean Harlow, and a Cheetos-loving grizzly bear (as I said, *unpublished*) all converge at once to bring an end to the hero. I figured this story would never see a shelf at Barnes and Noble, so I thought I might as well have some more fun and go all out by having said hero rescued by the ghost of the actress who, I had heard, jumped to her death from the sign in the 1930s.

But who was she? I had only known of the event, not her name.

I Googled "hollywood sign suicide" and was amazed to see that Peg Entwistle, this "Hollywood Sign Girl," was included in a great many books and articles about Hollywood, movie star scandals, unusual celebrity deaths, and the like. In every instance where the Hollywood Sign itself was the subject, Peg was mentioned. It wasn't hard to see that she was as much a part of the history of the sign as the sign was a part of Hollywood's history.

I became intrigued and fascinated by the girl, and never for a minute believed that a member of the prestigious New York Theater Guild would have ended her life so grotesquely simply because a few of her scenes had been deleted from a film. It didn't make sense.

Desperate to learn more, I looked everywhere for a biography about her. I was surprised and puzzled that such a mesmerizing starlet as Peg had managed to hover over Tinsel Town without a book for the better part of a century. The chroniclers of Broadway's Golden Age had ignored her, too. Angered and impassioned, I set the quirky novel aside and made a full-time job out of searching for the truth about this tragic girl. The work was often times frustrating, sometimes exciting, and always tedious. I started piecing together her career by viewing nearly every page of all the newspapers available on microfilm. There was no index or search engine to give me what I needed. I had to become a detective in a very real sense. For example, the *New York Times* had a daily feature called "Theatrical Notes." In it, there would be a dozen or so notices announcing things like "A second company of *Connecticut Yankee* will go on tour August 28," or "Beatrice Lillie, Noel Coward, and the cast of *This Year of Grace* will sail tomorrow on the *President Harding*." Then, every few days or so, I might find a "Peg Entwistle has been added to the cast of *Just to Remind You*, which goes into rehearsals next week." More information about Peg and her various stage engagements would eventually come to light as I collected all these little theatrical notes and followed leads and hunches and researched other cast members, writers, and producers of her plays. It was a very slow process.

I began to suspect that maybe the reason no one had ever written Peg's biography was because it was just too damn time-consuming.

I had an idea of when she started acting professionally, and so I began from there. The bits and pieces began to form a timeline, and a more complete photograph of her life started to come into focus. I obtained all the available legal documents about her and also spent four *very* frustrating days in the basement of the Los Angeles Hall of Records, looking for the files regarding her divorce from actor Robert Keith ... nothing. Then, just as I was about to give up, I learned that when a gal filed for divorce in Los Angeles in 1929 she had to use her first given name and the last name of her husband. The reason that divorce records for "Peg Entwistle," "Millicent Entwistle," "Millicent Lilian Entwistle," or even "Peg Keith" were not there is because she had filed for divorce as "Millicent (sometimes called 'Peg') Keith."

I began to suspect that maybe another reason no one had ever written Peg's biography was because it was just too damn tricky.

But as frustrating as it all was with the seeking, there was double the satisfaction in the finding. When I was doing research and Peg-related consulting for filmmaker Hope Anderson on her documentary *Under the Hollywood Sign,* I managed to track down Peg's brother, Milton Entwistle. Milt and his daughter Lauretta opened the family archives to us. Hope used what she wanted for her film, but I grabbed it all up — every letter, diary, address book, image, note, stamp and receipt. I took no chances; I thought it best to have what looked to be too much information, for I had a feeling that even the most obscure or seemingly unrelated name, date, or notation might lead to another missing piece of Peg's story. (This proved to be the case on numerous occasions, as you will see later in this book.)

Lauretta kindly loaned many items, and made photocopies of others. Milt also contributed charming memories about his family and life in Hollywoodland. An added bonus came by way of Peg's cousin Helen Reid, who shared many more anecdotes with me.

More and more it started coming together and more and more a very deep realization began to take hold of me ... I began to suspect that maybe the reason no one had ever written Peg Entwistle's biography was because it was meant to be written by me...

Prologue

What's Past Is Prologue—Shakespeare[1]

Bette Davis wants to be an actress, but she is sad, confused, her life seems hopeless....
January 1926. Bette's mother cannot afford to send her to a good acting school, one which could properly prepare her for Broadway. To ease her daughter's pain, Ruthie surprises the future Hollywood legend with a trip to see Henrik Ibsen's *The Wild Duck* at Henry Jewett's highly regarded Boston Repertory. Starring in the play is Blanche Yurka, the famous Broadway actress and director. Yurka will play the role of a mother named Gina Ekdal.

Filling the role of Gina's daughter Hedvig is a lovely new addition to the Boston stage, an English girl by the name of Peg Entwistle. When Bette sees Peg for the first time, she gasps; astounded at the face of this young actress. "My heart almost stopped," Bette would write in her memoir many years hence.[2] "She looked just like me!"[3]

They were both just seventeen years old.

Bette sits erect, mesmerized by the resemblance, her soul captivated by Peg's interpretation of Ibsen's tragic Hedvig—whose eyes are going blind. "I was watching myself. Miss Entwistle had lost herself in Hedvig. Now I did too. There wasn't an emotion I didn't anticipate and share with her."[4]

Bette remains hushed, attentive to every nuance Peg brings to her role, every subtle gesture, every word of dialogue. She is profoundly attached to Peg's Hedvig ... ache for ache, sigh for sigh, and tear for tear. Peg has given life to Hedvig and Hedvig has in turn changed Bette's. An epiphany has taken place fore and aft of the footlights—the three girls have become as one. In the last moments of the play, Bette watches with an intensity she has never before known. Hedvig agonizes. She is being shunned, rejected, abandoned by the father she loves—just as Bette had been, not long before.

"Father! Father! No, no! Don't turn away from me," cries Hedvig as she clings to him; hysterical and broken-hearted.[5] Enduring unbearable torment, the poor child is tossed aside and watches in horror as Father storms out of the house. Desperate for help, for love, for understanding, she runs frantically to the woman who only minutes ago confessed to her husband that Hedvig may not be his daughter. "Mother, you must get him home again! Why won't Father have anything to do with me any more?"[6]

The scene is gut-wrenching; the finale, more so. Hedvig takes a pistol and disappears into the attic to prove to Father that nothing is more important to her than he ... she will destroy her most treasured possession—a beautiful wild duck that had been wounded by a hunter and then nursed back to health by the love and innocence of Hedvig. But the play is allegorical—Hedvig is *The Wild Duck,* and her wound is beyond nursing.

A gunshot! The family rushes to the attic.

A moment later Hedvig is brought center stage, lifeless, carried down in Father's arms.

He had come to his senses and then desired to forgive his wife and once again love dear Hedvig with all his heart. But it is too late and poor Hedvig will never learn that Father really does love her.

The audience weeps for the girl but no one has as much feeling for her as Bette Davis ... "When 'the little wild duck' shot herself in the breast, I died with her."[7]

The curtain falls and Bette is more determined than ever to fulfill her dream. "A whole new world opened up to me," she said.[8] "I was thrilled with Miss Entwistle's performance."[9] As they were leaving the theater, Bette cried out, "Mother! Someday I will play Hedvig."[10]

Three years later Blanche Yurka needs a Hedvig. Bette Davis will be *The Wild Duck.* Bette begins her climb up the ladder to the top of the Hollywood heap.

Three years later Peg begins her climb up the ladder to the top of the Hollywood Sign.

Peg Entwistle wants to be an actress, but she is sad, confused, her life seems hopeless...

ACT I

*Go search the world and search the sea,
then come you home and search with me.
There's no such gold, there's no such pearl,
as a bright and beautiful English girl!*
   — W.S. Gilbert[1]

1

The Curtain Rises

Millicent Lilian Entwistle took her first breath of life on February 5, 1908, inside a modest house located at 5 Broad Street within the urban district of Margam, a small suburb of Neath County in Port Talbot, Wales. Her parents, Robert and Emily, were English. They resided in the comfortable London community of West Kensington, and had come to Wales to visit Emily's parents, John and Caroline Stevenson, specifically so Caroline could act as a midwife. John Stevenson was a metallurgist who plied and studied his scientific trade from his Broad Street home not far from the steelworks operations near Port Talbot's Swansea Bay. Thus, in the land that gave the world such notables as Geoffrey of Monmouth, Dylan Thomas, and T.E. Lawrence, the future stage actress known as Peg Entwistle had her debut.

The Entwistle name goes back to at least 1276, when it was spelled "Ennetwysel." It is derived from the locality where a man once lived or held land, in this case a small village of the same name in Bolton le Moors, Lancashire, in the Northwest of England. The name was derived from an old English term signifying "river fork frequented by ducks."[1] Had Peg's father been alive in the late thirteenth century he would have been known as Robert de Ennetwysel, meaning "Robert of (or from) Ennetwysel, the place where ducks frequent the river fork."

It isn't known exactly when or how Robert Entwistle first met Emily Stevenson, but they were living together as early as 1891 in the infamous Bath Row slums of Birmingham, in England's West Midlands region. Together they ran a public house, an inn that served alcohol. Robert was licensed as the victualler, Emily as the manageress. On a page of the 1891 census they claimed to have been married, but a license issued by the Established Church of England shows a wedding ceremony did not occur until November 3, 1904. The simplest explanation for this discrepancy is that the young couple lied in order to get their jobs and the required business licenses. It isn't known how long they had worked at the inn, but the 1901 census of Glamorganshire, Wales, lists Robert as an English actor on tour. Emily is not here recorded, but it's likely she wasn't far away, for her family's house in Port Talbot was just 23 miles from Glamorganshire.

Peg Entwistle was an adorable baby, born healthy and whole with features following classic English lines. Her delicate wisp of blonde hair accentuated eyes of vivid blue. She grew into an attractive, soft-spoken young woman who came to love the still camera with an affectionate, gentle gaze. Her Mona Lisa smile was simple, offering expressions of polite sentiment. And on rare occasions when she gaily flashed her bright teeth for a photographer, it usually meant she was celebrating something delightful.

Soon after the birth, when mother and child were able to travel, Robert and Emily said goodbye to the Stevensons and made for home in England. Their Victorian terraced house at West Kensington's 53 Comeragh Road was quaint, its location middle-class. For a community of West London this meant a castle or two and plenty of theaters full of Shakespeare.

From her start it seems Peg was destined for the stage. By the time she was born, her father and his closest brother, Charles Harold Entwistle, were full-fledged theater folk. And while her dad was able to keep his wife and child comfortable with minor roles and some set designing, it was Peg's Uncle Charles who excelled in show business and who later had the most influence on her stage aspirations. Charles, who was sometimes called Harold, was affectionately known to his family and friends as Enty. Peg liked to call him Uncle Charlie, but also gave him the pet name of "Mister E."[2] Her brother Milton recalled how she would sometimes prance throughout their Beachwood Canyon house in Hollywood, searching room to room for their uncle while whispering "Mister E? Oh, Mister E, where are you?"[3] Upon finding him she would throw her arms around his neck, then, in a soft, beautiful voice, parody the opening line of Ah! Sweet Mystery of Life, a famous Rida Young and Victor Herbert song from 1910: "Ah! Sweet *Mister E* of life, at last I've found you!"[4]

Peg's father Robert Entwistle (pictured) was not a force on the stage, but he and his brother Charles did once perform for the king and queen of England (courtesy Entwistle Family).

Although an actor, Charles Entwistle flourished more as a manager. Highly adept and respected, he controlled many of the business affairs of prominent actors, theaters, and theater owners, particularly during the late 1800s. He first studied theater and drama in Heidelberg and Paris before tackling the London stage, where he acted and had associations with Sir Henry Irving, one of England's most cherished thespians. It was during this relationship that Sir Henry was given knighthood in 1895 — the first actor to ever receive such an honor.

Still in his twenties, Mister E controlled or managed theater operations throughout England and beyond. He was given glowing letters of referral from employers Robert Arthur, J.B. Howard, and Frederick Wyndham — men whose theatrical empires covered Britain. During a four-year span that saw the turn of the century, Charles Entwistle was acting manager for the Revill family's Theater Royal Sheffield. While there, he incorporated a year managing theaters whose supervisors were appointed by the stringent Court of Chancery. In Scotland, he organized the staff, advertising and opening of the Grand Theater and Opera House at Glasgow. Leonard Rayae, well-known star of the South African stage, praised Charles for representing him in Capetown. Following his success managing the Buenos Aires season of famed British actor Seymour Hicks, the South American Theatrical Syndicate promised Charles a position should he ever return to Argentina.

It was during this period of his itinerant success that Peg's uncle was first introduced to Broadway. He was brought to America in 1906 by legendary producer Charles Frohman. While sources vary as to whether Charles Entwistle worked for Frohman as a publicist or manager (probably a bit of both), his obituaries in 1944 mention him helping manage Frohman's newest discovery, a talented ingénue named Billie Burke (still years away from her memorable film roles as Glinda the Good Witch in *The Wizard of Oz*, and the high-strung hostess, Millicent, in the delightful, star-studded *Dinner at Eight*). Burke had been discovered in England by Frohman in 1907, signed to a contract, and soon became one of Broadway's polished gems.

Charles Entwistle also managed Mrs. Patrick Campbell, one of the most successful English actresses of the era. Mrs. Campbell's take on the character Eliza Doolittle in *Pygmalion* (a role written especially for her by George Bernard Shaw) set the bar for Julie Andrews and Audrey Hepburn when it was adapted as the stage and screen musical *My Fair Lady*.

During his administrations and travels in those early years, Charles met stage pioneer Walter Hampden. Known as the Dean of Broadway, Hampden was one of the most respected Shakespearean actors of American theater. His portrayal of Hamlet placed him at the pinnacle of the A-list until a Romanesque profile named John Barrymore became perhaps the most celebrated Hamlet of Broadway's Golden Age. Notwithstanding the chiseled features and acting gifts of Barrymore, Hampden himself was hard to ignore. He was strikingly handsome, talented, and highly regarded in legitimate theater. He was elected president of The Players following the death of his predecessor, actor John Drew. Hampden would hold the office for nearly thirty years. The Players, whose library is named after Hampden, was (and still is) a gathering place for professionals of commerce and the arts. Modeled after London's famous Garrick Club, it was founded in 1888 by America's forefather of legitimate theater, Edwin Booth, who has the unfortunate distinction of being a brother to John Wilkes Booth, infamous assassin of President Abraham Lincoln.

Hampden and Charles Entwistle quickly became friends and remained so until Charles died. The families were very close, too. Milton Entwistle remembered the association fondly, recalling motor trips to Union Station to pick up Hampden and his wife, actress Mabel Moore, whenever they visited Los Angeles.

Peg's uncle received tremendous praise for his managerial skills over the years, but of every shining reference heaped his way, he was most proud of a letter written by Hampden just before the star embarked for Europe in early 1925. This letter gave Charles the highest recommendation to any potential employer without appearing to be a letter of reference. One sees a clever bit of writing by Hampden for Charles's benefit. Instead of the typical "To Whom It May Concern," followed by a synopsis denoting various attributes and accomplishments, it is addressed directly to Charles and comes off as a tome of gratitude more than anything else. It is written to let a reader know that over the years Walter Hampden and Charles Entwistle enjoyed a fine, prosperous business association *and* a warm friendship. Every important theater owner and producer in the world knew and admired Hampden; this gave Charles plenty of validation. Peg's uncle carried this letter with him until his death, and a good argument can be made that he did this not because it was from a famous employer, but from a friend.

But back in 1910, turmoil entered the Entwistle home. It has always been reported that Peg's mother Emily died when Peg was two years old (some say four), but she hadn't. Robert divorced her. It isn't clear on what grounds, but it must have been something very serious, for the court awarded Robert sole custody of Peg. As a single dad with a two-year-old,

Robert's life could have easily become a jumble of complication and worry, but there was plenty of motherly help from his sisters Rosina and Lilian and the wives of his brothers Henry and Ernest. And there was Emily's sister, Laura Seaton. Peg's Aunt Laura remained a close friend of the Entwistle family. Robert routinely allowed her to bring Peg on numerous trips to Wales, presumably so the little girl could see her mother but certainly so she could visit her maternal grandparents.

There was other turmoil in 1910, too, this time on a national level: King Edward VII died in May. And then in June 1911, after more than a year of mourning King Edward, coronation ceremonies began for his son, King George V. Because Charles Frohman's reputation as a theatrical producer had gained him international recognition, he was given a seat on the general committee overseeing a gala performance scheduled to occur at His Majesty's Theater in London. A thousand names from nations far and wide would be recruited to act out important moments from classic plays. And while the number of players seems large at first glance, it should be noted that the committee selected participants based on ability and responsibility; those who could not be trusted would have no place upon the royal stage during such a historic milestone as the crowning of a monarch.

The committee selected Robert and Charles Entwistle for Shakespeare's *Julius Caesar*. Peg's father and uncle would perform for the king of England and Queen Mary. It was here, at just three and a half years old, that Peg Entwistle had her very first exposure to the stage, sitting in a pushchair, watching her father and uncle from the wings of the world's grandest theater during the most regal of ceremonies.

Sir Henry Tree, well-known British star of the English stage and official Proprietor of His Majesty's Theater, directed the *Julius Caesar* scenes. The choreography was arranged by Granville Barker, an icon of England's stage who later helped usher Broadway into its Golden Age. One theater critic who was present during rehearsals wrote an article describing in almost tiresome detail the intricacies of all that was involved. When it came to pageantry the event was rivaled only by the Precession of the Equinoxes. Every actor had a mark, every gesture a cue, when the entire ensemble of 300 moved stage left or right; it did so with precision.

Beside the privilege of appearing on His Majesty's Stage, the actors were to be presented to the king and queen. After the final performance the army of costumed actors hurried to their dressing rooms to transform themselves into presentable subjects. For several hours they huddled in quiet groups, no doubt rehearsing in the individual theaters of their minds the bow or curtsy and polite greeting with which each would become humble. It isn't hard to imagine Robert and Charles fawning over each other, doting on each other's appearance, nervously checking immaculate details from top hat to shoe tip.

Peg's favorite uncle was Charles Entwistle. He sacrificed much in order to raise Peg and her brothers after they were orphaned (courtesy Entwistle Family).

Alas, any fears the brothers may have had regarding a lingering smudge of stage makeup or a vagrant thread upon a lapel could be laid to rest: King George and Queen Mary had other business to attend. The disenchanted thespians were eventually herded out, their priority reduced to a significance somewhere between the king's sumptuous banquet and the men who swept the gutters beyond the gates of Buckingham Palace. However, Peg's father and uncle were entitled to a coronation medal and ribbon for their participation, and perhaps the medallion's vibrant shine and handsome ribbon afforded a sense of validation.

When the festivities had ended, Peg's Uncle Charles returned to New York City. He continued his representative duties under Frohman, and between assignments dabbled in a bit of acting. Robert remained in England, raising Peg with the help of the Entwistle and Stevenson families while taking acting jobs in and near London. When not acting, he worked in his father's stationery shop, learning to make fancy gift boxes, a specialty trade he would later take to New York's Madison Avenue.

In 1911, during production of the play *Hobson's Choice,* Charles Entwistle met a stately American actress named Bertha Jane Ross. Jane, as she preferred to be called, was of well-to-do Ohio stock, her family having their home in Elmwood Place, a small village located a few miles north of Cincinnati in Ohio's Hamilton County. Jane's mother, Matilda, raised Jane and her siblings in all matters polite and religious while family patriarch Milton Ross prospered as a salesman for the Jergens Soap Company. Jane's father had opened up California for the company and was rewarded handsomely for his efforts.

Jane Ross was adventurous, athletic, creative, and active in civic organizations. She was an expert horseback rider and claimed to have traced her ancestry to John Ross, husband of America's seamstress darling, Betsy. Statuesque in profile and posture, Jane was fond of tailored suits with broad white lapels that brought attention to her handsome features. She made her own clothes and liked to paint. She enjoyed fishing, catching frogs and target shooting, and she was relentless at poker and billiards, proudly noting her cash winnings in a diary.

She was a hybrid dowager who mingled comfortably amongst the upper crust of Manhattan socialites and Boston bluebloods while remaining down to Earth enough to spirit a horse into a breakneck gallop or command her powerful Cole automobile to its limits. She wasn't afraid of getting a bit dusty or chipping a fingernail, although one would have been hard-pressed to ever find her in need of a bath or manicure. By the time she met Charles Entwistle she had made a fine living as an actress and owned a beautiful house by the bay in Santa Monica, California.

While giving interviews on tour, she would speak wistfully of her ocean-view home, fancy car, and of Don Caesar, a highly intelligent bay horse that followed her around like an affectionate dog. Jane and Don Caesar had a somewhat celebrated reputation and journalists never tired of informing their readers about the time she and her noble steed saved a young girl, an old woman, and another horse from catastrophe. It had been a harrowing few moments of real-life drama that could easily have been mistaken for a cliffhanger scene from one of Pearl White's *Perils of Pauline* serials.

The heroics hadn't surprised those who knew Jane Ross.

She had been riding Don Caesar on a rugged trail alongside a canyon near Santa Cruz, California, when a runaway horse came charging toward them. Seated in a carriage harnessed to the horse were a terrified young girl and her grandmother. The girl had been at the reins when something spooked the horse and it bolted at full speed. The girl lost hold of the straps and now had no way to control the frightened animal. Jane was familiar with the trail and knew that the carriage would never make the sharp corner it was fast approaching — there were no turn-offs, only a steep face on one side of the trail and the canyon on the other. The helpless passengers would be pulled into space, hurtling hundreds of feet to their deaths. Jane maneuvered her horse into position and held patient for the right moment. As the runaway came barreling by, she and Don Caesar gave chase. When they got alongside, Jane reached over and grabbed the horse's bridle, slowing the carriage to a stop. The girl, her grandmother, and the horse were saved.

It would not be the last time Jane Ross and a trusted partner came to the aid of a helpless trio in need.

* * *

Charles Entwistle and Jane Ross worked marvelously well together during the 1911 production of *Hobson's Choice*. Although Charles was nearly 20 years her senior, Jane was quite smitten by his handsomeness and intellect. She wasn't hard to look at, either, and so business soon turned to pleasure. In June 1912, Peg's distinguished Uncle Charles married the outgoing adventurer-actress in Ohio. They honeymooned their way across the country and then settled in at Jane's house in Santa Monica.

It was about this time that Jane and Charles were hired by Lee and J.J. Shubert to take the Broadway smash *A Butterfly on the Wheel* on the road during the coming winter. The troupe assembled and rehearsed in Los Angeles; opened in Utah, and then made its way east to New York. The Shuberts continued auditions while Charles, the tour manager, kept himself busy by scheduling theater venues and hotel and train reservations. Jane was engaged to play the female lead, a socialite named Peggy Admaston whose happy marriage turns sour when Mr. Admaston's business becomes more important than his woman.

When not being followed around town by her heroic bay horse or getting caught pilfering a neighbor's rose bushes (a diary confession focused more on embarrassment than repentance), Jane Ross studied her script earnestly.

On New Year's Day, 1913, after a champagne party for the company at the home of one of the actresses, the troupe headed to Salt Lake City, Utah. A few days later, Jane writes of the miserable conditions: "Nearly frozen to death and no water at the Seculoh Hotel. Pipes all frozen. Quarreled with Enty and took walk with Alice to find water."[5] Frozen pipes also plagued their January 7 premiere at the Salt Lake Theater. Water couldn't get to the steam boilers until just before curtain rise. For three hours an audience filling just half the seats shivered under wraps as a dismal breath of warm air trickled from the vents. The next day, Jane rented a sewing machine and "made warm bloomers for everyone."[6] She also "made up with Enty,"[7] but not before she and the rest of the cast took turns expressing their bitterness toward the hapless manager.

Such was the early twentieth century road life of an actor. Cross-country troupes suffered much in those days. It wasn't uncommon for entire companies to be stranded in small towns and railway stations, hungry, tired, freezing or sweltering while sometimes waiting days for producers to send additional funds. Actors' Equity, the union regulating theatrical contracts and productions, would be created in the coming spring, but even several years after its formation many actors on tour still endured brutal conditions. Not until a strike in 1919 — headed largely by Ethel Barrymore — would things finally begin to change.

Typically, each venue employed its own crew — stagehands, ushers, ticket sellers, etc. The top of the box office take from each performance went to the venue's owner to meet that payroll. If turnout was light, the acting company's business manager (i.e., Charles Entwistle) would have to pay the difference using petty cash supplied by the production's home office. Other times, even when ticket sales were good, the cash was quickly spent on unforeseen expenses such as a greedy hotel owner padding the bill; rebuilding damaged stage scenery; replacing the contents of lost or stolen luggage and costume trunks; or even removing an actor's decayed tooth.

Charles' frugality (he had booked Salt Lake's cheapest hotel) with the operating funds for *A Butterfly on the Wheel* was meant to help the money last as long as possible, but it nearly cost him his marriage ... this would not happen again.

From Brigham Young's city, the tour traveled to Denver where Jane hosted a poker game and picked the Savoy Hotel servants clean. In Cheyenne, Wyoming, she earned every blister of her eight-mile hike over the plains. In Lincoln, Nebraska, just before curtain rise of a one-night-only performance, she lost $9.10 to some stagehands in the dressing room but later won $10.20 from the staff at the hotel — her diary doesn't mention if the margaritas she served gave her an edge. Then it was off to Iowa — Sioux City, Mason City, Waterloo...

After a day in Quincy, Illinois, they arrived in St. Louis, Missouri, for a two-week engagement before heading to Jane's hometown, Cincinnati, for a week's vacation. Back on the road, they hit Louisville, Kentucky, for three days, and then Columbus, Ohio, for three more. It was here that Peg's aunt experienced an amazing event: Jane writes that she and Charles were having dinner at the train station, in a restaurant called The Track House, when ten young college boys who had seen her the night before in *Butterfly* approached the table. They presented her with bouquets of violets and lily of the valley and then proceeded to serenade the stunned actress. Still reeling several hours later, Jane had to be carried in tears by Charles onto the train destined for Detroit. Jane doesn't mention the lads' names, or from which college they hailed, but it's a good guess that the tour's miserable start in Utah was now forgotten by her, or at least forgiven. In early March, after five days in Michigan, the tour ended in Buffalo, New York.

In early April, Lee Shubert promised Peg's uncle another management position in the coming fall. There might also be a role for Aunt Jane. They were told to return in July to work out the final details of the unnamed production. A few days later, Charles and Jane boarded the liner *Olympic* and made for England to introduce Jane to Peg, her father, and the rest of the Entwistle family. Also on board the ship (and not without much fanfare) was theater mogul Charles Frohman, who was embarking on his yearly European jaunt to check on theatrical concerns and buy some plays. Jane's diary notes that she and Charles enjoyed drinks with the famous producer in his cabin; it is here that Frohman promised Charles that he would hire Peg's father as a stage manager and bring him and Peg to New York.

Following a night of "monstrous waves,"[8] Jane and Charles joined Frohman and his companions for a private dinner with the ship's captain. Ten days later they met Robert Entwistle in London. Charles informed his brother of Frohman's offer. Robert was impressed and readily accepted, but Jane's statuesque beauty impressed him too. Family lore has it that when Robert laid eyes on his brother's wife, he asked, "Are there any more like you at home?"[9] Indeed, Jane's eligible sisters were Lois, Lauretta, and Marguerite. A fourth sister, Helen, was living in Los Angeles with her husband. (Jane had one brother, Charles Ross.)

Peg arrived from Wales the next day with her mother's sister, Laura Seaton, with whom she had been staying while her father was on an acting tour. Peg took an immediate liking to her new American aunt, especially when Jane said she had a horse and promised to give riding lessons to the excited five-year-old.

Robert was interviewed and hired by Frohman several days later. After an emotional day that saw Jane brought to tears during farewell toasts at a dinner with all the Entwistle family and friends, she and Charles boarded the SS *Chicago* and departed England. They arrived in New York on July 29, 1913. Two days later they signed contracts with the Shubert brothers for a road tour of a musical comedy called *The Five Frankfurters,* a parody about the Rothschilds and their banking dynasty. Charles's success with the previous winter's tour of *A Butterfly on the Wheel* earned him a general manager's position several months earlier than promised. Jane was again contracted as a player. Notable among the cast was Henry Travers, now mostly remembered for his film role as Clarence, Angel Second Class, in Frank Capra's 1946 Christmas classic, *It's a Wonderful Life.*

With an open calendar until the scheduled rehearsals in September, Jane and Charles

Jane Entwistle and Don Caesar, a brilliant horse that followed her around like a well-heeled dog (courtesy Entwistle Family).

spent the next five weeks vacationing in Clarklake, Michigan, and at the Ross homestead in Ohio. Also scheduled to begin rehearsals in that September of 1913 was Peg's father. He was to have his Broadway acting debut in a Charles Frohman production at the Lyceum Theater.

It had been thought by many that Peg Entwistle did not arrive to America until 1916. This idea comes mainly from a ship's manifest showing her as passenger on the SS *Philadelphia* during a voyage from Liverpool to New York in March of that year. And while immigration records could not be found confirming that Peg came to the United States before 1916, there is no question that she and her father were in New York City as early as September 1913: in her diary entry for September 6, 1913, Peg's Aunt Jane says she visited "Babs and Robert" in their apartment at 233 West 45th Street.[10] (Babs was Peg's nickname.) Three days later, Jane records having lunch with them "on Broadway."[11] Eleven days after this she writes of meeting Robert at the New York Theatre, where she was rehearsing *The Five Frankfurters.* On September 26, 1913, a *New York Times* review of *The Younger Generation* lists

Robert S. Entwistle in the cast. In the New York Public Library, the White Studio Theatrical Photographs Collection contains 66 images from the Lyceum Theater's 1913 production of *The Younger Generation;* at least ten of these show Peg's father. Jane mentions being with Robert on several more occasions that September, including a visit to Pittsburgh by him and Peg while she and Charles were on tour in *The Five Frankfurters*. There is also a September 7, 1914, *New York Times* review listing Robert Entwistle in the Broadway production of *The Beautiful Adventure*. A 1914 license registered in Clarklake, Michigan, proves when and where Robert remarried, and among other items in the Entwistle archive is an adorable photo of Peg in an Easter dress, taken in 1914 by George Schmitt of the Fountain Square Studio in Cincinnati.

Any number of reasons might account for the lack of official records regarding Peg's 1913 maiden voyage to America, including document theft by memorabilia collectors in the years following her death. (This seems to be the case with her RKO contracts.) However, it's more likely Peg's 1913 records were lost or accidentally destroyed. This is not hard to believe in light of the era. Immigrant status-and-arrival record-keeping at the Port of Liverpool and at Ellis Island was archaic and hardly without problems, as illustrated by a clerical error during the aforementioned 1913 trans–Atlantic voyage of Jane and Charles. Jane, a native Ohioan, was mistakenly identified on the ship's manifest as a British subject. On her next voyage, in 1916, she was listed as a resident alien. Both entries are of course incorrect. In each case she should have been recorded on a separate U.S. Citizens manifest; this was never done. And it caused no small irritation for Jane; the United States government refused to acknowledge a mistake had been made, even when presented with documents and witnesses proving she was indeed an American-born citizen. (One item presented was a newspaper feature showing Jane sewing an American flag; the caption mentions her being a descendant of Betsy Ross.)

For over a decade she argued her case. Then in 1924, after jumping through countless hoops of inane bureaucracy, Jane Ross Entwistle was finally recognized by a United States District Court ... as *naturalized* citizen 2074157.

Absent immigration records for Peg Entwistle prior to 1916, the facts detailed above present enough evidence to support her 1913 arrival in the United States.

* * *

Robert Entwistle was never a force on or behind the stage, but the production in which he had his Broadway debut was given favorable reviews and ran a moderate 60 performances. This 1913 Charles Frohman production was a double bill. Robert played Mr. Leadbitter in Stanley Houghton's front piece, *The Younger Generation*. The second show of the production was called *Half an Hour,* a little playlet written by Sir James Barrie, creator of *Peter Pan*. It wasn't well liked and is considered one of Barrie's lesser works. But *Generation* was good enough to carry the weaker *Half an Hour* through the production's run. The *New York Times* thought *Generation* was cleverly written and performed by "a company of actors very evenly balanced in respect to merits."

Robert Entwistle hadn't achieved much attention in his first Broadway outing, apart from the cast list; the *Times* reviewer doesn't mention him at all. But this didn't bother him in the least. He wasn't a thespian to the marrow; being ignored by a critic meant little or nothing to him. Since his arrival to the States he had gotten some new ideas; acting and stage managing were now careers he could take or leave. Sure, gigs with Charles Frohman made quick cash, but Robert was a homebody at heart, a man whose real longing was to run a business and raise a family. His plan was to remain in theater's realm until he had earned enough money to open a shop specializing in stationery and gift packaging. He was off to a good start, and though not praised for his performance in *The Younger Generation,* he hadn't been singled out as a buffoon either. Moreover, his introduction to the Ross family had gone very well. As long as he showed up and did what was required, Robert's new life in America had much to offer. But the attention he cared for most was from his little Peg and the new gal they had met upon arriving to America — Jane's sister Lauretta.

About this time, many film companies on the East Coast were pulling up stakes and heading to Southern California for sun and scenery. Charles and Jane decided to try their luck in motion pictures. They began making arrangements for a return to California amid hopes of associating with some of those early trailblazers of this fast-growing entertainment medium. But first some important family business required their attention.

As the biggest westward migration since the 1849 Gold Rush was kicking up dust across the Continental Divide toward a young California town called Hollywood, love between Peg's father and Jane's sister bloomed: On July 29, 1914, while summering in Clarklake, Michigan, Robert married Lauretta Ross. Adorned with a dainty frock of white taffeta, Lauretta made her way down the aisle, the aroma of pink and white sweet pea blossoms emanating from the flower girls' baskets. A few minutes later, as Peg smiled from the pews, Robert kissed his bride. It was now official ... the brothers Robert and Charles were married to the sisters Jane and Lauretta.

And now six-year-old Peg had a new mommy.

Following the reception and supper, the bride and groom made their way to the train station for a trip to Niagara Falls, New York. Upon returning from their honeymoon, Robert and Lauretta picked up Peg at the Ross home and returned to New York. Robert soon began rehearsing for a play called *The Beautiful Adventure.* One of the featured players in this comedy was Frank Morgan, the whimsical character actor most remembered for his multiple roles in MGM's 1939 film *The Wizard of Oz.*

Meanwhile, Peg's uncle had been making gains in California. In July, Charles and Jane had gone to San Rafael, a picturesque town near San Francisco Bay. Charles had gotten his first motion picture job, a supporting role in *Salomy Jane,* a western melodrama adapted from *Salomy Jane's Kiss,* a story by Bret Harte, well-known writer of tales of the Southwest pioneers. This was the first movie produced by the California Motion Picture Corporation (CMPC). The central figure at CMPC was its star, Beatriz Michelena, a firebrand dazzler who (along with sister Vera) had trained professionally to become an opera singer like her father, Fernando, the famed Mexican tenor of San Francisco.

Peg took an immediate liking to Aunt Jane's sister, Laurette Ross. The doting mother and wife brought stability, love, and warmth to the Entwistle home (courtesy Entwistle Family).

On September 6, Peg and Lauretta went to Broadway's Lyceum Theater to see Robert in the premiere of *The Beautiful Adventure,* which the *New York Times* called "[a] comedy of great charm, played with exceptional skill by a wisely chosen company."[12]

In October a special invitation-only advance screening of *Salomy Jane* was held at the St. Francis Hotel in San Francisco. The St. Francis also hosted the premiere in early November. A few days after the premiere, Beatriz Michelena gave Uncle Charles a contract to direct her next picture, *Mrs. Wiggs of the Cabbage Patch,* a drama based on a 1902 best-selling novel of Kentucky poverty by Alice Hegan Rice. With a handful of players from *Salomy Jane* under his direction (including a budding star named Belle Bennett), Charles's first time behind the megaphone went well. It paid well, too. Robert Birchard, editor of the *American Film Institute Catalogue of Feature Films,* provided a payroll ledger showing Charles was paid $500 (over $11,000 today) for his directing. When it opened at the Lyric Theater in San Rafael, over the following Christmas holiday, the entire town turned out for a marathon viewing. For three consecutive days from 1 P.M. until midnight, *Mrs. Wiggs of the Cabbage Patch* was continuously shown to the ecstatic audiences. Much of the elation, however, was due to the locals seeing *themselves* on the screen: They had been filmed as spectators in a circus scene. But the most fun the star-struck citizens of San Rafael had with the film is here described by Marin County film historian Lionel Ashcroft: "During the course of staging one of the scenes of a robbery near Fairfax, the actor who played the bandit was arrested by local deputies for robbing a stage. They did not believe he was an actor, disarmed him and took him to the Courthouse in San Rafael, where he stayed in the County Jail. Several hours later the director came to the Courthouse and explained the 'robbery' to the judge, who then ordered his release."[13] The director, of course, was Peg's Uncle Charles.

* * *

In May of 1915, tragedy struck the on high seas near Ireland when a German U-boat torpedoed the British luxury liner *Lusitania.* Nearly 1,200 civilians were killed, 128 of them Americans—and one of those was Robert and Charles Entwistle's Broadway employer, Charles Frohman. Actor John Drew had warned Frohman not to go, but the producer was determined to see his good friend James Barrie in England. The ship sank in about twenty minutes. Witnesses reported that Frohman helped actress Rita Jolivet with her lifejacket and then escorted her into a lifeboat. Seeing that the small craft was overcrowded, Frohman refused to get aboard. When Jolivet and the others beseeched him, he brushed off the idea with a line echoing his favorite play, Barrie's *Peter Pan.* "Why fear death?"[14] he said as he stepped away from the lowering craft. "It is the most beautiful adventure in life!"[15]

Some survivors told the *New York Times* they saw Frohman standing on deck, walking stick in hand, calm and reserved as the ship listed hard and her bow dipped into the ocean, pulling him and over a thousand more souls to their deaths. His body was recovered several days later and brought to New York, where many more thousands turned out to pay their last respects.

It might be said that Charles Frohman was a theater unto himself. His galaxy of stars at one time or another included the biggest stage names of the era: Ellen Terry, Ethel Barrymore, Billie Burke, Maude Adams, John Drew, Walter Hampden, John Barrymore, William Gillette and 700 others. He controlled over 200 theaters in America and England. His power and influence in the theatrical world were unmatched, and yet he was as polite and respectful to a janitor sweeping a stage as he was to the king of England.

Peg and her father attended Frohman's funeral with Walter Hampden and Mabel

Moore. However, Charles and Jane were not able to attend as they were on the West Coast; instead, they paid their respects at a memorial for the famous producer in Los Angeles. Jane, always one for adventure, had forgone the typical dark and drab garments of mourning and opted instead for a flamboyant pink suit she had created herself. There is no doubt that the outfit caused some mourners to shift in their pews, but it was, after all, a memorial for a showman, not a head of state. Jane recorded the event in her diary without the slightest regret for her fashion statement.

A few days later Charles pitched some scenarios to the Nebraska Film Company in Los Angeles. When that didn't pan out, he got a few minor acting gigs at Universal Pictures. After a month, he left Universal and then was hired to direct a picture called *The Surrender,* a western drama produced by the oddly named 101-Bison. *The Surrender* had a small cast of players who never did much of anything considered "big" by industry standards. It was released in September 1915 and, like its small cast, just simply faded away.

* * *

Early in 1916, Peg sailed back to England with her father and stepmother. Uncle Charles and Aunt Jane accompanied them. The purpose of the trip was to attend an Entwistle family reunion. It was a strange time for transoceanic excursions.

The belligerents of World War I were in their second year of hostilities, and though far from peaking, death and destruction ravaged much of Old Europe's continent. U-boats of the German navy continually stalked and engaged French and Belgian frigates and cruisers. The Kaiser's battleships courageously challenged, and at the same time feared, the British Fleet's massive armadas of dreadnoughts, whose devastating broadside volleys of heavy cannon were second only to the wrath of God.

Yet, in the midst of all the terror, ships of United States registry were guaranteed safe passage through the Atlantic lanes. This came about as a direct result of the Americans who were killed in the sinking of the RMS *Lusitania.* Fearful that the United States would be drawn into the war because of American public outrage, Kaiser Wilhelm II ordered a halt to unrestricted attacks of civilian ships, particularly American vessels. This edict promised unmolested voyage of the SS *Philadelphia,* which was now steaming Peg and her family to Liverpool. Indeed, there would be little for Americans to fear from the Kaiser's navy until the spring of 1917, when President Woodrow Wilson urged Congress to declare war on Germany after learning they were enticing Mexico to invade the United States.

Unaffected by war, indifferent to the volatile and convoluted geopolitics of 1916, little Miss Entwistle was too busy to concern herself with such harsh realities of life. Upon arriving in London on January 30, she was met by a swarm of relations, including uncles Henry and Ernest Entwistle, their sisters Rosina and Lillian, Rendell Graham (Rosina's husband), Army Lt. Billie Rowley (Lillian's husband) and Ernest's wife, Vivienne. Laura Seaton was also there, having come up from Wales for the occasion.

After some hours spent reacquainting over lunch, the entourage retreated to Henry Entwistle's home in Kensington. Six days later, on Peg's eighth birthday, a grand lunch and high tea was held in her honor. Later that evening, dressed to the nines, they boarded a train for Oxford. There, at the New Theater, they enjoyed a performance of *Peter Pan.*

The next day, Laura took Peg to Wales for a visit while Robert remained in London with Charles and Jane. It isn't known how the eight-year-old spent all of her time there in Port Talbot, but she was quite a little actress and loved to command a room, so it isn't hard to imagine her entertaining the Stevensons with animated stories of her experiences in America and aboard ship. She returned with Laura to London on February 17. Aunt Jane surprised her with a beautiful blue and red plaid dress she had sewn from scratch. It featured a white broad collar similar to Jane's trademark fashion statements. Peg wore it to church the next day.

On February 26, 1916, the family reunion dinner was hosted by Henry Entwistle at the Restaurant Frascati, a fancy Mediterranean-style eatery just outside of London. The management gave every attendee special souvenir menus that were passed around and signed by each family member — much like graduating students will do with their class yearbook. Uncle Charles signed his name at the top; below him, Vivienne, and then Rendell. Lauretta inked her tidy autograph fourth. Now it was Peg's turn. She used a pencil; her child-like scrawl is careful and deliberate.

"Babs."[16]

When and why young Peg got tagged with "Babs" remains a mystery. It is normally recognized as a pet name for "Barbara." It may have been given to her by Aunt Jane or Lauretta, for it seems distinctly American. However, "Babbie" was a character in James M. Barrie's 1897 play *The Little Minister*.[17] In the story, a girl of royalty named Lady Barbara disguises herself as a gypsy named Babbie, and goes to warn villagers about her father's plans to arrest them. It is possible Peg saw a revival of this play, liked Babbie, and from that came "Babs." Whatever the origin, Peg's family and friends always referred to her as Babs, and she signed all her personal correspondence this way. Even after her death, Peg Entwistle's family continued to speak of her as "Babs." They still do today. (The genesis of "Peg" is detailed later.)

Two weeks after the reunion, Peg and her parents boarded the *Philadelphia* and steamed for New York. Again, Aunt Jane and Uncle Charles accompanied them. Jane notes in her diary how glad she was to leave England, and her entry two days later is a chilling reminder of war and the German Wolf Pack lurking below: "Very glad to be out of danger zone."[18]

Peg shared a good deal of time with her aunt during this voyage. They also shared seasickness for four straight days. When she was feeling better, Jane taught Peg the finer points of gin rummy. During a day of calm seas and a blue sky they sunned on deck chairs while Charles read to them from Jane's favorite book, *The Count of Monte Cristo*.

On March 19 the 527-foot *Philadelphia* entered New York Harbor at four o'clock in the morning. She docked at Pier 62, the historic Chelsea Pier which had been home to the *Lusitania*, and was the destination of the ill-fated *Titanic*. From there the five Entwistles retired to Peg's apartment in a hotel on West 45th Street. Several days later, perhaps because Lauretta tired of living in a hotel high rise, she and her sister went house-hunting with Peg. It didn't take long. That afternoon she rented a place at 1001 East 167th Street, the Bronx. The next day, as Robert and Lauretta supervised the moving company and set up their new place, Jane and Peg spent the day together, getting familiar with the Bronx neighborhoods, shopping, enjoying dinner and then taking in a show at the nearby American Theater.

Peg's father and uncle were still working for Frohman's company: Robert as a bit player, set designer, and stage manager, while Charles sat huddled in a theatrical office, arranging press releases, fielding inquiries, and using his position to get Jane noticed. It worked, too ... sort of. She was signed to play the supporting role of Maeve in Iden Payne's Irish tragedy, *Grasshopper*. It opened April 7 at the Garrick Theater on Broadway. The production was written up in a most confusing manner two days later. The *New York Times* first promoted *Grasshopper* as a quaint play containing touching colloquies. Then with hardly a breath expelled it is demoted to "laborious ... awkwardly written ... only fairly well acted."[19] But there was no confusion at the box office: The play closed after just three performances. Rehearsals had taken three *weeks*.

Jane was devastated. She was so terribly upset and embarrassed by the play's failure that Charles decided to get her far away from Broadway. Without hesitation, he quit his job and made train reservations for a getaway to Santa Monica. Jane still had her cottage home near the bay; Don Caesar would again earn Jane rave reviews from the amused townsfolk who watched "Donnie" follow her around on the beach like a well-heeled dog. It was just what the doctor ordered. Robert and Lauretta hosted a farewell dinner and poker party for them with a few close friends. Jane arrived with a pair of goldfish for Peg. To everyone's delight the imaginative little girl named the small one "Babs," and in homage to her father called the larger one "Bobs."

Almost immediately upon returning to California, Uncle Charles got a film role in *The Beggar of Cawnpore*. It was produced by Charles O. Baumann's Kay-Bee Pictures unit and released that same April. Also in the film was one of the most popular screen actors of early Hollywood, H.B. Warner. In August, Peg's uncle made *The Summer Girl*, a comedy by Francis Marion, another silent era pioneer.

In September 1916 Peg's father began rehearsals for the October opening of *Hush!* at the Little Theater on Broadway. The play was unremarkable for many reasons but managed to last into November. Its only real distinction: the Broadway introduction of two popular English actresses, Estelle Winwood and Winifred Fraser.

October and November saw Jane and Charles Entwistle reunited with Lee and J.J. Shubert for a northeast revival of *Hobson's Choice*. Prior to the November 6 opening at the Royal Alexandra Theater in Toronto, Jane and her powerful Cole automobile and death-defying thrill ride in the Santa Cruz Mountains with Don Caesar created a small splash in the Canadian press. She was heralded as a "stately beauty," an American heroine who maintained grace and calm in the midst of terrifying challenge.[20] *The Toronto Sunday World* published an account of her heroics and ended the article thus: "Although such rare nerve and self-possession accomplished a life-saving feat quite as thrilling as any ever devised by a scenario writer for the screen, Miss Ross speaks of the experience as though it were a matter of the moment, which is quite in accord with the athletic spirit of young America."[21]

* * *

Peg's father also once had a harrowing bit of adventure which required rare nerve and self-possession. No cliffs and no rampaging steeds here, though, just the terribly bruised ego of a clumsy actor: In 1926 Peg told the *Boston Globe* the story her father used to tell about his very first time on a stage. He had appeared in *Monsieur Beaucaire*. Robert, who was balding, was given a hat and wig. The rest of his costume included a cane, snuffbox, and a lace handkerchief. As he entered the scene he was to hold the items in one hand and remove his hat with the other while doing a courtly bow. But as he took his steps and began the bow, he tripped on the edge of a rug and stumbled headlong to the floor. The cane, snuffbox, and handkerchief went flying in one direction while the wig and hat came off together in another direction. Booth Tarkington's romantic opera had suddenly become a Vaudeville skit as the audience howled with laughter. The mortified young actor simply piled everything back into his hands and atop his head and continued on as if nothing happened. It was Peg's favorite story of her father's acting career.

In early 1917 Robert Entwistle moved his family back to the Upper West Side, into a large brownstone at 251 West 88th St. Peg had to say goodbye to her friends in the Bronx, but the aspiring actress was happy to be near Broadway again. Now she could more easily convince her parents (or visiting aunt and uncle) to take her to a play, and this she did often.

It was also about this time that Peg cajoled her father into giving her his small collection of scripts, which she liked to memorize and then recite to her family and friends at mixed gatherings. Peg thoroughly enjoyed pretending to be the star, and as a "director" she got a grand kick out of assigning roles to the people around her. In September, Peg's cast of players increased by one when her stepmother Lauretta gave birth to little blue-eyed Milton.

Robert Entwistle next appeared in the Empire All Star Corporation film adaptation of *The Beautiful Adventure.* He and three other cast members from the original 1914 Charles Frohman production were signed to reprise their stage roles. The film had no real star power (most films didn't) and the actors wouldn't get rich (most actors didn't), but Robert's screen debut was aptly titled. With a lovely wife and daughter, and a healthy new son to coddle and mentor, life in America was a beautiful adventure indeed.

* * *

Not long after Peg turned ten years old, she was enrolled in the St. Agnes Academy, a parochial school for girls. About this time, her father began rehearsing a Broadway production called *Humpty Dumpty*. It starred Otis Skinner, one of the top draws of the day. Meanwhile, Peg's Uncle Charles was in Glen Cove, Long Island, shooting *Too Fat to Fight*, an hour-long silent film about a lovable rotund gent who is turned away by the army but proves his mettle at the local YMCA, where he had gone to slim down. The film was terrible and starred no one of prominence. In an industry that was turning out hundreds of pictures a year, *Too Fat to Fight* was easy to overlook.

Robert's *Humpty Dumpty* fared somewhat better than his brother's film. Leading man Otis Skinner was given rave notices for his performance, and the *New York Times* review of this polite comedy is short, but complimentary to the entire cast: "It is not alone the performance of the star which rises above the play: half a dozen of the cast could be brevetted for distinguished service were their fellow-players less skillful."[22]

Also in the cast of *Humpty Dumpty* was Elisabeth Risdon, a handsome but petite English actress who trained (and later taught) at the Royal Academy of Dramatic Arts. In 1915 Risdon was voted England's most popular film star. During a rehearsal of *Humpty Dumpty*, Robert Entwistle introduced his ten-year-old daughter to Risdon, who was 21 years her senior. Despite the vast age difference, Peg and Risdon will become good friends while performing together in the Theater Guild's 1929 national anniversary tour.

On September 27, 1918, eleven days after the premiere of *Humpty Dumpty,* a birthday party was held for one-year-old Milton Entwistle. During the course of the festivities, a special card was made for him. It contains a six-line poem; each person originated a line to dovetail the one preceding it. Aunt Jane recorded each contribution. The final line was Peg's:

"Our little boy has lived a year." (Uncle Charlie)
"Let's hope he lives a hundred more." (Indecipherable)
"Anyway, here's to him with good cheer." (Auntie Jane)
"With luck he's crossed our house and door." (Mother)
"A breath of Heaven did appear." (Daddy)
"When he was sent to us last year!" (Sister)[23]

* * *

With a wife and two children to feed (and now a third on the way), Peg's father lost faith in the theater's ability to provide a steady income. His last play (*Humpty Dumpty*) had been pulled from the Lyceum Theater after just 40 performances; this prompted Robert

1. The Curtain Rises

to retire from the stage. He opened a unique stationery shop at 25 East 54th Street — smack dab at a lucrative corner on Manhattan's swanky Madison Avenue. To assist him, he hired a woman named Marion Gressing. Using natural creativity and skills he learned while working in his father's shop in London, Robert began making custom gift boxes for many of the city's wealthy residents; Gressing did all the stationery printing. By Christmastime, customers were called "clients" and orders for gift boxes were by appointment only. Given the specialized nature of this store and its elite location, one might expect a fancy name befitting the elaborations taking place therein; however, the logo on the window was simple: Box Mart. In a *New York Times* article some years later, Charles Entwistle said his brother's shop was the only one of its kind.

As Robert toiled pleasurably and profitably in his new vocation, Charles was busy in Washington, D.C., shooting a film called *In the Hollow of Her Hand*. The murder mystery starred Alice Brady, a Broadway sensation and, as luck would have it, the daughter of William A. Brady, arguably the most powerful producer of American theater (now that Charles Frohman was dead). Mr. Brady wielded his power with a heavy, sometimes greedy hand ... something Peg would come to unpleasantly learn near the end of her life.

Although she had been propelled upon the stage several years earlier with the help of her famous father, Alice Brady proved to be a charming actress of great talent. She starred in many stage and screen productions and in 1936 was Oscar-nominated as Best Supporting Actress for her role in *My Man Godfrey*, a much-loved comedic romp starring William Powell and Carole Lombard. A year later, her appearance in *In Old Chicago* won her the Oscar for Best Supporting Actress.

A young company called Select Pictures Corporation produced *In the Hollow of Her Hand*. Select was making a lot of noise in 1918. At its helm was Lewis J. Selznick (father of David O. Selznick) and Adolph Zukor (father of Paramount Pictures). They controlled the screen work of sisters Norma and Constance Talmadge and a movie star debutant named Marion Davies, longtime pet of newspaper tycoon William Randolph Hearst.

In the Hollow of Her Hand might have become a hit (thus helping Charles Entwistle's career) given that Alice Brady was the centerpiece; instead, the film was forgotten shortly after its release due to the phenomenal reception of another Alice Brady film called *The Better Half,* in which

In 1918 Peg joined the American Junior Red Cross and helped make care packages for the war refugees in Europe (courtesy Entwistle Family).

she played twin sisters. Moving pictures were no longer considered a gimmick by 1918; however, creative writers were always looking to include a bit of gimmickry that would otherwise have been impossible to flesh out in a stage production. Having Brady simultaneously playing a good twin and an evil twin was a spectacular plot device for the day.

Around this time, Peg joined the American Junior Red Cross. This came about after Broadway had gone dark for several weeks as a result of rising fears brought on by 1918's devastating Spanish flu pandemic. When theater owners closed their venues, they encouraged actors and their families to get involved with the overwhelmed and understaffed Red Cross. Peg was given a uniform and was assigned light duties such as fundraising and sorting Friendship Boxes, packages containing food, medicine, and blankets—gifts from generous Americans to the war refugees of Europe.

In 1919 Charles Entwistle made his last two silent features. January saw him once again at Metro Pictures, with Ethel Barrymore in *The Divorcee*. The script was adapted by June Mathis from W. Somerset Maugham's play *Lady Frederick*. Five months later, Tribune Productions Inc. signed Uncle Charles to support *The Woman Under Oath* with Florence Reed, one of the grande dames of Broadway and a board member of Actors' Equity. *Oath* was directed by John M. Stahl, one of the founders of the Academy of Motion Picture Art and Sciences.

Aunt Jane was busy herself during her husband's film excursions. On March 18, 1919, she and producer David Belasco signed a contract for the Irish comedy *Dark Rosaleen*. Also busy that same day was Jane's sister Lauretta: she gave birth to Peg's second brother, Bobby.

While Lauretta was doting on her newborn son, Jane went on the tryout road with *Dark Rosaleen* before opening to good reviews on April 23 at Belasco's theater on Broadway. It enjoyed a respectable three-month run. Notable among the cast was Charles Bickford, one of the most familiar character actors of Hollywood's golden age.

According to Jane Entwistle's diary she had roles in several films from 1913 to 1916, but she doesn't name these films or the studios that produced them. Entries regarding her film work are sporadic, with a minimum of detail. At least one news article mentions Charles directing her in a film, but here, too, no title or studio name is given. It seems Jane's film career consisted of only a few uncredited bit roles for flash-in-the-pan companies.

Peg's service with the Red Cross was over by 1919. With the Armistice in full swing and the flu epidemic in check, the playhouses of Gotham were once again bustling with drama, comedy, and song. When not attending classes at the St. Agnes Academy, Peg could often be found enjoying herself in the things she loved best. For there was a world of theater around her, and in her the theater was Peg Entwistle's world.

2

Peg O' Peg's Heart

The story varies, but generally goes something like this: In late December of 1919 Broadway producer Harry Herbert Frazee wanted to bankroll a three-act farce called *My Lady Friends,* but he was short on cash. So, in order to fund this show, Frazee, who also happened to be the owner of the 1918 World Champion Boston Red Sox, unloaded his most valuable possession ... he sold Babe Ruth to the New York Yankees. Ruth was the nation's top slugger at the time, but Frazee's deal was a theatrical home run. *My Lady Friends* became a comedy hit that later turned into a bigger hit musical called *No, No, Nanette.* The sale of Babe Ruth to Bean Town's most hated sports rival also gave birth to the mythical "Curse of the Bambino." But try telling a Bostonian it was only a myth: After winning the World Series four times in seven years prior to 1919, it was another 86 years before the Red Sox reigned as World Champs again. The Yankees owned the crown 26 times during the same span.

Thus began the decade known as the Roaring Twenties.

Peg Entwistle was 12 years old with the advent of the Jazz Age and the flapper (and the Bambino Curse). It was also the beginning of her stage career, as she played the title role in a school production of *Peter Pan.* Stepmother Lauretta sewed the costume; it wouldn't have the wardrobe departments of Broadway theaters knocking down her door, but Lauretta had given it her best and a surviving photograph of Peg modeling the finished product shows the young actress to be somewhat pleased ... somewhat.

Peg's father continued to profit steady and sure. Hardly could he and his partner have chosen a better location for their Box Mart. A block east was Park Avenue and some of the most expensive apartments and real estate in America. Many of Robert's clients lived in the area; they included bankers, advertising executives, and fashion designers. And his theatrical connections brought him a good deal of business from the Broadway set — actors, producers, writers, etc.

It wasn't hard to see why the store had become popular. Robert's gift boxes were cleverly decorated to fit special occasions and tailored toward children. A box containing a baseball glove for Timmy's birthday might have a wind-up train clicking along an oval track fastened to the top of the box, black licorice bits filling the coal car. Susie might have a tea set in her Christmas box, with perhaps a ballerina or two poised on top. There were numerous printing and stationery shops in town, but Box Mart was *the* place to go for turning a simple gift into a charming experience.

Now that Robert was familiar to the locals living near his store, he thought it would be wise to have his family reside in the area. It was a much more expensive neighborhood, but he was confident in his store's ability to make all the ends meet. And so, to the ritzy Upper East Side they did go, to a spacious four-room at 140 East 72nd Street, a block from

Park Avenue. The new place offered upscale comfort and was just a 15-minute walk (or five-minute ride) to Box Mart. And Central Park was only a stone's throw away. Although it was suffering some disrepair because of municipal power struggles (a few areas were filled with dead trees and overgrown brush, or marred by litter and graffiti), there was still plenty for Peg and her family to enjoy. A summer afternoon might be punctuated by a picnic on the Park's former military parade ground known as Sheep Meadow. Here, they could pet the resident flock of pedigree Southdown grazing under the watchful eye of a real shepherd, or even visit the sheepfold housed in the magnificent Victorian building that was to become the famous Tavern on the Green restaurant in 1934.

There was plenty for the children to graze upon as well, such as cotton candy and other treats sold by vendors: candied apples; all-day suckers the size of small plates; sweet and delightfully chewy taffy, licorice, hand-turned ice cream and shaved ice drenched in all the syrupy flavors of the rainbow. And a day at the Park just wouldn't be complete without a visit to the Menagerie, known today as Central Park Zoo.

Peg and Lauretta often loaded little Milton and Bobby Entwistle into strollers and took leisurely walks along the reservoir. Being true New Yorkers now, they would sit on benches and toss peanuts to friendly squirrels and popcorn to cooing pigeons.

Central Park was a grand place for a rookie teenager, but by 1921 New York for thirteen-year-old Peg was more than fond times with hungry critters and leisurely strolls with the family. The girl had aspirations.

During that spring, while Peg was still four years away from her Broadway debut, her Uncle Charles was busy managing the man who would make that debut possible: family friend and Shakespearian A-lister Walter Hampden. He was influential across the entire theatrical spectrum: He was an advocate for performers regarding disputes within the Actors' Equity purview, and as a feature writer for the *New York Times,* he contributed lengthy, erudite articles defending the virtues of the repertory style. He had just returned to New York with Peg's uncle after an extended tour and was now rehearsing for a Broadway revival of *Macbeth.* (During this period, Aunt Jane sold her Santa Monica house. When she wasn't acting or accompanying Charles on tour, she divided her time between her family in Ohio and her husband in New York.)

As the business manager for an A-list performer and producer, Charles was armed with the answers to nearly all of his niece's questions regarding the latest news of Broadway notables. Of course, Peg's aunt was also a reservoir of information. Jane wasn't just an actress, she was a fan. As far back as 1913 her diary mentions seeing a show nearly every night when she wasn't in one. A slow week might list three productions. When Peg was as young as five she sometimes went along. Every other week or so, Jane's journal names a half dozen or more family members and friends accompanying her to a play. But it's the stars who stand out in Jane's diary: John Drew, Fay Templeton, Lillian Russell, Forbes Robertson, Billie Burke, Ellen Terry and others, all of them the biggest headliners of the day. As a veteran and fan of the stage, there were few theatrical questions Aunt Jane Entwistle could not answer for her niece.

Because of her uncle's association with Hampden, Peg was able to go backstage after watching him perform. Many actors were fans of each other and regularly attended each other's performances, especially on opening nights. Some of Hampden's biggest fans included Maude Adams, Madge Kennedy, Ruth Chatterton, Ina Claire, Mrs. Minnie Maddern Fiske, John Drew, the Barrymore siblings and George Arliss, whose Beverly Hills address and number are listed in Charles Entwistle's date book.

There were other famous followers of Hampden, most of them celebrated on Broadway and in Hollywood, and it took just a polite request from each (if they hadn't already been invited) to come backstage before or after a performance. Peg was no exception. As the niece of Hampden's manager she was allowed behind the curtain with little more than a beckoning wave from her uncle. Sometimes she just introduced herself to an usher or stagehand as she walked briskly by, as if she owned the theater. In a way, she did.

Peg's interest in theater received much nurturing through this privilege, and she met many famous actors who happily answered her questions about acting and the actor's life.

Peg also buried herself in many periodicals such as *Guild,* the monthly organ of the Theater Guild. *Theatre Magazine, Theatre World,* and *Theatre Arts Monthly* were Broadway standards she could not do without. *Vogue* was important to her for two reasons; it covered the Manhattan stage as well as women's fashion (many times combining both). Every week came *The Billboard,* an industry catalogue that listed where auditions would be held, when rehearsals would begin, and want ads for stagehands, craftsmen, and so on.

There were numerous theatrical publications, but for the latest news, reviews, in-depth articles about stars, productions, and the like, nothing could beat the *New York Times.* The *Times* was the "go-to" daily for all things Broadway. Its theater section was the first thing actors, producers, and patrons turned to each morning and it would have been nothing short of theatrical blasphemy for an intelligent, stage-minded girl like Peg Entwistle to ignore it.

Although she was still years away from high-profile co-starring roles with two of Broadway's most cherished and successful leading ladies, you can be sure that Peg knew what was happening with both of these women, for scarcely could they buy a new hat or attend a tea without making the top fold of the *Times*: Billie Burke (wife of producer Florenz Ziegfeld) was back from Hollywood after shooting what became her final silent film, *The Education of Elizabeth.* And Laurette Taylor (wife of playwright John Hartley Manners) was currently wowing them at the Cort Theater in a hit revival of her husband's *Peg O' My Heart.* Miss Burke and Miss Taylor were magical, bigger-than-life Broadway royals in 1921. Thirteen-year-old stage hopeful Peg Entwistle could only imagine sharing curtain calls and ovations while standing at their side.

*   *   *

Peg was an actress. And an actress is part mimic; theater critic John Hutchens points this out in the June 1932 issue of *Theatre Arts Monthly.* In writing about impersonations of Laurette Taylor, Ethel Barrymore, and Mae West by impressionist actress Dorothy Sands, Hutchens noted that the technique used by Sands to capture exactness of personality, voice, and gesture were found deep in the mimicry where he believed acting has its basic security.

Indeed, as a girl Peg spent a good deal of time at the mirror, practicing Billie Burke's delightful sing-song voice while mingling the imitation with Burke's mannerisms, such as her dance-like shoulder-shrug accentuated with slight throwbacks of her head. (Perhaps the best example of this occurs during a classic scene in the 1933 film *Dinner at Eight,* when Burke's excited hostess, Millicent Jordan, contemptuously complains about her dinner plans going awry.)

Peg knew that her Uncle Charles helped manage Burke's affairs when she was under contract with Charles Frohman; she never let her uncle leave a get-together without first showing off her "Billie" and cornering him with questions regarding the famous actress.

But it was Laurette Taylor who had the greater influence on young Miss Entwistle. The seed of this influence was first planted in 1914 when Peg accompanied her Aunt Jane and other family members to a performance of Taylor's original Broadway production of *Peg O' My Heart*. In several family photographs taken in 1914 or 1915, Peg is posing in a manner similar to the way Laurette Taylor was often shown in playbills and publicity shots: a slight forward bend at the waist accentuated by a more pronounced crane of the neck, as if leaning into another's whisper. From a gentle tilt of the head a bright smile ignites the world as eyes peer fetchingly from their corners. The similar poses may be coincidental; then again, maybe not.

Like the original 1914 production, the 1921 revival of *Peg O' My Heart* was the biggest hit on Broadway. It saw nearly 700 curtain rises, almost a hundred more than the original production. Taylor's title character and her adorable mongrel sidekick were favorites among young girls. The photos of Peg at this time show a girl who may or may not be mimicking Laurette Taylor, but on Valentine's Day 1921, when Taylor and the revival of her trademark role opened on Broadway and again took New York City by storm, Millicent Lilian Entwistle, heretofore known to her family only and always as "Babs," left the Cort Theater with her aunt and stepmother and now began to call herself "Peg."

If Peg's primary interest had been ballet, she would have practiced form and movement such as standing *en pointe* and turning fouettes; she would have followed closely the career of prima ballerina Anna Pavlova, and gone to see performances such as Stravinsky's *Pulcinella*. Had the violin been her calling, she would have turned her ears to the strings of Efrem Zimbalist, learned to read music, and dreamt of enrollment at Juilliard. But, to paraphrase Shakespeare, "The Play Was Her Thing."

There were connections for Peg everywhere in this regard, and 1921 offered much to the girl who was just beginning her pursuit of Broadway dreams. But her dreams were about to be tragically interrupted, and, worst of all, those pleasant picnics on Sheep Meadow would just never be the same.

* * *

On April 2, 1921, Peg's stepmother Lauretta succumbed to bacterial meningitis.

Telegrams to Lauretta's parents, Henry and Matilda Ross, indicate that Robert was at her side. It isn't known if Peg and her brothers were there also. Milton and Bobby were toddlers, too young to understand the nature of this loss, but Peg understood it all too well. She had grown very close to Lauretta during their eight years together; for all intents and purposes the woman was her *mother*. The devastation felt by Peg was not unique, of course, but it was cruel nonetheless.

Lauretta undoubtedly loved the sons she had borne, but the place she had in her heart for Peg was just as special. In virtually every photo of her and Peg together, they are embracing, smiling, *bonding*. (Indeed, Peg loved her stepmother Lauretta enough to record her name, and not Emily Stevenson's, in the "Mother's Maiden Name" section of her marriage certificate.)

Because it was first thought she had a touch of flu, Lauretta was home for several weeks. Then her condition worsened and she had to be hospitalized. The battle had been lost, however, and now Peg's best friend lived only in her heart and in the memories of pleasant days in Central Park. On the same day that Lauretta died, Robert and Peg and the boys were on a train to Cincinnati with her body. She was buried in the Ross family plot the following day.

Many friends and neighbors joined the family in their grief. This was not surprising. All who knew Lauretta held her as a gentle soul; a good friend, sister, and daughter, and above all, a loving wife and mother. She was a woman of her time in an era of her type. As a girl growing up at the turn of the century she had learned to do most everything "the old-fashioned way." She churned butter, chopped wood, scrubbed clothes on a washboard and believed a tablespoon of castor oil cured just about *everything*. She ran her home and nurtured her family in a manner that could have been a model for a Norman Rockwell painting.

Lauretta Amanda Ross Entwistle was 35 years old.

* * *

After several weeks of mourning in Ohio, Peg was back in New York. Robert found the strength to return to work. Peg searched for strength of another kind.

At some point shortly after Lauretta's death, Peg realized that she was now a mother to her brothers; her chance to become an actress was put on hold, and perhaps even gone forever. The Entwistle and Ross families did not believe in using nannies or hired help to raise their children. Unless her father married again, Peg would be expected to help raise her brothers until they were of age. This could take 15 years ... it might as well have been a thousand. She probably remained silent on the subject lest she sounded selfish. She might even have believed she was selfish for just *thinking* such things. The Entwistles were kind people, but they also carried nearly every British stereotype of the era. Peg's duty now was to care for her father and brothers, and she needed to keep a stiff upper lip while fulfilling this duty. This is not to say Peg's father was being cruel or unfair; on the contrary, he was very mild and thoughtful, especially to his children. Moreover, he was chiefly responsible for allowing Peg access to all the theatrical opportunities she desired.

But that was when Lauretta was alive.

It's impossible to completely understand how all this affected Peg psychologically. Clearly the loss of her mom had broken her heart, but the thought of being a surrogate mother instead of pursuing her dream of walking the boards of Broadway scarred her all the more.

Keeping a stiff upper lip was not the medicine Peg Entwistle needed.

* * *

The Christmas rush of 1922 came early for Robert Entwistle's Box Mart. Each holiday season came a bit sooner and got a bit busier than the one before as word spread of the elaborate gift boxes he created. This meant that Robert would have to work late to keep up with the orders. And so, on the night of November 7 (Election Day in New York), as the returns were projecting a landslide win for the state's next governor, Alfred Smith, Peg's father locked his Madison Avenue store just before 10:00 P.M. He bid goodnight to his assistant, Mrs. Gressing, and then began the short walk home.

While crossing Park Avenue and East 72nd Street, with his apartment building in sight, Robert was struck down and crushed under the wheels of a limousine. Several witnesses, including a husband and wife who were parked at the curb, reported seeing a uniformed chauffeur get out, look down at Robert, and then hurry back into the car and speed away. It was too dark to get a good description of the driver. A partial plate number was given to the police, but it was not accurate enough to be of any help. Robert was put into the back seat of the couple's car and taken to nearby Presbyterian Hospital. However, his injuries were too complicated for the receiving doctors. He had compound hip fractures and his spine was snapped in two places; part of it had penetrated his brain. (The well-meaning people who lifted Robert into their car might have caused him further injury.) He was transported to the larger, better equipped Bellevue Hospital two miles away.

Uncle Charles was in Pennsylvania with Walter Hampden. Aunt Jane was in Ohio with the Ross family. Peg and her brothers were alone in their apartment when the call came. The police also called Mrs. Gressing. She and her husband hurried to Peg's and stayed with the children until Charles arrived. As a testimony to 1922 technology, it had taken two days to reach Charles and two more before he arrived to New York. His brother's condition was serious but in a telegram to Jane he said the prognosis favored a full recovery. Robert was alert and cheerful despite knowing he'd have to remain in a body cast for two months. A few days later he was moved to Prospect Heights Hospital, a long-term rehabilitation clinic in Brooklyn. Jane arrived in New York about two weeks later. She could see that the shock of what happened to Robert so soon after Lauretta's death was putting a monumental strain on Peg. Aunt Jane was acutely aware that a fourteen-year-old should not be expected to maintain responsibility for two boys, four and five years old. She thought it best to give her niece a much-needed break, so she returned to Ohio with Milton and Bobby in tow. Charles stayed with Peg at the apartment and worked out of Walter Hampden's Broadway office.

Thanksgiving came. Christmas drew near....

On the morning of December 19, Charles stopped by the hospital to visit his brother before going to work. From there he went to a telegraph office and sent a cable to his wife in Ohio. Then he headed back to Peg's apartment, two train tickets and a shipping invoice in his pocket, no doubt struggling to find the words he would need to comfort his late brother's daughter ... Robert Entwistle, 48, had succumbed to a brain hemorrhage related to his injuries. For the second time in 18 months, young Peg had to escort one of her parents to a graveyard.

They buried him next to Lauretta ... three days before Christmas.

The limousine driver was never found.

* * *

Aunt Jane turned 37 on the day of Robert's funeral.

A dowager's Birthday be damned, if children must bury a parent it should not happen at Christmastime! This was the kind of thought one might expect of Jane Ross Entwistle. She was feminine and polite, but her diary and letters paint a portrait of a woman most men would not dare provoke — even in an era where the fairer sex was still considered the lesser one (suffrage was barely two years old). The prime of Jane's life almost reads like a Hollywood embellishment of an Old West pioneer. She was a crack shot with a rifle, an expert on horseback (remember Don Caesar), and once went on an afternoon adventure — alone — through the Badlands of South Dakota and recorded it in her diary thus: "Went for a ten mile walk, very nice...."[1]

She had endured brutal conditions as an actress touring the continent, steamed at least twice across an ocean swimming with German submarines hungry for tonnage, and snubbed her nose at segregation because for the life of her she could see nothing wrong with a white woman playing poker with a Chinese cook or a Negro porter aboard a train. It was just this kind of courage and tenacity that helped Peg's aunt face her most important challenge ever.

Charles and Jane Entwistle had been married for ten years now and still had no children; this had been a career choice. They loved their profession and knew that having children meant one of them would have to retire. Stay-at-home dads were a rare breed in those days and Jane was not ready to give up the stage, so they had remained childless. But things were different now. Lauretta and Robert were dead. And come hell or high water the boys would not go to an orphanage and Peg would not be sent to her birth mother, Emily. Fortunately, Robert had arranged for the care of his children just before he died. Four days before his passing he dictated his last will and testament; in it, he gave complete and permanent charge of Peg and her brothers to Charles and Jane. And just in case the former Emily Stevenson Entwistle got any ideas, Robert stipulated: "My eldest child, Millicent Lilian Entwistle, is the daughter of my first wife, whom I divorced, and the custody of my said daughter was awarded to me. I do not desire my said daughter to be at any time under the custody or control of her said mother."[2]

The wording suggests a serious element behind their divorce, for Robert had not even mentioned Emily by name. It may also indicate that she was living in America then. Moreover, according to Peg's cousin Helen, Peg had deep resentment toward Emily: "Babs and Uncle Robert never mentioned her — no one ever did. I have no idea what she did to them. After he died, Babs always thought of herself as an orphan. Who were we to argue?"[3]

Robert had complete trust in his brother and sister-in-law, and 85 years later Milton Entwistle reverently reflected: "Jane and Enty gave up their lives for us kids."[4]

Contrary to what has been claimed by some writers over the years, Peg and her brothers were not left destitute after their father's death. Charles and Jane Entwistle, though not wealthy, were far from broke at the time. Jane's family was financially solid and Charles was still the business manager for one of Broadway's top draws ... there was no barefoot ragamuffin Peg Entwistle in a tattered dress selling pencils on a street corner.

Moreover, Peg's father left behind life insurance and a trust of several thousand dollars — not exactly Rockefeller money, but it was plenty in a time when a gallon of milk, a dozen eggs, 12 pounds of potatoes, and a pound of butter, bread, and pot roast cost all of $1.77.

Robert bequeathed half of Box Mart to Marion Gressing for "recognition of her faithful service."[5] He gave the other half to his brother. Charles then quickly sold that half interest to Mrs. Gressing for $2,000, the modern-day equivalent of about $25,000.

Intimately, Robert bequeathed to Milton and Bobby a pocket watch and silver cigar case, respectively. To Peg he left all his rings and other personal effects.

Shortly after Robert's funeral, Peg went to New York with her aunt and uncle to pack up her apartment. Everything was transported to Ohio. The children would live under the roof of the Ross household. Other than a brief screen appearance many years later, Jane would never act again. She became a fulltime mother to her sister's orphans without expressing a single regret. Indeed, she came to relish the role so much that one might wonder if motherhood had not been in her heart all along.

The parental influence Jane and Charles had on Peg is discussed later, but its effect on her brothers can be summed up by a note in a 1944 Easter card: "Dear Auntie Jane and Uncle Charlie, God bless you, my dears, with happiness, peace and comfort free from strife and worry for all of your days. [signed] Your loving son, Milt."[6]

Your loving *son*.

The years 1921 and 1922 had been devastating for Peg and her family. If life were fair they would have been given a lengthy respite from sadness and worry, but life isn't fair at all.

* * *

Mastoiditis is a malady involving inner ear infections. Today it is easily treated with antibiotics, but such medicine was not available until the late 1930s. In the 1920s, operations to drain the infection were risky. It was a leading cause of child mortality.

Revelry and echoes of "Auld Lang Syne" had barely ushered in the New Year 1923 when Peg's four-year-old brother, Bobby, fell seriously ill. He had a high fever and his ears began seeping pus—a symptom of the worst case of infection. Jane rushed him to a Cincinnati hospital where small tubes were inserted into his eardrums to drain the poison brewing inside his skull. They treated him in time, before the bacteria could spread to his brain. He recovered, but doctors said the boy had a defect of the mastoid and could die if he wasn't moved to a warm climate. Uncle Charles was making a good living managing Walter Hampden's affairs and was saving to buy a home in New York, but now everything changed with Bobby's illness. This new crossroad was inescapable—the decision clear. A move to Los Angeles offered the greatest benefit for the family: The climate would help Bobby and there were good hospitals and schools in the city. Added support would come from Jane's sisters Helen, who had a house in Hollywood with her husband, Charlie Rees, and Marguerite, who was a few miles away in Glendale. The only real obstacles facing the family (assuming Bobby would get well) were finding a house and securing a job for Charles. The latter had frustrating difficulties attached.

Charles was first and foremost a theater man; his reputation flourished on Broadway and in England and his résumé included a host of impressive names and assignments, but theater in early 1920s Los Angeles, while popular from the 1800s until about 1914, was now mostly passé. (A rebirth of the L.A. stage would come, but incrementally, such as in 1925 with the advent of the A-list–enhanced Masquers Club, and

Charles and Jane Entwistle never legally adopted Peg and brothers Milton (left) and Bobby (right), but the results were the same. They were a family in every sense of the word, as evidenced by this quiet portrait taken shortly after the family arrived to Hollywood (courtesy Entwistle Family).

in 1929 with the inaugural West Coast tour of the New York Theater Guild's repertory company ... featuring Peg Entwistle.)

Peg's uncle would be hard-pressed to find any lasting theatrical success in Los Angeles. That left the film industry as his second option, but here, too, his prospects were limited. His dozen or so film credits as an actor and director going back to 1914 qualified him as a pioneer of the silent era, but just barely, and it had been four years since his last Hollywood gigs, when he was in *The Divorcée* with Ethel Barrymore and *The Woman Under Oath* with Florence Reed.

Charles's connections in Hollywood were few, he'd been away too long. Nevertheless, he would give it a go, pitch himself to the studios and hope for the best. But deep down he knew that he'd probably have to spend much of his career traveling back and forth between the coasts in order to provide for his wife and the children.

When he got called away to be at his nephew's hospital bed, Charles had been with Walter Hampden in Baltimore — the last stop of a tour. When Bobby was stable, Charles met up with Hampden in New York and explained everything. Hampden fully understood the gravity of the situation. He gave Charles a paid leave of absence in order to get the family situated in Los Angeles. As an added relief, Hampden assured him that no matter how things panned out, he would always have a job to fall back on with the acting company.

When doctors confirmed that Bobby was well enough to travel, the Entwistle quintet headed to California by train. Peg was quite pleased. She loved to travel and this was to be her second cross-country trip in a year (she and her father had visited Jane's sisters Helen and Marguerite the previous summer). Moreover, Peg was happy to get away from Jane's mother, Matilda. The Ross matriarch, now in her sixties, had been born before the Civil War. A creature of her time, Matilda favored "old-fashioned" women like herself, the kind who lived for doing chores; dutiful wives who stayed home to raise broods. Actress-adventurer Jane Ross had been an exception to this ideal, but becoming a maverick under Matilda's roof would have been no easy task. Indeed, of the five Ross maidens, all but Jane had become homemakers. Peg admired this and wanted to be an actress just like her aunt, to be on stage, to travel, *to sleep late.*

In a 1927 letter, Peg says she always hated getting up early. If anyone resented this side of Peg Entwistle, it was the sternly up-and-at-'em rise-and-shine Matilda Ross.

Photos of Peg with Matilda in the frame are not always flattering. Peg looks positively annoyed at times, like she had just been scolded. In one such photo she has the frown of a girl who has just eaten a sour snail sandwich; standing in back is Matilda, looking strict and matronly with a smirk that seems to say, "Don't give me any trouble, because there are plenty more snail sandwiches where that came from."

Matilda's letters show she dearly loved her grandsons Milton and Bobby; she cared for Peg also, but seemingly with a lesser heart. This may have had to do with Peg being related to her by marriage whereas the boys were grandchildren through her flesh-and-blood daughter, Lauretta. Whatever the reason for the chilly air, Peg and Matilda never really bridged the tension; they simply tolerated each other. The irony of this strained relationship will play out in a tender but uncanny premonitory comment made in the same hour of Peg's fateful 1932 decision.

* * *

When Peg and her family arrived to Los Angeles in 1923 they stayed with Jane's sister Helen and her husband Charlie Rees at their house on Cheremoya Avenue, in a rustic area of Hollywood called Beachwood Canyon. After a few days of resting from their trip, Uncle Charles began shopping himself around at the studios and playhouses. Bobby was still a bit weak, so he was kept indoors and closely monitored for the next few weeks. But Milton was healthy and strong and soon Aunt Jane had him enrolled in public school.

Peg was another story.

Her father's horrible accident and slow death coming not so long after watching Lauretta die still weighed heavily on Peg's heart. Robert had been gone for just a few weeks and she missed him terribly. The trip to California and the knowledge that she was a continent away from Matilda had cheered her up, but she was still quite fragile and lacked the confidence to mingle with peers. This is not surprising; remember, for all intents and purposes Peg considered herself to be an orphan, and in those years orphans were generally frowned upon by kids with parents. Orphans were the outcasts of schools and playgrounds and often cruelly teased. Peg knew she would be a wounded seal in a sea of sharks during recess and lunch time. Being raised by an aunt and uncle, no matter how loving and parental they may be, didn't exempt an unfortunate like Peg from the wrath of schoolyard bullies and brats. Her English accent could only make things worse. She was determined to have none of this and resisted all attempts by Aunt Jane and Uncle Charles to persuade her to go to public school. Then Jane found an ad for a private academy for girls. A photo showed the teachers on horses lined up in front of the administration building.

Peg must have beamed with delight.

*   *   *

The Bishop's School is a well-respected boarding academy nestled in La Jolla, a small suburb of San Diego, California. It began in 1909 as an independent institution affiliated with the Episcopal Church and was supported financially by the famous Scripps Foundation.

Bishop's prided itself on instilling intellectual, artistic, and athletic excellence in its girls. The school's founder, Bishop Joseph H. Johnson, and primary benefactor, Ellen Browning Scripps, believed in commitment to community service and that this commitment should begin at the school itself. Tuition and room and board were completely free to any young lady who enrolled. The school's primary goal was to prepare girls for college by way of a structured and disciplined Christian approach to living and learning.

Dr. Molly McClain, an associate professor and chair of the History Department at the University of San Diego, had been a boarding student at Bishop's. In *The Journal of San Diego History,* Dr. McClain's article celebrating Bishop's centennial noted that the school's motto, Simplicitas, Sinceritas, Serenitas (Simplicity, Sincerity, Serenity), "expressed a desire to help students attain strength and poise in their physical, mental and spiritual lives."[7]

By 1923, Bishop's track record was already impressive; since its founding, virtually every one of the girls had gone on to obtain degrees from prestigious women's colleges such as Vassar, Wellesley, Smith, Bryn Mawr, and Ivy League and state universities. Dr. McClain quoted one student's recollection from that era: "Our preparation for college was so superior that many of us found college work much easier [than the work at Bishop's]."[8]

So, by train to San Diego went Peg with her aunt and uncle. Following an interview with head mistress Caroline Cummins (a Vassar grad), they were introduced to the principals and given a tour of the grounds. It's likely they met Bishop Johnson and Ellen Scripps that first day, for both the good bishop and millionaire philanthropist made a habit of maintaining close contact with all the girls and their families. Peg was welcomed warmly by her fellows upon admittance. Any apprehensions she might have felt during and after the minutes of kissing her aunt and uncle goodbye would soon be soothed away by the open arms of bright, friendly girls her age. She may have even been met by an orphan or two.

The schedule at Bishop's was a busy one. Not all the students lived there, but the ones who did were awakened at six o'clock in the morning. Any sleepiness that lingered was soon washed away by the cold bath each girl took to "stimulate intellectual activity."[9] Next, they put on white uniforms and headed outside for a brisk set of calisthenics. Then it was off to chapel for mandatory Morning Prayer followed by breakfast and five hours of classroom study. In the afternoon came lunch and then athletics and physical fitness. Here, the girls could participate in any activity they desired, including tennis, basketball, softball, track and field, or riding.

Peg headed for the horses.

Jane had prepared her well. Peg learned to ride from her aunt years earlier and had many hours in the saddle. She was not only proficient as a rider, she had command of the equestrian lingo and was familiar with all the equipment. If a teacher told her to round up a breastplate and running martingale from the tack room, Peg knew what to look for and where to find them. She could tell you an English bridle came with a snaffle bit and caveson, and that most Western rigs used a bitless bridle called a hackamore. She did have one major weakness, however: She was too small to lift and toss a saddle onto anything much bigger than a Shetland pony.

An evening at Bishop's included study halls from 4:30 to 6:00 and 8:00 to 9:00, with dinner in between. Afterward, hot baths and personal time kept the girls occupied until lights-out at 10:00.

Peg was enrolled in the prestigious Bishop's School shortly after arriving to Hollywood in 1923. This photo shows her seated in the middle row, center, with unidentified classmates. Her delight at something happening off camera is frozen in time (courtesy Suzanne Weiner and The Bishop's School).

Weekends and holidays meant an extra hour of sleep and no classes; the schedule was lighter but busy nonetheless. This was also a time of camaraderie and friendly interaction between the students and faculty, for in the end they were all sisters in Christ. This fellowship included sports competitions and other group activities. In helping to teach the girls the importance of gratitude, charity, and civic duty, the weekends were also a time to minister to the neighboring communities. Peg's experience as a Red Cross volunteer during the war and flu epidemic served her well here. One of Bishop's commitments included a children's hospital, and if there was one thing Peg Entwistle could relate to, it was a child's suffering.

At Bishop's, Peg did well academically and conformed obediently ... most of the time, anyway. A bit of her maverick personality can be seen in a yearbook photo: She is seated in the midst of her 16 classmates; her skin and frame are healthy looking and her hair is a beautiful coif of sun-bleached blonde. For the sake of formality as well as posterity the class was no doubt instructed to face the camera...

But with the click of a shutter time is frozen and Peg is forever off on her own individual adventure of merriment. There looks to be no intended mischief; nevertheless, she has set herself apart from the other girls; her head is turned conspicuously to her right and her elated expression reminds one of a kid watching a traveling circus parade through town. She seems to be speaking or chuckling at the delightful happening that has caught her eye ... probably frolicking horses.

* * *

By mid-spring 1923, Uncle Charles had not yet found work in Hollywood. Then Walter Hampden called from New York and offered him a gig managing the Players' revival of Richard Sheridan's famous 18th-century comedy *The School for Scandal*. The Players held annual Broadway revivals of classic plays and always cast stage legends for the roles. Ethel Barrymore, John Drew, and Albert Bruning would accompany Hampden behind the footlights of *Scandal*. Uncle Charles went to New York to get the contracts in order before the June engagement, and by the end of May was back in Hollywood. Peg was back in Hollywood, too. The seniors at the Bishop's School had graduated and classes were out of session until August. Peg could have stayed and enjoyed the summer activities that Bishop's offered its boarders, but she had worked hard for nearly six months and now wanted to share some time with her family.

After spending some days recovering from his New York trip, Uncle Charles decided it was time the Entwistles got their own house. As luck would have it, just few doors away from Peg's Aunt Helen's sat a dilapidated fixer-upper, vacant and half hidden behind an overgrown jungle of neglect ... 2428 North Beachwood Drive. Interesting light into Peg's mind was shed during an interview with her cousin, Helen Reid, the daughter of Jane's sister, Marguerite: Peg, whom Helen remembered as "smart and polite"[10] with "blue, blue eyes, and hair [color] like skinned almonds,"[11] felt really sorry for the place. She first saw it the previous summer with her father during their visit with Jane's sister, Helen. "She talked about how sad it was to be orphaned," said Mrs. Reid.[12] "She had meant the house, but thought of herself as an orphan, too."[13]

Using the power of persuasion (or what Matilda called "getting her way"[14]), Peg talked her uncle into having a look at the place. He did, and thought it had potential. The two-story single-family framed stucco was a mess and had only one bathroom, but the three bedrooms would accommodate the family nicely, and the boys would have a swell time running around on the acre of land. When Uncle Charles contacted the deed holder, he was amazed to learn it had been built in 1913. Tumbleweeds, overgrown trees, poison ivy and general disarray were to be expected of landscape long ignored, but the dwelling was in tremendously bad shape for being just ten years old. Other homes in the area had been built at about the same time, yet hardly could a shabbier newer house be found in Hollywood. It isn't clear why the property had fallen into such disrepair, or for how long it sat empty (no records of previous tenants were found), but after negotiating with the land owners a deal was agreed to and a contract signed.

Peg's sorry little orphan had been adopted.

Charles pooled $2,000 of his own cash, $2,000 more from Jane's father (at six percent interest), and another thousand dollars borrowed against some oil stock to buy and renovate the property: equal to about $62,000 today.

Studying the contracts he made with the McFadden Construction Co. and their subcontractors reveals how rundown the property was. Peg's comment about looking orphaned was not hyperbole. New plumbing and fixtures would be installed; floors refinished; tile was needed for the bathroom and kitchen, and there would be new plaster and paint inside and out. And then there was the landscape. Trees needed to be trimmed, bushes pruned, weeds pulled, soil tilled, grass seed planted ... on and on it went.

The work would take several months. Charles kept watch over it as if it had been a stage production under his management. He made sure every pipe fitting was new, every board of lumber straight, every ceramic tile smooth and grout line even.

* * *

For nearly 90 years the original contracts, invoices, receipts and canceled checks regarding the purchase and renovation of Peg's Beachwood Drive house sat in a box, forgotten or ignored until they were made available for research by Milton Entwistle and his daughter, Lauretta Slike. Most of these documents were found to be in pristine condition, dated and

Charles Entwistle purchased this home shortly after the family moved to Hollywood. No longer owned by Peg's family, it is still there and often visited by tourists on their way to the Hollywood Sign (courtesy Entwistle Family).

signed by Charles and the owner of the McFadden Construction Co. They are important in helping establish Peg Entwistle's timeline.

While Charles was busy overseeing the project, Peg was spending a lot of time studying plays (Broadway was never far from her heart). One day as she and Aunt Jane recited lines on Helen's porch, a noisy parade of men and machines began making its way up North Beachwood Drive. Giant steam shovels and monstrous tractors belching plumes of exhaust went creeping through the neighborhood at a snail's pace. Cousin Helen, who was watching Peg and Jane's performance, remembered some of what took place next: "Babs and Aunt Jane stomped off the porch in frustration and went to see Uncle Enty, who was by the road watching the trucks. She said something like, 'What is all this?' or 'What are they doing with all this?'"[15]

You see, all of Charles's contracts are clearly dated; the city's history is a matter of record. And in the late summer and early fall of 1923, 15-year-old Peg Entwistle stood in front of her Beachwood Drive home and watched all the pieces of the Hollywood Sign go by…

3

Hollywoodland

*"The history of the Hollywood Sign cannot be underestimated.
It's the only monument in the world that started out as a billboard."*
— Filmmaker Hope Anderson[1]

Milton Entwistle was in the mood for a little action.

The adventurous 12-year-old has just returned from watching screen idol Ramon Novarro in Louis B. Mayer's *Ben-Hur*. Like most lads who enjoyed the film's exciting chariot race, Milton wonders what it must be like to compete in such a thrilling contest of courage and skill; to earn laurels and salutations as had champion Judah Ben-Hur. He imagines the energy of the arena; the roar of the crowd. *Milton Ben-Hur! Milton Ben-Hur! All Hail and make way for Milton Ben-Hur!*

Unfortunately, no gilded chariots led by powerful teams of muscular, flared-nostril stallions are to be found in Beachwood Canyon — the milkman's delivery wagon and its docile swayback mare will have to do for now. Beachwood Drive will suffice as Circus Maximus.

Milton spies from the bushes. The milkman hops off his wagon and crosses the street. The swayback twitches her ear; swings her tail. The hero makes his move...

Milton Ben-Hur!

An hour later, Roman Centurions (played by Los Angeles police officers) manage to corner the "chariot" in front of the place where this whole itch first began — Sid Grauman's Chinese Theater on Hollywood Boulevard. When informed of this transgression, Emperor Uncle Charles Entwistle is not amused. Milton Ben-Hur is sentenced to corporal punishment. But the hero is resolved; he shall endure the chastisement of stripes with a stoic face of courage befitting a champion of Rome. Neither tears shall he shed, nor mercy's plea shall he beg ... and then the spanking begins.

Another day in Hollywoodland...

Peter the Hermit awakens from a nap and emerges from a shack near the horse stables in the hills at the far north end of Beachwood Drive. A trusty greyhound is at his side. Bedecked in a flowing robe of linen girded at the waist, and a lion's mane of snow-white hair matching his full beard, Peter the Hermit clutches a wooden staff and yawns while stretching the last remnants of sleep from his muscles. For a moment he looks like an Old Testament prophet calling down fire from Heaven. Indeed, while Cecil B. DeMille's 1956 remake of *The Ten Commandments* is still many years away, Peter the Hermit's resemblance to Charlton Heston's Moses is uncanny.

It is time to go to work. Beachwood Canyon's most unusual resident begins his daily hike into the city. Business should be good today. His business consists of receiving handouts from the locals and coins from amazed tourists eager to take his snapshot. Each day he strolls southward, passing the village market and the real estate office. A few minutes after walking through the archway of the clock tower marking the tiny village's entrance, Peter and his dog will have to pass the picket fence at 2428 North Beachwood Drive. Sometimes they pause in front of homes where generous families dwell ... this is one such home. The Hermit knows that a pretty actress lives there—she's not famous ... but maybe someday she'll do something big to get the town's attention.

Another day in Hollywoodland...

Albert Kothe is a German immigrant whose job it is to change burnt-out light bulbs from among the thousands affixed to his employer's massive 50-foot-tall billboard. Wired in three separate sections as well as one complete circuit the length of several football fields, the sign is programmed to intermittently flash a logo from dusk to dawn. When timed relay switches open, electricity is routed to the first section: the word "HOLLY" blinks on, and then a second or two later the next section follows suit with "WOOD," and finally the third lights "LAND." All three sections are now energized as one. The hill directly in front of the array becomes noonday bright as thousands of bulbs illuminate the outline of the entire logo:

HOLLYWOODLAND

The 30-foot-wide letters stay lighted for a few seconds before going dark so the cycle can begin all over again. Each bulb is relatively small, but there are 4,000 of them, spaced nine inches apart. A 35-foot-wide flashing dot was installed below on the hillside to help punctuate and draw attention to the monstrous structure, but it wasn't needed—a harbor master 30 miles away in Long Beach could see the illumination. For 16 years the southern face of Hollywood's Mt. Lee will rarely see darkness.

Before Kothe can climb the sign in order to reach his work, he must first descend the terrain behind it. The steep grade of the slope has inherent dangers and presents an arduous struggle for the strongest of men on the best of days. The task essentially involves mountain climbing; Kothe has to rappel with the help of a rope anchored to a pole at the summit 175 feet above the structure. Arriving at its base, he is then able to reach the highest light bulbs with the help of ladders permanently affixed to the back of each letter. Anyone at all could reach the top of these structures using the ladders, but Albert Kothe and his employers had little concern for trespassers; after all, who besides him would want to climb up the damn thing, anyway?

Another day becomes night in

HOLLY ... WOOD ... LAND ... HOLLYWOODLAND ... HOLLY ... WOOD ... LAND ... HOLLYWOODLAND ... HOLLY ... WOOD ... LAND ... HOLLYWOODLAND...

* * *

In 1903, Hollywood incorporated as a municipality. Seven years later, the need for an adequate water supply precipitated a vote by the townsfolk to join the community into the care of the City of Los Angeles. Then, in 1911, a developer named Albert Beach began paving a portion of road leading north from Franklin Street in Hollywood to Graciosa Street near the Hollywood Hills. When the paving ended at the lower portion of a lush, spacious canyon, Beach named the road and canyon after himself. In the ensuing years this road was developed further until it extended far and high into the hills. Today it is called North Beachwood Drive.

Beachwood Canyon would also see growth. During the peak of this growth, the canyon and surrounding area would come to be known by locals as Hollywoodland. The history of the town called Hollywood can be traced back to the 1850s, when it was just a small agricultural community of hardly 500 souls. But the *legend* of Hollywood, with all its "Tinsel Town" lore and tales of the big screen's Golden Ages of Silents and Talkies, could arguably be said to have had its birth in February 1923; it was then that developers Sidney H. Woodruff and Tracey E. Shoults, backed with finances from *Los Angeles Times* publisher Harry Chandler, land tycoon Moses Hazeltine Sherman (founder of Sherman Oaks, California), and ranch owner E. P. Clark, created the Beachwood Canyon real estate venture called Hollywoodland. Although the canyon was spread over thousands of acres, the venture only involved a 500-acre subdivision of a ranch owned by Sherman and Clark at the top of Beachwood Drive.

Part stunt and part advertising genius, the Hollywoodland promotional campaign began with enticingly printed ads promising such things as "The luxury of metropolitan living with the glorious freedom of the hills,"[2] "Clean, pure mountain air,"[3] and "Unlimited dividends in Joy and Prosperity!"[4] They also promised sewers, aqueduct water, and gas and electricity service to each home. Special financing was available for those on the lower economic level.

The pamphlets and print ads were tempting to be sure, but nothing would quite catch a prospective buyer's eyes like the giant electric sign near the top of Chuenga Peak on Mt. Lee, a part of the Santa Monica mountain range adjoining Griffith Park.

Originally constructed using telephone poles, pipes, wood framing, and panels of sheet metal, the sign was an eyesore to environmentalists, a landmark for pilots, and, according to Peg's brother Milton, a playground for kids living in the canyon — including Peg.

Near the top of Mt. Lee, about a half mile west of the sign, there was a massive H carved into the terrain. It's sometimes said this was made by the Hollywoodland developers, but it was made by students from Hollywood High School; it was there as early as 1922.

In the weeks before construction of the Hollywoodland Sign began, the company erected a test H ten yards east of where the actual H was eventually anchored. The test was to determine the best positioning of the letters, to get an idea of how the sign would look from the Los Angeles basin. Then, in November of 1923, when this audition and rehearsal of the sign was completed to the satisfaction of its producers, a small army of surveyors, electricians, carpenters, and laborers headed up the hill to begin its construction. Trucks hauled the poles, braces, tools, ladders, rope, and sheet metal as far up Beachwood Drive as they could go. From there, tractors and mules took over, dragging the poles and other heavy pieces up to the peak; behind them, scores of men carried the smaller items. In her documentary *Under the Hollywood Sign*, filmmaker and Beachwood Canyon historian Hope Anderson shows amazing footage of this event; one can see the crews in single file, each man laboring the burden of sections of framing over his shoulder while trudging upward and onward behind the tractors. Viewing the film, one is reminded of World War I tanks and infantry going into battle.

Construction of a reservoir southwest of the sign would begin later in August. Lake Hollywood, as it came to be known, would not be filled until 1925. To hold the lake's 2.5 billion gallons in place, Mulholland Dam was built. The developers had also planned to expand their subdivisions out to this lake, but the stock market crash of 1929 would shatter those dreams.

The HOLLYWOODLAND Sign became a playground for the more adventurous children of Beachwood Canyon, including Peg. The electric 35-foot-wide dot below was added when the sign had its light bulb array installed. The arrow shows the approximate spot where Peg's body was found (courtesy Bruce Torrence Hollywood Collection).

Later that month the sign was officially dedicated. Part of the ceremony involved pretty models posing for photos while riding sidesaddle upon the massive scoop of a steam shovel. The Hollywoodland Sign was now the town's newest celebrity.

But the sign was intended only as a temporary billboard. It was to be demolished once all the property was sold; the developers figured that would take about 18 months. Because of this, it was rather hurriedly and flimsily built in only four weeks. The cost was $21,000 (about $260,000 today).

Although the sign looked solid and impressively strong from afar, it was given just enough integrity to keep it upright for those 18 months. This resulted in numerous structural problems. Hundreds of holes were bored through the panels to lessen the effect of wind upon them, but sustained gusts from the notorious Santa Ana winds caused the letters to wag violently. Each letter was held by four telephone poles sunk ten feet into the ground, but the letters weighed thousands of pounds; when they wagged they created tremendous stresses, causing the poles to loosen in their sockets. Metal panels would sometimes be torn away by the winds, lumber would crack, and it wasn't uncommon for an entire letter to lean over precariously or even partially collapse. Repairs involved little more than adding more poles, rope, and baling wire. Historians of the area sometimes deny that the sign suffered any wind-driven calamity, but *Under the Hollywood Sign* has footage showing the sign twisting in the Santa Ana winds. There are also photographs of men repairing what appears to be windstorm damage.

The Sign was unattractive — downright ugly when seen up-close — and the terrain and construction flaws made it very unsafe to be near ... or on. A marvel of advertising, the Hollywoodland Sign could hardly have been called a marvel of engineering.

For the housing development itself, the company hired renowned Spanish and Mediterranean revival architect Jon Delario. He built an array of homes incorporating different styles reflecting a European touch. Stonemasons were brought from Italy to construct retaining walls and stairs leading up the steep slopes to the homes. Some of these walls and stairways are quite elaborate, colorfully decorated with glass gems and mosaic tiles, and are still popular with residents and tourists. The masons also built a stone entrance on Beachwood Drive to welcome visitors and residents into the quaint, distinctly European-flavored Hollywoodland Village.

Plans called for a security gate between the 30-foot-tall clock tower and the ten-foot-tall archway across the road. Guards were to be posted from sunset to sunrise, but neither gate nor guards came to be.

With private roads leading to secluded lots offering spectacular views of the Los Angeles basin, and its close proximity to the major film studios, it wasn't long before notables of the film industry began making their way into Hollywoodland.

While some stars moved into the homes already built by the company, other screen luminaries erected fantasy homes reflecting their iconic status. Gloria Swanson wasn't really a resident, but everyone knew about her love nest up on Woodhaven. It is sometimes reported that producer Mack Sennett was a partner in the Hollywoodland venture; he wasn't, but he did buy the highest lot above the sign and on at least one occasion snapped publicity photos of bathing beauties between the sign's Os. Sennett's title writer, Felix Adler, had a home on Beachwood Drive. Adler later became famous as a screenwriter for Harold Lloyd, lovable buffoons Laurel and Hardy, Abbott and Costello, and the Three Stooges. In his last years, Adler was a daily presence in the Beachwood Village Laundry, handing out candy and coins to children and regaling adults with tales of old Hollywood and all the famous people he knew.

Perhaps the most interesting Hollywoodland resident (Peter the Hermit notwithstanding) was silent screen legend Pola Negri, who was often seen piloting her spectacular lavender Rolls-Royce around town. Negri liked to take her pet leopard for strolls to the village. Her estate had a large collection of exotic animals and she loved to show them (and herself) to the community.

Other prominent names on the Hollywoodland marquee included Norma Talmadge, who lived next door to Negri and Douglas Fairbanks. Doug, Jr., is said to have once lived in the house at 2210 Beachwood Drive. Charlie Chaplin bought a home on 2222 Beachwood from a Russian land baron. From time to time a gangster took up residence in Hollywoodland. During Prohibition it was rumored that liquor was smuggled through tunnels into Beachwood Canyon speakeasies. In the late 1930s Hollywood's favorite hoodlum, Bugsy Siegel, ran a speakeasy out of the famous Castillo del Lago mansion on Durand Drive.

Busby Berkeley, the film director known for his elaborately choreographed routines involving dozens—or hundreds—of singers and dancers, eventually moved into the house adjacent to the Hollywoodland tract office. It is the first home one sees upon entering the village.

In spite of a bit of debauchery now and then, Hollywoodland was always far from anything resembling a den of iniquity. In fact, religion had a toehold long before the terms "speakeasy" and "love nest" made their way into the local vernacular. In 1912, the Theosophist Society pulled up its Chicago stakes and settled a colony into a snug elevation at the southwest corner of Beachwood Canyon; they called it Krotona Hill. By 1926 the colony had moved to Ojai, California, but the building they called home is said to have been the first silent film theater in Los Angeles.

After doing the Lord's work during the Roaring Twenties in New Jersey, a Dominican cloister of ever-praying nuns called the Monastery of the Angels migrated to the City of the Angels. The founder of the monastery, Mother Mary of the Eucharist, soon received word of a heavenly deal: A mansion with its own hill could be had for a song. Though nearly penniless, Mother Mary was able to raise the funds. In short order she moved her prayer business into the Giroux family mansion on Carmen Avenue, a few blocks west of Beachwood Drive. The Monastery thrives today as it did then, with nuns praying in shifts 24 hours of every day.

* * *

Exactly who came up with the idea for the Hollywoodland Sign is open to a bit of interpretation, for there are two versions of the structure's origin. One version credits Hobart Whitley. Known as the Father of Hollywood, Whitley was the first to coin the town's name. He was also one of America's most successful developers at the turn of the century. His real estate portfolio included Whitley Heights, a Mediterranean-style village in Hollywood nestled within a triangle comprising Cahuenga Boulevard and Highland and Franklin Avenues. Some of his residents included Rudolph Valentino, Gloria Swanson, W.C. Fields, and Charlie Chaplin. To advertise the Heights, Whitley used a large electric sign; it is said that he told *Los Angeles Times* publisher Harry Chandler that Chandler's Hollywoodland investment might do better if its wooden billboard was replaced with a sign similar to the one at the Heights. Chandler agreed. The Crescent Sign Company was contracted to erect a structure. Then Thomas Goff, a noted artist and owner of Crescent, created the design of the Hollywoodland Sign ... or so the story goes.

The second version is considerably more elaborate. It involves 26-year-old ad man John Roche. Roche had been hired by Hollywoodland to create a brochure for the subdivision. He drew up a rough draft of a map showing proposed home sites, streets, equestrian trails, etc. Above the layout, on the face of his Mt. Lee outline, he wrote "HOLLYWOODLAND."[5] However, Roche wasn't designing a sign; he was simply titling the brochure with the company's name. He showed this drawing to Harry Chandler; he liked it and asked Roche if the logo could be made into a sign and erected on the hillside. If so, would it be seen all over Los Angeles? In a 1977 *Los Angeles Times* interview, Roche says he went walking along Wilshire Boulevard and took photographs of the hills to see how much of Mt. Lee could be seen from the city streets. He figured if the letters were about 50 feet tall they could be read from as far away as two miles. He created a scale drawing of the logo—it was nearly eleven feet long and ten feet high. Said Roche, "I took it to Mr. Chandler's office about 11 one night ... and he said, 'Go ahead and do it.'"[6]

Roche also insisted that there were no lights on his Hollywoodland Sign. "They came sometime later," he told the *Times*.[7] Exactly when, he couldn't say, for by then he was 65 miles away in Orange County working on a Chandler-related development called Dana Point.

These two versions have caused confusion among researchers, writers, residents and tourists. Open any two or three books discussing the early years of Hollywood and you will meet both versions. However, if one blends these together, a more logical conclusion can be drawn: John Roche designed the original dimensions and positioning of the Hollywoodland Sign. Harry Chandler gave the go-ahead to build it. Thomas Goff, owner of the Crescent Sign Co., architected and blueprinted Roche's design. Crescent constructed it without a lighting system. Some time shortly after that, H.J. Whitley suggested to Chandler the notion of lighting the sign. Chandler liked the idea. Crescent was called again; Thomas Goff designed the 4,000-bulb perimeter array and his company installed it. This is probably when the big electric dot (sometimes called a searchlight) was erected below the sign.

* * *

Peg simply got tired of the Bishop's School. She wanted more free time and dresses that didn't make her look like a sailor. She wanted to sleep late and more than anything wanted to be an actress, not a scholar. She finished another session at Bishop's and in 1924 had bid goodbye to the goodly reverend and his gals and returned to Hollywood.

One can almost imagine Grandmother Matilda rolling her eyes with a sigh heard all the way from Ohio. Jane and Charles caught a lot of heat from Matilda because of the way they seemed to bend over backwards to accommodate Peg's wishes. But accommodating her wishes didn't mean that Peg had the run of the house; she was expected to obey and honor her uncle and aunt as any daughter would her father and mother (and she did). However, Jane and Charles recognized in Peg the same theatrical traits they themselves had, and often treated her as a peer. This was a rather liberal way to deal with a young teen in the 1920s, and as a result, they may have unintentionally spoiled their niece. Peg had to follow the rules of the house, but there is no question she had her way when it came to public school. She still refused to go and simply shook her head at any notion of a return to Bishop's. That meant a tutor, which to Uncle Charles meant another mouth to feed.

Fortunately, Walter Hampden's repertory was booked at the National Theater in New York for the entire 1923-24 season. Charles had been with him since September when rehearsals had gotten under way. Hampden was starring in ten productions, including a highly touted revival of Edmond Rostand's *Cyrano de Bergerac*. This was the first time he was interpreting *Cyrano* for Broadway and New York City was buzzing. (It had been 23 years since a *Cyrano* strode the New York boards, when Benoit Constant Coquelin portrayed the long-nosed lovelorn opposite Sarah Bernhardt's Roxane.) Hampden was also premiering *Othello, Romeo and Juliet,* Philip Massinger's *A New Way to Pay Old Debts,* and *The Ring of Truth,* a play based on Robert Browning's *The Ring and the Book*. The other five plays of the Hampden season were familiar favorites of his repertoire: *Hamlet, Macbeth, The Merchant of Venice, The Taming of the Shrew* and *The Servant in the House*. Hampden's *Cyrano* performances were sold out months in advance and it proved to be a very profitable year for all involved.

Because Peg's uncle was managing a major Broadway success and getting a share of the box-office take, he was able to engage the services of a professional tutor named Helen Baker. She lived on Laguna Street (now Martin Luther King Jr. Boulevard), just off the campus of the University of Southern California in South Los Angeles. Her primary clients were USC undergrads and she rarely took on a student below the high school senior level. But Peg was an exception; the tragedies that darkened her life had done little to dim the brightness of her intellect and Helen Baker knew a gifted student when she saw one. At home, Peg studied the same subjects and was given the same kind of homework she would have gotten at any school (including Bishop's).

Milton Entwistle recalled that the two brains in the family were Uncle Charles and Peg. He remembered his sister nearly always had a book in her arms and that Charles was a trained and practiced speed reader who could sift through several volumes in a day — hardly a surprise for a man whose world travels had made him proficient in German, French, Italian, Spanish and Latin. In Peg's letters, and in comments to reporters covering her career, one hears the words of an articulate, intelligent young woman who, as an actress, may have sounded a tad self-centered at times, but as a thinker exhibited flashes of profound introspect.

* * *

In early February the Jergens Soap Company assigned its western sales territory to Jane's father, H. Milton Ross. On its surface this doesn't seem unusual, considering Mr. Ross was the company's vice-president of sales. Such clout could earn any business executive in the east a transfer to the warm and sunny West Coast, but this transfer hadn't been the result of any corporate strategy hammered out in a boardroom filled with clouds of cigar smoke. No, this one had Matilda Ross written all over it.

With three of her four remaining daughters and grandchildren living in Los Angeles, Matilda's big house in Ohio echoed with loneliness. The determined matriarch called Jane and told her of glad tidings to come: She and Papa were going to live with Jane's sister Marguerite in Glendale. After disconnecting with Jane, Matilda called Marguerite to inform her of this news ... it seemed only right. Matilda also told Marguerite that Helen and Charlie (her husband) would be picking them up at the train station and that Charlie was a dear to let Papa use his car for work. Matilda then called Helen and Charlie to inform them of this news ... it seemed only right. When she finished altering their day, Matilda called the train station to reserve a sleeper compartment on the California Limited.

Can the baggage car hold a player piano? Excellent, charge it to Jergens!

She called a moving company.

Can a piano be crated for a long trip west? Very good, charge it to Jergens!

Finally, she called her husband's office to tell him they were moving and to be sure to thank Mr. Jergens for the transfer and travel expenses. When he began to protest, Matilda simply cleared her throat using exaggerated decibels. If Papa Ross knew what was good for him, he'd pull whatever corporate strings needed pulling and get assigned to California, *pronto*.

It had been a busy few minutes for busybody Matilda Ross.

Details are sketchy, a passing reference in a letter, and so his reason is not quite clear, but a few days later Charlie Rees packed his bags and left Jane's sister, Helen. The reader will remember that Charlie and Helen lived a few doors away from Peg's Beachwood Drive house, the house where Matilda planned to spend *lots* of time visiting her grandsons.

* * *

Except for Charlie leaving Helen, Matilda moving to California, and the addition of Boo!, a mixed-breed puppy Matilda gave to Peg and her brothers for a Halloween treat, 1924 would see no significant changes in the Entwistles' lives. Peg continued her tutelage under Miss Baker and spent much of her free time riding horses and visiting the beach and famous amusement piers in Santa Monica. But her favorite exercise of leisure was reading plays with Aunt Jane.

Jane and Charles had amassed a collection of scripts over the years; many were smash hits, still relevant and often revived, including those by the greatest playwright. But Shakespeare was not something to which Peg inclined — an interesting aspect given her English heritage and family's theatrical background. While Peg was never Shakespearean, she hadn't abandoned him, either. She went to many of his plays, and would perform in one of his most difficult works. There's no question she had the talent to make a living with Shakespeare, but as a simple matter of personal taste she came to prefer other playwrights, such as Henrik Ibsen for his tear-jerking realism and Bernard Shaw for his gruff commentary. She also greatly admired Eugene O'Neill, but said he left her feeling sad.

She and Aunt Jane would often drive to downtown Los Angeles to see a play. The larger houses included the Morosco, Orpheum, Mason, Pantages and Grand Avenue. There was also the new Biltmore Theater, adjoined to its famous hotel namesake. At these venues Peg got a taste of the drama, comedy, and vaudeville found in New York. However, she thought the productions were lacking. Even with such Gotham notables as David Belasco, A.L. Erlanger, May Robson, Eleonora Duse and David Warfield bringing a measure of legitimacy to theater in Los Angeles, Peg remained starved for the Broadway energy and romance she had come to love.

Ironically, the venues in downtown Los Angeles were on or near an avenue named Broadway. Angelenos called this the Theater District, a term that did not sit too well with Peg. She preferred New York's "Rialto" and the "Great White Way," which always added much more romance to her heart's Broadway.

She could swallow her pride and manage to support Los Angeles' so-called "Broadway" and its Theater District; at least she could recognize some of the names on the marquees, but the thing that gave her head-shakes were the theatrical goings-on west of downtown. In Southern California's suburban theaters, the plays had titles familiar to her, but the productions were usually done in small non–Equity community theaters comprised of local folks whose acting was more hobby than calling: grocers, cooks, schoolteachers, the dog catcher. One evening, while reading the actors' names on the playbill for *A Midsummer Night's Dream* at the packed Memorial Open Air Theater in Santa Monica, Peg absentmindedly shouted, "Auntie, who *are* these people?!"[8]

Not since she got caught looting roses a decade earlier had Jane been so mortified.

* * *

Peg's year at Bishop's helped her mature into a young lady. Yes, it was only a year, but it was a structured seven-days-a-week year, and for a 15-year-old that's a long time to spend nurturing body and mind. During her stay she had learned to cope with the lingering grief of her parents' deaths. In so doing, her life was enhanced with a new measure of self-confidence. Whereas a year earlier doubt and trepidation at being an orphan

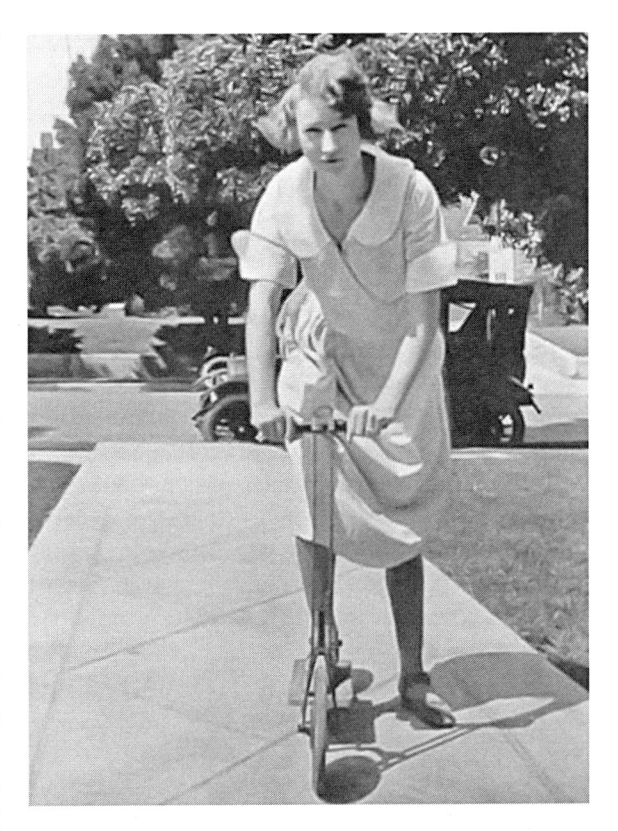

Peg scooters up the walk of her Aunt Helen's house on Cheremoya Ave., around the corner from her Hollywood home. By 1924 she had adapted well to Los Angeles, but New York's Broadway was in her heart (courtesy Entwistle Family).

caused her to rebuff public school for fear of ridicule, self-assurance now led her to believe public education would only stall her progress. Indeed, a year at Bishop's was worth at least two at a city-run high school.

Peg was 16 now and beginning to notice a bit more sunshine in the world. When she blew out the candles of the first day of that magic age it must have crossed her mind that she wouldn't be a kid forever. Soon she would be all grown up, able to do whatever she wanted; go wherever she pleased. And contrary to what has been said about her over the years, the evidence shows Peg Entwistle wasn't all too thrilled about Hollywood — not from the theatrical aspect of it, anyway. New York was on her mind, Broadway in her heart.

But for now she was stuck and for now she would make the best of it. She hadn't completely gotten over losing her mom and dad, of course, but keeping busy helped time pass more quickly, and time, she was told, was a healer of all wounds. Peg accepted that Robert and Lauretta were gone forever, but the thing that was hurting her now was knowing that Broadway, the *real* Broadway, was still alive, still thriving, and having a grand New York time without her.

She wasn't old enough to go off on her own, but she also wasn't too young to begin getting ready. Reading plays and interpreting scenes with her aunt was good practice, and Jane's stage experience was helpful for instruction, but it was now time for the next step.

Just down the street from her house sat the Hollywood Theater Community School (HTCS). Since 1916 it had taught "Stage, Screen, Voice and Diction"[9] to thespian-minded fledglings. There were a number of similar schools in Los Angeles, mainly operated by former actors of minor note who once upon a time had a Broadway fling and maybe a few moments of face time on the silver screen. HTCS was one of the pricier acting schools, but there was nothing fancy about it. The stage was just a humble half-foot-high platform; there were no footlights and no dressing rooms. Students simply rehearsed important scenes from famous plays and learned such stage techniques as how to project, animate, use pantomime and facial expressions and so on.

Peg signed up that spring and had her first taste of semi-formal guidance. The proprietor and instructor, a woman with the obviously contrived stage name Constance Cornell, met with Jane several weeks later and told her that Peg had great potential and exhibited flashes of brilliance. She was excellent at mimicking and diction and amazed other students with her knowledge of theater history. She also performed a good number of scenes without glancing at the scripts. Cornell also played up Peg's blonde hair, deep blue eyes, and petite frame. She urged Jane to get an agent and present Peg to the studios. Not surprisingly, Cornell knew of just such a person who represented fresh, new talent. But the conversation went no further, for Miss Entwistle had no desire to be in the movies.

The *play* was her thing.

* * *

Going back a bit, to February 1924: Uncle Charles, in New York with Walter Hampden, had fallen ill. He was prescribed bed rest by Hampden's physician. During his recuperation Jane had written him a Valentine's Day letter. This letter wasn't found in the family archive, but the 12-page reply was. Charles wrote it piecemeal during a three-day period. It helps discern some of what Jane had written and speaks to her concerns and some events taking place at home: She resented the film studios because they hadn't hired him. The boys were rambunctious. She was having trouble balancing her budget and worried the house might have been a bad investment. Helen's husband was still on the run. Milton was sick, and Bobby, bitten by the adventure bug, had a habit of running away to discover new worlds.

After telling his "Janey"[10] that her Valentine's letter "came like a shower of refreshing rain to a thirsty desert,"[11] Charles mentions he has "a grippe cold."[12] He begins the body of his narrative as might a novelist of the time: "In the teeth of a high and bitter wind" introduces her to the dramatic blizzard that left Manhattan buried in a foot of snow.[13] Next, he addresses her concerns about the new house. He admits it's a risk but feels "Fate" has played a hand in it.[14] He's sure it will "develop into a $20,000 property or even $25,000."[15] He tries to soothe her anger at the studio bosses. "I met a great admirer of Walter's who is influential in Hollywood and has promised to write glowing letters of introduction."[16] The unnamed admirer also promised to speak to the bosses (also unnamed) on his behalf. (This would never happen.)

As he continues—stopping now and then to welcome visitors or messengers delivering theater-related paperwork—we learn that "almost every cent" owed to the children's trust fund has been repaid.[17] Milton got ill from drinking bad water, so Charles suggests giving the children only Puritas bottled water. He regrets that the boys have been troublesome but tells her not to fret about Bobby's running away because Peg's father did it all the time when he was that age. He also promises to spend time "getting reacquainted with the boys" when he returns.[18] Matilda and Papa Ross have decided to buy their own house in Glendale and so Charles writes, "I am sure, as you say, that it is much nicer to have your mother near, but in her very own home."[19]

He wants to take Jane on a two-week vacation where she can have peace and quiet and "Old Enty can make love to his darling once more."[20] He talks about how important she and the children are to him and asks for trust. Everything he does is for them. He finishes by saying he will soon "write to Babs" about the latest Broadway news.[21]

Charles also discusses checks he sent to Jane; five dollars for the boys' shoes and "37.95 for the things for Babs."[22] Jane had taken Peg on an energetic shopping spree for her sixteenth birthday. Still more than two years away from appearing on a Broadway playbill, Miss Entwistle seems to have enjoyed herself like a Broadway star. Thirty-eight dollars was a week's salary for a lot of people in 1924, but Uncle Charles, himself married to an actress, makes no complaint about the check for Babs. For well does he know that a girl with stage aspirations must have the latest in smart fashions if she's to look her very best.

* * *

Peg had come a long way during 1923 and '24, and as 1925 drew near with a seventeenth candle, she was becoming more and more practiced in attributes impressed

By the time Peg joined the Hollywood Theater Community School at 16, the young stage hopeful was already enjoying the theatrical look of a grown-up actress (courtesy Entwistle Family).

upon her by Aunt Jane, Uncle Charles, the Bishop's School, Miss Cornell, and yes, even in those fostered by Grandmother Matilda. And suddenly Peg had become a young lady, soft-spoken, considerate, sober-minded and wholesome. Her eyes had opened to the realization that while hard work and discipline were a cornerstone to one's success, success was far from one's own doing — it took the help of others. The richest oil man was so because of men in the fields. The greatest composer was nothing without the skills and cooperation of musicians.

While growing up in her theatrical family, she had seen such teamwork many times on the stage, but the idea had escaped her until now: Even the best actors needed writers, directors, set designers, people to aim the spotlights and others to pull the curtains. No actress was a star alone; each was surrounded by a universe.

ACT II

When million-footed Manhattan, unpent, descends to its pavements ...
When Broadway is entirely given up to foot-passengers and foot-standers —
when the mass is densest;
When the façades of the houses are alive with people — when eyes gave,
riveted, tens of thousands at a time;
I too, arising, answering, descend to the pavements, merge with the crowd,
and gaze with them.
Superb-faced Manhattan!
   — Walt Whitman[1]

4

The Stage Is Set

I'm not quite sure that I want to be a Queen,
But I should like to be a well-educated Princess.
—Peg as Snow White[1]

Listening to a cluster of boring politicians speak was probably not what Peg Entwistle had in mind when she attended a gala dinner at Boston's Copley Plaza in October of 1927. The occasion was a celebration marking the 400th week of Henry Jewett's successful 1923 Jewett Repertory Fund. It was this Fund that gave birth to the highly regarded Boston Repertory—known formally as the Repertory Theater of Boston.

A dais crowded with long-winded government officials might tend to cause droopy eyelids for a non-political person such as Peg, but the list of special guests in attendance was impressive enough to keep any young actress wide-eyed and bushy-tailed. Some of those seated around Peg included Maude Adams, Winthrop Ames, William Gillette, and David Warfield.

President Calvin Coolidge had sent his campaign manager, former Massachusetts Senator William Butler, to present an American flag to Jewett and his wife Frances. Also on hand to bestow the state and city ensigns were Massachusetts Governor Alvan Fuller and Boston Mayor Malcolm Nichols. Dr. George Vincent, head of the Rockefeller Foundation, was there. And while it isn't known if Dr. Vincent brought a gift for the Jewetts from his boss, John D. Rockefeller, Sr., it would have been worth the hot air of a hundred politicians just to see Mr. and Mrs. Jewett given one of Rockefeller's famous and much cherished tokens of appreciation for jobs well done—a shiny new dime.

Frank Gilmore, the executive secretary of Actors' Equity, also spoke. Peg would have been quite sure to make a show of paying attention to *that* speech, for Gilmore was the lord and master of all things pertaining to rules of the Broadway boards. She would also have been alert during the speech by David Belasco, the famous actor and producer with whom Peg's Aunt Jane and Uncle Charles had worked during the 1910s. The night's Toastmaster, Dr. Daniel Marsh, read telegrams from presidents of several prestigious universities and Boston's Roman archbishop, Cardinal William Henry O'Connell. Here, Miss Entwistle may have again been tempted to nod off a bit—being Episcopal and all—but she would have perked instantly as soon as Dr. Marsh started reading congratulatory messages from Mrs. Minnie Maddern Fiske (distinguished actress and stalwart champion of repertory); Mary Mannering (turn-of-the-century Shakespearean A-lister), and musical comedy playwright Guy Bolton, who penned *Grounds for Divorce* and *Anastasia*, and later took turns pairing up with Jerome Kern, Cole Porter, George Gershwin and others to create a host of Broadway gems such as *Have a Heart, Anything Goes, Lady Be Good* and *Girl Crazy.*

Perhaps the most interesting telegram for Peg to hear that night was from a good friend of her Aunt Jane's: noted stage and silent film actress Viola Allen.

Renowned opera stars Queena Mario and Raphaelo Diaz had opened the program, treating the crowd to selections of *Faust, La Boheme,* and the flower song from *Carmen.* After the dinner and speeches had ended, the festivities moved a few blocks away from the Copley Ballroom to the Boston Repertory's handsome Georgian home opposite the Symphony Hall on Huntington Avenue. A ceremony took place as the flags gifted by the chief executives of the nation, state, and city were unfurled and hung prominently from their respective VIP boxes. Then it was curtain rise as Ernst Toller's *The Machine-Wreckers* had its American debut. Some in the audience may have wondered how it was that a German expressionist of Communist persuasion came to pen a story of England's 19th century Luddite disturbances, but Peg would have been wondering about other things, such as the November 1925 evening she helped open the Repertory Theater of Boston as the youngest member of the Henry Jewett Players.

The talented actress was now, these two years later, remembering the tingles and anticipation of her very first professional role on a stage — when near a thousand souls of prestige and prominence had been pleased to make her acquaintance in the theater's inaugural production, Sheridan's *The Rivals.*

Other tingles would soon follow — like the time a drama critic in *The Harvard Crimson* called her a prodigy, and the flirtations lavished upon her by certain young men of letters invited to rehearse with the company during special theatrical classes. And sweet was the recollection of a *Crimson* article titled "Miss Entwistle Crashes the Big Time," penned by a university drama critic who had seen her on Broadway after her Boston departure.[2] He had urged his fellow Ivy Leaguers to "Go and see the reason for the Harvard attendance at the Repertory last year."[3]

Peg Entwistle ... *Harvard girl?*

* * *

Henry Jewett, an Australian by birth, first brought his repertory style of theater to Boston in 1915. His season began at the Boston Opera House with three months of Shakespeare. A year later, he and his wife Frances took over the Toy Theater on Dartmouth Street. This small house was renamed the Copley, enlarged, and there until 1924 Jewett's acting company presented a successful, respected, notable list of plays. But the revamped theater was much more expensive to operate. Unable to afford the overhead, Jewett suspended his company and concentrated full time on raising funds for his grand experiment, a privately run profit-making theater and acting company subsidized by a tax exemption. Jewett and Frances had had a vision, and the reputation and connections to make it happen. They incorporated and then began selling "Gold Notes," beautifully designed bonds that are today valuable to collectors. These were hundred-dollar bonds that matured at five percent over 15 years. Some of the most prominent citizens of Boston, New York, and Washington, D. C., supported the Jewett fund, including President Coolidge and his wife Grace, who were the first to purchase some of the bonds.

Henry and Frances Jewett were able to raise $150,000. A site for the new theater was purchased in the cultural center of Boston. In November 1924, ground was broken. The entire cost from basement to weathervane came in at $800,000 (about ten million today).

But it wasn't just a fine and fancy tax-exempt entity that Henry and Mrs. Jewett wanted, it was about repertory, in the true sense of the style: a troupe of skilled players who presented a different play each night or week. It was the stuff of a time long ago when there were far fewer theaters and so shorter runs of many plays were presented to keep audiences happy and the cast sharp and diverse. But the main proposal with which Jewett approached Massachusetts and the city of Boston involved his theater company's tax exemption.

He proposed that his organization could be run in a way similar to the libraries and universities run by the government. However, he wanted no public funds going to his theater; instead, he wished only a permanent tax dispensation. Thus loosed of all obligations governing taxes on income and property, the company would use the extra money to present better, more prominent productions featuring famous actors, directors, playwrights, set designers, and so on. Jewett's philosophy was that productions involving the most recognized and brilliant names of the theater world could only complement and enhance Boston's cultural heritage.

Indeed, in covering the story of the Boston Repertory for the *New York Times* in 1925, Carter Irving, one of the most recognized and respected theater critics of the day, wrote, "The contribution to the public by which it justifies the tax exemption which will enable it to operate with much less overhead than its purely commercial rivals, is presumed to be in the character of the plays presented — the range of them, the quality of them, the serious purpose with which they are selected and the high level of the acting."[4]

As for new, young talent he planned to recruit, Jewett's desire was to put before the public the best type of drama and acting possible; hence, if a person should decide to go on the stage, and was willing to train at the Repertory, they would have the guidance of experienced actors and actresses to lead them along the way. The plan was to have students begin as all of the most famous actors and actresses had, by playing in minor parts until they were experienced enough to assume the more difficult roles. If they proved to be talented enough, the Repertory would be willing to lend them assistance toward greater stage success.

Granting the Boston Repertory tax-exempt status was ultimately up to Jay Benton, the Massachusetts attorney general. Part of his formal opinion read, "The Jewett Repertory Theatre Fund, Inc., was incorporated for the following purposes: To enlighten and educate the public concerning the value of the Repertory Theatre as a vital factor toward the higher development of dramatic art and to establish a permanent playhouse in the city of Boston, where the best plays of all times may be presented, where competent actors may be afforded an opportunity of appearing before the public under favorable conditions, and to encourage playwrights and actors in the best traditions of the dramatic profession...."[5]

The building was up and ready for action by October 1925. Jewett spared no expense and built a beautiful, modern venue that offered amenities not found in many Broadway theaters. The Boston Repertory was a Rolls-Royce whose appointments included roomy seats, a balcony with private boxes, huge orchestra and cyclorama pits, a rehearsal room nearly as large as the main stage, prop room, a set-designing studio, state-of-the-art lighting, ventilation, heating and air conditioning systems, numerous lounges, restrooms, and a spacious foyer and lobby. For subscribers and other high-profile guests, a private tea room was available even when no performances were scheduled.

As successful as Jewett's experiment had become, the 1929 stock market crash would have a devastating effect on ticket sales. By 1930 stage productions were over; in came sleep-inducing lectures on the mating habits of wildebeests; up went a movie screen showing third-run talkies. In June of that year, Henry Jewett was dead at 68. His widow, Frances, simply did not have whatever it was she needed to get the Repertory back into shape.

In early 1932 a new management took over. Jewett's lifelong dream was renamed the Guild Theater of Boston. Blanche Yurka and Mrs. Patrick Campbell headlined its premiere, the ancient fantasy *Electra*. But few had taken notice and there was little fanfare. And Broadway was appalled to learn that the new management was calling itself a Guild — no one in Boston had cleared this with New York. Such was the cheek and power of the Great White Way, home to the only Guild that seemed to matter back then.

The footlight and curtain-call days of Jewett's beautiful building were for the most part over. It next became the Esquire Theater, a movie house that featured art films such as *Henry V*, with Laurence Olivier. There was a rare occasion when a play found its way back, like in 1941, when Dorothy Gish and Louis Calhern starred in *Life with Father*, but its rightful place as a venue for legitimate theater would not fully return until 1953, when Boston University purchased the building. Today it is the School of Theater Arts at Boston University's College of Fine Arts.

Rumor has it that Henry Jewett's ghost haunts the place. One could hardly fault him.

And who could have faulted Peg had she decided to haunt the old Repertory herself? After all, she had been a part of its beginning, and in no small way. As with 1927's anniversary gala, the Boston Repertory's 1925 coming-out party captured the attention of presidents, kings, and ambassadors. The biggest names of the era had either attended that first curtain rise or had sent telegrams of praise and enormous floral arrangements. While some of these names mean little or nothing to most persons of the modern era, others have had their historical importance chiseled in stone. At some point during her engagement as one of the Henry Jewett Players, Peg Entwistle met, performed in front of, or had been included in the congratulations sent to Jewett from Calvin Coolidge, John D. Rockefeller, William Gillette, George Bernard Shaw, Eugene O'Neill, E.H. Sothern, Julia Marlowe, Maude Adams, George M. Cohan and a score of others.

And then there was the one whose name had not yet become chiseled in history.

Peg's ghost hasn't haunted the old Boston Repertory, but when she was alive and well on its stage she sure as hell haunted an unknown girl named Bette Davis.

* * *

In early March 1925, while Peg was still in Hollywood, Uncle Charles stood on a pier at the Port of New York with hundreds of Walter Hampden's fans and bid a boisterous farewell to the popular actor, his wife Mabel, and their daughter Mary. The family was sailing to Italy for a well-deserved vacation following a grueling theatrical season that had lasted nearly 18 months. Apart from being prohibited by Equity rules to perform on Sundays, and several weeks "down time" after breaking his foot during *Cyrano*, Hampden and his troupe had had very little time off.

As the Italian-flagged *Dante Alighieri* made for Naples, Charles Entwistle returned to his apartment and readied his bags for his own vacation to hearth and home.

Shortly after he arrived, Peg hounded him with questions regarding the exciting insider news he had leaked to her a few weeks before the official February press release: The New York Theater Guild had plans to start something called the Theater Guild School of Acting. It would begin in the fall. Uncle Charles filled her in on all the details and then gave her a surprise: His influence and assurance to the Guild that his niece had the stuff they were looking for in young, untried talent secured her a spot on the roster ... if she wanted it.

Broadway!

One might imagine Peg giving her uncle a tremendous hug, or squealing delight with her aunt. And then there was Grandmother Matilda. The reserved Ross matriarch would have been cautious with her reaction. She had seen this kind of thing before, Peg getting enthusiastic about some new hobby or adventure only to change her mind in favor of some other pursuit. While this impulsive part of Peg's personality irked Matilda, there was certainly no malice in changing horses during a race. It was simply a matter of a young girl experimenting with life ... searching for purpose and contentment.

Except for the usual bumps and bruises, the Entwistles' next few months were largely uneventful — but they did have their moments. Against Matilda's advice, Charles and Jane left Peg's education up to her own discretion. Matilda was livid; she argued that Lauretta and Robert would not have allowed Peg to be her own parent. The child needed to be in school, not lounging around the house, poisoning her mind, with *Photoplay* and *Vogue*. Charles pointed out that far from having a poisoned mind Peg was very probably the only aspiring actress in Hollywood who came to the breakfast table with Chaucer and Euripides under her arm.

Peg was starting to have fun again. She smiled more. Her face glowed; her eyes twinkled. Her countenance changed remarkably during this time; so much so that Aunt Jane had her pose for a special photograph in a fashion reminiscent of a formal coming-out portrait for a debutante — or perhaps a princess. Jane painstakingly hand-painted the entire photograph with what looks to be watercolor or pastel. Her work is amazing and although the colors have faded a bit, Peg's visage remains beautifully portrayed in a delicate, lovely light.

And so, Peg continued her acting lessons at the Hollywood Theater Community School until about mid–June, when she and her uncle boarded a train for the East Coast. Charles was returning to work for Walter Hampden, but first he would bring Peg to the Guild School to meet the director and enroll her into the program. Peg was to fulfill her dream and study performing arts with the highly esteemed New York Theater Guild.

Broadway!

But then she met Henry Jewett.

* * *

The Guild School was designed to be a stepping stone to professional acting for young stage hopefuls. It was also meant to be

This portrait of Peg began as a black and white photograph taken by her Aunt Jane, who then enlarged and painted it as a surprise for her. The slightly faded original adorns a wall in the home of Milton Entwistle (courtesy Entwistle Family).

a sort of clearing house for the hundreds upon hundreds of Broadway dreamers who were flocking into New York from all over the country. These novices had lots of heart, little money, and virtually no talent. Most wouldn't know how to find an agent even if one would take them on, and only the sharpest of the bunch knew about trade periodicals listing auditions.

Theatrical managers and producers were getting swamped — and annoyed — as these kids crowded into their offices every morning and throughout the day, each vying for a few minutes' chance to recite some lines or interpret a scene. What bothered the Broadway bosses was not that so many held such interest in the theater, but that the sheer number of these beginners made it harder and harder to find the time to find the ones with genuine talent.

Winifred Lenihan, the first director of the Guild School, writes about this in a *New York Times* article explaining the school's reason for being. She noted that all these "little girls" who secretly act Shakespeare in their rooms,[6] and all the "comical young men" who recite pieces at church festivals,[7] were without the understanding that "acting is a profession, and a difficult one ... [I]t is a craft that takes years to become even reasonably proficient in."[8] Lenihan goes on to quote the moans she heard from theatrical managers: "What can we do about these youngsters? Is there any way of weeding them out? Is there any way of helping the capable ones and sending the others back to their mothers?"[9]

To separate this wheat from the chaff, the Guild School was formed. Its primary goal, according to Lenihan, was in "training and development of genuine talent."[10] The means to this end was through a process of elimination. The skills, endurance, and discipline of each pupil would first be sternly tested by Lenihan, herself an accomplished and respected actress. Those who survived her correction made it to the next level. Their progress, if any, would be judged in the coming months by a panel of Broadway experts including actress Laura Hope Crews, producer Winthrop Ames, and New York Theater Guild co-founder Philip Moeller.

Lenihan began interviewing applicants in February 1925. She ended up with 700. Each was given a probationary period of 30 days to impress and improve. For example, a girl might have voiced a wonderful Juliet in Lenihan's office, yet nervously croaked like a frog while reciting "...wherefore art thou Romeo?"[11] on stage in front of the other hundreds of students.

Juliet would have just one month to turn her frog into a princess.

The school officially opened on October 1, the deadline for enrollment. By the first day of November, when the last probationary student had either sank or swam, only 105 of the original 700 had shown Lenihan they had something that might be considered talent. These 105 were next awarded a $500 scholarship to help make ends meet. As a condition of the scholarship, each student signed a contract: If they made it to graduation, their services would be optioned by the Theater Guild for the next theatrical season at a salary of $50 per week.

When this first senior term ended in May 1926, only 21 students — three percent of the original 700 — had earned the right to call themselves graduates of the Theater Guild School of Acting. They were then formed into an acting company and had as their June graduation ceremony a professional Broadway outing at the Garrick Theater.

The play was *Prunella*, a well-received poetic fantasy by Granville Barker and Laurence Houseman. In the title role (the equivalent, if you will, to a Valedictorian) was a girl named Sylvia Sidney. Sidney enjoyed Broadway; however, most of her long career was as a character actress on screen. She received a 1973 Oscar nomination for Best Supporting Actress in *Summer Wishes, Winter Dreams,* and won a Golden Globe in 1985 for her supporting performance *An Early Frost,* but is most remembered for her roles as Joel McCrea's soft-hearted ingénue in *Dead End* (1937); the chain-smoking gatekeeper of Purgatory in *Beetle Juice* (1988), and the grandmother whose yodeling Slim Whitman album saves the world in *Mars Attacks!* (1996).

Sylvia Sidney got rave reviews for her Broadway debut, and it can only be assumed that Peg may have done as good a job playing the lead in *Prunella*. Both girls were equally attractive and had similar acting styles. Peg, however, had the edge on Sylvia because of her family's theatrical background and years of exposure to Broadway, whereas Sylvia had no theatrical experience whatsoever prior to her enrollment into the Guild School. Add to this Peg's acting lessons in Hollywood and many hours spent rehearsing scenes with Aunt Jane, and she was arguably the more seasoned of the two ingénues. But Peg was never considered for *Prunella* because she was never really in the running.

She had been interviewed by Winifred Lenihan and readily accepted into the program, but shortly after her probation period began, Peg attended a birthday party for Walter Hampden. Many notables of stage and screen and social circles were there, old friends of Hampden's and familiar acquaintances of Uncle Charles. It was here that Charles introduced her to Henry Jewett. Peg told Jewett she had read about his plans for the Boston Repertory and was very intrigued by it all. They chatted for a while, discussing the repertory style and its history and importance to legitimate theater. Now it was Jewett who was intrigued. Peg had impressed him with her maturity and theatrical knowledge (Walter Hampden sometimes teased Charles about replacing him with his niece). Then, in an odd reversal of the norm involving those fledgling stage hopefuls taking place throughout New York City, a famous theatrical producer broke precedent and made a pitch to an unknown, untested talent.

Peg balked at first when Jewett asked if she would like to join his acting company. The Jewett Players was a fairly well-known troupe, but mostly in the northeast, whereas the Theater Guild was a prestigious and internationally recognized institution. And Peg knew very well that prestigious connections mingled with talent and charm were part and parcel of Broadway success for a young girl. Sure, Boston had Harvard and blue bloods and the Beacon Hill set, but the Guild was, well, the *Guild*.

Then Jewett told her whom he had engaged for the coming season, and that he still needed a young miss to support them. Peg's reasoning shifted gears: If she remained with the Guild School it would be almost a year before she could get any *real* acting done. But Jewett was promising a six-month contract at the same salary the Guild was offering its grad students, and she'd share billing with A-list stars Blanche Yurka and Emma Dunn. The Guild, of course, had a sizable number of associated stars, and popular Broadway veteran Laura Hope Crews was directly involved with helping to train the Guild's students, but there would be a lot of star-struck kids crowding around her all at once. In Boston, said Jewett, Peg could have individual and immediate attention from Yurka and Dunn. She would start rehearsals right away once construction of the new theater was complete, and she could also stay rent-free at the Repertory's living quarters (called the "Nursery").

Peg accepted Henry Jewett's offer.

Boston!

Jewett also told her that she would still be a student of sorts, trained in a manner similar to the Guild School's apprenticeship, only without the threat of elimination hanging over her head. He was aware she had talent and flair, but she needed to prove herself worthy of important roles. She would have to learn the mechanics of performing, such as how not to upstage a player by improper or inattentive crossing (something she will struggle with a bit, early on).

When the new theater was ready in mid–October he would send her a train ticket. He wrote down for her the names of 22 plays; he might not produce all of them during the coming season, but it was up to her to learn them nevertheless.

Years later, Walter Hampden will recall that moment: Jewett handed Peg the list of plays, she scanned it and exclaimed, "I know all but one of them by heart!"[12] Astonished, Jewett looked at Hampden, who nodded his head, affirming this was for the most part true. It was true enough for Henry Jewett. Convinced he had just uncovered something special, he opened his billfold and handed her $100 — a retainer worth two weeks of her promised salary.

Peg Entwistle had secured her first acting job.

The following day she asked her uncle to accompany her to Winifred Lenihan's office. He refused. This was something she had to do alone. But he promised all would be fine because she was only leaving the Guild's training program, not backing out of a theatrical contract. But he added that her handshake agreement — with Jewett's payment — was indeed a contract ... a *commitment*. When the Boston Repertory called and said it was time, she had better forget about fun and games for a while. She would have a big job to do and a lot of important people would be watching and keeping score. She must also remember her place in the troupe. For a while she would be looked upon as a novice, extremely gifted, but a novice nonetheless. She could expect, and indeed should welcome, correction and criticism from instructors and peers alike. And even when she thinks she's right, *knows* she's right, she must not argue the point. The time would come when she could have her say, but there were dues to be paid first, and that required a meek and humble spirit.

According to her cousin Helen Reid, the only play that Peg had not mastered on Jewett's list was *Snow White,* which is probably why Uncle Charles gave a metaphoric reference to it: "Boston," he told his niece,[13] "will welcome a comely princess, but they will not much care for a girl who thinks herself the *queen*."[14]

5

The Work Begins

In some incredible fusion, Entwistle, Hedvig and I were now one.
— Bette Davis, *The Lonely Life*[1]

Sylvia Sidney, "Valedictorian" of the Theater Guild School, will make her Broadway debut two days before Peg Entwistle's. However, Peg will have already performed in over a dozen professional productions at the Boston Repertory. If Henry Jewett's theater — which seated about 1,000 patrons — played to a full house for every performance of each production in which she appeared, it can be estimated that Peg would have taken well over 200 final bows in front of nearly 190,000 patrons by the time Miss Sidney had taken her *first* bow.

As staggering as those numbers are, consider this: Of the original 700 people interviewed by director Winifred Lenihan for enrollment into the Theater Guild School, only Sylvia Sidney and Peg Entwistle would go on to become professional, fulltime actors of note — a success rate of less than three-tenths of one percent.

The remaining 698 aspiring actors and actresses faded into obscurity, including the 20 who graduated with Sylvia and supported her in *Prunella*. A look into their careers shows only a handful of very minor acting credits between all of them. (The author's comparisons of Sidney and Entwistle are meant only to show that Peg's decision to join the Boston Repertory was, for her, the right one. This comparison is not indicative of their talents or quality of the institutions each chose to attend. Both girls were prodigies, each institution prestigious.)

As the bricks of the Repertory Theater building were being fit together during the summer of 1925, Peg spent her time brushing up on Henry Jewett's list of plays and taking in much of Broadway. In August, she and her uncle returned to Hollywood for five weeks to spend time with the family. By early September they were back in New York City, each one gearing up for their respective theatrical seasons.

A few days after their arrival, Hampden's wife Mabel invited Peg for tea at The Players, the exclusive club frequented by creative types. A short time later they were met by Hampden and Peg's uncle. The men came bearing exciting news: A deal had been agreed to between Hampden and *the* biggest name in theater. Hampden was a man of great insight and sensitivity, and as he shared the details of this theatrical agreement in front of Peg, he sensed a reserved longing coming from her. He knew she was too polite to ask, so he asked instead: Would she like to be on stage with Ethel Barrymore?

Hampden had engaged Barrymore, one of his oldest friends, for a season of Shakespeare. They hadn't been together on stage since the Players' production of Sheridan's *The*

School for Scandal two years earlier. Having worked intimately with the most famous actors and actresses of his day, Hampden was far from star-struck; nevertheless, the Barrymore contract was as exciting for him as it was for Peg. He had recently taken over the Colonial Theater and renamed it, to no one's amazement, Hampden's Theater. Ethel Barrymore's association with his repertory company for a season of Shakespeare guaranteed immense success for everyone involved.

When he was finally able to free himself from Peg's thankful bear hug, Hampden explained the particulars to her. She would have a walk-on in *Hamlet*; carry the king's train, bring in the poison cup, things like that. It wasn't much, but it would give her a taste of the footlights. And he couldn't pay her or add her name to the cast because of Equity rules, because he would give her no contract due to her prior agreement with Henry Jewett. Not that any of that mattered to a girl whose head was swimming with elation, for at that moment in time there was no one on earth richer than she ... no one.

Barrymore!

And so, on October 10, 1925, in front of more than 1,300 people packed into Hampden's where Broadway meets 62nd Street, 17-year-old Peg Entwistle, the richest girl in the world, cut her theatrical teeth with the most famous stage actress alive.

* * *

Peg basked in the Broadway glow for about two weeks before she had to bid farewell to Barrymore and the electricity surrounding her. In Boston, Frances Jewett helped her get settled into the Nursery, the living quarters provided for cast members of the Repertory. (Stars, such as Blanche Yurka, had their choice of high-end hotels.) Rehearsals began immediately for the company's inaugural production of Richard Brinsley Sheridan's *The Rivals*, a five-act comedy of manners that was first performed in England in 1775, which is also the story's setting.

Peg was cast as Lucy, the conniving maid to Lydia Languish, one of the story's principals, played by Olive Tell. Though Lucy was a minor role, it was not an insignificant one, especially for Peg. It was as much her debut as it was the Repertory's.

Wardrobe consisted of late 18th century flamboyant, which delighted Peg to no end, and there were humorous moments for her to shine. One such moment occurs in the first act when Peg's not-very-bright Lucy has just returned from book-hunting for Lydia:

> LYDIA: Well, child, what have you brought me?
> LUCY: Oh! Here, ma'am. [*Taking books from under her cloak and pockets.*] This is *The Gordian Knot*, and this, *Peregrine Pickle*. Here are *The Tears of Sensibility*, and *Humphrey Clinker*. This is *The Memoirs of a Lady of Quality*, written by herself, and here the second volume of *The Sentimental Journey*.
> LYDIA: Heigh-ho! What are those books by the glass?
> LUCY: The great one is only *The Whole Duty of Man*, where I press a few blonds, ma'am.
> LYDIA: Very well, give me the sal volatile.
> LYDIA: Is it in a blue cover, ma'am?
> LYDIA: My smelling-bottle, you simpleton!
> LUCY: Oh, the drops! Here, ma'am.[2]

The play was a smash hit with the Repertory's first audience, which included many dignitaries such as the governor of Massachusetts and the duchess of Rutland. Henry Jewett, who played the role of Sir Lucius O'Trigger, gave a speech, as did other prominent persons, including Governor Fuller and actor Francis Wilson, who played Bob Acres. Mrs. Malaprop was played by Emma Dunn, the noted stage actress who went on to make over 100 films.

It was a spectacular night, with the ushers dressed as footmen of 1775 England and a large number of audience members arrayed in a bewildering variety of the period's costumes. Throughout the evening, the patrons played their own little powdered-wig scenes amongst each other. After the play had ended, a grand costume ball was held in Repertory Hall.

The *Boston Globe* covered the event and dedicated nearly an entire page of newsprint to it the next day; a nameless theater critic for the paper wrote a glowing review. The critic hadn't noticed (or hadn't cared to report) Emma Dunn's frustration at Peg, who kept crossing in the wrong direction. In order to teach the nervous rookie a lesson, Dunn ad-libbed stage direction six times during a scene where she and Peg address each other. When the audience was supposed to see Peg's face they saw only the back of her head as Dunn casually, but most purposefully, lured Peg to turn upstage.

This somewhat humiliating lesson in stage manners in front of more than 1,000 people would have crushed the ego of many an actress, but Peg knew Emma Dunn wasn't being vindictive; she was teaching mechanics. She had driven home Winifred Lenihan's philosophy: "Talent and personality are not enough!"[3] Peg always looked back on that lesson with fondness.

But of all the interesting facets involving Peg's first speaking role on the professional stage, two are most noteworthy: First, she is credited in the production playbill as "Margaret Entwistle."[4] She chose Margaret because she believed this formal night required something more formal-sounding than "Peg." Of course, she might have used either one (or both) of her given names—they were certainly prim enough, but she was never very fond of Millicent Lilian, hence her nearly life-long usage of Babs and Peg. At any rate, she would use the name Margaret for the first two plays, from then on it was just plain Peg Entwistle.

The second most noteworthy facet of the night had been announced that morning in the *Boston Globe*: "The opportunity of hearing the first presentation of the Repertory Theater of Boston and what its founders are attempting to do will be afforded the radio listeners this evening at 8 o'clock from WBZ. This theater ... will broadcast the entire opening play, *The Rivals*."[5]

Peg was very excited to know her voice—and performance—would be heard throughout Boston perhaps even as far away as New York City. Of course, at that time WBZ was not very strong, only 5,000 watts, and home receivers were primitive. Nevertheless, it is a marvelous little discovery to know that Peg's first professional role on stage had been heard live in thousands of homes beyond the doors of the Boston Repertory.

Entire plays, operas, and Broadway musicals had been going out over the airwaves since early 1922. But those had all been performed at radio stations, the plays being read in sound booths by actors holding scripts. The Boston Repertory's presentation of *The Rivals* seems to have been the first time an entire play was aired live during its actual stage performance in front of a audience. One might argue that young Peg "Margaret" Entwistle was one of the pioneers of performing arts broadcasting ... and she was just getting warmed up for a solo radio debut, playing one of the world's most famous characters.

* * *

Rip Van Winkle awakened to become the second production of the new Boston Repertory. This adaptation of the Washington Irving short story opened on November 23. It featured all of the players from *The Rivals*. In *Rip*, Peg ("Margaret Entwistle") played Hendrick, the innkeeper's son. She was also still acting in *Rivals*, which had several performances scheduled each week into the opening of *Rip Van Winkle*. She was also rehearsing or studying her key roles in Jewett's next three productions, Ibsen's *The Wild Duck*, Gilda Varesi's *Enter Madam*, and Winthrop Ames' 1912 adaptation of *Snow White*.

Such was life for Peg during her time at the Boston Repertory: Within a few days of arriving she was simultaneously performing or rehearsing multiple plays each week. There would be little time for anything else: "We started rehearsing at 10 [A.M.] and remained at the theater, either rehearsing or acting, until nearly midnight," she told one reporter.[6]

Nearly *every* midnight...

Usually, there were two different plays each day (afternoons and evenings) from Monday through Friday, with a third opening as one of the other two ended a run. (The Repertory's most popular and successful production, *The Wild Duck*, would have numerous revivals.) On Saturdays, throughout the holidays and into the New Year, there was a triple bill that included morning presentations for children. For the 1925-26 holiday season it was *Snow White*.

The labor was intense, but Peg relished the tasks. She was honing her craft at a feverish pitch, and though the days were long the time went by quickly. Before she knew it, it was the evening of December 7, 1925, opening night of *The Wild Duck*.

Blanche Yurka, the famous Minnesota-born bohemian of stage and screen, was the star and director of *The Wild Duck*. A former opera singer (at this time near the end of a four-year marriage to Ian Keith, an actor twelve years her junior), Yurka was highly respected and one of the most popular actresses of the day, having attained stardom in 1922 playing Queen Gertrude opposite John Barrymore in *Hamlet*. Yurka was reprising the role of Gina Ekdal that she had so successfully interpreted on Broadway earlier in 1925. Notable among that cast was Romney Brent, who will be paired with Peg in Shaw's *Getting Married*; Warburton Gamble, who will travel with Peg on a national tour; and Helen Chandler, whom fans of horror flicks may remember as Mina Seward in 1931's *Dracula*.

Yurka loved *The Wild Duck*. She performed it hundreds of times and was adamantly protective of her interpretation of Gina, as evidenced by one Boston interview: "Reviewers and ignoramuses have sometimes asserted that Gina was a slut and a rather frowsy hausfrau. I am convinced that Gina, as Ibsen saw her, was nothing of the sort."[7] (In Yurka's era the word "slut" didn't have the connotation of a promiscuous woman, it meant a "slovenly" one.)

Yurka was the most gruff, demanding director Peg would ever work with; years later, Bette Davis said Yurka could give you a scowl that hurt more than a punch to the face. But if you were sharp, committed, and true to the craft, then in Yurka's hands you could be molded into a star. Just don't criticize her cooking: During this Boston production of *The Wild Duck*, Yurka's recipe for "Wild Duck Sauce" was published in newspapers as far away as Oxnard, California[8]: "Melt Crisco, add the onion and chopped pepper and then the flour ... just before removing from the fire, stir in the chili sauce and Worcestershire...."[9]

The theatrical season of 1925 ... could it have tasted any better?

More than just a main course for Yurka's dinner, *The Wild Duck* is a beautiful play, a complex allegory whose humor does little to soften its overwhelmingly tragic end. It was crafted in 1884 by Norwegian playwright Henrik Ibsen. He is considered the father of modern drama and his plays were quite fashionable with the American stage for much of the 20th century. Along with *The Wild Duck*, his most famous and most revived works include *A Doll's House, Ghosts, An Enemy of the People, Hedda Gabler* and *The Master Builder*.

The Wild Duck helped propel Peg to Broadway. And because her performance in it so profoundly affected and inspired screen legend Bette Davis to pursue her dream to become, well, *Bette Davis,* and because Bette will play the same role as Peg, and, like her, act it alongside and under the direction of Blanche Yurka, the Boston Repertory's 1925-26 production of this Ibsen tear-jerker deserves a bit of a look...

Central to the plot are Hedvig, her mother Gina, and Gina's husband Hjalmar, who may or may not be Hedvig's biological father. Hedvig is to be 14 years old in two days. She loves to read but must shade her sensitive eyes while doing so—she hasn't been told she is going blind. She is a naïve adolescent, but in all the story there is no one more innocent.

Gina is the backbone of the family, practical and hardworking. She has to run her husband's photography business because of his neglect and folly. She is not very sophisticated but has common sense, a firm grasp on reality, and juggles the house and business admirably.

Hjalmar is a lazy, egocentric fool gallivanting in two worlds of fantasy, one with his senile father in an attic menagerie, the other in a quixotic pipe dream regarding a revolutionary invention he will never advance past the bragging stage. Hjalmar's self-centeredness is sickening, in one instance drawing another's sympathy away from Hedvig's coming blindness and onto himself. But Hedvig lives for him and worships the water he thinks he walks upon.

Also key to the story is a wealthy manufacturer named Werle; 14 years earlier, Gina and Werle had an affair. Their tryst occurred close enough to Gina and Hjalmar's marriage that she has doubts as to which of the two men fathered Hedvig.

Caught in the mix are poor Hedvig and a little wild duck. Her life revolves around her father Hjalmar, but the duck is her most treasured possession. It had been wounded by Werles while hunting, then rescued by a family friend and given to Hedvig. She nursed it to health but it was too badly hurt to ever fly again. It became her pet. Later, after Gina confesses to her husband that she and Werles spent a night together just before the marriage, and that she isn't sure which of the two men fathered Hedvig, Hjalmar comes to hate the duck, seeing it as a symbol of the child—as a trophy of Werles' hunt.

When a discussion arises about how the little duck has no family as do the rabbits, hens, and chickens of the house, Hedvig remarks, "There is so much that is strange about the wild duck ... nobody knows where she came from either."[10]

Hedvig is indeed *The Wild Duck.*

For her birthday, Werles gives Hedvig a lifetime stipend worth a fortune. This pushes Hjalmar over the edge, and he now believes Hedvig is not his daughter. The thought of it disgusts him. He has a fit and hurls insults at mother and child. Hedvig has no idea what is happening; she becomes confused and hysterical and rushes to him, clinging desperately to the only father she has ever known. She holds tight, crying, begging him to stay. He tosses her aside and storms out of the house.

Because Hjalmar had mentioned wanting to wring the duck's neck, Hedvig becomes convinced that if she kills the duck it will make her father happy and prove to him her love and he will return home.

The next morning—Hedvig's birthday—she goes to the attic with a pistol. She intends to shoot the little duck but then her heart breaks at the thought of it. Unable to sacrifice the helpless creature, but unable also to suffer the loss of Father's love, she turns the gun on herself.

* * *

Although Ibsen gave no such stage direction when he wrote *The Wild Duck,* Henry Jewett ended each performance by having Peg placed into an open coffin. The men of the play became grim pallbearers who silently paraded Peg's poor Hedvig off stage, up through the middle aisle, past the weeping audience. It was brilliant theater.

The above synopsis does little justice to *The Wild Duck*. Reading the play in its entirety, or better yet, seeing it performed with capable, impassioned actors, can leave one with a sense of empathy for Hedvig long after the final curtain has come down. Indeed, such an impression has even been known to last a lifetime.

Just ask Bette Davis.

Bette, whose film career shaped her into an American icon and one of the greatest actresses in Hollywood history, saw *The Wild Duck* at the Repertory in 1926 and was mesmerized. She never forgot that night and many times credited Peg as the driving force that steered her toward her goal. Some have said that Bette's inspiration came from Valentino and Pickford, but in her own memoirs, numerous interviews, and in documentaries and biographies, Davis is seen pointing to Peg's "little wild duck" time and time again:

"It was my first serious theater and a whole, new world opened up to me. I was thrilled with Miss Entwistle's performance."[11]

"My heart almost stopped. She looked just like me."[12]

"I was watching myself. Miss Entwistle had lost herself in Hedvig. Now I did too."[13]

"When 'the little wild duck' shot herself in the breast, I died with her. I had no pulse whatsoever as Hedvig was carried from the stage in a little casket ... everything in my life fell into place ... I was in focus for the first time ... this was the vision ... I knew now that more than anything — despite anything — I was going to become an actress."[14]

Indeed, that evening had such a profound effect on Davis that even her mother Ruthie remembered it more than 30 years later. In 1957 Ralph Edwards and his popular television show *This Is Your Life* honored Ruthie. Bette's mother reminisced about how her famous daughter was inclined to pursue acting. She spoke of Peg's performance in *The Wild Duck,* and while she remembered it a bit differently than Bette had recalled in her memoir, Ruthie said this with regard to their reaction at the

Peg as Hedvig in Ibsen's *The Wild Duck*. Of all the plays she did at the Boston Repertory, none was as popular as this tragic allegory (author's collection).

play's end: "We didn't applaud. We just sat there, and everybody filed out, and she looked at me and she said 'Mother, if I can live to play that part I shall die happily.'"[15]

Bette soon began her quest and in short order started making some noise on the boards. And then Blanche Yurka heard about her, and wanted to know if Bette would be interested in playing Hedvig. "Interested! I had never forgotten nor not believed that one day I could play this part—ever since I saw Peg Entwistle at that matinee in Boston."[16]

So, in 1929 the eager young ingénue with the Entwistle-blue eyes joined Yurka on tour ... Philadelphia, Washington, and eventually Boston, Bette's hometown. Bette recalled how important that first night playing Hedvig in Boston was to her. She sat in her dressing room a few minutes before curtain rise, very concerned about how she would do in front of the hometown crowd: "Could I conceivably do for someone else what Peg Entwistle had done for me?"[17] She could—and probably did, for Bette's Hedvig was a smash hit.

It speaks well of Bette Davis to have carried Peg in her heart for so long: In November 1976, a full half century after Bette saw Peg play Hedvig, Al Cohn of *Newsday* asked, "Were there any actresses after whom you patterned yourself?"[18] Bette replied, "One. The reason I wanted to go into theater was because of an actress named Peg Entwistle...."[19]

The two-time Oscar winner and ten-time nominee (eleven if one includes the 1934 write-in campaign for her role in *Of Human Bondage*) continued to laud Peg all the way into the final several years of her life as she toured France and granted interviews.

It isn't known if Bette Davis and Peg Entwistle ever saw each other again following that January evening in 1926. It's assumed they exchanged pleasantries following the performance, a common occurrence between the Henry Jewett Players and patrons that normally took place shortly after the actors had changed clothes and removed their makeup. Given the enlightenment Bette received during Peg's performance, it is virtually certain that she would have wanted to meet Peg, and that they chatted, if only for a few moments.

Bette got her first film contract shortly after working for Yurka, this other "little wild duck" becoming known on the Universal Studios lot as the "little brown wren."

The rest is Hollywood history.

6

As Broadway Nears

Peg Entwistle, the 18-year-old actress who scored heavily in the Repertory Theater Production of The Wild Duck *will be heard on the WBZ wave each evening at 6 o'clock.*—Boston Globe, 1925[1]

After three rousing successes in a row for the Repertory, it was time for yet a fourth.

After two matinees the week of December 14, *The Wild Duck* went on hiatus until January. But there was little rest for Peg. On the evening of December 14, the Jewett Players opened the Boston revival of *Enter Madame*, an interesting little comedy about a prima donna, written by Gilda Varesi and Dolly Byrne. However, only Byrne knew that Varesi, who starred in *Madame* during its phenomenal 1920–22 Broadway run, had co-written the play, for Varesi had used the pseudonym Giulia Conti. This was because the story parodied Varesi's mother, celebrated opera star Elena Varesi. Exactly when Conti's true identity was revealed is hard to say, but by the time the play hit Boston, Gilda Varesi and Byrne were credited as the playwrights.

It isn't known how Mother Varesi took to her daughter's mischief.

Among the cast of that Broadway production was Gavin Muir, a respected leading man who will soon play a leading role in Peg's career. Muir had played Madame's son. For the Repertory, this part was filled by Ross Alexander, who would kill himself in 1937, reportedly with the same gun his actress wife, Aleta Freel, allegedly used on herself in 1935. (There would be doubts.)

In Boston, Blanche Yurka had the title role of *Enter Madame*. Peg played Aline Chalmers, the fiancée to Madame's son, John. It was not as important a role as Hedvig, but she portrayed Aline wonderfully, prompting the *Harvard Crimson* reviewer to tell the city, "Peg Entwistle deserves commendation also ... [C]onsidering her youth and her work in *The Wild Duck*, we predict for her a bright future."[2]

Rip Van Winkle was about to go back to sleep as the company ended rehearsals for *Snow White*, and the comedy *Mrs. Partridge Presents* by Mary Kennedy and Ruth Hawthorne. Peg had gotten a head start playing the famous princess. Before the company began gearing up for the actual play, she had already been presenting solo performances as Snow White on nightly broadcasts at WBZ radio. Given the allotted time slots, these look to have been basically advertisements, five-minute productions used to announce that she and her Seven Dwarfs would begin presenting their play at the Repertory starting December 21.

Snow White and the Seven Dwarfs was an adaptation from the stories of the Brothers Grimm. It was scripted in 1912 for Broadway by producer Winthrop Ames under the pseudonym Jessie Braham White. Marguerite Clark was the princess then (and in the 1916 film). Ames's version has much in common with the more famous Disney-animated production of 1937, but there are a few glaring differences: Bick, Flick, Glick, Snick, Plick, Whick and Quee gave way to Doc, Grumpy, Happy, Sleepy, Bashful, Sneezy and Dopey. And Disney's music was original, so while the Repertory's production did have music and song, its dwarfs did not sing "Whistle While You Work," and Peg did not croon "Some Day My Prince Will Come." But she did get to sing.

When her Snow White—lost in the woods and very hungry—comes upon the dwarfs' house for the first time, they are gone, yet their dinner table is prepared. The princess must eat, but is certainly no glutton. As she goes to each of the seven plates she takes one item, singing a ditty while doing so.

Boston loved everything about the play. Set designers Jonel Jorulesco and Carl Rockstrom were paid much tribute. The *Boston Globe* called the scenery "[e]xceedingly lovely ... especially beautiful was the forest."[3] The costumes were lauded too: "Peg Entwistle made a delightful Snow White and looked as pretty as every fairy tale princess has a right to be."[4]

"Miss Entwistle was a little princess who might have stepped out of an illustration of tales by Grimm," proclaimed the *Boston Herald*.[5]

From the *Boston Transcript* came, "The pretty heroine was entirely satisfying. Miss Entwistle made her a merry little person, ready to dance blithely. A true fairy tale bride for the Prince when the happy ending was at last brought to pass."[6]

For Peg, all this praise and attention must have indeed seemed like a fairy tale come true.

But Princess Entwistle had little time to bask in the glory, for her schedule was a busy one. *Enter Madame* had an evening performance six nights a week and there was added to these a Tuesday and Thursday matinee. *Snow White* played each Monday, Wednesday, and Friday afternoon and on Saturdays at 10:30 in the morning. And there was her radio schedule, which, during the holidays, was to be expanded from five minutes to thirty. The *Boston Globe* announced: "Peg Entwistle, the 18-year-old actress who scored heavily in the Repertory Theater production of *The Wild Duck,* will be heard on the WBZ wave each evening at 6 o'clock. Miss Entwistle will broadcast a Christmas story for the entertainment of the younger members of the radio audience. The popular young actress will also take part in the impressive celebration program which will be broadcast Christmas Eve. She will appear in the Yuletide festivities in the *Snow White and the Seven Dwarfs* costume."[7]

The Yuletide festivities spoken of was an annual celebration put on by the city of Boston. It took place on the Boston Common. The *Globe* called 1925's "more elaborate than ever."[8]

At five o'clock that evening, Beacon Hill came alive with joy. The weather was mild, with clear skies and temperatures in the low 40s dropping to just the high 30s. Mayor Curley spoke—with Snow White at his side—and then from the Samuel Parkman Bandstand sounded the orchestra and Choral clubs. WBZ radio broadcast the entire event live from the bandstand.

Peg wasn't scheduled to go on the air until 9:30 P.M., so until then her job was to mingle in character. She got to act without a script for almost four hours—pure joy. She no doubt looked beautiful in her Snow White costume; and to the children, second only to Santa in popularity.

There were hundreds of carolers marching through the streets, thousands of candles illuminated Beacon Hill and the State House. There, the tree-lighting ceremony took place, and a nativity pageant made its way twice around the Common. There was also a community open house; those who lived in the area encouraged friends and neighbors to come in and share Christmas pleasantries such as eggnog, cookies, and good old-fashioned holiday cheer. The party was to continue until midnight.

Among the Common and all over Beacon Hill, Peg Entwistle merrily played the princess for all it was worth, for Peg liked to be noticed — particularly when she was worth noticing. And as the city's papers touted this night as the largest Christmas Eve celebration Boston had ever seen, her fetching portrayal of Snow White could not go unnoticed among the many thousands who were mingling about. Her delightful manner would have warmed the heart of any Scrooge. Indeed, after *The Billboard* noted Peg was America's youngest regular member of a repertory company, it added, "The part of Snow White is a particularly happy one for Miss Entwistle."[9]

Exactly what Christmas story she told over the air that fantastic night isn't known. An attempt to discover if any of her broadcasts had been archived proved unfruitful. But at 9:30 she was on the bandstand, speaking (and probably singing) into the microphone, doing her thing as thousands stood among her and thousands more huddled around shortwave receivers in cozy Christmas homes, listening to Snow White comfort them — to Peg Entwistle charm them...

* * *

Three days after Christmas, *Enter Madame* was shown the exit, but not Blanche Yurka. She was next given the title role in *Mrs. Partridge Presents.* In early 1925 this three-act comedy had enjoyed a fine Broadway reception with Blanche Bates as its star. Also notable in that production was Sylvia Field, a fine actress who will share footlights with Peg in 1931, and Ruth Gordon, whose talent will bring Peg one of her biggest career disappointments.

In the Repertory's *Mrs. Partridge Presents,* Yurka played Maisie Partridge, a wealthy New York widow who attempts to make her two children independent. The ironic twist here is that Maisie's idea of independence is to see to it that her son Philip (Ross Alexander) becomes an artist, and that her daughter Delight (Peg) becomes an actress. But Philip desires to be an engineer and Delight wants only to marry the man she loves. The siblings hatch a plan to fool their mother into thinking they are following her wishes, yet all the while they are secretly pursuing their own. But this is a comedy, so the deception involves humorous situations.

How ironically fun it must have been for Peg, who could no more *not* be an actress than alter her gender, to act the role of a girl who despises becoming an actress but must pretend to be an actress by acting like one. In the end, with the approval of the audience, the youths get what they want and all feel a sense of pity for the well-meaning Mrs. Partridge.

Mrs. Partridge Presents opened December 28, to what the *Boston Globe* called "a distinctly high-class audience"[10] that "found abundant entertainment and hilarious amusements."[11]

Of the cast, the three most prominent were Yurka, Peg, and a new addition to Jewett's company, Carlotta Irwinn, who played Katharine, a dizzy, giddy friend to the Partridges. ("If the top could be lifted off, feathers would fly out," says one character about Katharine's light head.[12]) The *Globe* noted that this trio "shared the evening's triumphs about equally."[13] It also mentioned, "All three were called before the curtain repeatedly after each act."[14]

It seems Miss Entwistle was beginning to get the hang of this acting thing.

She was also getting the hang of the theatrical upper-crust social circle. On December 30 the first official meeting of the Boston Repertory's season was held by its officers in Repertory Hall. This "meeting" was actually an afternoon program of tours, recitations, readings, and songs. More than 300 guests and members of the Repertory Theater Club and the Repertory Acting Company were in attendance. Mrs. Alvan Fuller, wife of the Massachusetts governor, was the guest of honor. Henry and Mrs. Jewett spoke of their struggles to establish the Repertory, and Blanche Yurka gave a speech extolling the importance for all young actors to acquire repertory experience. "One needs elasticity," said Yurka.[15] "One must play a variety of characters to enrich the content of the color of one's character [in any given play]."[16] Then Yurka, who loved to remind everyone she met that she was of Bohemian parentage, sang several Czecho-Slovak folk songs. Esteemed theater notables E.H. Sothern, Cyril Maude, and Louis Mann attended the event, and Yurka told reporters the three had "declared [the Boston Repertory] a perfect place, with permanent equipment for a national theater."[17] A reception was held in the Repertory Club library, with tea served by Mrs. Fuller and Mrs. Jewett. In the receiving line, guests were greeted by Peg Entwistle and other players of the company.

* * *

Peg turned the corner of 1925 and '26 playing Snow White and Delight Partridge. Her radio days ended early in the New Year. On January 4, *The Wild Duck* went back on the boards. It was about this time when Bette Davis showed up and found her stage hero. And then on January 11, Peg became a hero of another kind in William Shakespeare's *Much Ado About Nothing*. Although Peg lacked a certain zeal for Shakespeare, she did have a passion for getting paid, so when Jewett decided to tackle one of the Bard's most difficult comedies, Miss Entwistle could only sigh and brush up on her *thee*s, *thy*s, and *thine*s. She wasn't half bad, as it turns out.

Much Ado About Nothing involves two pairs of lovers, Benedick and Beatrice, and Claudio and Hero. Peg played Hero. Chicanery and mischief are the order of the day; the story has too many twists and turns to detail here, but in the end, Hero has not really died, was never unfaithful, and will live happily ever after with her love, Claudio.

On opening night, as Peg was getting ready in the dressing room, floral bouquets arrived for her. Her stomach turned when she read the accompanying cards. This was her first real go at Shakespeare, and there in the audience was one of Broadway's most preeminent Shakespeareans, Walter Hampden, sitting with his wife Mabel and Peg's Uncle Charles. Peg's cousin Helen picks it up from there: "It was one of Enty's favorite stories. Babs had been gone [dead] for a time, but when [Walter and Mabel] visited, they talked of the old days ... Babs was shivering and pale as milk. She kept her hands to her hips so no one might see them shaking, the poor thing! Mabel said Babs was crying later because she just knew she was awful, but Walter said she really was very good. They all liked to smile about that one!"[18]

But Peg needn't have worried about tripping up. Everyone — actors, directors, producers, critics, even Walter Hampden and perhaps Shakespeare's own ghost — knew what a difficult piece of theater *Much Ado* could be. This is also seen in the number of its productions — or rather the lack of them. It had been thirteen years since *Much Ado* was last seen on a professional stage in Boston *or* Broadway. Almost no one wanted to go near it. Sure, it was Shakespeare, but Hampden wouldn't touch it with a ten-foot pole. *For god sakes, this was the play that embarrassed Julia Marlowe, E.H. Sothern, and John Drew!* remembered the veterans. Some things were better left alone, many thought, but Henry Jewett knew he had a very talented group of players in his company.

As Hero, Peg had to wrestle Shakespearean dialogue such as:

> Why, you speak truth. I never yet saw man,
> How wise, how noble, young, how rarely featured,
> But she would spell him backward: if fair-faced,
> She would swear the gentleman should be her sister;
> If black, why, Nature, drawing of an antique, made a foul blot;
> If tall, a lance ill-headed;
> If low, an agate very vilely cut;
> If speaking, why, a vane blown with all winds;
> If silent, why, a block moved with none.[19]

Of course, it would help if Peg knew what she was saying. And she did. The entire cast knew what they were saying—and doing—for the play was a success. The *Boston Globe* admitted, "The production of such a difficult piece was indeed a courageous thing for Mr. Jewett to even attempt,"[20] and called it "sprightly and pleasing performance."[21] The Globe also had this to say about the nervous little actress who had thought herself so awful that night: "Peg Entwistle, as Hero, as usual, delightfully girlish and pleasing."[22]

So then, any apprehension Peg had concerning her role as Hero was really, what ... much ado about nothing? Well, not quite...

Peg told a reporter the story of a comical, almost slapstick stage mishap during one of the later *Much Ado* performances. She had been watching the scenes from the wings and became so engrossed in the story that she completely forgot the time. She caught sight of one of her co-stars, Bill Mason, frantically waving at her from the wings on the other side of the stage. Peg needed to get to that side in a hurry, for that was the side from which she had to make her entrance into the scene, and her cue was coming up very shortly. In a panic, Peg made a dash for it behind the scenery backdrop, but she found her way completely blocked by stacks of boxes and barrels. Quickly she made her way downstairs to a doorway leading to a tunnel that traveled under the entire length of the stage. But as she was about to rush through the door, it was violently pushed open from the other side, striking her in the head. The culprit was Bill Mason. He had come running to see where she had disappeared to.

But that was just the beginning...

Peg wasn't bloodied, but she had an immense lump on her forehead and her hair was in complete disarray as she finally made it to the other side. However, she must have been suffering a mild concussion, for the blow to her head had dazed her and she ended up rushing onto the stage and making the wrong entrance. She couldn't remember just exactly where she was supposed to be. Disoriented and disheveled, Peg wandered around on the stage in the wrong scenery while Beatrice, Leonardo, and the prince were trying to keep the audience from realizing something was wrong. They started adlibbing lines of "Hero, where is Hero?" as they pretended to look for her over other parts of the set.[23] Finally, to the relief of all concerned, Peg rallied and made the proper entrance. "Miss Entwistle didn't forget her lines, either, although she was in such confusion," said the *Boston Globe*.[24]

The Hero was ever the trooper.

* * *

The work never seemed to end. Still busy with *Much Ado* and *The Wild Duck*, Peg also had to rehearse as an understudy for Agnes Scott's role of Lady Cicely in Bernard Shaw's comedy *Captain Brassbound's Conversion*. The play was a hit but Peg isn't listed in the opening night cast.

Now for John Galsworthy's absorbing drama *Loyalties*, about a Jewish fellow who is tolerated in higher English social circles because of his wealth. When $500 is stolen from him during a house party, he refuses to accept the loss "as a gentleman should."[25] He accuses Capt. Ronald Daney, a war hero who also happens to be the most popular and well-loved man of the party. Peg played Daney's wife, Mabel. Critics were loyal to *Loyalties* and tell us the cast enjoyed cheers and applause throughout their individual performances.

Then it was time for *Caesar and Cleopatra*, also by Shaw. Charles Quartermaine and Mary Servos had the title roles. It was the most ambitious production yet for Jewett's company. Dozens of cast members were involved, some of them playing several characters. It lasted more than four hours. (To shorten it, many producers omitted the third act, but not Jewett.)

Despite its length, the play was highly regarded in Boston. Peg played Charmian, one of Cleopatra's maids. She only had a few lines, but at least she got to wear a toga.

Caesar made it into March, but not quite to the ides: On March 5 it closed. Three days later, Peg starred as Ellie Dunn in another Shaw production, *Heartbreak House*. Ellie is perhaps the most difficult role she ever interpreted. The part is of a relatively nice girl who manifests several personalities. If she isn't perfect, the entire show has been a waste, no matter how well the other players had performed. Peg was very concerned about interpreting Shaw exactly as the great playwright intended. "I must have studied for hours ... one must study every word of Shaw. You can't ad lib, or slide over lines as one can in comedy. It was a dreadfully hard task to be letter perfect on a Shaw role when opening night came."[26]

The *Globe* said she excelled as Miss Ellie, but the *Harvard Crimson* explained, "Of all the performances of the evening the playing of Peg Entwistle as Ellie Dunn was the most interesting. When the play opened upon its strange first scene, the room like a ship's cabin in [the] Heartbreak House, Ellie was a living character. Before the play was half over she had turned from a young and attractive girl with her own personality to a type hard and cold and self-seeking. And when the play ended she was again become a living personality. It was this transition which illustrated most exactly the difference between Shaw's characters and his types."[27]

On March 15 came the wistful *Minick* by Edna Ferber and George S. Kaufman, the story of Old Man Minick, an aged widower who goes to live with his son and daughter in-law. The young folks think he hasn't any sense, Old Man Minick *knows* they don't. It's a battle of generations as the elderly gent meddles in business he shouldn't. This was the Boston premiere of *Minick,* and Peg, who played Lil Corey, did a fine job with the rest of the cast. There wasn't a bad review to be found in the city.

Question: Should a young wife, who finds she has nothing in common with her prig of a husband and knows another man who loves her and whom she feels she could love, elope or not? This is the dilemma facing Peg Entwistle's Elizabeth Champion-Cheney in W. Somerset Maugham's satirical comedy *The Circle*. Peg had the leading role in this well-received production. The *Boston Globe* called her "[e]specially noteworthy."[28]

The Circle and *Minick* took Peg from late March well into April. Then it was once again time for another *Wild Duck* revival. Blanche Yurka had gone on to other things, and so the role of Hedvig's mother was filled by Ruth Taylor, a wonderful actress who had been making some noise at the Repertory during the previous weeks. The Yurka-Entwistle magic was lacking but there were no complaints to be heard or read with the pairing of Miss Taylor and Peg.

As Peg again walked the boards with her popular Hedvig, she also appeared as Babbie in James M. Barrie's *The Little Minister*. (The reader will recall this Babbie as the likely inspiration from which Peg had begun to call herself "Babs.") Babbie is really Lady Barbara, who leaves her castle and disguises herself as a gypsy in order to warn villagers that her father plans to send soldiers to arrest them for protesting economic conditions. The play was a smash and it seems the *Boston Globe* never tired of one particular adjective to describe Peg: "Miss Entwistle is delightful as Lady Babbie."[29] And it is quite probable Peg would have done a delightful interpretation of Lady Babbie even if she had not known that the great Maude Adams, who originated the role, was on the Advisory Board of the Boston Repertory.

Peg's last hurrah at the Boston Repertory began on May 10, as Arsene in Ferenez Molnar's *The Swan*, a dramatic comedy about the trials and tribulations of royalty and ambition. Though not a spectacular success, *The Swan* glided effortlessly with a "[v]ery pleasing performance."[30] The *Boston Globe* also observed that Molnar's play was "most fortunate in its handling by Mr. Jewett's players."[31]

And that's generally how things went during Peg's apprenticeship. But maybe "apprenticeship" is too simplistic a term to describe what she actually experienced and accomplished as a Henry Jewett Player, for Peg had attained a significant amount of fame among the Boston set. Her interpretations of Hedvig, Snow White, Ellie Dunn, Elizabeth Champion-Cheney and Babbie had been especially well-received. She achieved high marks in her other roles, too. And there was the radio gig and her starring Christmas Eve role on that outdoor stage, whose footlights and spotlights were thousands of bright eyes and gleeful smiles of beaming children who delighted as much in a Christmas song from Princess Snow White as they did in a candy cane from Santa.

At the start of her apprenticeship, Peg had begun to excel and expand her talent at an uncanny rate. Apart from the episode in *The Rivals,* when Emma Dunn had to upstage her in order to drive home the importance of crossing, and the time she was nearly knocked out during that episode of inattentiveness in *Much Ado About Nothing*, Peg hadn't stumbled over difficulty. Some of her roles were minor, where stumbles were easy to avoid (and for critics to overlook), but most of the time she was in lead or supporting roles where flubs would have all the subtlety of a china cabinet crashing to the floor.

Her schedule had been physically demanding and mentally taxing. For eight months she worked a minimum of 12 performances of two and three plays each week. And there were constant rehearsals for the next premiere or revival. Sundays were "off" days, but only for performing in front of paying audiences; she still had to rehearse and study scripts. And a legal holiday didn't mean a day off, it meant an extra matinee. But no matter how tired she might be after an emotionally draining performance, she was required by Henry Jewett to smile and engage patrons and special guests after each show. Peg was a dynamo. She was as much in her element as a fish in a pond and admirably held her own alongside some brilliant stage veterans.

In fact, she had sometimes outshined them.

After heaping almost embarrassing praise on Blanche Yurka for her performance in *The Wild Duck*, the *Boston Globe* added, "Yet even she is out shadowed by the child. Peg Entwistle, young member of the Repertory company, gave a magnificent interpretation of the innocent little girl. In every movement, as the play swings now into comedy, now under the sudden touch of Ibsen's whip-like touch to bitter sarcasm and threatening tragedy, from the time we first see her, hands to those tortured little eyes, the figure of Hedvig moves like a wraith through the gathering storm—flaxen hair that now lights up in wan smile, now falls into bewilderment. In voice, in action, she dominates the entire piece, and it is her death by her own little hand that ends it."[32]

It was no small thing to have "out shadowed" the likes of Blanche Yurka, one of the best stage actresses of the day and a card-carrying member of Broadway's elite. Realistically, the best any apprentice could hope for playing opposite Yurka was a simple, honorable mention.

But along came Peg Entwistle.

A year after her debut as Hedvig, a theater critic for the *Harvard Crimson* saw her Boston pre–Broadway performance in *Tommy*. The writer referred to Peg as an "Erstwhile Repertory prodigy."[33] If Harvard University didn't know a prodigy when they saw one, then who did?

Peg could have stayed at the Boston Repertory much longer if she had been so inclined. Her popularity there hadn't waned and she was getting better with each production, but she was exhausted; the 14-hour days were taking a toll on her petite frame. She was just plain tired of Jewett's grueling schedules. "I want to play stock summers, perhaps, but I don't think I ever want to go back to playing in repertory the year round," she said upon reflection of those months as a Jewett Player.[34]

So it was time to move on—to rest up and renew her strength so she could more easily reach out and grab the brass ring ... her Broadway dream.

7

At Last!

Someday, I may have the ineffable joy of having a play written for me by Barrie. I would rather be Maude Adams than any woman in the history of the stage. — Peg Entwistle[1]

Lights! Energy! Excitement! Tingles and Glitter Galore!
Broadway!
Mixed reviews ... mediocre productions ... less-than-full houses ... fickle leading men ... broken promises ... busted hearts...
Broadway?
It would be nice to say that Peg's professional entrance to the big-time ballyhoo boards of the Great White Way had come with all the zing! and pop! to which she had grown accustomed while in Boston, but it didn't.

She arrived to Manhattan in early June and stayed with her uncle at his apartment near Hampden's Theater. Peg's plans were to take a trip to Hollywood so she could visit Aunt Jane and her brothers and while she was there maybe join a stock company for the summer. But Peg wasn't in New York City for more than few days when she met Gavin Muir, a Chicago-born character actor who became so good at faking an English accent that many thought he was British through and through. He told her he was currently rehearsing a play called *The Man from Toronto,* but one of the actresses hadn't worked out and the production was in desperate need of a blonde English girl. Would she care to give it a go? Peg must have chuckled — the whole thing was so very convenient and pat that she probably thought Muir was hitting on her, but she accepted.

The Man from Toronto, written by Douglas Murray, involves one Fergis Wimbush (from Toronto, of course) who has been left a fortune. Because of a clause in the will he must go to England and before a certain time marry a certain widow he has never met or else he gets nothing. It was a popular play in England going back to World War I, but its success there had much to do with the British themes and English humor that permeates it curtain to curtain. When tried on Broadway in 1918 it was known as *Perkins* and starred the legendary actress and aviatrix Ruth Chatterton. But even she could not help the dismal affair. American audiences just didn't appreciate the English funny bone and *Perkins* closed after just a score of performances.

But the play continued to flourish in Britain and was even enjoying success (as *The Man from Toronto*) when Muir met Peg. Muir took her to the Selwyn Theater on 42nd Street, a half block from where Broadway and Times Square meet. The Selwyn — named after producers Edgar and Arch Selwyn — wasn't exactly *on* Broadway, but was close enough to be considered a Broadway venue by those who drew the boundaries— and that was close enough for Peg Entwistle. After reading a few lines for director Albert Bannister, she was given a contract to play the relatively minor role of Martha, a daughter of Mr. Wimbush. Peg postponed her trip to Hollywood and joined the company that night for rehearsals.

(Coincidently, this role was played by Entwistle family friend Frances Goodrich during the 1918 Ruth Chatterton production. Goodrich married Albert Hackett and they became the most successful husband-and-wife screenwriting team in Hollywood. Their stunning résumé includes Oscar nominations, Writers Guild Awards, and a Pulitzer Prize for Drama. When Peg's aunt and uncle nearly lost their house after falling behind on a bank loan, Frances and Albert covered the debt and let them repay what they could, when they could.)

The cast had been rehearsing *The Man from Toronto* for nearly two weeks when Peg joined them, but she jumped in with ease. A few days later, on June 15, the production had its pre–Broadway tryout in Stamford, Connecticut. Virtually all plays destined for Broadway were first tried on the road, usually for no more than several days or a week. It was during these tryouts that directors, writers, and cast members fine-tuned the product, adding or deleting scenes or dialogue, adjusting stage direction, and so on. It isn't known what changes were made to *The Man from Toronto,* but two days later it had its Broadway premiere at the Selwyn Theater.

The reception was less than stunning. Although a *New York Times* drama critic wrote that the production was, "[c]ast suitably and played crisply," the play was panned.[2] It hadn't bombed, but it hadn't wowed the city, either. In the *Times* review, Peg was alluded to only in the most distant sense: "Nor do the Wimbush sisters make for good contrast."[3] There is no mention of a "prodigy" from Boston.

But Clarence Taylor of *The Billboard* took a bit more notice. After first complaining that the play had more exits and entrances per act than seemed possible, he lauded the charming ingénue above all: "The most delightful member of the cast is Peg Entwistle, who brings to the role of the real maid in the little household a charming personality that is difficult to describe. The part is not awfully important, but Miss Entwistle makes it important."[4]

Lucy Jeanne Price, a syndicated columnist, thought the cast gave a "pleasing, time-whiling performance,"[5] and when *Toronto* was still drawing an audience ten days later, the producer announced it would remain at the Selwyn for the summer and tour Canada in mid–September. But strife arose within the ranks, most notably in the form of an actor named Curtiss Cooksey. Before joining *The Man from Toronto,* Cooksey was the lead in *One Man's Woman,* but days later he quit, citing "interpolated business that was degrading."[6] What that meant is hard to say but it possibly had something to do with him not getting his way. At any rate, Cooksey was now feeling "interpolated" in *Toronto* and abruptly quit to sign on with producer David Belasco for one production or another. His replacement was Jack Roseleigh, an actor of minor note. Alas, after just 30 performances *The Man from Toronto* went dark. It was July 10. Only a month had passed since Peg had been the talk of Boston circles ... and now Harvard's favorite ingénue was just another New York City actress without a job.

Despite her disappointment with *The Man from Toronto,* Peg chose to remain in New York rather than take a much-needed break to see her family in California. She was determined to go home to Hollywood as a full-fledged Broadway star, but *Toronto* had failed her. So she stayed in Manhattan to regroup. The new theatrical season would start in the fall, and that meant plenty of opportunities during the rest of the summer to find a suitable production.

Peg no doubt started perusing trade publications like *The Billboard,* which listed auditions and casting calls. And while it isn't known whom she contacted in New York, or where she auditioned during this time, it is certain that she called her "agent" in Hollywood...

In the course of researching Charles Entwistle's address book there was found some faint writing that looked to have been erased long ago. Written over these erasures were phone numbers and names unrelated to Peg. Guided by curiosity and a hunch, and with the help of a magnifier, the author was able to determine the titles of two plays: *Gentlemen Prefer Blondes,* the Anita Loos comedy now mostly associated with the film starring Marilyn Monroe, and *An American Tragedy,* a drama by Theodore Dreiser. Both of these plays were slated to open in New York in the fall of 1926. Auditions took place during and after Peg's engagement in *The Man from Toronto.* Charles Entwistle had no reason to write down the titles of those two plays for his own sake; he had no connection to them. But he would have written them down if his niece asked him if he could get her an inside track with the producers.

Theatrical notices of the day show that hundreds of ingénues were lining up to audition for both plays. For *Gentlemen Prefer Blondes,* a thousand girls tried for the role of Lorelei Lee; 270 were brunettes in blonde wigs, including June Walker, who won the part.

Peg Entwistle, though far from "stuck-up," could never accept being crammed inside tiny outer offices with dozens of other hopefuls vying for a part. And why should she have to (she likely reasoned)? With tireless effort she had paid her dues and proven herself at the Boston Repertory, and her uncle had connections—why not use them? So she called him ... was there *something* he could do for her? He would have jotted down the titles of any plays in which she had an interest. He would have promised to make some calls.

It isn't known if Charles got her an audition through a side door for the Loos or Dreiser plays. But this much is known: Miriam Hopkins was nearing the end of a run in a hit play in Chicago at the same time the producers of *An American Tragedy,* unhappy with the results of its New York auditions, decided to take their casting calls to the Windy City. After hundreds of girls auditioned in New York, and then hundreds more in Chicago, Miriam Hopkins was awarded the co-starring role of *An American Tragedy.* Coincidentally, the play that Hopkins was working in closed the same day that news of her role in *An American Tragedy* hit the papers. For over three months she had been playing a flapper named Beth Calhoun in George M. Cohan's *The Home Towners.* Cohan had also been making arrangements to bring this production and much of its Chicago cast to Broadway, but now he was short an actress to play Beth Calhoun. He tried, but couldn't find a girl in his cast or even all of Chicago who was good enough to replace Miriam Hopkins. He hoped New York had someone to offer.

* * *

Of all the legendary theatrical producers during the 20th century there is none more famous and synonymous with America than George M. Cohan. But he was no mere producer. Cohan was a playwright, actor, singer, dancer and composer of more than 500 songs. Some of those songs helped make him a legend and an American icon for the ages.

James Cagney's Oscar-winning portrayal of Cohan in the 1942 film *Yankee Doodle Dandy* helped imprint the heart of the nation with a singing spirit of patriotism not seen since the First World War. Cohan's rousing melodies, such as "Over There," "You're a Grand

Old Flag," and "The Yankee Doodle Boy," helped puff the chests of America's fighting forces headed overseas. For his contributions to the morale of the country during that war, President Roosevelt awarded Cohan the Congressional Gold Medal. George M. Cohan personified patriotism and became a hero to the heroes, but he wasn't a slouch on Broadway, either.

The Home Towners was a comedic farce from Cohan's own pen. Its Chicago run was the inaugural production of his new theater, and it had been well received. In New York, as he had done in Chicago, Cohan would produce and stage it, as well as supervise the new director, John Meehan. Usually Cohan starred in his own productions, but not this time. This was notable enough to be mentioned in virtually every announcement and review regarding *The Home Towners,* and according to at least one theatrical critic this contributed to a slightly less than full house for the New York premiere.

Besides Miriam Hopkins, a few other original cast members did not accompany Cohan to New York, but notable among the principals was Chester Morris, a character actor whose future film career would include an Oscar nomination (*Alibi,* 1929) and 14 title roles as the popular detective Boston Blackie.

Although it hasn't been firmly established, bits and pieces of information culled from family archives seem to hint that Uncle Charles may have contacted Lee Shubert on behalf of his niece. Charles had successfully managed a few of Shubert's productions some years earlier, and Peg's Aunt Jane had roles in several of them. Shubert was a friend of Cohan's going back many years, so it's entirely possible Peg got an audience with Cohan through this association. Of course, this is only speculation; it is just as likely Peg did all of her own footwork here. At any rate, she met Cohan and was given a contract to play Beth Calhoun. A *New York Times* article titled "And Who Is Peg Entwistle" says she rehearsed one week with the director (Cohan supervising), and a week with the cast.[7] This was remarkable to the *Times,* for Peg was the last player to join a cast that had already been rehearsing for some weeks.

Because the production had played in Chicago for months, there was no need for a road tryout; the play was suitable and Cohan had complete trust in the new members. On August 23, 1926, *The Home Towners* had its Broadway premiere at the Hudson Theater. Once again Peg was a half block off Broadway proper, but it was still "Broadway," and she was of course thrilled to be working for the great George M. Cohan.

The plot of *The Home Towners* involves two old friends from Indiana. Bancroft (played by Robert McWade) has become successful in New York and plans to marry Beth (Peg), but when Bancroft's friend Vic (William Elliott) arrives for the wedding and meets Beth's family he thinks Beth and her kin are just after Bancroft's money. Nothing could be farther from the truth, but that doesn't stop Vic from stirring up hornets. Beth breaks off the engagement after Vic insults New York ("six million bandits!")[8], New Yorkers ("All crooked, all deadbeats!")[9], and then her family in particular ("Charlatans and gold-brick salesmen!")[10]. On the way to a happy ending there are laughs galore, and nearly every reviewer loved the second act, particularly the over-the-top farce and wisecracks.

While some critics put on airs regarding Cohan's absence and his script's jabs at New Yorkers (calling folks from Indiana "pin-headed hicks" was apparently fine with these critics[11]), others thought it hilarious and highly amusing. *Time* magazine tagged it as a comedy of much effectiveness. Brooks Atkinson of the *New York Times* called it "the most enjoyable of the new comedies,"[12] and said, "Miss Entwistle, as the young Calhoun maiden, reveals herself as an actress competent to play in more than a single key."[13] Across the pond, London's *The Stage* received a cabled review by a special correspondent in New York. The unnamed critic noted quite boldly that Peg had been the Boston Repertory's leading draw the previous season. The writer commended her acting and complained that her role was all too brief.

The Home Towners closed in October after nearly 70 performances. It wasn't quite the run Peg had hoped for, but it was Cohan, and she had been his female lead. No one compared her to Miriam Hopkins and the critics had mentioned her favorably ... life was good.

Her money was good, too: $250 a week was an amazing salary for an 18-year-old stage actress at that time. And a share of one percent of the box office added weight to her purse. Peg had taken a significant hit to her ego with *The Man from Toronto*, but in *The Home Towners* she more than made up for it. Having Cohan's name on her résumé was a key that could open most any door, and yet, even with Cohan, Broadway stardom had still eluded her.

This was about to change.

8

Tommy

Before it changes its name again for Broadway consumption and you lose sight of Peg, go and see the reason for the Harvard attendance at the Repertory last year.—Harvard Crimson[1]

In early August 1926, three weeks before Peg Entwistle opened in *The Home Towners*, playwrights Howard Lindsay and Bert Robinson began testing a new comedy at Lindsay's Lakewood Stock Company in Skowhegan, Maine. It was soon announced that this play, called *Tommy Helps Himself,* would have a Broadway opening in the coming fall. (In Maine, the title role was played by Albert Hackett; as previously mentioned, Hackett was an Entwistle family friend and future spouse of Frances Goodrich.)

By then it would be known simply as *Tommy.*

The story involves a girl named Marie Thurber who is determined not to marry the goodhearted Tommy Mills for the simple reason her parents want her to.

A quick look: At curtain rise, Marie chats in her living room with Bernard. Now here is a lad full of self-assurance, this Bernard, a real go-getter making his way in the car sales game. His only character defect is in entertaining the minor vices of youthful ego. (One critic described him as the type who would go to a window and take a bow following a peal of thunder.) Bernard wishes Marie's hand in marriage and dotes on the young lady in no small way, wooing her with piano and song. He is bound and determined to have her, even going so far as planning an elopement. He has obtained a marriage license, forged Marie's name on it, and hired a preacher who now awaits them in a town far away — minor details which the zealous hopeful has yet to share with Marie.

But Tommy also wants Marie, and comes courting the old-fashioned way, by attempting to win her folks' approval. It seems to be working, for Marie's parents remain upstairs when Bernard calls on their daughter but always hurry down when Tommy comes a-calling. And why shouldn't they? He routinely brings lovely chocolates for Mother and grand cigars for Father. The fact that Tommy owns land and will one day inherit the town's bank might also have a little something to do with Mr. and Mrs. Thurber's bright smiles and friendly welcomes.

Enter Marie's Uncle Dave; a Republican boss senator whose doctrine in life is that no girl really knows what she wants until her family is against it. Dave knows that while Marie is quite smitten by Bernard, Tommy is the better man for her, and so he gets busy with some fancy meddling in order to sway her toward Tommy's side by turning her parents against him. But the ever-confident car salesman with the voice full of song and pocket full of forged marriage licenses is never far away—Bernard brings to the table just enough charm and pluck to keep things interesting.

With Tommy and Bernard tugging her heart to and fro, and her mind made up by everyone except herself, Marie will have quite a time of it all. Whom will she choose?

The spoiler is built into the play's title, of course. Marie will pick *Tommy*. Every ticket buyer knew this going in, but Broadway patrons were an experienced bunch; they knew if the title told them something of the ending, there must be some fun in getting there. And indeed there was. However, before delighted audiences could enjoy the fun of getting there, Peg Entwistle had to first get the part.

* * *

In early October 1926, producer George C. Tyler acquired the rights to *Tommy*. Not much was said about it at the time. But a week later, after *The Home Towners* closed on Broadway, Peg heard that Tyler was producing Margaret Kennedy's *The Constant Nymph*. The town was abuzz with this play's potential, and Peg wanted in. She rushed to Tyler's cloistered office at the New Amsterdam Theater on 42nd Street. She managed to get in the door, but Tyler had to let her down: All the female roles had been promised to other actresses.

Peg's hopes had been dashed, but she wouldn't remain crestfallen for long.

George C. Tyler was one of Broadway's shot-callers, one of those movers and shakers who got ink in the *Times* whenever he had indigestion or a toothache. He was also a friend of George M. Cohan's and had seen Peg in *The Home Towners*. And he hadn't forgotten her.

Tyler was a big shot all right, but one of few words, fewer words still if he saw no reason to waste his precious time on an actress or a project with no potential.

He handed Peg the script to *Tommy*. This moment both delighted and intimidated her. The fact that she was still in his office and that he had just handed her a play indicated he liked her—this would delight any actress. But Peg also suspected she might be in for one of his famous, intimidating hoodwinks.

Tyler's reputation was of a producer whose cryptic style easily frustrated reporters and press agents and often left young actors harried during auditions in his office. A favorite ruse of his went like this: After spending a few nervous minutes studying lines as Tyler sat staring from behind his desk, the audition would begin by a prominent clearing of the producer's throat and a circular wave of his cigar-clutching hand. On hearing the first word or line of the interpretation, Tyler would march over to hand the confused, intimidated actor a script of another play he had all along intended them to read.

Tyler rarely made his true intentions known before the last minute, choosing instead to drop hints sprinkled in ambiguity (if he dropped any hints at all). A favorite rejoinder to press agents went, "You may tell them I said 'yes and no' but don't quote me."[2] During a *New York Times* interview, while it was thought he was solidly committed to producing just one play for the season (*The Constant Nymph*), he said, "I might also do a piece called *Tommy*, but don't quote me on that because I may not present it after all."[3] But he did, and six others that season.

So Peg read him a few lines. No other girls were tested. Tyler had his Marie Thurber.

Tommy went into rehearsals in mid–November. Directing the production were its authors, Bert Robinson and Howard Lindsay. (Lindsay will share a 1946 Pulitzer for the play *State of the Union*, and a 1960 Tony Award for *The Sound of Music*, which he wrote with Russell Crouse.)

William Janney had the title role; Alan Bunce acted the rival suitor, Bernard, and Sidney Toler played Uncle Dave. Toler, a descendant of Pocahontas, was the most experienced and best-known actor in the cast, but he is most remembered now as Charlie Chan, having played the Chinese detective in 22 films—remarkable for a man who wasn't the least bit Asian. Ben Johnson, who was with Peg in *The Home Towners,* was also in the *Tommy* cast.

On November 21, 1926, after just ten days of rehearsal, the troupe was ready for a tryout. Said the *New York Times*, "A play called *Tommy*, which is sliding into view with unusual quiet, will be presented in Atlantic City tomorrow night.... It goes a week hence to Boston, and upon its reception there, presumably, depends its metropolitan career."[4]

The notices were good in New Jersey, but when the curtain at Boston's Park Theater went up to reveal Peg in the opening scene, she was so warmly cheered and applauded by a huge gallery of friends and fans from Harvard and the Boston Repertory that she openly gasped and struggled a moment to compose herself.

In its review the following day, the *Harvard Crimson* noted, "The audience at the Park, most of whom never saw the inside of the Repertory, loved Peg almost as much as her nursery mates ... which would seem to assure Miss Entwistle of a long career and a merry one, with IT safely in her possession. That she has sex appeal, which cries out even above the saccharine mouthings of *Tommy*, is evident. It is only to be prayed that her advent to Broadway in a nice, sweet, sticky little homey comedy won't sentence her to the sugar bowl for life."[5]

The *Tommy* tryout wasn't all work for Peg, but even on her time off it was still all theater. Shortly after the first week of that December she decided to visit the old grist mill and take in a matinee of Kane Campbell's *The Enchanted April* at the Boston Repertory. With laughter Peg described her leisure plans thus: "I shall sit out front and watch the show like a member of the audience, as if I didn't know every inch of the stage from the back. It will be such fun!"[6]

The company ended its road tryout after a few weeks and returned to New York in time for a short Christmas vacation. Then would come 1927, and the usual last-minute rush and anxieties attached to every Broadway opening known to history.

*　*　*

Billed by George C. Tyler as "An American Comedy,"[7] *Tommy* opened to a packed house at the Gaiety Theater on Monday night, January 10, 1927. The Gaiety was situated in the heart of Broadway ... *on* Broadway...

Finally!

Reviewers liked *Tommy*, but didn't *love* it. Like the relationship between Marie and the title character, it took a bit of time for hearts to truly warm, but warm they did.

Percy Hammond of the *Herald Tribune* said it was "a delightful comedy."[8] *Time* magazine predicted it would be "seized upon by all the stock companies in the land."[9] Robert Benchley over at *Life* said, "*Tommy* has the refreshingly sanitary air which comedies used to have...."[10] *New York Times* guru Brooks Atkinson gave Sidney Toler a rave review, but with Peg he was reserved: "The fresh and pretty Peg Entwistle is attractive in the manner of a number of other fresh and pretty ingénues."[11]

Atkinson also said the play wasn't very exciting; however, he did like it—and when Brooks Atkinson liked a play, not much could stop its success. Early on, within the first week or so, and as the show began to gather steam, there was talk that the district attorney might not take kindly to several scenes, the first when Tommy gets drunk and the other when Marie's parents come on stage in nightgowns.

City and state officials had serious concerns regarding morality in stage productions. New York Governor Al Smith was about to enact the Padlock Law, which gave police the power to close a theater for a year if a production was deemed indecent, obscene, or immoral. Broadway was put on notice and closely monitored by the ever-watchful eyes of the Society for the Suppression of Vice, religious and political leaders, and a hypocritical newspaper publisher, gossiper, and flagrant adulterer named William Randolph Hearst.

In spite of Hearst's two faces, these watchdogs (and the Padlock Law) had teeth.

On the morning of February 9, just a few weeks after *Tommy* opened, Police Commissioner James Warren announced his intentions boldly in the *New York Times*: Later that evening, his squads marched into the Empire Theater to halt production of *The Captive*, a play about lesbians. Fearing unrest, the cops waited for the show to end before stuffing their paddy wagons with the cast, including Humphrey Bogart's wife Helen Menken, Basil Rathbone, and Winifred Fraser, who had acted with Peg's father in 1916. In that same hour, police also stormed the Daly's Theater to put a stop to *Sex*, which featured drag queens and Mae West playing Margie LaMont, a kind-hearted prostitute. Other raids followed.

Of course, Peg's *Tommy* had nothing even remotely similar to the content mentioned above. And while the nightgown scene was harmless (a stout gray-haired actress and balding pot-bellied actor draped in flannel robes resembled anything but Mae West and a drag queen), it was still 1927, a time of Prohibition. Having a young man hug a jug of John Barleycorn while staggering about the stage in a stupor was generally considered a no-no. But the drunken scene in *Tommy* avoided the Padlock Law because the story has a character getting intoxicated for an acceptable reason: He is out of sorts with the parents of the girl he loves, but it is not of his doing. The lad has already proved to the audience (and watchdog groups) that he is benevolent, and a fine fellow to be sure. It was enough to get *Tommy* a nod of city approval.

Also in *Tommy*'s favor were reviews that pronounced it clean and wholesome, and other such soap. (Somewhat humorously, Robert Benchley in *Life* magazine said, "[W]hile you are there it is a not-inconsiderable relief to feel that the chances of a pervert's appearing on the scene are negligible...."[12]) Moreover, the writers had an ace in the hole. The play's script included alternate scenes and dialogue which omitted Tommy's imbibing and most all references to liquor. These script changes were designed to be used in the event *Tommy* went on tour and found itself surrounded by puritanical villagers wielding pitchforks and torches. But the changes were never needed and *Tommy* enjoyed a clean, wholesome, harmless run wherever it played.

Just as today, actors and actresses always did well to involve themselves with charitable work. While altruism certainly had center stage, everyone knew that publicity went hand in hand. On January 23, Peg and the other members of *Tommy*'s cast performed short skits at a dinner and entertainment program for the Catholic Actors' Guild. Leo Carrillo, a star of the stage long before his high-visibility role as television's Cisco Kid, also joined Peg and her crew in the fun. The keynote speaker was famed humorist Arthur "Bugs" Baer, who co-penned at least one Broadway revue with the Georges White and Gershwin. (Baer is also said to have nicknamed New York Yankees slugger Babe Ruth the Sultan of Swat.) Catholic leaders of Gotham were pleased with the event, and so word of *Tommy* and Peg's pleasantness in it began to spread quickly. The play was catching on. Every performance was now

Peg's Broadway debut as a professional actress was not spectacular, but her third production, the romantic comedy *Tommy,* made her a legitimate star. Here she is flanked by co-stars Sidney Toler (right) and the Jimmy Stewart–esque William Janney. This image was used around the country to promote smaller, non–Equity productions of *Tommy* more than a year after Peg's final performance in it (author's collection).

sold out. Reservations were made weeks in advance and ticket brokers worked hard to obtain more passes from George Tyler's office.

Tyler's publicists were also working hard.

The *New York Times* article, "And Who Is Peg Entwistle?"[13] came out two weeks after her nineteenth birthday. It touched on the theatrical background of her family and associations with Henry Jewett, Blanche Yurka, Walter Hampden and George M. Cohan. Peg also told the paper about Emma Dunn's embarrassing stage-crossing lesson at the Boston Repertory. The *Times* writer then reminds readers that most actors got their first leading roles in places with fewer lights and less attention. The article ends, "And the next thing she knew she was playing a lead on Broadway — not on one of the side streets that come under the collective heading, but right smack on Broadway at Forty-Sixth Street."[14]

And the pay wasn't bad, either.

Feeling all grown-up and Broadway-actressy when she worked for Cohan and earned $250-plus weekly, Peg had left her uncle's place and moved into her own on Beekman Street, near the Financial District, 15 minutes away from Times Square. Her new apartment was in a women-only building run by a Mrs. Macdonald. The residents were mostly professional women such as actresses and executive secretaries for the Wall Street elite. But Peg was now getting $500 a week (equivalent to about $6,000 today). Sidney Toler was earning $1,500 ($18,000). Moreover, their contractual share of the box-office take added significantly to these salaries. (Bit players and understudies were getting between 40 and 100 dollars per week, *sans* box office.)

Tommy was going into its second month and becoming more popular. This meant longer hours at work — especially after evening performances when scores of friends and fans came to the after-show meet-and-greets. Sometimes Peg wouldn't be able to leave for home before 1:00 A.M., and probably without having had dinner. In order to be closer to the theater she moved out of Mrs. Macdonald's building and got an apartment in the swanky Shelton Hotel, just across the street from the legendary Waldorf Astoria.

The Shelton was a newer high-rise that offered short or long-term rentals. For fifty dollars a week (assuming she took a two-room unit) Peg got maid service and other amenities including the use of the hotel's spas, lounges, two swimming pools, fully equipped gymnasium, squash court, bowling alley, game rooms, club houses, library, rooftop garden, solarium, restaurants and, of course, those famous Manhattan doormen whose uniforms reeked of admiralty and whose whistles caused taxis to magically appear out of thin air.

Peg Entwistle had hit the Big Time.

In April, about four months after *Tommy* opened, George C. Tyler moved the production four blocks away to the 900-seat Eltinge Theater on 42nd Street. This came after producers A.L. Erlanger and Marcus Klaw (owners of the Gaiety) decided it was more profitable to turn their theater into a full-time movie house (it had been a part-time movie house since 1926). The move to the Eltinge (named after female impersonator Julian Eltinge) worked out well for *Tommy*. It brought added income because it had a hundred more seats. The dressing rooms were larger and the air conditioning (created by swamp coolers) and lounges kept the actors and audiences cool and comfortable. There was also a unique three-size seating system that allowed a choice for patrons of slender, medium, or stout body shapes.

Tommy kept to the same rigorous schedule: Monday through Friday evenings at 8:30, and matinees on Wednesdays, Saturdays, and holidays. There were a few adjustments coming, including a new director and leading man, but *Tommy* was the talk of the town. In fact, it was the talk of other towns.

In a letter to her Aunt Jane, Peg said she thought the play would run through June, then after a little vacation she would go with it to Chicago. She was right, the play did go through June, but it was enjoying so much success that Tyler decided to hold it over. He announced that *Tommy* would continue at the Eltinge until late August and then open in Chicago on August 28. But then a sweltering heat wave hit New York in July. Dozens of people died throughout the city and hundreds more fell prostrate each day. Broadway patrons stayed away in droves. Many theaters had trouble filling seats, including those whose advertisements mentioned air conditioning ("refrigerated" was the more common term). Business picked up as the heat wave subsided, but Tyler didn't want to take a chance on what a New York City August might bring. So on July 23 he dropped the curtain on *Tommy* after a final matinee and evening performance. In spite of this, the *New York Times* called the play a success when noting its closing.

There were better plays, to be sure; however, *Variety* listed *Tommy* as one of the country's most successful attractions of 1927. It ended up in the top-ten of nearly 300 Broadway productions which opened that season. Tyler would never again have such a successful Broadway run. It had an original run of more than eight months in Atlantic City, Boston, and New York, eight shows a week — nearly 300 performances. Those are tame numbers for a successful play today, but in 1927 this was beyond the expectations of most producers.

* * *

When *Tommy* made it to Chicago, it did so without Peg. For reasons detailed below, she opted out and chose to stay in New York. A capable actress named Gay Seabrook took over the role of Marie Thurber and worked alongside most of the original cast, including Sidney Toler. The Chicago run lasted over four months and played to capacity audiences each day and night. From there it headed west, to small towns and big cities where it broke box-office records in Reno, San Francisco, and then Los Angeles. Tommy Mills and Marie Thurber warmed hearts and charmed audiences for two solid years on the road after the Broadway run ended. Its national success was owed in no small measure to Peg Entwistle, whose popularity in her originating role had given the production a great deal of recognition.

While Peg was with it on Broadway, the play had become immensely popular around the country in high school and college theater programs; it was a summer favorite with stock companies from sea to shining sea. Her association with the play had become so familiar that even a year after she and *Tommy* had parted ways, a newspaper in Bedford, Pennsylvania, *The Gazette*, advertised a local production with a photo of Peg in a scene from the original play. To drive home the story's wholesome theme and attract older and younger playgoers alike, the ad included a line from a Broadway review: "A page from everyday American life, touched with the glory of youth."[15] It shows Sidney Toler holding a large portrait of Abe Lincoln as Peg and William Janney (Tommy) look upon the Great Emancipator with much interest.

Peg Entwistle worked hard and achieved true Broadway success in *Tommy*. As in Boston, she drew the attention and affection of an entire city. But not just any city, this was New York ... this was *Broadway* ... the world capital of stage, the *Great White Way*.

When Peg was working the Boston tryout of *Tommy* back in December 1926, a critic in *The Transcript* described the production's stage setting as "unmistakably of the American middle-class earth,"[16] and the characters as "true to the type."[17] He spoke of the audience, too, taking particular notice of their response once they perceived the overall warmness of the play: "Every spectator with a homely American background drew up a chair and settled into it for the duration."[18]

In essence, the reviewer was telling his readers that the audience felt a kinship to the characters in *Tommy,* that the loves and losses and misunderstandings in the Thurber living room were not much different from those in their own homes. And so, after the last clap and the final "bravo!" had echoed, and after one more bouquet had landed at the foot of the ingénue, the audience members would retire to the comforts and trials of their own abodes, hoping that Marie Thurber's real-life Peg Entwistle would one day find lasting happiness with an honest, warm, sincere and gentle man like Tommy Mills.

She found Robert Keith instead.

9

Little White Lies on the Great White Way

We get along splendidly, he's a sweet thing and I love him terribly.
We've been married eight months and haven't had a real honest to God fight yet.
And I don't think we ever shall...— Peg to Aunt Jane[1]

On April 18, 1929, exactly two years to the day after marrying actor Robert Lee Keith, Peg Entwistle testified under oath in Los Angeles Superior Court to the following (in part):

That on said 16th day of April, 1929, defendant came to the theater where plaintiff is working so drunk that the doorkeeper at the time didn't know who he was; that thereupon defendant told the doorkeeper that he was the husband of plaintiff and wanted to see her, and the doorkeeper recognizing the fact that the defendant was too drunk to see her, refused to let him go into the theater, but members of the cast who knew him saw him as they were about to pass out the door and turned and came back saying that plaintiff's husband was outside and that he was drunk again and that they refused to pass out by him, and refused to go out as long as he was there...

... That the defendant's first act of extreme cruelty towards the plaintiff took place in the following manner: when he married the plaintiff he had a living wife from whom he was divorced, and had a child of the age of about six years; that he said nothing to the plaintiff about ever having been married, or about having a child; that on about the second day of plaintiff's marriage, she and the defendant's mother were sitting in the parlor of their apartment [when] the plaintiff saw [a] picture of a little boy upon the piano and asked her mother-in-law who it was and the mother-in-law replied "Why, that is Bob," and the plaintiff asked who "Bob" was and the mother-in-law replied "Why, that is your husband's little boy...."

... That while playing in Detroit, Mich., about the 1st of December, 1928, the defendant became very much under the influence of intoxicating liquors, and while the parties hereto were in bed together, the defendant took the plaintiff by the hair and raised her up from the bed several times, pulling great handfulls [sic] of hair each time, until plaintiff finally screamed several times, whereupon the house detective came to their room and thereupon the defendant ceased pulling her hair.[2]

"And he's so sweet and lovely and patient ... and proved to me what kind of stuff he's made of ... he's really such a peach."[3]

* * *

Robert Lee Keith was born Rolland Keith Richey in Fowler, Indiana, on February 10, 1898 ... or so the story goes. It's often said that Peg met him when they appeared together in the Broadway production of Eugene O'Neill's *The Great God Brown*. Keith was the star of this play but Peg was never in the cast, she was at the Boston Repertory during that time and was working in other Broadway plays when *God Brown* was running.

Keith was a theatrical veteran by 1927, having walked the boards since 1921 when he appeared in Carlos Wupperman's *The Triumph of X* with future Bogart spouse Helen Menken and prolific character actor Frank Morgan. Keith was well-liked among his fellows and there's no question he had a goodly amount of talent and stage presence. He'd been on the screen, too, having done at least one picture, a 1924 silent called *The Other Kind of Love*.

Media reports of a whirlwind romance and spontaneous wedding between Peg and Robert Keith were not completely accurate. On April 19, 1927, the *New York Herald Tribune* ran the headline "Peg Entwistle Marries After 4 Days Wooing: Actress and Robert Keith Meet on Thursday, Engaged on Friday, and Wed on Monday."[4] The article began, "After a four-day courtship, Peg Entwistle, who plays the ingénue role in *Tommy*, and Robert Keith, author of *The Tightwad*, and one of the leading players in *The Fog*, were married yesterday by the City Clerk in Port Chester. They met for the first time Thursday at a party given at the home of Mr. and Mrs. George Meeker and became engaged the following day."[5] (George and Eleanor Meeker were appearing in *Judy*, a Broadway play starring Queenie Smith.) Two weeks later *Time* published a similar article.

The *Herald Tribune* included brief biographies of Peg and Keith, but the most interesting aspects of their wooing had never been publicly known until now. And if the marriage hadn't ended so tragically, it all might have made for some wonderfully romantic memories.

Peg once again manifested the impulsive (but well-intentioned) side of her personality by marrying a man she didn't really know, on a whim — and without first telling her family, who took great pride in traditional courting and suitable weddings. Shortly after getting married, she sent her aunt a letter detailing the events. She is sorry for having left her family out of the loop and so opens with apologetic self-deprecation: "Lady Jane, I don't know what you think of me, but I know you are perfectly justified in whatever you *do* think. I feel [like] a swine. Please forgive me."[6] Peg says she met Keith a year earlier, but doesn't say where. (It was most likely in Boston, at the Repertory.) Then she says, "I met him again recently,"[7] but, "had no more idea of marrying him than I had of flying!"[8] This second meeting occurred at the Meekers' party, on the Thursday mentioned in the *Herald Tribune* article. She confirms newspaper accounts of a whirlwind romance: "The speed of our 'courtship' (as you might call it) was terrific!"[9] At some point during the party Keith asked her if she would join him Saturday night to see Fritz Lang's *Metropolis*. She said yes. He would pick her up at nine o'clock. Later, as Keith was mingling elsewhere, Peg ran into a few of her friends. One of them suggested they all have dinner together — on Saturday. To help insure she wouldn't be late for her movie date, she suggested they dine at the Shelton Hotel. (It isn't clear why, but Peg kept her date a secret from these friends. Perhaps it was shyness because of their age difference; he was ten years older.) After agreeing to the Shelton, Peg told them she had "an engagement"[10] for nine o'clock that night; she would have to excuse herself early.

With a full Saturday night scheduled, Peg continued to schmooze at the Meekers' party and eventually met up with Robert Keith again. Apparently she hadn't told him about her dinner plans even though the couple remained together and "talked of life and art until five in the morning, when they practically put us out."[11] Keith escorted her home that morning but they wouldn't see each other again until Saturday. They both needed sleep and recuperation before and after appearing in their respective plays Friday night. There had been no wedding engagement on Friday, as the *Herald Tribune* claimed.

On Saturday evening Peg enjoyed dinner with her friends. After excusing herself she went up to get ready for her date. When she came to the lobby a bit later she was stunned to see Keith talking with the dinner mates ... all of whom were friends of his from Broadway. "None of them knew who I was going to meet. So you can suspect my feelings when I came downstairs ... to find the whole gang standing in the lobby talking to him! My God, what a fool I felt, after all the fuss I had made!"[12]

Instead of seeing the movie, they met with mutual friends and went to the famous Crystal Room at the Ritz-Carlton Hotel. Peg says the room had "hoards of smartly gowned ladies and gentlemen, most of whom Bob knew—and a Jazz band was going so loud we could hardly hear ourselves think!"[13]

Ah, but with Roaring Twenties romance in the air, who needs to think? "It was in this setting that he said 'I love you!' Boy, what a thrill I got!"[14]

They partied at the Ritz until 2 A.M. It was Easter Sunday. While escorting her home to the Shelton, Keith asked Peg if she would like to come to his apartment later for cocktails and to meet his mother, "I replied that I would."[15] At 4 P.M. he picked her up. Peg wants to describe the apartment in detail but says, "Uncle Charlie will be able to do it so much better than I."[16] However, she does mention it belonged to Rudolph Valentino (dead just eight months) and was designed by Natacha Rambova (his wife from 1923 to 1926), the famous set designer and artistic director of silent films. Peg was smitten by the place. She loved the glass-encased sun porch that extended further into an open-air balcony. She called it "futuristic."[17] Next, she tells Aunt Jane of their late-night shenanigans: "We went out on the open balcony and the night was enough to make a hog romantic. There is the whole view of Central Park, with the Skyscrapers all lighted around the edge. The sky was marvelous and the stars were very bright."[18]

And so it was there, in a nest once owned by the most famous romantic film idol in history, in the wee small hours of the morning, that Robert Keith popped the question. "When I said I would marry him it was five o'clock,"[19] Peg wrote. Keith then called a friend, actor Frank Allworth, to come over with some money (it's astounding that two working Broadway stars were out of cash). Then he got his mother out of bed and within 20 minutes the group piled into a cab headed to Stamford, Connecticut, for a marriage. But Stamford had a five-day waiting period, so to Port Chester, New York, they went—the town in which the *Herald Tribune* said they were married. But the *Tribune* was wrong, for Port Chester said residents of New York City proper must get a license there. To Manhattan's city hall they went, where, finally, after a round trip of more than 82 miles—*in a taxi cab*—Peg and Robert Keith tied the knot at precisely 12 noon.

Peg also describes the clothing she and her husband were wearing. She seems astounded that without having planned it they had both dressed so similarly: "Bob had on a black suit with a black hat and shoes and black ebony cane! [I] had on a black satin dress, black hat, black shoes and black stockings, with white gloves and a string of pearls."[20] She also said her face was dirty and that he was unshaven. Moreover, in their nuptial rush to and fro from state to state and city to town and back again, they had overlooked one not-so-minor detail: "We had no ring so Bob used the prop ring that he had used in the play he was playing in!!"[21]

* * *

It is certainly reasonable to ask, "What the heck was Peg Entwistle thinking?"
She wasn't ... she was infatuated.

Robert Keith was regarded as a handsome leading man of the stage; Peg was an attractive, popular upstart on Broadway. As a thriving young woman with desires, it was quite natural for her to want a relationship with a successful man in her profession. She had probably fantasized about such a union since those early days primping in the mirror while mimicking famous actresses. If it hadn't been him, it would have been some other actor.

Their whirlwind romance occurred during a whirlwind weekend. On that Saturday a play penned by Keith, *The Tightwad*, had its debut at the Forty-Ninth Street Theater on Broadway. Peg doesn't mention to Jane if they had seen it; they probably hadn't, as he had nothing to do with the actual production. Keith may have been satisfying to Peg, but his ability as a playwright left *New York Times* drama critic Brooks Atkinson wanting. His review of *The Tightwad* included the following: "Mr. Keith has [written] a rather humdrum piece, pleasant and dull by turns, perfunctory in plot, sometimes bright and sometimes tame in conversation."[22] Indeed, *Tightwad* left all of Broadway wanting: It lasted a dismal week of just nine performances despite being produced by Lee and J.J. Shubert.

But the rookie playwright and his bride cared little for theatrical reviews now, for love was in the air; besides, they had too much to do on the heels of their marriage ceremony. Peg wanted to move her things out of the Shelton Hotel that afternoon, but she didn't have much time. Her Easter Monday matinee of *Tommy* had a 2:30 curtain. (Keith had one for 8:30 at the National Theater.) When the last hat box and dress trunk found its way into her new home, the famous apartment at 91 West 81st Street, Peg had no time to arrange His and Hers towel sets in Valentino's old bathroom, she needed a taxi, fast: "I had ten minutes (when I finally got to the theater) to change from the skin out, put my makeup on and do up my hair. And I made it!"[23]

Peg explained her last-minute arrival to the cast. "I didn't know anything could create such a sensation! When we called up everyone and told them, they wouldn't believe us. The thought that I should get married at all and then that I should marry Bob, of all people, was almost too much!"[24]

Following her 8:30 show that evening, Peg says they went to two parties and didn't get home until 3 A.M. Tuesday. She had been up since 3 P.M. Sunday, an hour before Keith picked her up to meet his mother. It had been a non-stop 36-hour nine-course feast of fun, love, and work: "Bob took me home and I just gave way. I almost went to sleep standing up ... I hadn't taken my clothes off until three o'clock [Tuesday] morning!"[25]

It wasn't called the Roaring Twenties for nothing.

Peg assured her aunt that she got along splendidly with Keith. To validate his reputation, she writes, "I will leave the drawing up of his character to Uncle Charlie."[26] (It should be assumed that Peg's uncle had concerns about her marrying a man she hardly knew. But Keith would certainly have been polite and respectful to Charles; not only for Peg's sake, but also as an actor, for he would want to impress the manager and friend of Broadway's Walter Hampden. Indeed, between the lines of Peg's courtship letter is found indication that Charles had a measure of fondness for Keith, for she trusts her uncle to speak favorably of him to Aunt Jane.)

Peg closes this letter by giving her love to her brothers. "They certainly are getting splendid looking, aren't they?"[27] She adds, "I am sending you something for your anniversary,"[28] and then signs, "Lots of Love, Babs."[29]

Her postscript is an interesting three-part sign off: "By the way, I'm a Lucy Stoner!"[30] Peg is referring to 19th century American suffragist Lucy Stone, who championed the right of women to retain their maiden or birth names after marriage. She's telling her aunt she will still be known as Peg Entwistle, rather than Peg Keith or Mrs. Robert Keith. Women who chose not to take their husband's names were called Lucy Stoners and Maiden Namers.

Peg adds, "My singing is coming splendidly and I will soon be able to hang my golden hair over the balcony!"[31] This confirms she had not cut and dyed her hair brown, as seems to be the case in theatrical photographs taken of her during *Tommy*. She was using a wig on stage. And speaking of her golden hair, the *Washington Post* noted, "Peg of the wild hair they call her in the theater."[32] Indeed, the lovely-locks ingénue was rather fond of a sexy, slightly wind-swept look upon her head. (This is particularly evident from 1929 on.)

Peg ends the above letter with a humorous tale: "A stenographer, one day, was making all kinds of mistakes and spilling things and knocking things over and her boss said, 'For God's sake, what's the matter with you, are you sick?' and she said, 'Yes, thank God!'"[33]

It was a riot in 1927...

* * *

Let's back up a bit, to the minutes immediately following Peg's marriage, when Robert Keith's mother, the widowed Mary Robinson, and Frank Allworth (destined to drop dead on a Philadelphia stage in 1935) had both just signed Peg's marriage certificate as official witnesses. It isn't hard to imagine the glowing young bride cuddled up to that handsome peach of hers, leaning prettily against him in the taxi as she stared wide-eyed and excited at the marriage certificate — a document that she, her husband, his mother, and Frank Allworth had just signed under penalty of law. "*WE hereby certify that we are the Groom and Bride named in this Certificate, and that the information given therein is correct....*"[34]

Where the certificate compelled an answer to "Single, Widowed or Divorced," Keith responded, "Single."[35] In the box titled "Number of Groom's Marriage," he had the clerk indicate this was his first marriage.[36]

And so, on that blessed wedding day, as she and her new husband gaily made their way through the gridlock of Gotham, Peg laughed and sang with the giddiness of a new bride, of a heart swimming with love and hope, all the while not knowing she was now the stepmother of six-year-old Robert Alba Keith, her husband's son from a previous marriage to a woman named Helena Shipman. But her husband's mother and best friend knew and conspired to keep this from her going so far as to sign a legal document attesting that Robert Lee Keith had never been married. And why not? It was just as easy to lie to city hall as to a gullible teenager.

Complicating matters further: a specific quirk in Peg's personality ... she *hated* kids. Well, not *all* kids, she certainly loved her brothers and cousins. Nonetheless, another letter to Jane lends insight into Peg's thoughts on motherhood: "Needless to say, the last thing in the world that I want is a child. I wouldn't do that for any man ... I'm positively rabbid [*sic*] on the subject...."[37] Peg never bothered to hide her feelings about it to the press, either: "Electric lights appeal more to me than a rose-covered cottage with babies playing around the doors."[38]

Peg would only know her husband's son as Robert Alba Keith, but the reader might know him by his stage name, Brian Keith, the actor fondly remembered for such film roles as Teddy Roosevelt in *The Wind and the Lion* (1975); Mitch Evers, the father who gets hoodwinked by his twin daughters in Disney's original *The Parent Trap* (1961), and as Uncle Bill in television's *Family Affair* (1966–71).

* * *

"That is your husband's little boy...."[39]

One can almost imagine Peg sitting there in her apartment, in the moments immediately following her mother-in-law's statement: Peg staring at the photo of the boy Brian Keith ... her eyes welling with tears, her heart sinking to unfathomable depths, devastated at the realization that her husband so boldly lied to her about his life. She was humiliated; made to look like a fool. *Who else knows?* she would have thought. *What else has he lied to me about?*

Peg Entwistle, a girl highly proficient in things theatrical, had a perfect opportunity here to become a four-hankie drama queen. She had every right to make herself the center of the universe with flooding tears and howling sobs. Instead, all the indicators are that she remained composed in front of her mother-in-law; completely in control of the emotions tugging inside her. If this is indeed true, it would have been some of the best acting of her short life.

But Peg was also very intelligent and therefore quick to understand that it wasn't really the marriage to Helena Shipman her husband had been keeping secret, it was the boy; because he knew how much Peg disliked the idea of motherhood. But Peg didn't panic; she had no reason to panic. She understood that being the child's stepmother didn't mean having a role in raising him. He lived with his birth mother and even if he did come to Manhattan, his grandmother was there to care for him. Peg's career was safe; she wouldn't have to miss a performance or audition because her stepson had the mumps, or because she couldn't find a babysitter.

When all things are considered, it becomes obvious that Robert Keith told his mother (and friends) to say nothing to Peg about his son. He of course knew it couldn't be kept secret for long; he did intend to tell her, but only in *his* time. The photo on the piano was probably supposed to have been removed until he planned to break the news to her. At any rate, the ruse was discovered. And yet, in spite of being deceived and humiliated by the man who supposedly loved her, Peg will for now say nothing about it to him. It seems she asked her mother-in-law to do the same. But why did she not want her husband to know that he had been found out?

There are two answers for this—each a different side of the same coin: Heads: Peg didn't want to embarrass him, to put him on the spot. Tails: She was worried how he might react to being put on the spot.

Peg Entwistle will enter the parlor incident into the court record later on, but again, there is nothing to indicate she told her friends or family about it immediately afterward. If this is true (it does seem to be the case), then it's largely due to her feeling ashamed.

Telling her friends about it all would invoke any number of reactions in varying degrees, but to the family (particularly to her stringent Uncle Charles and the ever-stern Ross matriarch, Matilda) such an admission would crumble the grand pedestal upon which Peg had placed her man. Moreover, she probably had some passing thoughts that it would make her seem to them that she was nothing but a naive and silly girl for having fallen in love with such a cad. But her family adored her, and while they surely would have disowned him, she would have received only love and understanding from them.

Deep down she had to know this was true. If anyone was going to think of her as naive and silly, it would only be Peg Entwistle. But to her thinking, she had an image to protect, namely that of a mature, reputable Broadway actress happily married to an esteemed actor, a professional leading man and playwright. As a girl growing up in the theater, it was often these kinds of marriages she saw in her family's theatrical friends and associates. Such people left an indelible impression on her; she admired them and wanted to be like them — noble, respected thespians whose talent and integrity earned invitations to the king of England's stage. Peg was working hard to achieve honor and delighted in showing off her successes and in no small way believed Robert Keith was one of these. But now she knew her marriage was really just a house of straw on a foundation of sand and telling anyone the truth would only compound the shame.

So for now Peg put diplomacy into action ("From my earliest memories I have practiced diplomacy. It's the best place," she once told her aunt[40]), and through diplomacy managed to retain a measure of dignity while keeping her home life peaceful and public persona free from scandal and gossip. Besides, she was in love, and if a loving wife can't forgive her husband's poor judgment and little white lies, who can? Sure, she was hurt and saddened, embarrassed and ashamed, and she was being a bit of a coward, but it wasn't the end of the world. On the contrary, *Tommy* was getting a lot of notice and playing to full houses. She was making good money and had her name in lights. The city's papers heralded her marriage in theater sections, and she had even been featured (with her husband as second banana) as a special guest on a May 20 program of Terese Rose Nagel's popular radio interview show on WGBS, New York. She was frequently invited (along with second banana) to formal dinners hosted by socialites and stars of stage and screen. She had now become one of Gotham's favorite ingénues.

But Peg Entwistle wasn't quite there yet.

Down Broadway lay New York's exalted Theater Guild, still her goal and dream. The biggest names and the most prestigious productions were of the Guild. This was theater's elite; their members were a select, specially chosen few, and if you were good enough to be recruited and stay with a production from rehearsal to box party, you had finally arrived.

The Guild's talent-seeking was perpetual and they scouted productions and took note of unique actors in America and abroad, but their executive director, Theresa Helburn, was looking for more than just parrots of Shakespeare and Sheridan, or Ibsen and Shaw. Every actor had memory, but Helburn had standards—the *Guild* had standards ... *impeccable* standards.

And so a-scouting they did go, this Theresa Helburn and her company of like-minded thinkers and artists of the Theater Guild's board of directors. They sought only the finest talent mingled with impeccable character and high moral fiber. Guild actors must be *gentlemen*; the actresses, *ladies*. Each was expected to be conservative in all manners of speech and dress. They must be temperate, polite, and slow to anger, because when you were in the Guild, you *were* the Guild. The organization wasn't puritanical, but Helburn didn't mind if *you* were — not as long as you could command a stage, anyway.

And this was Peg's desire, to be asked to join the New York Theater Guild (one didn't simply walk into their office uninvited). She had been creating a buzz since her Repertory days and the Guild's ears perked. She remained true to her craft, and being married to a noted actor would seem to only help her chances with the organization. In fact, the Guild liked to cast husbands and wives together, most notably Alfred Lunt and Lynn Fontanne.

So, in the terrible realization that her marriage was steeped in deceit, Peg remained calm and publicly composed, lady-like and level-headed, because she knew she was Guild material and that they were feeling her out, and she wanted in with them, and *no one* was going to hold her back. Nothing had changed since the day she told a Boston reporter, "If I have to give up love and marriage to get to the top of my profession, well and good. If I must give up happiness as well to have my name in electric lights on Broadway, then I shall never complain."[41]

Neither a lying husband nor a conniving mother-in-law would get in her way. No, nothing would stop Peg Entwistle ... not even the child growing inside her.

* * *

In August 1927, soon after closing on Broadway, *Tommy* went to Chicago (and points west) with most of the original cast. As mentioned earlier, Gay Seabrook would now become Marie Thurber. Peg had opted out. Producer George C. Tyler gave her no trouble, for she had two good reasons for him: She wanted to explore other character types, those a bit less sugary; and she wished to remain in New York to be with her husband. So, with Tyler's blessing (the fact she worked for him in a later production proves as much), Peg was allowed to back out of the *Tommy* tour. Now she was free to pursue more mature drama and to play the dutiful wife to Robert Keith, who, as it turns out, hadn't worked on stage since the previous May, and whose ability as a playwright was also bringing nothing to the table except a thirst for liquor and constant requests for money from Peg. She was supporting his mother, too.

During this time, Robert Keith finally admitted to a previous marriage and having a son. Peg will later tell the court that during this confession he was very drunk and remained so throughout much of their marriage. His confession was hardly volunteered out of repentance. Peg had grown weary of his antics and so she forced him into a corner and chided him. The jig was up. But there was more to the story: Keith was in desperate straits. The police were actively seeking him, he said. If he didn't pay his court-ordered alimony, he would go to jail. This was no lie. And he was known well enough in Manhattan to be rather easily found. Peg was moved by his predicament (and no doubt by a torrent of crocodile tears). She wrote him a check. It wouldn't be the last he time he asked her to rescue him. And it wouldn't be the only time he used the money to get drunk rather than obey the court order.

Peg's success in *Tommy* had made her so popular in New York that she was able to find another role only a few days after Tyler released her. Much to her empty-pocketed husband's relief, she was contracted to head the cast in Bernard McOwen's train wreck *The Uninvited Guest*. It became the first flop of her career (Robert Keith notwithstanding).

Peg's agreement to do this play was an amazingly bold and courageous move. She wanted a less sugary part, and now she would have her chance. Dark and grim, *The Uninvited Guest* starred Peg as Johanna Jackson, a barefoot country girl with a distinct drawl living in the Ramapo Mountains of Upstate New York. She is married to a jerk 50 years her senior who cannot give her what she truly desires ... motherhood. The audiences do not at first realize just how badly Johanna wants a baby — they believe the young woman plays with a doll because she's mentally ill ... she is, but not in the way they think she is. Johanna wants a *real* baby now, and gets so desperate she seduces the local minister (a character the *New York Herald Tribune* called "a half-brother to Elmer Gantry"[42]) and gets pregnant by him. Her family wants her to abort the baby (the uninvited guest), and after it's born they want her to give it up. But Johanna has the "overpowering maternal urge" and will keep the child at any cost.[43] She dotes on and loves the infant, but after its mysterious death she grows suspicious of the minister and murders him.

The Uninvited Guest had a tryout in the Bronx before opening at the Belmont Theater on Broadway in late September 1927. Harold McGillicuddy of the *New York Telegraph* didn't think it was an entirely bad play, but believed it wouldn't last long given the current competition. Richard Watts, over at the *Herald Tribune,* panned it severely, but said Peg gave "actual sincerity to her heroine's role."[44] Joseph Mulvaney at the *New York American* didn't like it either, but he thought Peg was an excellent actress. The *New York Times* said, "Through it a frail and wan Peg Entwistle gave a performance considerably better than the play warranted."[45] "Frail" and "wan" were not words normally used to describe the usually sprite and lively Peg Entwistle.

Not long after the miserable failure of *The Uninvited Guest,* she wrote a letter to her Aunt Jane, in Hollywood:

> Dear Jane ... I didn't do my stuff on my monthly menstrual period and began to get worried, so I bought up all the medicine I could find to start it again but it didn't do any good, so I betook myself to a doctor — a friend of Bob's. He gave me some more dreadful medicine to take and told me if that didn't work he would send me to someone who would perform an abortion.
>
> So we dug out $160 ... and I went and had it done. And boy! What a relief! They had to give me gas twice because I was fighting so in my sleep. That put us in quite a hole as far as money is concerned. But olé! God Save the King! What a relief!![46]

Peg goes on to discuss "less morbid subjects," such as her police dog, Otto (a wedding gift from actor Alan Mowbray), comparing it to Shecco, one of her childhood dogs.[47] She complains about money again, about how broke she and her husband are. She is still owed two weeks' salary for *The Uninvited Guest.* (She will never receive it.) She hasn't worked since its closing, and with Christmas coming she apologizes for not being able to send any gifts. She and her husband have had to dismiss Georgia, their housekeeper. Peg seems sincerely moved for having to let her go: "She's a perfect old darling ... looks after us like a couple of babies. Darns his socks ... washes my things and runs *everything* and we never know what we're going to have for dinner!" (Meaning Georgia was an inventive cook.)[48]

After eight pages Peg signs, "Packs of love, Babs ... (P. S.) Bob sends his best."[49]

The whole affair is really rather pathetic.

* * *

When the timeline is laid out, one can see why the *New York Times* described Peg as "frail and wan."[50] Abortions were hardly a pretty thing in 1927, and Peg had hers just before opening *The Uninvited Guest.* She told her aunt about being sedated several times because she was fighting in her sleep. This hints of substandard anesthetization. She started regaining consciousness during the operation. One might wonder how much damage had been done during this fighting as surgical instruments intruded into her. She didn't mention hemorrhaging, but it's possible she suffered considerable blood loss. The archaic procedure left Peg anemic, physically weak, mentally drained, and possibly with a tinge of blood poisoning.

She was rehearsing *Guest* during her recovery, too. As she was the star, a request for even one day off would have been met with considerable scrutiny from the producers (L.M. Simmons, Inc.). She couldn't dare mention an abortion and wouldn't want to be caught tripping over contradictions in a lie, so it was best to simply work through the pain and discomfort.

As of this writing, aborting a fetus as a method of birth control is a legal and common medical practice in the United States, but in 1927 New York City it was a felony. It was so abhorred in the public eye that periodicals such as *Time* and the *New York Times* rarely (if ever) used the word "abortion," preferring instead to publish terms like "illegal operation."

One can peruse the city's papers of the time and read of doctors being sent to prison for performing abortions. Sometimes things got really ugly: On the same day Peg got married, a young woman named Loretta Enders died during her abortion at the hands of Dr. Amenti Rongetti. He was tried for murder and sentenced to the electric chair. Rongetti escaped Old Sparky, but in another case a doctor was given 25 years to life in prison when his patient died.

Many abortions were performed in the patients' homes, often in unsanitary conditions. But even when performed in a doctor's office there were inherent dangers, as blood transfusions and antibiotics had yet to be invented. Infections, particularly in the bloodstream, were rampant.

There's no question that Peg wished to remain childless, and the irony of her having an abortion while engaged to play a woman who desperately wants a child is astounding. Perhaps even more astounding is that she seemed to have had little or no concern for what might have happened to her career — and freedom — if word of the abortion had gone public. The New York state laws called for imprisonment of the mother for up to four years. According to Section 80 of the Penal Code, first enacted in 1908, she would have been charged with manslaughter. Peg could have even gotten a year in the county jail just for ingesting the inducing medicines she mentions in the letter to her aunt. Obviously, though, she thought it worth the risk.

And what influence did Robert Keith have in it all?

Peg writes to her aunt that the doctor who set up the abortion was "a friend of Bob's."[51] It's not surprising that her husband knew such a fellow. Keith's associations would have included all sorts of felonious characters given his taste for liquor during this era of Prohibition, when things like whiskey were obtained through bootleggers and speakeasies. In the Roaring Twenties, an alcoholic like Keith would know all types of underworld denizens.

Of course, no one actually *forced* Peg to have an abortion — the decision ultimately was hers. But she had to know that if word of this ever made its way to Theresa Helburn, executive director of the our-actresses-are-cleaner-than-snow Theater Guild, she would have been blacklisted from the Guild before even getting there. And Peg also had to know that Helburn was the kind of person who might very well inform important Broadway producers and agents about her "illegal operation."

That's the way it was done in those days. Word of an actress's illicit behavior made its way to Broadway moguls, and to them abortion was *most* illicit. It is also important to note that Helburn was a representative to all the Broadway producers in the Clean Play Committee, an organization of theatrical notables formed in early 1927 that sat as jury to productions whose morality was questioned for whatever reason. This committee was one of the several groups that had given the cast and production of *Tommy* a stamp of approval. This was likely when Helburn first became impressed with Peg's talent and clean living. Knowledge of Peg's abortion would have distressed her not a little.

Peg could escape the law, but the work, the *good* work, would have dried up. She wouldn't have been allowed to audition for meaningful roles in important productions. Agents and producers would have stopped returning her calls. If she cornered them on a sidewalk or coming out of an office or theater she'd get the brush-off, sometimes politely, sometimes rudely, but always quickly. Peg Entwistle would have been told in so many words that familiar cliché, "*You'll never work in this town again!*" Eventually, in a few years, she could have found her way back into decent Broadway roles, but the Guild would remain out of reach as long as Theresa Helburn was at the helm.

If she knew this could happen to her career, why didn't she just have the baby and then give it up for adoption? How did a girl like Peg Entwistle come to decide that aborting her baby was worth the chance of destroying her reputation on Broadway?

Another look at a portion of the "abortion letter" to her aunt (emphasis added by the author): "[H]e would send me to someone to have an abortion. *Needless to say,* the last thing in the world that I want is a child. I wouldn't do that for any man. I don't know what is it [sic], but it must be *a streak of insanity* with me. I'm positively *rabbid* [sic] on the subject. *I've tried all my life to fight it, but it gets worse all the time.* The doctor told me *I was abnormal.* At least I'm being a little bit original...."[52]

Peg claimed the doctor told her she was abnormal. However, not wanting to be a mother in and of itself hardly made a 19-year-old career-minded girl abnormal, even in 1927. Certainly an intelligent man like a doctor would have known this. So what exactly was it about her that prompted him to say such a thing? Peg told her aunt she was positively rabid about the idea of having a child. In this context "rabid" means fanatical, militant, blind to any other opinion. It would seem that Peg made vehemently charged comments during an examination, leading the doctor to remark she was reacting in an abnormal manner, not that she was abnormal *per se*.

But from where had such vehemence come?

It may have begun when Peg was ten and eleven years old, when she witnessed her brothers being born. Seeing a woman give birth (twice), and the painful, graphic nature involved would leave many girls apprehensive at that age. Whether or not this was the case, the year 1921 should be remembered: when Peg thought her chances at becoming an actress were forever gone after her stepmother died; when she believed she'd have to be a surrogate mother to her very young brothers. Losing Lauretta had crushed her spirit, but the burden of perceived shattered dreams for the future added continents of weight to the motherhood world that fell upon Peg's thirteen-year-old shoulders.

The brutal death of her father in 1922 also cannot be overlooked. Until Aunt Jane and Uncle Charles came to the rescue, Peg thought she would be the *sole* caregiver to her brothers. Granted, it was for no more than a few days or so that she believed this, but it had clouded her mind and overwhelmed her heart nonetheless, and a few days is like an eternity when one's life is awash with dread and despair.

Peg's psyche could not have endured these rattling, emotional storms at such a young age without suffering some kind of post-traumatic affliction. She never resolved these issues and so they followed her into adulthood. This is why she came to embrace an "abnormal,"[53] over-the-top dislike at the thought of being a mother. Untreated and unresolved, this fear of the possibility of her own motherhood festered into a glaring, irrational character defect.

"*Needless to say,* the last thing in the world that I want is a child."[54]

Needless to say, she made these feelings well-known to her family during the years.

Peg correctly surmised she had a "streak of insanity,"[55] but she was not *insane*. Truly insane people do not ponder their sanity. She was no more mentally disturbed than someone who is afraid of flying, or who is claustrophobic, or who slept with a light on as a kid in order to keep monsters from crawling out from under the bed.

Peg told her aunt she tried to fight the rabid feeling all her life but it kept getting worse. Of course it did; because in her own strength she had been fighting the traumatic motherhood-related events of her early years. She'd been wrestling alone, without the help of therapy or counseling, because that's how such things were done in the "good ol' days," particularly if you were born with a British "stiff upper lip" *and* had a grandmother named Matilda Ross.

And now as a pregnant wife just 19 years old, Peg's worst fears threatened to become a reality. Horrified at the thought of becoming a mother, she became willing to go to jail or suffer Broadway's scorn. This "streak of insanity"[56] made perfect sense. After all, one could always get paroled, and scorn may come and go ... but motherhood lasts a lifetime.

In light of the overall history of Robert Keith's abusive, self-centered behavior toward Peg, it's tempting to think he might have manipulated her into having the abortion. The record shows he cared little for the financial well-being of at least one child he sired; another child would only add to the burden of his already thin wallet. Whether he behaved as a fatherly provider on his own or by court order, he'd be obligated to support Peg's baby for as long as the law dictated. His interests were clearly best served by an abortion. But temptation to lay blame solely on him must be avoided. Of course Keith's role in it all was not insignificant, and it will be shown that he was the most destructive force to ever enter Peg Entwistle's life. However, in this matter the obvious becomes apparent in its own light: Peg's body was her own and she had complete control over what went in it, and what came out.

10

Between Curtains

"It looks as though this business has retired me." — Peg Entwistle[1]

Early December 1927.

"Dear Jane, don't faint! I think I hold the world's record for non-letter writing! I don't know exactly how to begin — first of all, I have no job...."[2]

Late January 1928.

"Dear Jane, as usual my letter writing is always a bit late. I haven't got a job. It looks as though this business has retired me...."[3]

Peg's first (and longest) theatrical dry spell began with the closing of *The Uninvited Guest* in October 1927, and continued until her first wedding anniversary, when she and her husband were signed by the Theater Guild in April 1928.

It's possible — but doubtful — she may have gotten a *very* minor part now and then, a part so insignificant no trade publication or city newspaper thought it worthy enough to note; one that had no lines, such as "Woman at Table." But it is certain she hadn't been signed to a production as a star or supporting player for nearly five months.

Fortunately, Robert Keith's drinking had not yet turned him into the animal he will become in the months ahead. Such an added burden of abuse and heartache piled upon her extended unemployment might have been enough to push Peg out a Manhattan window long before she climbed a Hollywood ladder. But from April of 1927 and through much of 1928 she and Keith got along quite well together. Apart from his lying about his son and ex-wife, periodic drinking, and past-due alimony, Peg's marriage was for now still far from disastrous and even included genuine moments of affection. There's no question that she was in love with him, but deep down she seemed to doubt if it was still okay to be *married* to him.

Knowing full well that her husband is at least ten years older than she is, Peg tells Aunt Jane, "We're only five days apart in our birthdays."[4] Peg is not trying to put forth a lie that they are nearly the exact same age; she is *validating*, reaching; grasping at what she can to convince herself that they *are* compatible. It's almost like saying, "We're both Aquarius! We were made for each other!" Her remark may have been a cute sentiment at the time she wrote it, but when it's examined in proper context with regard to the dysfunction already evident in the relationship, there's no question she was attempting to construct a rationale to her own satisfaction. Peg may have been writing to her aunt, but she was speaking to herself.

"When we were married, I knew about as much about marriage and love as the back fence ... I didn't realize it then, but I do now."[5] This is true enough, but within the context of the letter, the idea Peg's conveying is that her husband has helped to enlighten her, remove the scales from her eyes; empowered her with some sort of matrimonial maturity. Peg has put him on quite a pedestal for her aunt. Not until 1929 will Jane learn that her niece's happy-marriage guru was really a child-neglecting alcoholic divorcée who took Peg's hand behind a veil of deceit.

The back fence knew more about marriage and love than had Robert Lee Keith, but he and Peg have ironed out their differences. And though she may have some doubts, and be in denial, and from time to time seek validation, Peg will make a go of it come hell or high water.

After dismissing their housekeeper Georgia, the newlyweds had to fend for themselves. (It isn't known if Keith's mother was still living with them.) Peg describes how they "agreed to split up on the work."[6] Ever yearning the actress lifestyle since her earliest days, Miss Entwistle writes, "Bob asked me what I disliked most, and I said the thing I disliked most was to get up in the morning, to get breakfast, and to wash dishes."[7] (If one is given eyes in the Great Beyond, Matilda Ross is probably still rolling hers.)

Peg says Bob agreed to make the breakfast and do the dishes. She didn't say what her chores entailed. But she loved the Valentino-Rambova apartment and was particularly smitten by the living room area with an open fireplace: "It is my own special domain."[8]

Winter has arrived and Peg says she couldn't wait for the weather to get cold so she could have a cozy fire. She may have been the only person in New York City who complained about the unusually warm December. As she tells Jane these things, Peg's police dog, Otto, whose head is so beautiful "that everyone remarks,"[9] is in the corner "gnawing on a huge bone."[10]

We know Charles Entwistle was still working in New York because "I see Uncle Charlie occasionally."[11] Peg asks her aunt to give her love to her brothers and then she tugs your heartstrings: "I'm most tremendously happy. I hope you'll be pleased to hear that. I hope you don't wish me any bad luck for not writing to you. I really feel ashamed."[12]

Peg asks about all the excitement Marie must be causing. It seems the long-time family friend had gone "mad for a time"[13] during some sort of "chain of circumstances."[14] But Peg says, "Marie is really a peach ... she was awfully, awfully kind to me."[15] Aunt Jane next receives well wishes from her niece and a request not to worry too much about anything. Peg asks that she convey her love to everyone and promises to send money when she gets back to work. (Why Peg sent money to her aunt so often is a bit mysterious. Uncle Charles was making a fine living as Walter Hampden's manager. Nevertheless, throughout her career, Peg sent money to her.)

"If you can make heads or tails of this letter you're a wonder. It's most incoherent."[16]

Actually, it isn't. But it does lack a certain confidence. And why shouldn't it? It was inked by Peg Entwistle, who just a short time ago was the talk of the town; she can see Broadway from her window, yet not a single theater features her name...

"Here's to an awfully happy Christmas and a better New Year ... Packs of Love, Babs."[17]

* * *

Things began looking up financially for Peg and her husband sometime just before, or very soon after, Christmas 1927. Peg remained jobless but Keith picked up acting work of some kind. There are no press releases of him opening a production or replacing an actor, but in January 1928 Peg told her aunt, "Bob is playing in the same play. A terrible thing!"[18]

Because there is nothing mentioning Keith in any New York plays during this time, Peg's referring to his job as a "terrible thing"[19] could mean he was a bit player ("Man at Table"), or was working for a small company out of town. If the latter is true, Connecticut or Massachusetts would be the likely places. Peg could not have meant that the play itself was terrible, for terrible plays lasted only a few days and it is clear that he had been working for about a month.

Whatever Keith was doing, he seemed to be bringing home some bacon. Peg tells her Aunt Jane, "Christmas was lovely. Bob gave me a locket and a bracelet to go with it. It [is] old silver — sort of antique. It's lovely."[20]

Indeed, it is. Although the matching bracelet is lost, the locket is owned by Peg's niece, Lauretta Slike, who allowed this author to examine it. It is oval, with one hinge, and tooled by expert hands. There are diamond patterns along the outside edge, and two exquisite heart-shaped designs intertwined and inlaid with royal and light blue. It still holds a photo of Peg, which she cropped from a larger one and fit snug into the locket. She is beaming with a bright, ecstatic smile, looking admiringly upward at what was probably her husband. She would also have cropped his face from the larger photograph and placed it in the locket ... it is no longer there.

"Dear Jane, thanks terribly for your sweet little pillow you sent. There is a blue moiré cover on the bed, and the pillow, being yellow, looks awfully pretty."[21] Peg also got silk stockings, "which were more of a necessity than anything else,"[22] and presents from her brothers. "Thank the boys for their lovely Christmas gifts to me, will you? Tell Bobby I loved the little bird he sent me."[23] Peg gives her best to family friend Harry Haven, a script consultant at Paramount. Haven was renting Peg's old room at the Beachwood Drive house.

Peg tells Jane she is waiting and hoping to hear about a "marvelous" part: the title role in *Serena Blandish*.[24] Before becoming a hit play, it was a novel titled *Serena Blandish: Or the Difficulty of Getting Married*. It was published in 1924 by Enid Algerine Bagnold, who also wrote *National Velvet*.

Nearly every actress under 30 loved the *Serena Blandish* book and yearned to play the role on Broadway. Manhattan was buzzing. Many girls, including Peg, tried for the part. But the producers were in a quandary; so many talented and qualified actresses had auditioned that no one girl stood out among the others. A press release did little to allay the suspense when it was announced that the producers had whittled the list down to a definite final four: Miriam Hopkins, Ruth Gordon, Fay Bainter, and "perhaps even somebody else."[25]

Peg remained hopeful. She was as much "perhaps even somebody else" as was the next girl. Moreover, she knew she was as good as Miriam Hopkins, because George M. Cohan had thought so. That's why he hired her to take over Miss Hopkins' role in *The Home Towners*.

"And it's a gorgeous part. The only thing that will stand in my way is that they might want a Name [sic] for it, because the part carries the whole play."[26]

Ruth Gordon was the Name. And *Serena Blandish* kept her busy for a while.

Peg had gotten every part she wanted until now. According to her cousin, Helen Reid, this was a role she had *desperately* wanted. Losing it was a bitter pill to swallow. It became one of the top three toughest letdowns of her career. It isn't known how many auditions she went on during her drought. It could have been several or several dozen. In the meantime, as her husband worked at his nondescript job and from time to time partook of his nondescript drink, Peg puttered about as a dutiful wife and made the best she could out of the winter months. She was still full of hope, though, and knew right well that she'd get back on top — or at least close to it. Because she was young and pretty; in love and without child; and she knew she had as much talent as Miriam Hopkins, Ruth Gordon, and Fay Bainter ... or perhaps even somebody else.

11

The Guild

Robert Keith and Peg Entwistle have been engaged by the Theater Guild for its touring company next season. — Press release, April 1928[1]

The New York Theater Guild had its beginning on a Thursday evening, December 18, 1918, in the Brevoort Hotel on lower Fifth Avenue in New York City. This was when Lawrence Langer, a daring Welsh-born expert of theater, shared a bottle of wine and an idea for a new project with a masterful, idiosyncratic director named Philip Moeller, and an eccentric actress named Helen Westley, who kept cash and bank books in her stockings and several young men on her arms wherever she went. (There's only so much room in a stocking.)

Several days after the Brevoort wine session, a meeting to discuss the details of Langer's notion was held at the home of Josephine A. Meyer, a spiritualist friend of Langer's. Actor and artist Rollo Peters, son of the highly regarded California painter Charles Rollo Peters, was also there, along with Edna Kenton, the erudite author of books covering such fantastic subjects as space travel, Atlantis, the Great Pyramid of Giza, and center-of-the-earth civilizations.

This eclectic half-dozen agreed on three fundamental aims: They would form a group to carry out the idea of a specialized theater organization made up only of artists who were experts in their work; secure a theater building with a seating capacity over 600; and govern absolutely by a committee which would delegate executive and administrative powers to its members. Later, these aims were condensed to a single sentence: "To produce plays of artistic merit not ordinarily produced by the commercial managers."[2]

By the time Peg Entwistle came to Broadway, the Theater Guild had become the most admired and prestigious theatrical organization in the country, perhaps the world. For many years its board of directors comprised these six: the abovementioned Langer, Moeller, and Westley; also Maurice Wertheim, a millionaire investment banker and world-renowned chess patron; Lee Simonson, noted architect and painter whose set and scenery designs for the Guild became the delight and envy of the theater world; and Theresa Helburn, a Bryn Mawr College alumna and drama critic for *The Nation*. She became the Guild's first play reader. It wasn't long before Helburn was elected the organization's executive director. It was she who first proposed, and vehemently insisted, that the Guild make Lynn Riggs's *Green Grow the Lilacs* into a musical that eventually became the world-famous *Oklahoma!*

In the second week of April 1928, Peg and her husband were contacted by Cheryl Crawford, the Theater Guild's casting director. Theresa Helburn wanted to know if the couple would be interested in joining their Repertory Company for the coming season. Peg would have joined a show in a remote army outpost if Helburn asked. The young actress's drought had just received the most refreshing of all theatrical rain — an invitation from the executive director of the Theater Guild ... *the Guild!*

Because this was the organization's tenth anniversary, the 1928-29 season was to be its busiest, and Peg would be spending most of a busy year traveling to places that had not seen a Guild production. There would be a lot of publicity and a lot of work ... *lots* of work. (It's important to keep in mind that apart from its acting school, the Theater Guild comprised two main bodies: the Acting Company and the Repertory Company. Peg is here part of the Guild's Repertory Company.)

There was no audition for either her or Robert Keith, only a meeting with Helburn in her office at the Guild Theater on Broadway and West 52nd Street. Philip Moeller was also there. Peg and her husband were given a basic overview and itinerary: The Acting Company was to be divided into four sections, two of which would stay in New York for slated productions of *Strange Interlude* and *Faust.* The other two sections would go on a limited tour. One of these, featuring the Acting Company's crown jewels, Alfred Lunt and his wife Lynn Fontanne, would bring *Arms and the Man* and *The Guardsman* to Baltimore, Pittsburgh, Cleveland, Boston, Philadelphia and Chicago. The remaining section, with Claude Rains, Earl Larimore, and Henry Travers, would present *Volpone, Marco Millions,* and *Porgy* to four of the six mentioned cities (Boston and Philadelphia were the exceptions).

Peg's ambition was to be as famous as Maude Adams, who was once the highest-paid actress in the world. Peg voiced hopes that James M. Barrie would write a play with her in mind, just as he had done for Adams. The prestigious Theater Guild was to be a means to that end ... or so she had thought (courtesy Entwistle Family).

Each of these sections of the Acting Company employed 40 to 60 actors and technicians and would be on the road for about four months. A separate troupe was slated to bring *Porgy* to London. (Later, yet another troupe of the Acting Company would travel to Los Angeles and present Eugene O'Neill's immensely popular *Strange Interlude.*)

Peg's mission in the Theater Guild Repertory was to represent the organization across the United States in some of the towns and cities not being visited by the Acting Company. The Guild Repertory would feature four productions: George Bernard Shaw's stab and satire of the medical profession, *The Doctor's Dilemma;* S.N. Behrman's light and frothy *The Second Man;* Sidney Howard's comedy-drama of sordid New England bootlegging, *Ned McCobb's Daughter;* and the earthy and Irish *John Ferguson,* by St. John Ervine.

Besides Peg and Keith, the principal cast members included Elisabeth Risdon and Alan

Mowbray. Risdon, the reader may remember, was introduced by Robert Entwistle to his three-year-old daughter when they were appearing together on Broadway. Mowbray was a favorite leading man of stage who would personally finance the Screen Actors Guild during its founding in 1933. An ironic thing, this, for Mowbray never intended to have anything to do with screen acting — he didn't feel he had a face for films: "I saw myself in a newsreel once. Paid 35 cents to see it, too ... felt awfully cheated."[3] Also accompanying the Guild Repertory was Beatrice Hendricks, the comedic Broadway prima donna who had become a vaudeville sensation with impersonations of Sarah Bernhardt, Ethel Barrymore, Laurette Taylor and Eleanora Duse. Miss Hendricks had also appeared with Peg in *The Man from Toronto*. These five would have the lion's share of the work and notice throughout the tour. The other players were Brandon Evans (Risdon's husband), Warburton Gamble, Neal Caldwell, Lawrence Leslie, Lowden Adams, Payson Edwards, Paul McGrath, Edwin Maxwell, Hugh Rennie, Jack Quigley and P.J. Kelly, who appeared with Peg's Aunt Jane on Broadway in David Belasco's 1919 production of *Dark Rosaleen*. From time to time a Guild cast member would be replaced for one reason or another, but for the most part the troupe would remain intact for the duration of the tour.

The money could have been better; Peg would earn $175 per week (equal to about $2,000 today), but she wouldn't see a paycheck until late September, when the last two weeks of the month-long rehearsals began. (Equity rules allowed producers to squeeze up to two weeks of free rehearsals from actors.) And there would be no percentage of the box office for her to share, as had been the case with *Tommy*, but all her meals and travel expenses were covered. There's little doubt she would have agreed to a lesser salary, or even worked for free; after all, she was now a headlining actress with ... the *Guild*! Peg Entwistle had really, truly, finally *arrived*. She was just twenty years old.

The meeting with Helburn and Moeller took place on April 13, 1928 ... a Friday. It isn't likely that this traditionally unlucky date factored into her request, but Peg asked if signing the contracts could wait until Wednesday, her one-year wedding anniversary. This sentiment had gone over very well with the Guild directors; after a handshake agreement, Peg and her husband left Helburn's office and then returned to the Guild Theater a few days later and made it official. Peg was also given permission to bring her German Shepherd along. Otto would be the company mascot, and a warning to any small-town wolves who might feel compelled to behave naughtily toward the troupe's attractive women.

It was all so wonderful. Hardly could a girl — an actress married to an actor — have received a more fitting anniversary gift than to be signed by the New York Theater Guild.

Babs Entwistle truly was "most tremendously happy."[4]

The New York Police Department was not.

* * *

A few months later, about the middle of August, Peg and Keith were having breakfast at the Shelton Hotel's restaurant when a police detective approached their table. He handed Keith a court order and said, "You have until two o'clock today to pay up this back alimony, and if you don't you are going to jail."[5]

Keith was embarrassed, of course, but Peg was mortified. According to her account of the incident, the detective had been anything but subtle, choosing intimidation through public humiliation. Like most cops in the city he was probably a family man, and he would certainly have known that Keith was a noted actor. And as a policeman's salary was only a fraction of the salary of an actor, this detective would have much in the way of contempt for a deadbeat Broadway father, especially one enjoying a substantial meal in a luxury hotel. The detective would have glanced down at the plates, cups, bowls ... *What had the lad and his mother eaten today, gruel?*

If there was ever a moment when a gruff detective needed to punctuate his point by twisting his cigar into a man's Eggs Benedict, this was certainly such a moment.

A cop's mind would also have a hunch that any woman who kept company with such a man as Keith had to know he neglected his son's welfare ... the detective would feel it was his duty to make Peg feel ashamed of her husband and herself. (Of course, the detective had no idea that Peg had already given Keith several checks to pay the debt, or that Peg has just now learned the money never reached the boy.)

The restaurant at the Shelton was a popular one and was probably busy at the time. And it would figure that the staff and a number of the regular customers knew Peg from her days as a resident guest. Peg said the detective had his badge hanging from his coat pocket — a hard-to-ignore attention getter. There would be an awkward hush followed by whispers from the nearby tables as the cop boomed his voice authoritatively: "Pay up this back alimony.... If you don't you are going to jail!"[6]

Keith was $1,000 in arrears (about $12,500 today). That buys a lot of food and clothing for a little boy — and a lot of contempt from a forty-dollars-a-week flatfoot.

Keith didn't have the money. Peg didn't have the money. She could borrow it from Walter Hampden, but that would mean her uncle would find out, and then Aunt Jane, and then Matilda ... no, that would *never* do. They scrambled all morning and into the afternoon to raise the money but their efforts came to naught. Several officers must have been following Peg and her deadbeat, for at precisely two o'clock he was arrested and hauled off to jail.

Poor Peg must have imagined her husband suffering all sorts of horrid indignities ... cold coffee, soggy toast, stale cigarettes. Desperate for help, she swallowed her pride — what little of it might have lingered — and went to see the Guild's boss, Theresa Helburn. Peg explained the situation and then asked if the Guild could see it in their hearts to loan them the money. One wonders how many employers shell out $12,500 for a new employee who hasn't actually started working yet ... and who is sitting in jail.

Helburn had grace, undoubtedly more for Peg and little Brian Keith than for Robert. A contract for the loan was drawn. Peg signed and brought the cash to the police station.

Keith was released from custody and then he and Peg reported to Helburn so he could put his signature on the contract. In the end, most of the repayment would come out of Peg's paychecks ... it was par for the Robert Keith course. "Thereafter from time to time the plaintiff aided and assisted the defendant in paying his alimony."[7]

* * *

The Guild troops were marshaled on September 3, 1928. All nine of the coming season's productions began rehearsals at the same time. Hundreds of actors, actresses, understudies, writers, set designers, painters, electricians and other technicians went to work. The Guild Theater could seat 900 patrons, but only two or three acting groups at once. Other theaters and church halls were rented to help accommodate this unprecedented undertaking.

The actors had already been studying their scripts for weeks and this went a long way in shortening the rehearsal time. They spent the first few days sitting through table readings. This is exactly what it implies — the players would simply sit around a table and read the play. The environment was usually quite casual; the actors and actresses smoking or sipping coffee or tea as they interpreted roles and experimented with inflections, accents, and pauses and pacing with respect to their character's dialogue. Oftentimes, there were interruptions as questions were asked of each other or the director, or the playwright if he or she were present: *Mr. Moeller, might my girl be more likable if I gave her a bit of Southern Belle? Alan, when you deliver that line to her, try ending it by blowing a kiss ... yes, that seems to work very well, what do you think, Peg? Oh, I think that's an awfully nice touch, Mr. Moeller, but, Alan, maybe next time you could blow the kiss to me instead of Bob?*

If such an exchange as the contrived example above brought forth the intended laughter from the group, it meant camaraderie was building, and for an extended tour this was invaluable.

The entire schedule for the Guild Repertory Company is much too detailed to include here, but it basically went like this: In a metropolis like Los Angeles, all four plays (*The Doctor's Dilemma, The Second Man, Ned McCobb's Daughter,* and *John Ferguson* would be presented during a four-week stay. Each play would run one week with nightly performances (except Sundays) and several matinees. In cities the size of Kansas City, Missouri, they would stay a week and perform each play twice. In smaller cities, such as Memphis, Tennessee, or larger towns like Sandusky, Ohio, the company would generally stay three days and present one-night-only performances of three plays. Matinees were added if demand warranted it.

For rural America, the stops were strictly single-performance one-night stands. Those city slickers with their fancy hair and pretty talk would be up and out and on the rails before they had a chance to beguile any farmer's daughter.

When a town didn't have a legitimate theater, the troupe would perform in college theaters, high school auditoriums, vaudeville houses, and even movie theaters. Elisabeth Risdon thought this was a good thing. "We had crowded audiences, and mostly of this young generation which have been denied the chance to see the spoken drama. They find us an attractive novelty, and the colleges are providing the theaters where the trade fails."[8]

As to acting style, it was repertory in the strictest sense. The actors and actresses constantly changed roles. Peg might be the female lead in *Doctor's Dilemma* during the Topeka stop, but Miss Risdon would have that part in Omaha, Miss Hendricks in Houston. The cast members were very fond of this system; it allowed each of them to get a bit of the spotlight. The repertory philosophy of the Guild's managers was reflected in part by drama critic Alama Whitaker of the *Los Angeles Times*: "The Theater Guild company has no stars—and all are stars."[9] Risdon said, "I think it is good for us, the play should be more important than any of its participants."[10] In essence, every actor and actress was both a principal player and an understudy to their peers.

One of the amazing things about Peg and her co-players is that each one had to learn the lines and direction of *all* the characters in the four plays. The *Santa Monica Outlook* published an article featuring the Guild tour and Beatrice Hendricks. Hendricks noted that she had to memorize 90,000 words of dialogue contained in 600 pages covering the eight feminine roles in the four plays. (Consider the task of memorizing the dialogue—and action—of a typical novel, which runs maybe 70,000 to 80,000 words.) She had to perfect a mental photograph of it all. This, of course, means that Peg and Elisabeth Risdon had done likewise. But it was more than memorizing the dialogue; they all had to remember the entire action of each character in every scene. They needed to be aware of the business at hand in the storyline—the entrances, exits, cues and so on. In the following quote from her interview in the *Outlook*, Hendricks may just as well have been speaking for everyone in the company: "The mental photograph needs constant retouching. Every day [we] have to reread each part, to repeat the lines word for word to [ourselves]. Then the subconscious mind is ready to be called to duty."[11] It took more than a modicum of skill to keep all the information in its proper space, lest a line from the *Doctor's Dilemma* matinee inadvertently found its way into that evening's performance of *The Second Man*.

One of the great privileges afforded them by the Guild was the organization's insistence that no one was to mimic the other; each player was encouraged to interpret the roles as guided by their creativity. Hendricks said, "Do not imitate [we were told]. Play the roles, not necessarily as others do them, but as you feel them."[12]

They were really a very talented bunch. For the Acting Company's New York production of *Strange Interlude*, those players needed seven weeks to master that one play. Peg and her gang had mastered *four* plays in just one month.

While on the road, the troupe would get its stage direction from one of their own, actor Edwin Maxwell, who had a good deal of Broadway directing experience. Guild cofounder Philip Moeller supervised Maxwell's direction of the rehearsals. Moeller would also personally direct the New York and Los Angeles rehearsals of *The Doctor's Dilemma* and *Ned McCobb's Daughter*. He was the original director of these plays when they premiered on Broadway.

Moeller was a brilliant and elegant man, often wearing his overcoat, or a cape, over his shoulders and a thick wool scarf wrapped around his neck during the winter months, but more so for style than function. He was considered one of the best stage directors alive.

Raymond Sovey, a future two-time Tony Award nominee, would handle stage settings and wardrobe. Some of the costumes and jewelry that Peg wore in *The Second Man* were worn by Lynn Fontanne when she starred in that play for the Guild a year earlier on Broadway.

Robert Sisk, the Guild's press agent, traveled ahead of the tour, as did a Guild subscription secretary: Sisk to deliver the hype, the secretary to sell theater reservations and subscriptions to the Guild's magazine. She also hosted special readings of certain scenes from the four plays being featured. These events were basically tea and luncheon socials for target groups, such as women's book circles, garden clubs, and civic organizations.

* * *

Peg and her companions began the tour in Montclair, New Jersey, in early October. Several lengthy chapters could be used to detail the journey. (The author has chosen to spare the reader and himself such monotony.) By the time the tour ended nine months later, Peg had visited dozens of cities and towns in at least 18 states and appeared in each play as many as 100 times. (Guild production numbers published in the *New York Times* in November 1929 noted that *The Doctor's Dilemma* was given exactly 100 performances on the tour. Most of the time all four of the plays were scheduled to be presented as a package, so it is reasonable to assume Peg enjoyed well over 300 curtain rises.)

Scores of reviews of the four plays were found in small town and big city newspapers. There were also a number of articles and interviews featuring the individual cast members or the production in general. There isn't a bad notice among them. To put it simply, the Guild Repertory Company and Peg Entwistle were *magnificent*.

It's too bad Robert Keith had to cause her yet more shame and humiliation.

* * *

The Guild managers chose Keith to head the company; in essence, he was the captain of the team. It isn't known how soon he began drinking once the company left Manhattan, but for the first six weeks on the road he seems to have managed without causing serious problems.

When the company landed in normally Guild-friendly Rochester, New York, in late October, there came an astonishing lack of patronage. Oh, the reviews were terrific, but ticket buyers had stayed away in droves for the entire six-night run. The house was mostly empty for every performance and the Guild did little more than break even at the box office. Rochester had historically been one of the most theatrically enthusiastic provinces in the nation, and the troupe was dumbfounded by all the empty seats. The mystery was solved after *The Billboard* reminded everyone that the presidential and gubernatorial election campaigns were peaking and most of Rochester's patriotic citizens had been busy attending political meetings, conferences, and workers rallies. (Franklin Delano Roosevelt won the Governor's Mansion by a slim margin.)

Later that month in West Virginia (after the troupe had come up from Georgia), Peg's husband caused a ruckus loud enough to make the papers in Ohio, the next leg of the tour. Said the *Steubenville Herald,* "Failure to bring to trial the case of the state versus Robert Lee Keith, indicted on a second offense of operating an automobile while intoxicated, in the Brook County (W.V.) circuit court, scheduled for Tuesday morning, brought forth a lecture to court attachés and attorneys from Judge J.B. Somerville."[13]

Judge Somerville was furious; first because Keith wasn't in court, and secondly because his attorney had filed a motion to postpone the trial, claiming an unnamed "star witness" could not be located.[14] After scolding the prosecutor and defense attorney P.J. McGuire, the judge ordered McGuire to present the defendant to the court for trial on March 1, 1929. The four-man jury was excused. Keith stayed clear of West Virginia.

In late November and early December, after playing in Cincinnati, Sandusky, and Toledo, Ohio, the company arrived to Detroit, Michigan. On the first night there a drunk and crazed Keith viciously attacked Peg in their hotel as she was lying in bed. He grabbed "great handfuls" of her hair and pulled her into the air, off the bed, then threw her down and repeated the hair-grabbing and -pulling a number of times.[15] She agonized as tufts of hair were wrenched from her scalp. Her desperate screams for help finally drew the attention of the house detective; he barged into the room and stopped the assault. Possibly because there was no such thing as "zero tolerance" for spousal abuse in 1929, Keith wasn't arrested for assault and battery or domestic violence. And perhaps Peg didn't prefer charges. Or maybe he managed to sweet talk his way out of trouble; it was likely a little of all of the above.

The battered wife packed her things and moved to another room, fully intending to get a legal separation. She managed to stay clear of him for a week. He took some time off, managed to sober up, and spent much of the next few days begging Peg to forgive him. She did, because she loved him, and he promised he'd never lay another hand on her in anger, and would never "be cruel to her again."[16] And he would never drink again; not another drop, *ever.* He was done, through, finished. Like most alcoholics who swear-off drinking following a bout of trouble, he probably meant it. And, as a true enabler, Peg probably believed it. She agreed to go back to him, but only under the condition that they sleep in separate, adjoining rooms. However, by the time the company arrived to Milwaukee, Wisconsin, for their Christmas week performances, he was back at it. Peg said he was worse than before.

Theresa Helburn was finally informed of his behavior. In an attempt to steer the Guild away from bad press involving one of their actors abusing one of their actresses, Keith was fired for "acts and actions upon the state caused by his drinking intoxicating liquors,"[17] namely, the drunk driving arrests and pending trial in West Virginia. Peg licked her physical, mental, and emotional wounds in tormented silence.

Blacklisted by the Guild, and therefore Broadway, Keith made his way west. Two weeks later he was working the annual men-only frolic at the Masquers Club in Hollywood, California. He was in a skit called *Brothers*. From there, he got a gig as a celebrity greeter for James Gleason, who was hosting the Western Actors' Equity Ball at the Biltmore in Los Angeles. It isn't known if Peg knew this, but as she and the Guild Repertory headed for the coast, one town and city at a time, she remained heartbroken and humiliated.

* * *

Keith knew he would see his wife soon again. The company was scheduled to do four weeks in Los Angeles. The premiere of the first play would be just a few days before their second wedding anniversary. He would meet with her, reconcile, bring her flowers, apologies, promises ... more promises than ever before. She loved him, he could tell. He might have lost his job with the Guild, but he would not lose *his* Babs. He'd do anything for her, anything at all. So, she wanted him sober, did she? Then damn it, that's what he would become. Robert Lee Keith made a vow—he would never drink again ... *ever*.

And *this time,* he *really* meant it.

* * *

On April 14, 1929, following four and a half months of peace from Keith's abuse and drunken tirades, the Guild Repertory Company arrived to Albuquerque, New Mexico. It was the last stop on the Midwest leg of the itinerary. They had come to present a one-night-only performance of *Ned McCobb's Daughter*. Large newspaper ads published a month in advance of the show featured the names of the entire cast, but the only face associated with the production was Peg's. She was heralded as a "Star of the Theater Guild."[18] The photo of her was an official Guild photograph, but it is a bit less than flattering. Peg is hardly unattractive, but she is stern-faced, determined-looking, all-business. If she was a football player, it would be said she was wearing her "game face."

Two days later the troupe arrived at Grand Central Station in downtown Los Angeles. Peg was bright and cheerful when she saw her family waiting on the platform. After a hugfest and jovial introductions between cast members and the Entwistle clan, Peg and her German Shepherd went to Hollywood for a delightful day and evening of merriment with her family.

Peg and the cast went to work the very next night at the Figueroa Playhouse, located in the heart of Los Angeles City proper. As mentioned, each of the four plays on the bill would run a week, evenings and matinees. First was Bernard Shaw's *The Doctor's Dilemma*, the story of a distinguished doctor who has the ability to save only one of two men who are dying. Should he save his friend, a fellow doctor and kind-hearted healer of the poor who dedicated his life to the impoverished sick and saved countless lives, or should the miracle serum go to a wealthy scoundrel, a selfish, self-centered artist whose genius and creativity brings joy to millions?

The answer would be a simpler one if the distinguished doctor wasn't in love with the artist's beautiful wife—and if the wife wasn't willing to do *anything* to keep her artist alive ... and if the doctor wasn't perhaps tempted to procure himself a fetching widow.

Peg had a supporting role in the Figueroa premiere. She played the maid. Elisabeth Risdon played the wife, and it was she and Warburton Gamble who carried the night. But, as mentioned earlier, each of the cast members enjoyed the spotlight at various times.

On their wedding anniversary, Peg and her husband were signed to a national tour by the Guild. Left to right: Robert Keith, Peg, Elisabeth Risdon, and Alan Mowbray, a founder of the Screen Actors Guild. The dog is Otto, a wedding gift to Peg from Mowbray. She titled this tour image "The gang" (courtesy Entwistle Family).

As usual, the company was very well received. "The Guild players act it to the very hilt," noted a review by Marquis Busby of the *Los Angeles Times*.[19] Drama critic Robert Hutton, writing for the *Santa Monica Outlook*, said, "The production is magnificent. There is not a weak spot in it. Philip Moeller has shown such skill in direction as Los Angeles has not seen in many years. The cast is, without exception, splendid, and without the usual stage artifice."[20] Hutton also saw the play's final Los Angeles performance a week later, and wrote, "The acting is supreme. It is not acting at all, so far as the audience may discern. Which means that careful study and constant rehearsal plus intelligence not usually found of the stage makes the thing seem very real."[21]

Florence Lawrence, whose Hollywood beat covered stage and screen, wrote in the *Los Angeles Examiner* that Peg, Risdon, and Hendricks shared equal performance honors. And she was smitten by their "beautiful and colorful voices, and enunciation that delights the ear."[22] Indeed, for here you had the highly polished elocutions of two Brits and a Romanian (Hendricks). Lawrence added, "Miss Entwistle, with her [character's] bit of pathos, warmed the audience quite out of the judicial mood established by the calmness of the other performances."[23]

Pathos on her stage, pathos in her life...

"That on said 16th day of April, 1929, defendant came to the theater ... so drunk that the doorkeeper wouldn't let him in ... that thereupon defendant told the doorkeeper that he was the husband of plaintiff and wanted to see her, and the doorkeeper recognizing the fact that defendant was too drunk to see her, refused to let him go into the theater."[24]

Not only couldn't Keith get inside, but the members of the cast couldn't get out, not without having to be confronted by him. Peg said her fellows were on their way out (this following an afternoon matinee), but when they saw her husband outside the entrance with the doorman they quickly hurried back to the dressing room to warn her.

Peg was yet again humiliated by the man who claimed undying love for her. Mortifying her in public became his second favorite hobby. Keith refused to leave until Peg met him at the door. She did, and promised to meet him the next day—but only if he was sober. As soon as he was out of sight, Peg made a phone call. An hour or so later, she met attorney Gesner Williams at the nearby Superior Court and filed legal separation papers and a divorce action. The next day, April 17, Peg borrowed her aunt's car, met Keith, and took him for a ride (why not, he'd been taking her for one for two years). It isn't known where they went. But apparently he was sober, for Peg trusted him enough to allow him in the car. She told him how sick he had made her with his cruelty and abuse and drinking. Peg was straight and tactful, upfront and forward when she told him it was over, and that he needed to accept it. She loved him, but was no longer *in love* with him. She cared for him and worried for his safety and hoped he could turn his life around, but he would have to do it without her.

Peg seemed very strong that day—brave and confident. But she was an actress. And the truth is she was dying inside. A photograph in the *Los Angeles Times* shows her and Warburton Gamble in a scene from *The Doctor's Dilemma*. Peg, as Emmy the maid, looks forlorn, sad. Yes, she was acting, but she was certainly not acting frail and gaunt. She looks fifteen pounds lighter than when the tour began. Keith had no idea just how much of her life he had crushed ... he wouldn't have a clue until September 1932.

And then again, maybe not.

* * *

The day after Peg's drive and talk with Keith was April 18, their second wedding anniversary. Gesner Williams sent court process server Edward Soutter to hand-deliver a summons to Keith. He was ordered to appear on April 30 and give an answer to the action. Meanwhile, as Soutter was tracking down Keith, Peg was spending the morning of her second anniversary with Williams, giving a sworn affidavit detailing the cruel actions against her. Peg did not want alimony or property. She just needed to be free of him, and to be well enough in body and soul to give the stage her best. As it was, she could barely function: "That by reason of the actions of the defendant hereinbefore set forth, plaintiff became and now is sick, sore, and ill mentally so that she is unable to continue her work upon the stage except by using her greatest efforts and then is not doing the best she should towards her [fellow] employees; that if she is not separated from the defendant by judgment of this court, her health will be so impaired that she will be forced to stop her work...."[25]

It was no surprise when Keith failed to appear on April 30. Judge Marshall McComb allowed a default in Peg's favor and set a trial date for May 2. She returned two days later, as instructed, confident the humiliation would all be over now. She entered the building with a broken heart, but her soul was becoming a bit more at ease, for Keith was nowhere to be seen. He was gone for good. That meant shame and public humiliation would also be gone for good ... *finally*!

Peg wore a stylish dress and fashionable hat, her hands tucked inside driving gloves. She looked pretty walking through the swinging doors of Department 39. She took a seat next to her attorney. Gesner Williams assured her it would all take just ten minutes.

No more shame ... no more embarrassment ... no more public humiliation...

Miss Entwistle! How 'bout a smile for the Press!

She wasn't smiling when the reporter's flashbulb popped. It almost looks a like a smile, but it isn't, it's a smirk; a sort of "yeah-I-should-have-figured" simper that people often accompany with a short, sarcastic puff of air from the nostrils. Her lips are tight, bunched to one side. She's leaning forward a bit, elbows on the table arms folded atop her purse. Expressionless eyes stare straight ahead, not at the camera, toward the judge's bench — only she's not looking at the bench, she's looking *through* it beyond the wall behind it ... out into nowhere, to a nowhere place only she could see...

An A-list movie actress would have made the top fold of the front page, but Peg was Broadway B-list, so to mixed-blessing page eight she went: "STAGE FOLK AIR DISCORD IN ROMANCE: Peg Entwistle Says Actor Mate Was Cruel to Her, and Wins Divorce."[26]

Whoever said there is no such thing as bad publicity had never married Robert Lee Keith.

* * *

Peg was granted her divorce but it would not be final until after one year passed. She would still be legally married until May 6, 1930. This annoying aspect of the California law was no secret, but for a time Keith's marriage to an actress named Dorothy Tierney was. Keith met Tierney through actress Dale Winter. In June 1930, the *Oakland Tribune* featured an article about them. Apparently (although the article does not specifically say when) Keith and Tierney got married prior to May 6, 1930. The paper says they were married "some months" after they met while each was appearing in San Francisco.[27] This would have been some time in the late summer or early fall of 1929 — long before he was legally divorced.

The article teased Keith about how he accidentally blew the cover of this secret marriage when an unnamed fellow actor saw him walking an Airedale terrier in the park. The headline read: "Actor Forgets Lines, and Marriage Secret Is Out."[28] When asked by the actor where he got the dog, Keith began to reply, "It was a wedding present," but caught himself and stopped short of finishing the answer.[29] He avoided going into details, but one thing led to another, rumors persisted, and soon the "secret marriage" had come to light.[30]

Keith said that only Dale Winter (giver of the Airedale) knew of the marriage. If Keith was legally divorced from Peg, why did he want a secret wedding to Dorothy Tierney? Why had it remained secret for so many months? Keith and Tierney had become fairly popular actors in the San Francisco area. Publicity of their nuptials could only help their careers, especially after they began working together. Secret weddings were for Hollywood superstars who wished quiet ceremonies without interference from tabloid journalists and gate-crashing fans, not B-list stage players with nothing to hide.

A search of marriage records in San Francisco and Oakland between Keith and Tierney could not locate a certificate. It's possible the ceremony had been performed in another town or state. Keith's family did not respond to the author's queries. But the evidence suggests that the marriage between Keith and Tierney may not have been legitimate under law. However, in all fairness to the relationship, it must be stated that their love for each other was enduring enough to keep them together for 36 years until Keith's death in 1966. In fact, it looks as though Keith and Tierney enjoyed a marriage that in many ways Peg had hoped to have had with him.

Even scoundrels are not beyond redemption.

12

The Show Must Go On

*It will be fine if I can have love and a career, but of the two
I prefer the career to a husband.*—Peg Entwistle[1]

Peg exhibited an amazing amount of courage as the tour made its way west. She expected her husband would show up at any time. In the days immediately after the Guild fired him, Peg's anxiety nearly caused her a nervous breakdown. She feared he would storm in during a performance, drunk and violent, loud and obnoxious. Her fellow cast members were sympathetic toward her, of course, but for a time rehearsals were not the same. The jovial atmosphere among the players; the banter and kidding, the ad libs and parodies of each other ... the *fun*, had all but vanished. (Sometimes during rehearsals, Peg's dog would roam the stage and Alan Mowbray would recite lines to him. He nicknamed Otto "Rin," after the famous movie dog, Rin Tin Tin. "He's more ham than dog," Peg said.[2])

Everyone was on edge. But during those four and a half months when Keith did not show up at any of the theaters or hotels along the route, the company had become more and more at ease. And then when he appeared in Los Angeles, it was like an earthquake rattling inside her. But Peg had tapped into her reserves; she mustered courage and resolve and faced him, more so for her fellows and the Guild than for herself, but she did it.

And now he was gone—this time for good. Peg's heartache lingered, and the mental wounds were deep. Nevertheless, she pressed on, and did an excellent job during the Guild Repertory Company's remaining weeks in Los Angeles, and beyond to the tour's last curtain.

The show must go on...

On April 22 the curtain went up at the Figueroa Playhouse for S.N. Behrman's light comedy *The Second Man*. Robert Hutton called it an "Oscar Wildeish giggle from one end to the other."[3] Peg played Monica Grey, whom Hutton described as "a sort of fundamentalist flapper who refuses to forget a number of unessential fairy tales."[4]

The play has only four characters: An author (Alan Mowbray) fancies himself too intelligent to write commercial fiction, yet incapable of writing great stuff. So he will make a living marrying a wealthy window (Elisabeth Risdon), while a lovesick scientist (Neal Caldwell) tries to seduce Monica.

Edwin Schallert of the *Los Angeles Times* opened his review with, "See *The Second Man* for a delightful two and a half hours in the world of intelligent make-believe.... [A]n excellent play excellently played, it stands forth as one of the most worthy of the season's stage presentations ... Elisabeth Risdon and Peg Entwistle are the most able."[5]

The Guild Repertory Company program consisted of four productions. Here, in a scene from *The Second Man,* are Elisabeth Risdon, Robert Keith, Lawrence Leslie and Peg. Keith's drinking caused serious problems for the Guild, and especially for Peg (author's collection).

The day before *Second Man* opened, the company publicist released a lovely ink portrait of Peg and Neal Caldwell in a scene from the play. It captures a quiet, touching look at Peg's demure stage presence. It's a simple, lovely image.

A week later came Sidney Howard's comedic melodrama *Ned McCobb's Daughter,* with Risdon in the title role. Of the three bills so far presented by the Guild at the Figueroa, Los Angeles critics covered this production more (and more favorably) than the two before it. The story takes place in Maine. Carrie, the daughter of Ned McCobb (Brandon Evans), has married that good-for-nothing George Callahan (Neal Caldwell). George forces Ned to mortgage his farm so he can pay for an abortion for his mistress Jenny, played by Peg Entwistle. (One might pause at how often abortion held the spotlight in her life in so short a time....) And now the farm is in danger of foreclosure. When George is arrested for stealing money from a ferry, his bootlegging brother Babe (Lawrence Leslie) offers Carrie a deal: He will give her the money to pay off the mortgage and get George a good attorney if she will let him store his illegal whiskey in her father's barn. There are plot twists a-plenty as Carrie accepts the cash, pays the bank, and then cooperates with the state in order to rid her life of both Callahan brothers. Mowbray, ever the professional, enjoyed a very minor role, a cameo, really, as Carrie's brother, who has a stroke and dies within the first few minutes of Act I.

Four months earlier, Pathé Studios had released a film version of *Ned McCobb's Daughter,* with Irene Rich in the title role. Portraying Jenny was a 20-year-old Carole Lombard. It isn't known if she had gone to the Figueroa to see Peg's interpretation of the role, or if Peg had done likewise to see Miss Lombard's take, but it's quite possible each had done so. In fact, it would have been unusual if both actresses had not done so.

Miss Lawrence over at the *Examiner* noted the enthusiastic audience at the Playhouse, and said of the performance, "It brings new possibilities to each player, and last night's presentation proved scintillant in action, and vital in its fast-moving sequences of incident ... and will entertain hundreds to whom the dialog form of stage entertainment is sometimes lacking in power."[6] She continued, "Peg Entwistle, as Jenny, won admiration as the weakling girl, and her big scene in the third act merited warm applause."[7]

Edwin Schallert wrote in the *Times,* "The Repertory Company again evinced the effectiveness and the adequacy of their schooling.... [A]ttention might be duly drawn to Peg Entwistle as the romantically depressed Jenny."[8]

If only Schallert knew the irony of his statement, of how easy, and how not so easy, it was for Peg to play a romantically depressed girl in need of an abortion...

Perhaps the most interesting aspect of the show was the delegation of law enforcement officials in the front row. When word got out that the story was about bootlegging, Los Angeles Police Chief James E. Davis decided some "discreet balance" might be needed. He brought with him to the opening a large number of government officials closely identified with prohibition forces. These included high-ranking Federal agents and administrators, a presiding judge of the municipal court, officers of the district attorney's office, Captain James Benton of the sheriff's liquor detail and Captain W.F. Weyerman of the city's vice squad.

Peg likely breathed a sigh of relief that Robert Keith and his jug were absent.

On May 5, 1929, after rehearsing for the next night's premiere of the final Guild Repertory production, *John Ferguson,* Peg went to work racing a deadline, polishing a short article she penned for the *Los Angeles Examiner.* It was published the next day in the paper's theatrical section. In "L. A. Wins Praise as Show Center," Peg compares the drama audiences in Los Angeles to some of those she's seen across the country:

> Los Angeles really loves the theater. In other cities people go to a play not because they love the drama more, but because they love the furnished flat less. On winter nights they can't bear to be anywhere else. It is because they go there to keep warm. On summer nights they go there to keep cool. All this, of course, in cities that do not have a [tropical] climate.
>
> No dweller of the Southland would ever go to a playhouse for lack of anything better. Nothing as pallid or negative as that could lead him to the box office. He must be driven by an honest passion, an authentic urge.
>
> For this reason, Los Angeles should be the Louvre of the American drama. Nothing of indifferent merit can survive here. Only the really good offerings can compete with the meteorological and domestic attractions. Yet when a play is up to the standard, the response is overwhelming and gratifying. Los Angeles is a play town if the plays are good enough.[9]

In anticipation of the Guild's arrival to San Francisco, the *Oakland Tribune* came to Los Angeles to interview Peg. Under the heading "English Actress with Guild," the *Tribune* ran a May 5 article that covered a bit of her background and successful early start in theater.[10] It mentioned her work in comedy but noted how she desired to play emotional character parts. Peg elaborated:

I would rather play roles that carry conviction. Maybe it is because they are the easiest and yet the hardest things for me to do, if you know what I mean. I mean easy because I seem to fit into them, but difficult because I am never sure of myself. To play any kind of an emotional scene I must work up to a certain pitch. If I reach this in my first word, the rest of the words and lines take care of themselves. But if I fail I have to build up the balance of the speeches, and in doing this the whole characterization falls flat. I feel that I am cheating myself. I don't know whether other actresses get this same reaction or not, but it does worry me.[11]

The final installment of the Los Angeles stop was as emotional as it gets on stage.

St. John Ervine's bitter drama *John Ferguson* is about an 1880s poverty-stricken Irish family in the Country Down. In 1919 it became the Guild's first major success, and saved the fledgling organization from financial collapse. If a play could be fashioned into a memorial, the bronze giant in the lobby of the Guild Theater would be *John Ferguson*. Drama critic Marquis Busby, remarking on the Guild Repertory's 1929 revival, said, "I imagine playing a role in this drama must be regarded as a sacred privilege by all Guild players."[12]

John Ferguson is an aging, sickly, Bible-thumper who believes vengeance is the Lord's ... *no matter what.* He and his family (wife Sarah, daughter Hannah, son Andrew) are about to lose their farm to the despicable (of course) money-lender, Witherow. Ferguson has written to his brother in America and asked for a loan, but many weeks have passed and no answer has come. Hannah, played by Peg, makes an attempt to save the farm by agreeing to marry the cowardly, but financially secure, Jimmy Caesar. Witherow relaxes his pressure on the family, for he knows Jimmy has money. But Hannah reneges; she just cannot stomach the idea of marrying a man frightened by his own shadow. She backs out of the marriage and goes to Witherow's home to tell him that her family will not be able to meet the debt after all. Later, while pretending to escort Hannah safely to her home, Witherow drags her into the woods and rapes her. But Ferguson will not seek revenge, for God is the only Judge and his daughter's rape is simply a part of the divine plan. Ferguson doesn't budge even after his son angrily reminds him about that Biblical eye-for-an-eye thing.

Jimmy Caesar has a moment of bravado and sets out to kill Witherow, but when his gun accidentally fires on the way, he gets scared and goes into hiding. Hannah's brother steps up and defends her honor with a rifle shot through Witherow's heart. And now Andrew will have to face the hangman. Mother Ferguson anguishes that she will lose her son forever and blames Hannah for all the trouble. "It's *her* that ought to be hanged!"[13]

To be sure, the tragedy could not have come full circle unless it turns out the money to save the farm had indeed arrived from America, and was sitting in the local post office as Andrew had been taking aim at his sister's rapist.

This play was the Guild Repertory Company's biggest hit in Los Angeles. Three more matinees were added to meet the demand for tickets. Marquis Busby at the *Times* said, "It is their outstanding achievement ... Peg Entwistle scores as the tragedy-ridden daughter."[14] Robert Hutton also thought Peg was well cast, and that the Theater Guild players "are certainly giving us such performances as the west has not seen for many moons."[15] Florence Lawrence at the *Examiner* was impressed with the way Peg "gripped the audience with a note of suspense as the action progressed."[16]

The company then hit San Francisco, opening at the Geary Theater on May 13. Each of the four plays had its own week and was well received by enthusiastic audiences and drama critics — it was a mirror of the Los Angeles stop, *sans* the Robert Lee Keith welcoming committee. From there the troupe went to Salt Lake City for a week that featured all four plays on the bill. The City of Mormon was surprisingly receptive given the production's sexual themes (mild) swearing, portrayed use of booze and tobacco, and implied rape and abortion. The tour then had it last days in San Diego. It had been an amazing run.

History shows that this cast of players is perhaps the best repertory company ever assembled for a national tour. Theresa Helburn and the Guild directors were quite pleased. The mission had been accomplished: Tens of thousands who had only heard of the Theater Guild finally got to see it in action, and a good many subscribers had been enlisted.

The Guild's Board of Directors had awarded the players cash bonuses before they left Los Angeles, and when they arrived in San Francisco congratulatory telegrams and floral bouquets from the Guild managers and notable Broadway producers were waiting for them at the hotel. Only about six weeks remained before the tour production closed, and so the cast began thinking of their futures. They knew that producers, playwrights, and directors on both coasts were already contemplating suitable plays and players for the coming season, and the Guild Repertory had created lots of buzz. The cash bonuses and telegrams were promising indicators that everyone in the tour would be busy come the next fall, winter and spring.

Back in New York, Helburn decided that P.J. Kelly and Warburton Gamble were going to be sent back to Los Angeles to replace several actors in the Guild's West Coast production of Eugene O'Neill's five-hour, nine-act smash hit, *Strange Interlude*. Elisabeth Risdon will take over the feminine lead in *Interlude,* and then go with it to Oakland and San Francisco. Brandon Evans will join her.

Along with Lawrence Leslie and Neal Caldwell, Risdon was also given a contract to work with the Guild Acting Company in New York for the 1929-30 season.

Alan Mowbray and Beatrice Hendricks declined Helburn's offers. Mowbray had written a play called *Dinner Is Served* and wanted to direct and act it on Broadway with Hendricks. (They'll wish they took Helburn's offers when *Dinner Is Served* lasts just four performances.)

And what of Peg?

Nothing came her way ... she was shunned by Helburn and the Guild. The reason is ridiculous, but quite obvious, really: Theresa Helburn did not want to risk having Peg in their employ until it was absolutely certain that Robert Keith would not make any more trouble. Moreover, there was that little matter at the courthouse. The Guild could overlook Peg's marital problems as long as they had stayed close to hotel rooms and theater exits; but having them published in the *Los Angeles Times,* while the organization was trying to promote itself as a prestigious company made up of conservative, polite players, embarrassed the organization. So Peg was reduced to maintaining a stiff upper lip (yet again) as she watched more than half the cast members being given Guild contracts for the coming year.

Peg walked a tightrope since that night in Detroit, when her "Peach" became a pit, and she was on the verge of a nervous breakdown most of the way to Los Angeles. In spite of this, she had done her job wonderfully during the tour, which is why Helburn let her remain aboard until the end. But there is no question that if she had begun to miss work or falter on stage, Helburn would have canned her.

On its face, Robert Keith was the chief reason the Guild had not optioned Peg for the coming season, but one might wonder if word of her abortion had reached certain New York ears, too. At any rate, Peg would also have guessed — if she hadn't been told — that time away from Broadway could only help her cause in the long run. So, after the tour's end and all the farewells, each actor and actress went their merry way, and Peg took Otto and returned to Hollywood to stay with her family.

* * *

12. The Show Must Go On

In this curious photo taken during Peg's Los Angeles stop of the Guild tour, her brothers Milton (front left) and Bobby (front right) seem to get a scolding by Aunt Jane as she grips their arms. Peg, wearing a hat, is behind Milton as Ross family matriarch Matilda glowers behind him. The others (left to right): Boo!, Harry Haven, Uncle Charles, H. Milton Ross, Charlie Rees and Peg's cousin Helen Reid (courtesy Entwistle Family).

It was June 1929. Peg's name and face were still familiar to many Angelenos.

Living off the money she saved, Peg got an apartment almost directly behind her family's house. She then set about getting reacquainted with Hollywood: driving her aunt's car around, shopping, taking in plays. Elisabeth Risdon was still in the city, working in *Strange Interlude*. One evening, Peg, her cousin Helen, and their Aunt Jane met her for dinner at the Brown Derby on Wilshire Boulevard. Peg liked to show off a bit and so enjoyed herself when several fans recognized her and Risdon and asked for autographs as the actresses were leaving the eatery. It was just the lift she needed; for a few minutes, Peg Entwistle was a star again.

And then came some darkness around the end of June and into early July. Peg became extremely depressed. She contacted a close friend in New York, young socialite Anne Caparn, whom Peg had met in 1927 while working in *Tommy*. Peg told her about Keith's abuse, and the heartache, shame, and embarrassment he wrought upon her, and the unfair treatment she received by the Theater Guild. At some point Peg either confided suicidal ideations to Caparn, or Caparn surmised them. Clues from an amazing poem written by Caparn for Peg indicate that the despondent actress had given some thought to ending her pain by a leap from a high place. From reading the poem (seen later), it would be a very good guess that Peg had the Hollywoodland Sign in mind during her talk. The resemblance described in the poem is just too remarkable.

"Babs was happy when she came [to Hollywood after the tour]," said her cousin Helen. "We all went out to theaters and shopping and things like that. But then she got very quiet....

[She was] polite to everyone, but she stopped talking, really."[17] Helen never met Anne Caparn, but remembered Uncle Charles getting angry about the $45 call to New York. "She paid Enty and was happy again after talking to Anne ... I know it was Anne, because Enty fumed for lots of days about the call ... about Babs getting her own telephone company! And she seemed more her old self after that. I think Aunt Jane knew her [Caparn]."[18]

One of the other things that helped Peg through this difficult time was her love of horseback riding. She, her brother Bobby and Aunt Jane took to the hills and equestrian trails of Beachwood Canyon. It was just like old times again in HOLLYWOODLAND. Otto also liked the hills, but according to Helen was happiest when running along the shoreline in Santa Monica, giving chase to seagulls. (Otto will live out his life in Hollywood, with Jane's sister Marguerite.)

It isn't known if Peg dated anyone that summer, but she was socializing within the celebrity circuit. The 21-year-old, who had sipped her first cocktails when her name first went up in Broadway lights, was still infrequently imbibing, as evidenced by a guest book she signed on July 8, 1929, following a weekend-long party at the home of Mabel "Ma" Webb, mother of stage and screen leading man Clifton Webb. Other guests who signed the page included Harold Ross, founder of *New Yorker* magazine; actor, writer, and producer Jerry Wald; Ziegfeld Follies girl Joan Carter-Waddell; and Michael Farmer, the husband of Gloria Swanson. Each of them wrote a small "thank you" comment to Ma Webb; Peg's is below:

"To the 'It' girl of the Webb Estate. (The one with the curl in the middle of her forehead)."[19] Then Peg signed using a nickname Ma Webb had given her: "Pentwistle."[20] Her penmanship is a bit messy, as if she was writing with a shaky hand or blurred eye, and she had trouble remembering the date. She first wrote "8/8/29" before including her comment, then remembering it was July, not August, she inked a 7 over the first 8.[21] After signing her nickname she wrote another date, this time getting the month correct, but not the day ... "7/18/29."[22]

The "It girl,"[23] of course, is Peg light-heartedly teasing Ma Webb, comparing her to screen legend Clara Bow, the original It Girl.

It isn't clear how long Peg planned on remaining in Los Angeles, or if she was shopping herself to local theatrical producers (she expressed no desire to work in films). Peg could easily have gotten into one of the stage companies in town. Perhaps that's what she was going to pursue before Walter Hampden called from New York. His old friend, stage legend William Gillette, was going to come out of retirement and take his signature play, *Sherlock Holmes*, on an eastern states "farewell tour" beginning in the fall. Hampden asked Peg if she would be interested in playing the feminine lead, a young damsel in distress who falls in love with the famous detective. Would she like to be rescued and loved by Sherlock Holmes while the president of the United States and the first lady looked on from their box?

Peg would have to give it some thought; one just didn't jump at the first offer to come around, one must project an aura of professional reserve. It involves contemplation and study; deliberation and forethought; careful consideration of the details and due diligence...

A fraction of a second later, she gave Walter Hampden her answer.

13

Elementary, My Dear Entwistle!

*It is not enough to say that William Gillette resembles Sherlock Holmes;
Sherlock Holmes looks exactly like William Gillette!*—Orson Welles[1]

There is a somewhat apocryphal tale of how the great American stage actor William Hooker Gillette met Sir Arthur Conan Doyle for the first time in person. It's said that Gillette traveled to England where Conan Doyle was waiting for him at a train station. When the train halted, Gillette, dressed in the now familiar costume of Sherlock Holmes, stepped onto the platform and approached Conan Doyle. "Sherlock Holmes" clenched a large, curved briar pipe between his teeth and stared at his surprised, open-mouthed inventor for a moment. In a flash Gillette whipped out a large magnifying glass, examined Sir Arthur's face, and then in full character exclaimed, "Unquestionably an author!"[2]

If such an event never actually occurred, it should have.

William Gillette was born in 1853. His early years and career are best described in *William Gillette: America's Sherlock Holmes,* by biographer Henry Zecher; but it may here be said that Gillette was an amazing personage on and off stage. He was the son of Francis Gillette, a U.S. Senator and crusader of abolition and women's suffrage. William's mother, Elisabeth Daggett Hooker, was a descendant of the Reverend Thomas Hooker, the founder of Connecticut.

Tall and handsome, Gillette had his stage debut in 1875. Zecher notes that Mark Twain was a close friend of the actor and helped finance several of his productions.

Exactly how Gillette came to write the stage adaptation of *Sherlock Holmes* is detailed in Zecher's book, but when Gillette wanted to have the famous detective fall in love, he wrote to Arthur Conan Doyle, "May I marry Holmes?"[3] Sir Arthur replied, "You may marry him, or murder or do what you like with him."[4]

In his stage adaptation of *Sherlock Holmes,* Gillette has the hero rescue the damsel, but just before the stage fades to dark, the great detective romantically embraces the young ingénue, for they have now fallen in love. Sherlock Holmes purists have been agitated by this ever since.

If this storyline is difficult for a traditionalist to digest today, it may have been even more unpalatable to chew on in 1929, when Gillette's Holmes, looking every bit the actor's 75 years of age, makes love to Alice Faulkner, played by 21-year-old Peg Entwistle.

In August 1929, Gillette announced he was coming out of retirement to present a farewell tour of *Sherlock Holmes.* It was to begin in November. The producer, George C. Tyler (the reader will remember him from *Tommy*), had been negotiating with Gillette for nearly a year. One factor they had to consider was Gillette's desire to use professional Broadway actors; this meant negotiating with Actors' Equity, a union to which Gillette had no affiliation. A vote had to be taken, but Equity unanimously agreed that Gillette should be given a dispensation allowing him to employ card-carrying members of the organization.

In a letter obtained by Zecher, Gillette notes he had a say in selecting the cast for this production. Peg had to audition for the role, but a favorable recommendation from Tyler and family friend Walter Hampden would have carried some weight. It is likely, too, that Gillette had already heard of Peg, or saw her act; this might also have helped persuade him to cast her in the role of the ingénue.

Rehearsals began in October and the show opened at the Court Square Theater in Springfield, Massachusetts, on November 15. (Also in the cast was Walter Hampden's brother Charles.) By all accounts, this production was the biggest theatrical event of the season. Gillette was a superstar during his heyday, and his body of work was certainly not limited to *Sherlock Holmes*. Among his other great successes were productions which he had written and starred in, such as *Held by the Enemy* and *Secret Service*. However, it is *Sherlock Holmes* for which Gillette is most remembered ... and not surprisingly, for much of what we today associate with the character comes not so much from Arthur Conan Doyle as from Mr. Gillette. His inventions include the immense, curved briar pipe (a prop incorporated to prevent a straight pipe from obstructing the actor's face); the deerstalker cap, and, perhaps most famously, the legendary line, "Elementary, my dear Watson!"[5]

Actually, though, the above quote should be credited to actor Clive Brook. When Brook was playing the title role in the 1932 screen adaptation, he shortened and tweaked Gillette's "Oh, this is elementary, my dear fellow!"[6]

From a director's standpoint there was great interest in Gillette's original use of dimmer switches and theatrical lighting to bring about the opening and ending of a scene or act through the "Fade In" and "Fade Out." This, of course, is a common technical aspect in today's stage and screen, but in Gillette's era it was nothing short of genius. Another clever invention of Gillette's involved the use of a cigar: A room is pitch black and when thugs storm inside to subdue Holmes, they open fire in the direction of the glowing cigar — believing it is held in the detective's hand. Holmes suddenly turns on the lights from the other side of the room; he has the drop on them with his own revolver. The flabbergasted criminals stare dumbfounded at the cigar resting quite alone on a window ledge. This scene, a favorite among drama critics, was mentioned in nearly every review.

Gillette performed the role of Sherlock Holmes about 1,300 times and was so associated with the Baker Street gumshoe that news of his farewell tour made headlines in England and Europe. When the revival had its Broadway premiere at the New Amsterdam Theater, a congratulatory letter from former President Calvin Coolidge was read aloud to the thousands in attendance. Coolidge remarked that Gillette was performing a real service for dramatic art. Letters were also read from Corrine Roosevelt Robinson (Teddy Roosevelt's sister), John Phillip Sousa, Otis Skinner, and novelist Booth Tarkington, who said, "I would rather see you play Sherlock Holmes than to be a child on Christmas morning."[7]

Gillette concentrated this farewell tour in the east, going no farther west than Chicago. It lasted seven months, but along the way it was often held over (as was the case on Broadway, when the three-week engagement ran nearly two months). The play received rave reviews everywhere it went; however, critics for the most part ignored the performances of the supporting cast, concentrating instead on the star. Many of the write-ups are thousands of words long and spend a great amount of ink reminiscing about Gillette and his associations with the many great thespians and dignitaries of his era. The few reviews mentioning Peg and the other cast members are favorable, though brief. (In Peg's obituary, the *Hartford Courant* wrote more glowingly of her performance than they had during the tour.)

Regardless of the lack of attention in the press, this was a *very* good job for Peg. Having her name on the same bill as William Gillette was an immense boost to her résumé. He was a living legend and Peg was on her way to becoming one of the elite.

* * *

After the initial openings in Springfield and Boston, and then the Broadway run that had broken box-office records, the troupe zigzagged its way along the east — Philadelphia, Baltimore, Chicago, Saginaw, Madison, Columbus, Cleveland, Cincinnati, Pittsburgh, Hartford and a score of other cities and towns, large and small. It was when 1929 turned the corner into January 1930 that the tour had had it most prominent moments, for this was when Peg's Alice Faulkner was rescued and loved by Sherlock Holmes at the National Theater in Washington, D. C. She opened there with Gillette on January 6. Accompanying the cast now was Burford Hampden (another relative of Walter's) playing the role of Billy, the part played by Charlie Chaplin during Gillette's 1905 London production.

On the day the tour arrived to Washington, the president and Mrs. Hoover honored Gillette with a luncheon at the White House.

Had Peg chatted theater with the first lady? Lunched with President Hoover?

It cannot be ruled out.

Matthew T. Schaefer, archivist with the Herbert Hoover Presidential Library, confirmed that Gillette's lunch at the White House was noted on Hoover's calendar for January 6. Schaefer also noted that Mrs. Hoover was usually in charge of such affairs, but her White House Social Affairs files do not mention Peg Entwistle or the luncheon.

It cannot be proven conclusively that Peg and the other co-players were entertained by the president and Mrs. Hoover, but at the time of this writing nothing had disproven it.

If Peg did not attend the luncheon, she wouldn't have been too disappointed, for earlier that morning, newspapers across the country announced that the Hoovers would be attending that night's *Sherlock Holmes* performance.

Peg's father and uncle had performed on His Majesty's Royal Stage for the King and Queen of England when Peg was a three-year-old lazing in a stroller in the wings; now here she was, not yet 22 years old, and about to rival her theatrical family's accomplishment — gearing up to do what she loved most, on America's stage, for *America's* royalty. The young actress had every right to be proud of herself for what she was about to achieve that evening; she had worked very hard the last several years to maintain her sanity and keep her professional edge in the wake of the suffering and humiliation brought by Robert Keith, and the rejection by the Theater Guild. But now she was just a few hours away from the biggest night of her life. Such a privilege, and a fine performance, would go a long way in healing her wounds.

Unfortunately, Mrs. Hoover had fallen ill after the luncheon. President Hoover refused to attend the play, choosing instead to stay at his wife's bedside.

It may never be known with certainty if Peg accompanied Gillette to the White House, but one thing is most certain: She endured yet another major disappointment in her life and career. She had spent the day preparing to walk the boards in front of the leader of the free world, only to be told just before curtain time that the president's box would sit vacant.

Peg as Alice Faulkner, the maiden rescued and loved by William Gillette's Sherlock Holmes. Here the great detective (center) protects his damsel from menacing co-star Montague Shaw (author's collection).

Moreover, Hoover had official business to attend and so could not make any of the other performances later that week. Having been scheduled to perform in front of a sitting president is an astounding aspect of Peg's career. But the disappointment of a canceled once-in-a-lifetime event had to have run very deep. Other dignitaries did attend the premiere, including members of President Hoover's Cabinet, Justices of the United States Supreme Court, and the State Department's Diplomatic Corps ... not a bad gallery, to be sure. And not a bad performance, either: "In fact," said John J. Daly at the *Washington Post*, "the supporting cast for Mr. Gillette is excellent, with Miss Peg Entwistle playing the pivotal role of Miss Faulkner, about whose plight all the action centers."[8]

This *Sherlock Holmes* tour had its final performance at Princeton University, in New Jersey, on May 12, 1930. It had been a demanding seven months for Peg, but it had come with rewarding and unforgettable experiences. Moreover, she had been an important part of what even today may be considered one of America's most significant events in its theatrical history.

In December 1931 a second farewell tour will be produced. And while Peg had proven to be a fine enough actress to have remained in Gillette's graces for the entire 1929-30 season, he now wanted a different cast. So a girl named Betty Hanna became his next Alice

Faulkner. It's not likely Peg was disappointed by this, for almost immediately after she kissed Sherlock Holmes for the final time, she was heading north to Maine, to a beautiful lakeside resort about 350 miles off Broadway...

* * *

Located just a few minutes from the banks of Wesserunsett Lake, about six miles away from the town of Skowhegan, Maine, Lakewood Theater was (and still is) a nice little summer getaway for theatrical types. The resort itself — known as The Colony — offered comfortable cottages, dining, horseback riding, golf, tennis, swimming, fishing and wonderful views of the serene lake. But the theater itself was the real center of attraction. Many of Broadway's finest actors, directors, writers, and producers were recruited every summer to participate in the Lakewood Players repertory company. As mentioned earlier, this was where Peg's Broadway hit *Tommy* had its first tryout in August 1926. It was probably no coincidence that Peg was chosen to join the resident cast of the 1930 Lakewood Company by that season's director, *Tommy* playwright Howard Lindsay.

Typically, the Lakewood Players presented 18 different weekly productions during its season from May to September. In 1930, Peg Entwistle acted in eight of their productions.

The rehearsal schedule was a joy for all the actors. "For the players a summer at Lakewood becomes a real vacation," said the *Lewiston Daily Sun*.[9] Rehearsals began early but were always over by noon, and there was no practice at all on Thursdays. Most of Lakewood's plays opened on Monday evenings at 7:30 P.M. with an occasional matinee added for holidays and special occasions. And per Equity rules there were no performances on Sunday, so Peg had lots of free time to mingle and take advantage of all the amenities the resort had to offer.

The season's first production, Leslie Howard's comedy *Elizabeth Sleeps Out*, was absent Peg. She had arrived just days before the May 26 premiere of Howard's play and was busy getting settled into her cottage and new surroundings. She was also getting familiar with the script for her Lakewood stage debut. Notable among the cast of *Elizabeth Sleeps Out* was Peg's longtime family friend Frances Goodrich, wife of Albert Hackett, with whom she will share four Oscar nominations for screenwriting.

On June 2 Max Marcin's melodrama *Silence* premiered. Peg was also absent from this production. But Frances Goodrich received "hardy applause" for her performance.[10] On June 9 the curtain went up on Myron Fagan's comedy *Nancy's Private Affair*. Fagan was not a prolific playwright, but from 1945 until his death in 1972 he was very much a prolific anti–Communist and published many warnings about the so-called Illuminati and its control of world events.

As of this writing, no readable reviews of *Nancy's Private Affair* were found. And while the *Lewiston Evening Journal* mentioned Peg's arrival from New York, and that she would make her first Lakewood appearance in *Nancy's Private Affair*, she is not listed in any of the production's cast notices published in the local papers. Moreover, the current manager (2013) of Lakewood, Jeff Quinn, was gracious enough to provide this author with copies of all the Lakewood Theater playbills featuring Peg, and *Nancy's Private Affair* was not among them. It is possible she had a walk-on or filled in for another actress, but it's more likely that the *Evening Journal* was simply mistaken.

Peg was also not in the cast of the following week's production, *The Witching Hour*, a melodrama inked by Augustus Thomas, whose famous play *The Copperhead* made a star of Lionel Barrymore in 1918.

On June 23 came *Little Accident,* a Broadway comedy hit by Floyd Dell and Thomas Mitchell. While Dell's career is mostly forgettable, Thomas Mitchell prospered as a popular character actor. He is most remembered for his film roles as the father of Scarlett O'Hara in *Gone with the Wind* (1939), the drunken Doc Boone in John Ford's *Stagecoach* (1939), and Uncle Billy in *It's a Wonderful Life* (1946). Mitchell was also the first person to win an Oscar (*Stagecoach*), an Emmy (*The Doctor,* 1953), and a Tony Award (*Hazel Flagg,* 1953).

Little Accident was the story of a man about to be married, who discovers he has fathered a child with another woman. Peg was featured in this production. As with many of the plays at Lakewood that summer, reviews and other notes published in the local papers were damaged by age and are now mostly unreadable. But she did get some good ink in the production's playbill, including a full-page photograph showing her in smart fashion, bedecked in strands of pearls and a sharp-looking cloche; author Eve Golden described her as resembling Iris March in *The Green Hat.* The caption noted Peg was "a piquant young actress" and had played opposite William Gillette.[11] There was also a short article about her, with a corny introduction: "The forbears of Peg Entwistle were weavers of silk ... but in after generations the Entwistle progeny preferred to be weavers of dreams and therefore adopted the stage."[12] The reader is then given a synopsis of highpoints of her career. After some important namedropping we read, "With a foundation, inherent and by training, of the finest quality it is assured Peg Entwistle will go far in the theatre."[13] Well, there was certainly nothing corny about *that.*

Family friend Frances Goodrich was also in *Little Accident* and it must have been a real joy for her and Peg to finally share a stage.

Peg then had a week off the boards during the run of *Just Married,* a farce by Ann Nichols, whose *Abie's Irish Rose* had recently become the longest running Broadway play ever produced up to that time (five straight years). For the week of July 7 Peg portrayed Linda Seton, the female lead in *Holiday,* which was written by Philip Barry. His most notable play, *The Philadelphia Story,* was made into the famous 1940 film starring Katharine Hepburn, Cary Grant, and Jimmy Stewart. The Lakewood production of *Holiday* was an immense success and Peg was given top honors for her performances: "Peg Entwistle ... is always brilliant and ever intelligent. Miss Entwistle revealed the real spark of genius," said the *Lewiston Evening Journal.*[14]

In anticipation of Lakewood's next production *A Butterfly on the Wheel,* in which Peg was cast in the starring role the *Evening Journal* drama critic wrote, "The role of the harassed wife ... the sort that can only be done by a player of exceptional merit. Peg Entwistle is cast for the role of Peggy Admaston and, judged by her work thus far at Lakewood, she will give a memorable interpretation of the role."[15] Additionally, the playbill for *Holiday* had this to say in regard to Peg's forthcoming role in *Butterfly*: "In it Miss Entwistle will be able to show us her art at its best."[16] Indeed, Peg had done just that while portraying the same character her Aunt Jane had played during the Lee and J.J. Shubert tour of 1913. "The outstanding role ... is notably played by Peg Entwistle. The contrasts between the light-hearted butterfly society girl and the woman striving to prove her innocence against false charges were strongly limned and Miss Entwistle drew from the speeches every atom of value."[17]

Lakewood began the week of July 21 with A.A. Milne's comedic detective mystery *The Perfect Alibi.* And while Peg was not cast in this well-received production, she likely celebrated the newfound success of her friends Frances Goodrich and Albert Hackett, who had just sold their play *Let's Get Married* to Lee and J.J. Shubert.

July turned the corner into August at Lakewood with *The Plutocrat,* an Arthur

Goodrich adaptation of the Booth Tarkington novel. The stars of this production were Charles Coburn and his wife Ivah. Charles was a favorite player of stage and screen; his trademark monocle helped distinguish him throughout a career in which he earned an Academy Award for Best Supporting Actor (*The More the Merrier,* 1943) and two other Oscar nominations in the same category (*The Devil and Miss Jones,* 1941; *The Green Years,* 1946). Peg played the role of Olivia Tinker, daughter to Mr. and Mrs. Tinker as portrayed by Mr. and Mrs. Coburn. The play was a smash at Lakewood and given rave reviews, most of which were heaped upon Charles Coburn. According to critics, the highlight of the three-act play came just before the end of the last scene in the second act: Peg's Olivia falls in love with Hardie Albright "at second sight," which prompts Coburn to order a drink for himself: "Scotch for five!"[18] The *Lewiston Evening Journal* says these antics brought repeated curtain calls for the principals.

On August 4 Peg played a flapper in need of saving in the Rachel Crothers comedy *Let Us Be Gay.* It wasn't a big role for her, and the local press hadn't paid her much attention here (neither had the playbill). It was simply stated that she "was always in the picture."[19] The next week came *Escape,* a nine-episode drama by John Galsworthy, the future Nobel Laureate. In Peg's day Galsworthy was famous for writing *The Forsyte Saga. Escape* deals with the interactions between an escaped killer and the people he meets while on the lam. Peg's role was of The Girl of the Town. This almost sounds like a bit part but in fact most of the characters are known by their positions in life; The Policeman, The Maid, The Fellow Convict, etc.

Before the play began, there had been a special historical prologue written and presented by Howard Lindsay. This was in honor of the Tercentenaries of Massachusetts and Maine. Among the notables in the audience that evening was those states' respective governors, Frank G. Allen and William T. Gardiner. The most famous special guest in the crowd was theatrical producer Daniel Frohman, brother of the more famous Charles.

During the week of August 18 Peg played Elaine Bumpstead in *Broken Dishes,* a comedy by Martin Flavin, future winner of a Pulitzer for his novel *Journey in the Dark* (1944). The star of *Broken Dishes* was Donald Meek, a veteran actor in his sixties who had just ended a successful Broadway run of the same play. One of his co-stars during the New York production was a young hopeful who was just beginning to make a little noise ... it had been Bette Davis' second Broadway outing. Notable among the cast of the Lakewood production was Jean Adair, perhaps most remembered today as Cary Grant's Aunt Martha in Frank Capra's classic 1944 romp *Arsenic and Old Lace.*

Because of a special opera program at the Lakewood Theater the following week, Frances Goodrich and Albert Hackett would have only four days to present their comedy *Western Union Please.* It opened on Wednesday evening, August 27. The principals again were Donald Meek and Jean Adair. Nothing is known of Peg's performance. The play was a hit, with Meek and Adair receiving rave notice.

There were four more plays held at Lakewood that summer but Peg wasn't in any of them. It isn't known how long she remained in the colony following her appearance in *Western Union Please,* but it is very likely she stayed for the rest of the summer, enjoying the shows and the company of theatrical personalities.

14

Flops, Flappers, Folly and Fun

*Peg Entwistle will give up even love and marriage
to gain stage fame.* —Boston Daily Globe[1]

In late autumn, Peg visited her family for the holidays in Hollywood. Shortly after the New Year 1931, she returned to Manhattan. Within days she had secured a role in Samuel Shipman's *She Means Business,* a comedy-drama that, according to some reviewers, contained neither drama nor comedy. It's the story of a woman whose husband runs off with a blonde floozy (Peg). The husband has not only left his wife; he has left his once very successful business, the Ladies' Bag Establishment, in a shambles. The wife must fend off the creditors but along the way she's able to save the company and make it more successful than ever before. The husband returns, wanting a piece of the profitable action, but he is foiled and decency prevails.

It was a fine, capable cast; notable among the players was Bob Cummings, who will enjoy a long and successful career in films and television; including his popular NBC sitcom *The Bob Cummings Show* (1955–59). Also notable were Wallis Clark and Kate Byron, with whom Peg had shared the boards in *Sherlock Holmes* and several Lakewood productions. However, the talent in *She Means Business* did little to persuade patrons they had seen a hit. And while Ward Chase of *The Billboard* said Peg's performance helped relive the tedium engendered by the script, he opened his review by firing both barrels: "*She Means Business* is a second-rate piece of work."[2] The *New York Herald Tribune* called it "the best play ever written about the ladies' handbag industry."[3] After just eight Broadway performances, the producers called it a day. Peg packed her own bag and went home.

* * *

Luckily, February is a short month, for Peg found no work until March, when she was engaged by the Theater Guild for a revival of George Bernard Shaw's *Getting Married.* But this is Shaw, and so the story is really not about a young couple betrothed (Peg and Romney Brent); instead, what we really have is a two-hour indictment of the institution by an eclectic bunch with a bunch of eclectic ideas on this notion of getting married.

Philip Moeller directed this revival. Several members of the Guild's A-list were cast, including Margaret Wycherly, a future Oscar nominee most remembered as James Cagney's mother in *White Heat,* and Henry Travers, earlier mentioned as Jimmy Stewart's angel in *It's a Wonderful Life,* and for his work with Peg's aunt and uncle in *The Five Frankfurters.* Also in *Getting Married* was Theater Guild co-founder Helen Westley; Actors' Equity co-founder Reginald Mason; and Dorothy Gish, the younger of the two legendary sisters. The elder, Lillian Gish, was a silent era pioneer, while Dorothy preferred the boards of Broadway. Others in *Getting Married* included Hugh Buckler, Ernest Cossart, Irby Marshall, Ralph Roeder, Hugh Sinclair and Oscar Stirling.

The production went into rehearsal on March 3. Two weeks later it opened in Boston, as part of the Guild's seasonal commitment to its subscribers there. On March 30, some sixteen years after it had last been performed in New York, the curtain at the Guild Theater went up for *Getting Married*. Drama critic Brooks Atkinson described the situation a bit like this: We have a green grocer who is the village sage, and a bishop who thinks reasonably in spite of his vestments, yet horrifies his pompous brother by declaring that marriage cannot be divine until it is sane. There is a mayoress full of infidelity; the spinster who wants children but not at the price of a husband; the divorced lady who wants both her husband and her lover, and, of course, Peg Entwistle and Romney Brent, the young lovers who rebel against the marriage laws even as the guests are all assembled at the church. Peg's bride has just learned that marriage enslaves a woman forever and ever, whereas Brent's bridegroom has discovered that marriage will give him no redress. Such was to be expected in a puppet-filled universe of Bernard Shaw.

Brooks Atkinson liked the play, but thought it was a bit long-winded. Overall, the entire cast was wonderfully thought of, and then Atkinson writes, "Peg Entwistle has impertinence enough to be a Shavian flapper in good standing."[4] That meant he thought she was very good.

The most familiar name (today) in this revival is Dorothy Gish. It isn't known how she and Peg got along, but it has been said that Gish was not the easiest girl to work with. It would be surprising if she and Peg had become friendlier than was professionally required. It's not likely the two ingénues went out on the town together. However, Peg was taken under the wing of Henry Travers, who had fond memories of being on tour with her Aunt Jane and Uncle Charles. On at least one occasion during the production, Travers and Peg had dinner with her uncle at the home of Walter and Mrs. Hampden.

Peg also found a close friend in Romney Brent, the slightly impish Mexican-born son of a diplomat. Just four years older than Peg, he was a quiet, sober bachelor, and a favorite thespian of the Guild's managers and subscribers. He didn't have rugged good looks like most leading men, but he would have been considered "cute" by a girl like Peg (or perhaps "delicious" by Helen Westley, who was often seen with very young men at her side). Peg and Brent dated for a time, but there had been no serious romantic involvement.

Getting Married ran until early May, giving Peg close to three months of work and a few more notable names for her résumé.

Unfortunately, this was the last time she walked the boards of the Guild Theater. It was also her final Guild production of any kind. A high percentage of players with the Theater Guild were given recurrent roles in productions three or four times a year, year in and year out ... but not Peg. For an actress of her talent, range, and experience, this was an anomaly, and can only suggest a lingering resentment in the front office with regard to the Robert Keith debacle during the national tour, and possibly even direct knowledge or suspicion of her abortion.

It's rather probable that Theresa Helburn had a file of news clippings of Peg's divorce, Keith's drunken driving arrests, and even notes of details of cast members' accounts of the screaming, abuse, fear, and violence with which Keith had subjected them all.

It's important to remember that while Peg was Keith's victim, she had also been a central figure in the glaring embarrassment that affronted the Guild's impeccable public persona at the time the organization was trying to win Los Angeles as a subscription satellite. Remember, too, the tour hadn't even begun rehearsals yet and here was Peg, innocent, but Peg nonetheless, who Helburn had in front of her desk, begging for today's equivalent of $12,000 — pleading for a small fortune to get her irresponsible husband out of debtors' prison (after she had already given him the money over the months). In Helburn's mind it was Peg's face she saw time and again in matters troublesome. Also, as stated earlier, word of Peg's abortion may have reached Helburn's ears. If this is true, it would only compound matters. Whatever the case may be, and as circumstantial as the evidence is, there is enough to suggest that Helburn had given Peg a "scarlet letter," and had no desire to cast her in any productions in the foreseeable future.

Well then, it might (and should) be asked, if all this is true, why had the Theater Guild given her a role in *Getting Married*? The short answer is they had no choice. When Peg and her husband signed to go on tour with the Guild Repertory Company back in 1928, they

George Bernard Shaw's *Getting Married* was Peg's final production with the New York Theater Guild. Right to left: Romney Brent, Peg, Reginald Mason, Henry Travers, Dorothy Gish, Hugh Buckler (standing), Irby Marshall, Margaret Wycherly, Helen Westley and Hugh Sinclair. In the Guild's official article announcing this play, Peg's name was the only one omitted. Why? (photograph by Vandamm Studio, © Billy Rose Theater Division, The New York Public Library for the Performing Arts).

also agreed to perform in one other production in New York City for the Guild Acting Company. Every actor and actress in the Guild had to agree to this—it was one of the house rules. If you were signed to do a play in New York, you also had to agree to do a play in one of the subscription cities, such as Boston or Chicago. If you were engaged to a tour, whether or not it covered a subscription city, you had an obligation to also appear in a Guild production in New York City. (Because Robert Keith had been fired, his contract was null and void.)

It wasn't that the Theater Guild *wanted* Peg in Shaw's revival as much as they were *compelled* by their own rules to offer her a part before the clause expired (two years beginning the day following a final performance of the first engagement). Peg's clause was near the end of the two years and *Getting Married* was the last production within the time limit.

The Guild could have chosen to let the clause expire without hiring Peg, but then there would have been an arbitration hearing with Actors' Equity. She would have easily won a settlement, and the Guild would have been forced to answer some embarrassing questions.

While it doesn't seem that the Guild *actually* told Peg she would no longer perform for them following *Getting Married,* the poor girl had to have seen the writing on the wall at some point during or soon after the production.

There's no question Peg was deeply hurt when she realized she wasn't really, *truly* welcome by the single most important theater group to which she had always aspired. It is through such events and circumstances that one later gains a better understanding into her mysterious, tragic last words.

* * *

Peg didn't have to dwell on the turned backs of the Guild managers for long. Several days after *Getting Married* had its last curtain call, she was invited to join the Lakewood Players for the 1931 summer season. As with the 1930 season, Lakewood Theater would present 18 productions by notable playwrights and feature a good number of Broadway stars, including Humphrey Bogart and his wife Mary Phillips. Peg was slated to appear in the first seven productions beginning with George M. Cohan's comedy *Whispering Friends.* When she arrived at Maine's theatrical colony, she had a family member in tow, which the *Lakewood Theatre Magazine* announced thus: "If you see a youthful blonde girl dashing around Lakewood at top speed followed by a small black and white dog you may be sure it is Peg Entwistle, accompanied by Robin. Robin Entwistle is almost as well known at Lakewood as its owner who returns for her second summer to the Lakewood Players."[5]

The above write-up is rather interesting if looked at closely, for it seems to show Peg as a perky, energy-filled dynamo of activity. It wasn't likely that she had gotten over the Guild's rejection, but she was certainly not acting or looking like a reject.

Upon her arrival, Peg settled into a large cottage with actresses Sylvia Field and Gladys Hurlbut. Field was a very popular stage actress and today is most remembered as Mrs. Wilson in the television comedy *Dennis the Menace* (1959–63). Like Peg, she was an avid horse rider and every day she and Peg could be seen on the equestrian trails, dressed in togs, atop their mounts, with Robin giving playful chase. Local newspapers also mentioned Peg riding daily with other players in the Lakewood colony, including family friends Frances Goodrich and Albert Hackett.

As mentioned above, the Lakewood season opened with the Cohan comedy *Whispering Friends.* As with all the first-night openings at Lakewood, there was plenty of pomp. Unable to attend due to some unnamed but pressing matter, Governor Gardiner of Massachusetts sent a telegram of congratulations. Many other telegrams from famous producers, directors, writers, actors and others were also read aloud to the audience during the warm-up. Among the senders of good wishes were famed playwright Owen Davis (his son, Owen Davis, Jr., had a role in the play), Howard Lindsay, George M. Cohan, actors Jack Oakie and Skeets Gallagher, and legendary theatrical and industrial designer Norman Bel Geddes. Dr. E.B. Merrill, the speaker of the House of Representatives, was in the audience along with other notables of politics, commerce, stage and film.

In *Whispering Friends* Peg played the female lead, a wealthy young bride of two months whose friends begin to wonder if the groom's intentions were purely out of love. For her performance as Emily Sanford, Peg received kindness from the critic: "[She] is very charming, with personality and good to look at ... Miss Entwistle won many admirers [here] last season."[6] The play went over smashingly with the audience and a curtain call between the first and second acts was answered by the entire cast. There was, however, a somewhat ironic twist to the production: The role of Joe Sanford, groom to Peg's bride, was played by leading man William Harrigan a close friend of Peg's ex-husband Robert Keith. Together they had originated the principal roles in Eugene O'Neill's Broadway hit *The Great God Brown*. While it is true that Peg had — and will — play opposite other actor-friends of Keith, this was the first time since her divorce that she had acted with someone who was so close to him. One can only guess how Peg had truly felt inside playing the role of suspicious wife in a questionable marriage opposite one of her real-life's ex-husband's closest friends. There is nothing to suggest that Peg and Harrigan had not gotten along swimmingly behind the curtain, but it is interesting to ponder any private conversations they may have had regarding Keith.

Following that Saturday's performance of *Whispering Friends,* Peg and about half a dozen of the Lakewood Players headed to the Westchester Country Club in Rye, New York, about 380 miles away. The occasion was a charity event to raise money for the Actors' Fund Matinee Club, which helped unemployed theatrical types in need. The special program was headed by famed tennis champion Bill Tilden, who also happened to be a member of Actors' Equity. During short matches between pro tennis players and celebrities, Peg and the others in the Lakewood crew sold programs or raffled off autographed racquets and balls. A number of other notable actresses had also been recruited, including Laurette Taylor, Selena Royle, and Shirley Booth. Later that evening a testimonial dinner was held in Tilden's honor. One of the special guests and celebrity players was Walter Hampden; he was likely the prime reason Peg made the exhausting 760-mile round trip within a 36-hour time frame.

On June 8, Peg opened in George Kelly's dramatic magnum opus. *Craig's Wife.* Kelly, who was the uncle of the actress (and princess of Monaco) Grace Kelly, had won the Pulitzer Prize for Drama with *Craig's Wife* five years earlier. Peg had a supporting role in this play and was only given passing mention in reviews. The night before the curtain went up, the Lakewood Players were honored at a party held at the summer home of actor Arthur Byron and his wife. This was an annual event. One of the high-profile guests there was silent film star Marie Walcamp, still five years away from her suicide at just 42.

The week that *Craig's Wife* had its Lakewood run, the playbills ran a contest called "Can You Guess These?"[7] It was a list of Lakewood Theater–related trivia questions. First, second, and third prize winner received pairs of orchestra seats for the next production. (Is it unfair that the runners-up got the same award as the champion?) Question number three asked for the title of the play in which Peg made her Lakewood debut the previous summer. (If you guessed *Little Accident*, you win!)

On June 14 Donald Ogden Stewart's comedy *Rebound* was presented. Stewart was a member of the famed "Algonquin Roundtable" and his friends included Dorothy Parker, Robert Benchley, George S. Kaufman, and Ernest Hemingway. Stewart is today most famous for *The Philadelphia Story* (1940), which earned him an Oscar for his screenplay. Peg had a supporting role while her roommates Gladys Hurlbut and Sylvia Field shared center stage. No readable reviews were found, but the *Lewiston Daily Sun* made passing mentions of the play's record attendance despite several days of rainy weather.

The following week Peg was featured as Helen Trent in Bayard Veiller's *The Thirteenth Chair,* a murder mystery in which a man stages a séance to trap the killer of his friend. Peg was to again share the stage with her *Getting Married* co-star Margaret Wycherly, who had the principal role of spiritualist, Rosalie La Grange. Wycherly had enjoyed great Broadway success in this role when she originated it in the 1916–17 production. She had also played the spiritualist in the 1929 Tod Browning film. (Wycherly and Veiller were married from 1901 until 1922 and their son Anthony was twice nominated for screenwriting Oscars, for 1937's *Stage Door* and 1946's *The Killers*. Wycherly arrival at Lakewood was much heralded, for she was considered by many to be an actress of high esteem. Peg must have been thrilled to see her name mentioned in the announcement: "At Lakewood, Miss Wycherly met two former friends in Peg Entwistle and Gladys Hurlbut with whom she had been associated in New York productions."[8] Again, as with a number of the Lakewood plays, newspaper reviews of the performances were too badly deteriorated to discern. However, Peg's mutual respect with Wycherly was validated after the final curtain of *The Thirteenth Chair*: "Miss Peg Entwistle entertained at a super party for Miss Margaret Wycherly, following the final performance...."[9]

Next up on the Lakewood stage was *Love 'Em and Leave 'Em,* a comedy by John Weaver and George Abbott. Reviews of this play were not found, but the *Lewiston Daily Sun* did publish an article about the cast. It focused on their film credits and, surprisingly, included this mention: "Peg Entwistle and Gladys Hurlbut both have been seen on the screen."[10] An exhaustive search of film archive databases by the author could not find Peg in any films prior to her work at RKO in 1932. Several variations of her name were tried, but to no avail. If Peg had done any film work before, it was very minor — probably uncredited bit parts such as Girl at Table.

Two days after Independence Day, one of the most anticipated productions of the summer opened: Owen Davis' *Just to Remind You,* a cornball patriotic sermon preaching against the evils of New York City gangsters and racketeering. Davis was one of the most famous playwrights of the time and had an impressive résumé of nearly 320 plays. He was the first to bring F. Scott Fitzgerald's novel *The Great Gatsby* to Broadway, and had won the 1923 Pulitzer Prize for Drama with *Icebound*. His arrival to see the premiere of *Just to Remind You* (and the performance in it of his son Owen Jr.) brought added prestige to everyone involved with the production. Notable in the cast was Humphrey Bogart, who played Peg's love interest. Bogart's real-life wife Mary Phillips had the female lead.

Bogart's iconic status notwithstanding, the most interesting member of the cast was Paul Kelly, who was still on parole after serving two years in San Quentin Prison for the beating death of Ray Raymond, one of Florenz Ziegfeld's song-and-dance men. Kelly, who first became famous at Brooklyn's Vitagraph Studios as a child actor in silent pictures long before anyone heard of Jackie Coogan, was a fine stage actor, a rugged, handsome leading man long on muscle and short of temper. The synopsis of his crime reads like a yarn out of *Police Gazette*...

Ray Raymond was married to Dorothy Mackaye, a vivacious Hollywood actress. She and Kelly began a love affair. Raymond made his suspicions known around Hollywood, and as everyone knows, lusty news travel fast in Tinsel Town. This displeased Kelly and so, on April 16, 1927 (the exact day Robert Keith told Peg he loved her), as Miss Mackaye lounged in Kelly's Hollywood apartment, Kelly went to her home and challenged her husband to fight.

According to the testimony of Mackaye's maid, Kelly immediately began punching him. Despite Raymond's pleas that he was 50 pounds lighter, intoxicated, and in no shape to fight, Kelly continued pummeling the physically inferior man even as the maid begged him to stop the assault. After a final crushing blow, Kelly left. Raymond retired to his bedroom, bruised and bleeding. The next morning he was found on the floor, unconscious. Mackaye claimed she could not find a doctor for several hours and also tried to persuade the police that her husband died of natural causes. The coroner said a brain hemorrhage killed him. The cops pinched Kelly for murder and Mackaye for being an accessory after the fact.

The trial was sensational, of course, and the defense was able to convince the jury that Raymond's alcoholism played the larger part in his death. Kelly was convicted of manslaughter and sentenced to serve one to ten years but was paroled for good behavior after serving just 25 months. For her part, Mackaye served ten months.

In early 1931 the lovebird felons were married. The bride retired from acting to become a housewife while the groom continued working in films and on stage (he will win a 1948 Tony Award for *Command Decision*). The couple was well on their way to "happily ever after" when Dorothy succumbed to injuries resulting from a 1940 car accident. She was 38.

But in *Just to Remind You*, it was Paul Kelly who died. The play is about a fellow who opens a laundry business with his wife. Local gangsters demand protection money; the fellow refuses to pay. To remind him of what can happen without the gangsters' protection, his delivery truck gets smashed; the customers' clothes are ruined with acid; a bomb is tossed into his store, and in the end the fellow is shot dead — in the back — on the Fourth of July, as a crooked judge reads the Gettysburg Address to revelers in front of a flag pole and a band plays the National Anthem. It must have looked and sounded as ridiculous as it is to describe, but in Lakewood it was well received.

This will not be the case when Peg and Kelly arrive with it on Broadway...

Sometime during this production, the entire company of the Lakewood Players was assembled for a group photo on the front porch of the theater. Peg sits on the front step, smiling brightly and looking very pretty next to Sylvia Field. Charles Coburn stands in back; Bogart and Mary Phillips in the middle row. Paul Kelly is in front of Coburn, wearing a tight-fitting shirt and looking like he could take anyone there ... even Bogie.

On July 13, 1931, Peg opened in Lakewood for what is believed to have been her last production there: *So This Is London*, a comedy by Arthur Goodrich that had great success when George M. Cohan produced it on Broadway. Other than a few passing mentions about the play and the cast in the local newspapers, not much is known about the Lakewood presentation. This was the second play in which Peg had appeared with the headlining husband-and-wife team of Charles and Mrs. Coburn. It isn't known how exactly Peg came to get signed by Owen Davis for his New York production of his *Just to Remind You*, but shortly after the final curtain dropped on *So This Is London*, Peg took her leave of Lakewood's season to get ready for a pre–Broadway tryout of the play in Asbury Park, New Jersey. Also tagging along were her roommates Field and Hurlbut, the playwright's son, and several others, including Paul Kelly. After having such great success in Lakewood and Asbury, it was likely that Davis and his cast and crew of *Just to Remind You* expected a rousing welcome to compliment the play's over-the-top patriotic feel-good finale. But New York was not very fond of the story and it closed after 12 days. It was panned awfully and the nicest things to be found in the *New York Times* review was "Sylvia Field and Peg Entwistle contribute their personal charm to the hand-me-down parts they are taking."[11]

In 1931, machine-gunning, bomb-tossing, pay-up-or-else hoodlums ruled plenty of territory in cities like New York and Al Capone's Chicago, but citizens (and theater patrons) wanted real-life justice, not "message" plays that painted judges as corrupt and cops as helpless.

When *Time* magazine wanted an explanation for this hack melodrama, Davis said that he had never written a play for any reason other than he thought it would make a good show. But indignation got the better of him: "I burned with it ... I wanted to say what I could say, in my way, against organized crime. I honestly believe that the theater can arouse public opinion. I honestly believe that the theater can stir popular indignation. That's what I tried to do."[12] Whoever said "you can't blame a guy for trying," hadn't seen *Just to Remind You*.

In the Owen Davis gangster drama *Just to Remind You,* Peg co-starred with handsome leading man Paul Kelly, who was still on parole for killing Ziegfeld song and dance man Ray Raymond. Kelly later married his victim's widow and went on to a busy stage and film career (courtesy Tom Gregory).

* * *

Peg was out of work for about two months when she got a part in a revival of Marian de Forest's dramatization of Louisa Alcott's novel *Little Women*. But it was really just a part-time engagement, scheduled for morning and afternoon matinees four days a week through December and into the New Year. The producer, William A. Brady, tailored the production to appeal to children and presented it every year during the holiday season.

Early in his *New York Times* review of *Little Women,* Brooks Atkinson writes, "Happily, a quartet of excellent actresses has been assembled for this staging."[13] The four: Peg, as the artistically inclined Amy; Lee Patrick as Meg, the first of the little women to learn the facts of life; and in interpreting Jo and the dying Beth, Jessie Royce Landis and Joanna Roos left nary a dry eye in the Playhouse Theater. (Atkinson noted there was more sniffling and eye-dabbing owed to these women than could be found in a whole season's attendance at the modern plays.)

Brady (whose son, William Brady, Jr., was the stage manager) told the *New York Times* he carefully chose the four actresses. Though hardly stellar, Peg's co-leads compiled interesting résumés: Lee Patrick is most remembered as Effie, the secretary to Bogart's Sam Spade in the 1941 classic *The Maltese Falcon*. She revamped the role in the 1975 parody *The*

Black Bird, starring George Segal. In her 1954 autobiography *You Won't Be So Pretty,* Jessie Royce Landis said she concluded early on that she was not the ingénue type, so she became a character actress. In Hitchcock's 1959 thriller *North by Northwest,* Landis played Cary Grant's mother even though she was just eight years his senior. Joanna Roos was a Brooklyn-born tough who became a favorite Shakespearean at many festivals. She also co-founded the prestigious New Dramatists Committee and is probably best remembered for her portrayals in soap operas during the 1960s and '70s, such as *The Edge of Night, As the World Turns,* and *Love of Life.*

As he did every year for this revival, William A. Brady invited 500 children from hospitals and orphanages to attend the opening matinee. It was always a festive occasion, with Brady providing plenty of post-curtain eats and treats for his very special guests.

* * *

As she looked out over the footlights and absorbed the energy children are known to create, and as she later mingled with them and shared eggnog, Christmas cookies, and hugs, Peg Entwistle had likely remembered that 1925 Christmastime in Boston, when she was Snow White, when throngs of squealing, delighted youngsters converged on her. She wasn't the star this time, but Peg loved her role in Brady's revival and embraced it with a fresh nuance. One reviewer of her next Broadway show will mention *Little Women* and note how she had given her portrayal of Amy a unique, amusing personality not directed by the script. No one complained.

Perhaps it was the long, thick, corkscrewing pigtails of her fun stage hairdo that caused Peg to interpret the role in a distinctive light. Or maybe it was hope in the eyes of the orphans that influenced her — she certainly identified with them. Or was it the unfolding of the holiday season that gave her inspiration, with its cleanness of fresh snow and festive window displays mingled with the din of traditional hymns from within Gotham's historic churches? Maybe it was all of these things, maybe just some, or maybe none at all. It may have just boiled down to the simple fact that the young woman *loved* acting.

During the *Little Women* run, William Brady allowed the cast to seek work in other productions. On New Year's Eve the *New York Times* announced that Peg was replacing Claudia Morgan (niece of character actor Frank Morgan) in a mystery play called *Son of Satan.* No reason could be found as to why Miss Morgan had bowed out of the production, but the play was scheduled to open on January 11 at the Ambassador Theater.

The last performance of the *Little Women* revival took place on the morning of January 2, 1932. Peg began rehearsals with the *Son of Satan* cast two days later. On January 9 the *Times* announced that the playwrights, Ernest and Louise Cortis, had postponed the opening, and that it would be "presented at a Broadway house, to be selected later, on January 18."[14] The next day the *Times* said the play would open at the Ambassador, but this never happened. Two days later came word that the production had been called off altogether. No reason was given, but it might be guessed that the husband-and-wife playwright-producer team of Ernest and Louise Cortis were, frankly, out of their element. They were vaudevillians by trade, not created for legitimate stage. Their résumé speaks for itself: They have only one Broadway opening to their credit, a 1927 venture called *One for All,* and it had gone dark after just three performances and perhaps the most devastating review ever published by Brooks Atkinson.

William Brady had been impressed with Peg's work in *Little Women.* When she called and related her Cortis-related woes to him, he was sympathetic and promised to get her something in one of his next projects. He had several high-profile names and productions in mind and asked her not to audition for anyone else ... *especially* vaudevillians. He suggested she stay close to a phone.

Brady was not a show-off who dropped names and made promises that never materialized; he was one of the most influential producers in America, and he made things happen. Peg knew this, too. She stayed close to her phone — and far away from Vaudeville.

The man kept his word and a few weeks later Peg was gearing up for the second most talked-about revival of Broadway's golden era (the *Sherlock Holmes* farewell being the first most talked about). She was going to play opposite the only actress in the country, perhaps the world, who could outsell (and outshine) the likes of Billie Burke, Ethel Barrymore, Maude Adams, and yes, even Mr. Brady's own A-list daughter, Alice.

When Millicent Lilian sat in the Cort Theater on Broadway during a Valentine's Day performance in 1921, she decided to give herself a new first name. Young "Peg" Entwistle knew it was fine and dandy to use the name, even though she could never, *ever* actually play the lead in *Peg O' My Heart*, for there was only one actress worthy of that role ... the original Broadway Peg, the one and only Laurette Taylor.

ACT III

Though Death fling wide gold gates to magic lands,
Beyond that silver, meager, mystic moon,
We pray you, do not take away your hands
From earthly gestures, nor refuse the boon
Of your sweet, tragic presence on our stage.
We pray you, do not climb too high, too far,
Those wistful stairs to Death,
Nor Turn the page of storied Life too soon.
Death cannot mar nor mold your body to a thing forgot.
We know this well, but tremble for your soul,
Lost in a distant world where fame is not.
Madame, give pause before you pay the toll
Of wealth and glamour to a new strange god,
And set too sure a foot on unguessed sod.
   — Anne Caparn to Peg[1]

15

Give My Regards to Broadway

There was a radiance about her art which I can compare only to the greatest lines of poetry... — Tennessee Williams, of Laurette Taylor[1]

Broadway enchantress Laurette Taylor had been in relative seclusion since the 1928 death of her playwright husband John Hartley Manners, and hadn't graced the stage in nearly four years. But in January 1932, William A. Brady persuaded her to speak before the Ways and Means Committee in Washington, D. C. Brady and other prominent theater people had gathered in the nation's capital to protest added federal taxes on theater tickets. In her 1954 biography *Laurette*, Marguerite Courtney describes how her famous mother so enamored the Committee that U.S. Senator Carter Glass told the beautiful actress the theater would be tax-free forever if there were more speakers like her.

With eyes once again bright, and a spirit filled with exuberance and renewed confidence from delighting her first audience in years, Laurette Taylor and William Brady made immediate plans for her return to the stage.

Taylor was one of the Broadway Queens, but there were personal demons in her court. They loved to perform almost as much as she did, often manifesting themselves at the most inopportune time in the role of chronic alcoholism. Brady knew all about this, so in order to somewhat protect his investment and recoup some of his losses should the actress become "ill," he had her agree to a moral conduct bond that held $5,000 of her salary advance in a trust.

Though her malady often caused headshakes and disappointment, Taylor's reputation as a brilliant actress and a pleasant soul preceded her everywhere. So admired was she that when the press announce a Laurette Taylor engagement, many fans did not ask *which* play she was to perform; they only cared that *she was to perform.*

And it was no wonder, for the woman was mesmerizing — almost hypnotic. Her big, expressive eyes were brightly alive one moment and deeply haunting the next.

As detailed earlier, Taylor's trademark play was *Peg O' My Heart;* after that, she is best known for originating the role of Amanda Wingfield in Tennessee Williams's 1946 drama *The Glass Menagerie.* This play ran 563 times during a two-year Broadway run while five subsequent revivals over a forty-year period featuring stage luminaries Maureen Stapleton, Jessica Tandy, and Julie Harris totaled just 521 performances.

Peg's role opposite Taylor was every bit as spectacular in scope as her time with William Gillette — perhaps more so, for Gillette had been in his sunset, but Queen Laurette was awakening to the potential of a bright new day.

* * *

The production chosen by Brady for megastar Taylor and ingénue Entwistle came from the pen of J.M. Barrie, creator of *Peter Pan*. *A Night of Barrie*, or The Barrie Revivals as it was also called, was a double-feature consisting of *Alice Sit-by-the-Fire* and *The Old Lady Shows Her Medals*. Peg was cast only in *Alice Sit-by-the-Fire*, the front piece (presented before *The Old Lady Shows Her Medals*). Unlike traditional "curtain-raisers," *Alice* actually held more prominence than the play which followed. In fact, once upon a time, Barrie considered it more valuable than *Peter Pan*. He had given it to Charles Frohman as insurance against the failure of *Peter Pan* (then titled *The Great White Father*). Barrie, who apparently doubted *The Great White Father* would bring success, reportedly handed Frohman both scripts and offered *Alice Sit-by-the-Fire* as compensation against any loss his fairy play might bring.

Peg's role in *Alice Sit-by-the-Fire* was that of Amy, the daughter to Taylor's Alice. Alice has just returned from a long sojourn in India. Amy is displeased her mother has been gone so long and resists Alice's re-acquaintance. Amy also suspects her of having a lover, but there is no lover. Alice hatches a plan to win back her daughter's affection by pretending the imaginary lover has dishonored her. She slyly leads Amy into thinking she has put herself in her hands. In feeling needed by her mother, Amy's love for Alice is renewed.

The Barrie Revivals began on March 3, 1932, with a three-day tryout in New Haven, Connecticut. Notices were terrific. A few days later, Taylor's much-anticipated return to Broadway was met by a packed, standing-room-only Playhouse Theater. This was exactly three months after Peg had opened there as Amy in *Little Women,* and four years to the day since Taylor had last taken a curtain call.

Reviewers not only loved Taylor in the Barrie Revivals, they seemed insane with giddiness. Of particular note was the normally reserved *New York Times* theater critic, Brooks Atkinson. At first he held to his usual temperament and simply noted that Peg performed with a "green and willowy manner."[2] (He liked her.) However, when it came to his feelings about Taylor, Atkinson bursts into near cardiac arrest: "Please God, may she never be absent again! ... superb actress ... a wondrous thing ... an actress of inspiration ... she irradiates every scene!"[3]

(Atkinson probably had to inhale at this point.)

"...Her undulating motion, the receptive tremor of her listening, her liquid speech, her limpid gestures, her awareness of the whole comedy, and, best of all, her tender, beaming smile bathe *Alice Sit-by-the-Fire* in genius!"[4]

There was more of the same from the hyperventilating drama critic, and then after he scolds other critics for often using "magnificent" recklessly, Atkinson ends his review with that very same word. Yet there is little doubt, Laurette Taylor truly had been magnificent.

In 1905, James Barrie and Charles Frohman first presented the play to audiences in London. It wasn't well received. One critic said it had a ludicrously stupid plot. It was a complete disappointment from the start despite England's beloved Ellen Terry as Alice. Then in 1905 Frohman opened the play in New York, where Ethel Barrymore fared no better. The *New York Tribune* said then, "As a whole it is formless, spineless, indirect, incoherent, exceedingly pretentious ... a whirling mass of vacuous prattle ... often insipid, never strong ... no character, no action, no dramatic effect ... flimsy...."[5]

Taylor was able to do what the most winsome actresses of England and America before her could not: turn Barrie's sow's ear into a silk purse. Twenty-seven years later, the same *Tribune* that so caustically panned Ethel Barrymore's *Alice* called Taylor's "A triumph of a magnificent actress!"[6]

Peg Entwistle was always mentioned, too, of course, albeit in a more subdued light and generally in line with John Hutchens at *Theatre Arts Monthly,* who said that she had struck a clear note amid the surrounding whimsy.

From the start it seemed this Taylor-Entwistle pairing was destined to extend well beyond the scheduled run. Not since Peg starred in *Tommy* had things looked so favorable for her. True, she had received a lot of notice during her time with the Guild Repertory Company, and with Gillette in *Sherlock Holmes*; however, those were tours. What Peg really desired now was a Broadway run, a real, honest-to-goodness *run.*

With the triumphant return of bigger-than-life Taylor being so well received, Peg was within reach of the brass ring ... a Broadway engagement lasting a solid year or more. Taylor's contract with Brady was a long-term agreement involving the Barrie Revivals and at least one other unnamed production. If the revivals continued as they had begun (and it certainly looked as if they would), the team of Taylor and Entwistle might remain in New York until 1933, and then maybe go on tour, perhaps even to England.

Peg was very excited and hopeful because she knew that Brady had the juice to make it happen. Unfortunately, Taylor had too much of the wrong kind of juice...

* * *

"Please God, may she never be absent again!" went the prayerful printed clarion of Brooks Atkinson's review.[7] God and prayer notwithstanding, Taylor went absent a week after the premiere.

Peg played peacemaker between stage legend Laurette Taylor (left) and Charles Dalton in a 1932 revival of James M. Barrie's *Alice Sit-by-the-Fire.* It was the last Broadway production of Peg's life (author's collection).

On March 14, 1932, Brady canceled that evening's performance just minutes before the scheduled curtain rise. Nine hundred broken-hearted fans were given refunds. Brady refused to answer questions about the cancellation, referring all inquiries to Frank Gilmore, president of Actors' Equity. Gilmore also refused to discuss the matter and referred reporters back to Brady, saying, "It is Mr. Brady's enterprise, therefore it is up to him to make a statement."[8] Attempts to reach Taylor were intercepted by her physician Ed Devol, who simply said she was ill. Theatergoers were mystified, but theatrical insiders were not.

Taylor was a "periodic"— an alcoholic who will completely abstain from liquor for a time and then suddenly go on a binge lasting days or weeks. Some experts attribute the underlying cause of such drinking in creative people as a fear of failure coupled with feeling undeserving of success.

The Barrie Revivals were scheduled for a show every Tuesday and Wednesday evening, and an afternoon matinee every Wednesday and Saturday. Several days after the cancelled performance, Brady released an odd statement announcing a sudden change in the play's schedule. He pulled all the evening shows and replaced them with Monday and Friday matinees. It really is quite obvious that such an unusual move was simply an effort to allow Taylor her nights for drinking with the hope that she would be sober for the afternoon shows.

While this new schedule favored the star, Peg and the rest of the cast were in danger of taking a significant hit to their cash bonuses. Tickets to evening performances generally cost one to three dollars more than a matinee. Multiply the value of a 1932 dollar by 900 seats twice a week for the scheduled eleven-week run, and the drop in Peg's share of the box-office isn't unnoticeable, especially during the Great Depression.

It seems Brady didn't really like the thought of this, either, so the evening performances were quickly resumed. Peg's sighs of relief were short-lived, however, for Taylor's dysfunction had not yet reached its zenith ... nor was it limited to the stage.

A few days later the Catholic Actors' Guild invited Taylor to speak on their radio show at WOR. First she arrived to the station fifteen minutes past her time slot, and then when she got on the air she began reading poems that hadn't been cleared with management, a legal violation of recital rules of the American Society of Authors, Composers and Publishers.

Ignoring the producer's hand signals to stop her recitation, Taylor continued reading a poem by Edna St. Vincent Millay. Someone actually had to pull the plug on her microphone. When this event took place, the Barrie Revivals still had nearly two months remaining on the contract. But the next day Taylor again missed work. The packed Tuesday-night house was offered a choice of a full refund, tickets to a future show, or admittance to *Child of Manhattan*, a Preston Sturges play which was showing at the Cort Theater across the street.

As with the first cancellation, Brady again referred questions to Gilmore at Actors' Equity. Gilmore again told the press it was up to Brady to make a statement, and the good Dr. Devol again would only say that Taylor was ill and unable to comment.

The following afternoon, April 6, Taylor showed up for the Wednesday matinee. The director told her it had been canceled, but couldn't (or wouldn't) say why. Unable to locate Brady, she went home in a huff, fully intending to return for that evening's performance. A few hours later she got a call from a reporter asking what she thought of Brady's announcement, the dumbfounded actress demanded to know what he was talking about. He read her a press release: "Laurette Taylor's engagement in the Barrie Revivals at the

Playhouse will not be resumed. Miss Taylor's inability to appear resulted in the cancellation...."[9]

The stunned superstar ended the call without comment.

Peg Entwistle never took another Broadway bow.

Twenty-two years after Peg's death, Laurette Taylor's daughter will recall watching her 62-year-old bedridden mother cry out in agony as she made a painful, dramatic entrance into the next world just moments after taking a drink.

16

Mad Hope

By the time you get your name up in lights you have worked so hard and so long, and seen so many names go up and down, that all you can think of is: "How can I keep it there?"— Billie Burke[1]

In late March of 1932, as problems were mounting with the Barrie Revivals, Romney Brent was three blocks away at the Morosco Theater, starring in the title role of *The Warrior's Husband* (pre-famous Katharine Hepburn was also in the cast). As busy as Brent was with this production, he managed to pitch a play he'd written. In 1931, *No Money to Guide Her* had been tested in summer stock in South Hampton, Long Island. Brent then renamed it *The Mad Hopes*. His script drew attention on both coasts and with the help of New York producer Bela Blau, he cut a deal for a pre–Broadway West Coast tryout with the Los Angeles theatrical partnership of Edward Belasco and Homer Curran. Blau and Edgar MacGregor would direct.

Joseph Urban, the famous architect and scenic designer, added prestige to the mix when he agreed to create the stage settings. Urban, whose architectural masterpieces include the Ziegfeld Theater and Metropolitan Opera House, was legendary for his exact-to-scale, highly detailed miniature replicas of the stages on which his set pieces would be assembled. (Even tiny paintings would hang on the wee walls.) *The Mad Hopes* would be among his last stage designs before his death in 1933 and the first and only he would ever do for a West Coast theatrical production.

Still more prestige will come from the work of a man named Adrian Adolph Greenberg, but his credit on *The Mad Hopes* playbills will read, "Gowns by Adrian." This was the trademark of the world-renowned fashion designer who today is probably most remembered for creating the costumes (and ruby slippers) for MGM's 1939 classic *The Wizard of Oz*.

A few days after Brent and Blau sealed the deals with Belasco, Curran, Urban, and Adrian, they engaged stage icon Billie Burke for the starring role. A week after that, Humphrey Bogart was signed to play the male lead.

The Mad Hopes was a comedy centered on two frenzied weeks in the lives of Clytie Hope and her trio of grown children. The Hopes own a lovely villa on the Riviera but are in desperate financial straits because of the fiscally irresponsible Clytie. (She does things like buy gems on credit when she still owes the grocer for the only food in the house — bread and cheese.) A wealthy, good-hearted American (Bogart) becomes aware of the family's dilemma and offers to buy the villa at a very good price. Although Clytie knows the sale would solve her financial woes, she pretends not to need the American's money or his friendship.

Burke was a perfect fit for the role; the *Los Angeles Herald-Express* described Clytie Hope as a flighty woman whose vagaries keep everyone around her in an amusing state of turmoil. Billie had come to master this type of character during her previous 25 years on stage. To get a feel for how Clytie behaved (and sounded), the reader is encouraged to absorb Billie's magnificent performance as Millicent Jordan, the high-strung hostess in the 1933 film *Dinner at Eight* (which also stars Jean Harlow, John Barrymore, Lionel Barrymore, Marie Dressler and Wallace Beery).

Burke's birth name is almost as amusing as her character interpretations: Mary William Ethelbert Appleton Burke was given the "William" (Billie) portion of her moniker by her father, a singing clown named Billy Burke. Since 1914, Miss Billie Burke was also known as Mrs. Florenz Ziegfeld, because of her marriage to the legendary *Follies* showman. She was one of the most famous stage actresses in the world and her association with *The Mad Hopes* gave Brent and others involved in the production a substantial boost to their résumés.

Bogart was a suitable pick for Henry Frost, the American savior who brings sanity to Clytie's life, and love to her beautiful daughter Geneva. Bogart had made a few films and was fairly well known in Hollywood, and although he would soon get a lot more notice at Warner Brothers in 1932's *Three on a Match* (with Peg Entwistle fan Bette Davis), he was still four years away from his Duke Mantee–launched super stardom in *The Petrified Forest* (also with Davis). Bogart was also in the Theater Guild and had worked rather steadily on stage since before 1922.

Several weeks before the targeted premiere, all but one of the three principal roles had been cast. Who would play Clytie's daughter, Geneva? Belasco, Curran, and director MacGregor wanted a uniquely talented actress—an experienced performer charming enough to complement Billie and lovely enough to make a believable romantic interest for Bogart. Moreover, they needed a girl they could trust, one who wasn't so star-struck that she would freeze like a deer in headlights when caught in Billie Burke's glow. And just as important, they needed an actress who would not try to upstage the star or outshine the footlights.

Auditions were held on April 14. (At this time the play's title had temporarily been changed to *The Merry Mrs. Hope*.) By ten o'clock that morning, over a hundred actors and actresses had filled the main lobby and upstairs reception hall of the Belasco Theater. But after several days the role of the ingénue had still not been filled. Edgar MacGregor was beside himself and wondered how it was possible that of all the girls who had auditioned, not a one was right for the part. But then the producers remembered the New York Theater Guild's 1929 visit to Los Angeles ... and as producers they of course knew all about the recent trouble with Laurette Taylor and the Barrie Revivals. Edward Belasco contacted Brent, who was still in New York, and asked him if Peg was available. A short time later, Brent called back: Peg had no theatrical obligations until early June, when she was slated to join the Lakewood Players for her third summer season in Skowhegan, Maine. The smiling producer opened his checkbook.

The next day she was on a train with actor Rex O'Malley. O'Malley, a friend of Brent's, was between jobs when the call for Peg came. Brent, out of a chivalrous heart and concern for her traveling alone across the continent, managed to convince Belasco that for her safety the attractive young woman must have a male escort. The producer was more than happy to provide all of Peg's expenses but wasn't thrilled at the thought of paying for a bodyguard. After some haggling, a deal was struck wherein O'Malley was signed to play Clytie Hope's eldest son, Claude. Walter Byron, the actor previously engaged for the role, was well compensated for his trouble. Belasco promised him a part in a future production and also helped get him a supporting role in Alan Mowbray's *Dinner Is Served,* at the Hollywood Playhouse.

On May 4, the *Hollywood Citizen News* announced that *The Mad Hopes* was in the midst of rehearsals, and that Belasco and Curran had brought Peg out from New York especially for the production. Three days later the *Los Angeles Times* also noted that Peg was brought from Broadway *especially* for the new play. Other papers throughout the country followed suit, including the *New York Times.* This is important to note because until now it had always been said that Peg came to Los Angeles in 1932 for the express purpose of landing film roles after appearing in a series of Broadway flops. (One version has her doing this in 1929. Another says she did in fact come out in 1932 to act in *The Mad Hopes,* but that the deal fell through, the play was never produced, and so that was the reason she decided to try her hand at films. There are other variations.)

Since her death, Peg Entwistle has very often been portrayed much like that stereotypical girl from Small Town, USA, newly arrived in "Hollywood," standing forlorn by her worn suitcase in the bus terminal, frightened and alone in Tinsel Town, hoping to "make it big" in the movies ... *no matter what.* And while Peg will indeed get bitten by the motion picture bug, she had no film aspirations whatsoever when she arrived to Los Angeles at the request and expense of Edward Belasco and Homer Curran.

As Peg began rehearsing *The Mad Hopes* (and doubtless talking over good times with Bogart about their work together at Lakewood), the smoke of Laurette Taylor's devastation continued to rise in New York. On May 12, the American Arbitration Association held a hearing to determine William Brady's liability in the cancellation of the Barrie Revivals. At issue was disagreement over the contracts Brady had with Peg and her co-players involving compensation for the early curtain drop of *Alice Sit-by-the-Fire.* Brady gave the cast a severance package, but they felt they should have been paid full salaries and an estimated percentage of the box office gross equaling what the play would have earned had the production completed its scheduled run.

Brady argued the agreement stipulated that the salaries and shares of box office receipts were contingent upon completion of an *entire* run from the scheduled opening to the scheduled final performance. He said he was as much a victim of Laurette Taylor as they were, and so he shouldn't have to pay more than the two weeks' severance required by Equity rules. Brady also contended that no percentage of receipts should be paid since there was no more box-office.

On May 13, the arbitration board made their ruling: The actors were entitled to two and three-eighths weeks of salary. This amounted to the full two-week severance governed by Equity, plus their salaries covering the last three performances of the cancellation week. (The schedule called for eight shows per week, hence the "three-eighths.") Agreements regarding box office percentages were not governed by Equity, and the board said they had no legal control in that matter. The actors would not get a share of the tens of thousands of dollars the production had earned. In all, Peg's total loss would be equal to about $120,000 today.

On May 15, *The Mad Hopes* went to San Diego for a few days—a sort of pre-tryout tryout. Then on May 20 and 21 they played the Lobero Theater in Santa Barbara. The road tryout was a well-received success: Billie Burke was enchanting, Peg Entwistle was dazzling, and Humphrey Bogart was, well, *Bogart.*

On May 22, the company headed back to Los Angeles for the next evening's premiere at the Belasco Theater. The Belasco seated 1,600 but more than 2,000 patrons attended, including many film industry notables. When Billie walked onto the stage she looked so beautiful and youthful in her Adrian gown that someone in the seats hollered, "Why, she looks only 20!"[2] (Billie Burke was 48 years old in 1932. Many find it unbelievable that she was in her fifties when she played Glinda the Good Witch in *The Wizard of Oz*.)

Robert Garland, a founding member of the Drama Critics' Circle and drama editor for the *World Telegram,* had come from New York for the opening curtain. In his nationally syndicated column "Cast and Miscast" he wrote glowingly of Billie Burke, adding, "Peg Entwistle ... shines most brightly. Then, again, there's Humphrey Bogart, who, according to the editor of this column is constantly content to play himself over and over again."[3] Florence Lawrence at the *Examiner* included many high points in her review, among them:

> An audience which packed the Belasco Theater to the doors welcomed Billie Burke back to the footlights in a new play last night. In *The Mad Hopes,* the beautiful actress has a role with wide opportunities for the display of her talent. It calls upon a thousand facets of expression, rises to high emotion and carries a comedy vein of consistent whimsicality.
>
> Belasco and Curran have staged the new play most effectively and have endowed this Romney Brent opus with every distinction of cast and direction. Bela Blau, notable New Yorker, has developed the comedy to its highest points. Costumes and settings are delightful and every detail makes the production entirely fit for its translation to the New York stage.
>
> In the cast, Peg Entwistle and Humphrey Bogart hold first place in supporting the star and both give fine, serious performances. Miss Entwistle, as the earnest young daughter of a vague mother, presents a charming picture of youth, while Mr. Bogart made an immediate impression of finesse and subtlety in his every move as the young American who proves a good angel to an English family in financial difficulty.... [T]he final curtain was raised for a dozen or more calls before the audience was willing to leave the theater.[4]

Some who have attempted to chronicle Peg's final days claim *The Mad Hopes* was a flop. Honestly, it's not like these reviews had to be excavated from a dig in Egypt.

Edwin Schallert, a drama critic at the *Los Angeles Times,* fell into line with his peers in reviewing Burke, Bogart, and the production values, but to Peg he blew an extra special kiss: "One must, of course, take into large account such clever work as that of the assured, earnest, and often very sprightly Peg Entwistle. She rated a place high and efficient, owing to several of her scenes, notably in dealing with troubled romance. An exit during the second act brought her a very fitting tribute of applause for the well-played episode that preceded it. She attracted the audience throughout by her sincerity in playing her role."[5]

Of course she did. Peg Entwistle could do no less.

* * *

Hollywood was flooded with talented, well-trained, experienced Broadway actors and actresses in 1932. It's been estimated that after the stock market crash of 1929, two-thirds of Gotham's stage players migrated west to try their luck in films as theatrical producers slashed the prices of seats (thus, salaries) in order to compete with breadlines and soup kitchens. It is astounding that when Belasco, Curran, and MacGregor auditioned so many talented, attractive local girls, not a single one made a suitable enough Geneva Hope. So the call went to Peg. And with the Great Depression in full swing and *The Mad Hopes* less than two weeks away from its first curtain, the producers paid first class travel expenses for an actress 3,000 miles away, whom they had seen only once *three years earlier* ... a girl who had yet to read for them a single line of their new play, and who would have less than a week to rehearse upon her arrival. How often has such a thing been done? Even in times of plenty?

But Belasco and Curran wanted Peg. Romney Brent and Bela Blau wanted Peg. And, not surprisingly, Humphrey Bogart wanted Peg ... and Bogart *always* gets the girl.

Bogart had a house in Beachwood Canyon, not far from the Entwistle home. It turns out he and Peg had become quite chummy during *The Mad Hopes*, no doubt due in part to their having worked together during the 1931 season with the Lakewood Players. Peg's brother recalled for this author Bogart's visits to the house and remembered the actor as "a very polite, quiet-spoken young man."[6] Milton insisted there was nothing "haughty" about him.[7] That may have been true of the actor, but Uncle Charles Entwistle knew something of Bogart that Milton had not known at the time his sister was dating the future Hollywood legend: He was still married to Mary Phillips, who was 3,000 miles away on Broadway with Ed Wynn in his popular musical comedy *The Laugh Parade*.

Milton Entwistle said their uncle was like a protective, stern father. When Peg's suitor called the house to see if she could come out and play, Charles made no bones about the fact that Bogart was to come inside the home and properly go through the motions of making his intentions known before taking one step out the door with his attractive young niece. As far as can be determined, the dating wasn't serious, just two friends having some fun in town.

Milton also remembered an event that took place the day after the *Mad Hopes* premiere. A special delivery arrived to the family's house from the management of Hollywood's famous eatery, the Pig 'n' Whistle. They sent Peg a giant box of chocolates, a glorious bouquet of flowers, and a bag of English tin soldiers (presumably with her brothers in mind). The card congratulated her on an outstanding opening night. Peg gave her brothers the toy soldiers, and as they played with them on the floor, she pranced around, sharing chocolates with everyone and delighting in how her name and that of the eatery sounded so much alike.

She started singing, "Peg Entwistle, Pig 'n' Whistle! Pig 'n' Whistle, Peg Entwistle!"[8]

* * *

On June 4, 1932, *The Mad Hopes* closed its Los Angeles tryout as scheduled. About a week earlier, the *New York Times* announced the play would open on Broadway in the fall. Peg was asked by associate producer Bela Blau if she would like to commit to the New York production. Blau was more than impressed by her stage presence and the reception she was receiving from audiences and critics. Peg had proven to be an actress of such exceptional quality that when she introduced Uncle Charles and Aunt Jane to Blau and Romney Brent at a party following the premiere, Blau said, "No, sir, thank *you*," in response to Charles having thanked them for agreeing to bring their niece to Los Angeles.[9] This was Blau acknowledging the way Charles and Jane Entwistle had mentored her career.

So Peg had gleefully accepted Blau's offer. Her next season on Broadway was secure, and a handshake secured the commitment for each of them until a detailed Equity contract could be drafted and signed in New York. The deal was as good as done. The only problem was Peg's previous obligation to Herbert L. Swett, the managing director of the Lakewood Players. And while it isn't known if Peg had backed out of a *signed* contract with Swett, she most certainly had promised him the 1932 summer season, for the Lakewood Company had been announcing her June arrival there since the previous May. There should be little doubt that Swett was displeased at Peg's bowing out so near the Lakewood opening. Such reneging rarely — if ever — went over well with theatrical producers and managers.

Billie Burke, who for months wanted to do *The Mad Hopes,* was also onboard with Blau's plans for a Broadway run. "We are scheduled to play this in New York later on," she told the *Los Angeles Times*.[10] "So we are doing everything as perfectly as possible."[11] Bogart, on the other hand, already had agreements with Warner Brothers; he would make screen time with Bette Davis and Joan Blondell.

Blau would not have fretted about Bogart, for there were plenty of actors who could easily play his part. But Billie and Peg's agreement to reprise their roles on Broadway meant a great deal to him (and no doubt to Romney Brent). The delightful whimsicality of Billie and the charming fluttering of Peg could more than compensate for the lack of Bogart's presence.

If the West Coast run was any indication, it promised to be an amazing Broadway season.

But for now Billie and Peg were still in Hollywood, where the alluring pull of Tinsel Town so easily and so often upstaged Gotham's Great White Way...

* * *

Unbeknownst to Bela Blau, there had been some inter-office chatter taking place at Radio-Keith-Orpheum Studios (RKO). On May 31, an RKO executive named Charles Richards sent David O. Selznick, vice-president in charge of production, a memo saying he "found out from an inside source" that Paramount Studios wanted Billie Burke.[12] "However," said Richards, "She is very much interested in playing the part of the mother in *Bill of Divorcement*."[13]

It seems Billie was negotiating with the studios despite her public announcements that she would go to New York with *The Mad Hopes*. Selznick forwarded the memo to George Cukor, RKO's top director and the man slated to helm *Divorcement*. At the bottom of the memo, Selznick scrawled, "Cukor, work fast if we want her."[14]

They did want her and Cukor did work fast. And now Billie was going to make her first movie in more than ten years. She had done a number of silent pictures, but *A Bill of Divorcement* would be her first talkie.

It isn't known how or when she broke the news to Blau and Romney Brent, or to Peg for that matter. Peg would very likely have committed to the New York production without the enticement of Billie Burke, but she was nonetheless crestfallen that Billie jumped ship. Blau and Brent were extremely disappointed as well; losing Billie wasn't the end of the world, but casting a replacement of her caliber would be difficult.

In her 1948 memoir *With a Feather on My Nose*, Burke contradicts the research for this book with regard to the closing of *The Mad Hopes* tryout. She said she was at home in Santa Monica listening to her husband's radio show *The Chrysler Hour*, broadcast from New York, when she noticed he sounded ill. Worried about Florenz Ziegfeld's recent poor health, Billie claimed that she immediately contacted Homer Curran, co-producer of *Hopes*, and asked him to close the play so that she could rush to New York to be with Ziegfeld.... "He did not hesitate.... He closed at once and I was on my way to see Flo."[15] But the Los Angeles papers make no mention of the play closing early for any reason. Moreover, playbills of *The Mad Hopes* gave the dates of the run at the Belasco Theater, and the scheduled closing date was June 4. Ads in the *Los Angeles Times*, *Los Angeles Herald Examiner*, and the *Hollywood Citizen News* also reveal a scheduled June 4 closing.

Extensive searches of Los Angeles newspapers found no mention of Burke having to close the play in order to rush to her ailing husband's side; however, there were numerous ads announcing the last matinee and final performance for June 3 and June 4. If Billie's recollection of this event was accurate, there would have been something mentioned in the newspapers, for this was the most popular play in Los Angeles and it starred one of America's most popular and beloved stage actresses who was married to one of the most influential producers on Broadway.

The Mad Hopes simply did not close in the way Miss Burke remembered in her memoir.

She was also mistaken with regard to being offered her role in RKO's *A Bill of Divorcement*. She said in her book that George Cukor told her John Barrymore and Katharine Hepburn were on board; however, as the reader will see in the following chapters, Hepburn had not yet been chosen at this time: There was a short list of several actresses (including Peg later on) but no decision had as yet been made for the role eventually given to Hepburn.

Burke had gone back on her word to Blau regarding the Broadway production of *The Mad Hopes*. It had very likely stung him; however, he most probably thought that no matter whom he got to play Clytie Hope, all would be fine, for Peg Entwistle still had some magic, and if the new Clytie proved a bust, Peg's Geneva would somehow make up for it.

But the magic that was *The Mad Hopes* had been the work of Billie and Peg, not Clytie and Geneva, so is it really any surprise that on the same day David O. Selznick told George Cukor to work fast to get the one, he also told him to get the other:

"...Cukor, I hear great things about a girl named Peggy Entwhistle [sic], who is appearing with Billie Burke downtown. I have never seen her, but I suggest you look her up for *Bill of Divorcement*. D. O. S. [David O. Selznick]."[16]

Selznick was not one to *suggest* anything to a subordinate. This was an order.

The call had come quickly, within a day or two of the memo. Peg was astounded that one of the most important movie directors in the country had reached out to her. "She raved about it for days," said her cousin, Helen.[17] "At first she thought it was one of her friends, an actor having a joke at her expense. She nearly hung up [on Cukor]."[18]

The film that Peg would actually do at RKO, *Thirteen Women*, had not been discussed with her yet. If it had, Peg may very well have rejected RKO's offer. But when she was told Selznick was considering her for Billie Burke's picture, and that the male lead would be John Barrymore, it was too much allure for her. Peg said yes without much hesitation. And in so doing she completely forgot — or chose to ignore — what her uncle told her back in 1925 just before she went to the Boston Repertory, when she had shaken hands with Henry Jewett: "A handshake agreement was a theatrical contract ... a promise — a *commitment*."[19]

Bela Blau and Romney Brent knew as much, also.

Peg Entwistle had upstaged herself, and not even Emma Dunn would be able to save her.

17

Thirteen Women

If you saw Billie Burke in The Mad Hopes *at the Belasco, you will have a happy recollection of Peg Entwistle, who played the role of the daughter. Miss Entwistle is an accomplished actress, and although she was brought here from Broadway, she grew up in Southern California.*

She is a niece of Harold Entwistle of Beachwood Drive, who is a film actor. She was all set to return to New York when the play closed Saturday night, but Radio Pictures called her for a screen test. Now it is very likely that she will remain here for one of the featured roles in Thirteen Women.[1]

It's a very pretty signature ... a lovely hue of jade—not green, *green* would have been tacky; black, too common. *Jade*. Her trademark underscore emphasizes the last name with just a hint of feminine bend. The penmanship is clean; the pressure delicate, close to expert.

Peg Entwistle could handle a fountain pen.

On June 13, 1932, Peg signed a one-picture deal with RKO. She was to report on or about the second of July to begin preparing for her role in the screen adaptation of Tiffany Thayer's novel *Thirteen Women*.

The film involves a group of women who were once sorority sisters at St. Alban's, an exclusive college for girls. One of these girls was a mixed-race orphan placed there through the goodness of a missionary. After she was shunned and mistreated by the girls for being poor and only half-white, the humiliated half-caste ran away. She spent years studying the occult and became an expert in the powers of astrology and hypnotic suggestion. Now she has returned with a diabolical plan to exact revenge on the cruel school girls through the use of hypnotism and contrived horoscopes containing dire warnings of things to come...

Murder. Mayhem. Women in peril. Women insane.

Delicious.

One by one the victims fall prey to the supernatural—or at least *the suggestion* of the supernatural. Among these hapless ne'er-do-wells is Hazel Clay Cousins (Peg). Hazel is married to a fine sort, a man with good looks, a man with money, a man with a knife handle protruding from his chest. "Hazel!"[2]

It isn't Hazel's fault ... not really. After all, she was being hypnotically influenced into murdering her husband by the powerful weapon of the mind ... or was she? ... Was she *really?*

As tragic a figure as Hazel will become in the film, the book made her more so. Author Thayer (who was actually a man) wrote Hazel Cousins as a virgin who has remained so for the simple reason she is too pretty. Half the men who see her assume she must be married or engaged, and so they look away. The other half are sure and certain that such a beautiful girl, if single, can only break their hearts or spend them into the poor house, so they also look away.

What is such a one as Hazel to do? Thayer's novel takes a novel approach. Hazel becomes a lesbian, seduced by Martha, the wife of a wealthy lung doctor. Hazel will never know the touch of a man, and after Martha abandons her, she comes to believe the dreadful horoscope sent to her. She wilts away from tuberculosis, haunting memories of Martha, and ultimately starves herself to death.

Except for the omission of Hazel's death by tuberculosis, despair, and anorexia, RKO screenwriters Samuel Ornitz (whose alleged Communist ties will get him blacklisted in 1947) and Bartlett Cormack (an Oscar nominee of 1929) retained the basic premise of the book's forbidden love between Hazel and Martha. But the pre–Code era was coming to a close. Powerful, politically connected protectors of decency and morality will have their say. Dutiful film editors at RKO will obey orders. And Peg's saucy role as a young wife seduced into lesbianism, who stabs her husband to death following a bedroom tryst with the much older Martha, will now become just another insane heterosexual knife-wielding connubial murderess.

This was much more agreeable to the family-friendly puritans of 1932.

* * *

Peg looks slim and pretty in the film and carries herself with a reserved, smooth mingling of expression and poise. Her nose is a bit prominent on camera, but only in a British sort of way. (Jimmy Durante had nothing to fear.) Having retained a fair amount of her English accent, Peg's voice and diction are delightful. She presents a young lady of refinement and if one were not in the know, one might assume a girl of heraldry, or perhaps training from some New England finishing school.

It has often been said that Peg's role in *Thirteen Women* was a bit part. Indeed, as the film stands today, she has little more than a cameo comprising a few lines and screams of horror. It is also often reported that Peg "starred" or "co-starred" with Irene Dunne, Myrna Loy, and Ricardo Cortez, but other than a few publicity shots and a photo of her used by Myrna Loy in a scene, Peg never appears with them. This was true of her deleted scenes, as well.

RKO production reports show Peg's original scenes totaled 16 minutes and 15 seconds. Of this, approximately 12 minutes (75 percent) of her performance hit the cutting room floor.

All this editing lends itself to some confusing moments in the released version of *Thirteen Women,* but overall the film was well made and contains a few flashes of brilliance that in some ways put it ahead of its time.

Along with its (then) unique and daring approach to racism, there is use of the latest law enforcement technology for 1932, such as an all-points bulletin going out from actual police dispatchers to real patrolmen in radio cars, and a "telephoto" being sent and received using what we know as a fax machine. Also, a few well-directed location shots make for some brief but interesting background views of early 1930s Los Angeles, which are always fun to see.

As released in 1932, and as it stands today, Peg's remaining four minutes in three scenes of *Thirteen Women* look something like this...

Trapeze artist June Raskob (Mary Duncan) sits in her dressing room at the Joe E. Marvel Circus. She looks troubled while reading a horoscope made especially for her. The news is far from swell: Someone close to June will soon die because of her. In walks her sister May (Harriet Hagman) with their old classmate, Hazel Cousins. (It's inferred the girls haven't seen each other in quite some time.) Hazel tells them she was on a motor trip with a friend and when she heard the sisters were here, "I simply had to come in and say hello!"[3]

When May leaves the dressing room for a minute, June's happy-to-see-Hazel smile vanishes. She wrings her hands nervously and seems deeply troubled. Hazel is puzzled: "What's the matter, June?"[4]

"I have to tell you ... I've got to tell somebody! Hazel, I shouldn't go on with this act!"[5]

Mary Duncan's over-the-top performance here is 1930s camp at its finest. She isn't terrible, but she seems to almost be parodying her role, like a comedienne in a television skit making fun of early Hollywood (think of Carol Burnett's classic spoof of Scarlett O'Hara and *Gone with the Wind*). Although Duncan's presentation here is priceless to watch, it's surprising to see from a respected actress with 22 years of experience.

As June continues her speech, we learn how the girls have come to receive horoscopes from the great seer, Swami Yogadachi (C. Henry Gordon). June tells Hazel about the swami's prediction of a less than sunny future for the two sisters: "Hazel, he says something terrible was going to happen to one of us ... an accident!"[6] When they hear May calling June's name as she makes her way back to the dressing room, June gives Hazel a subtle look and gesture: *Quiet! She mustn't know!*

Makes sense, really; why worry the poor girl? After all, May already has enough on her mind. In a few minutes she has to be at work ... high over the center ring, soaring end over end through the air toward her nervous sister's trembling arms ... sweaty palms ... without a net.

Alas, it is show time. Hazel puts a hand on June's shoulder: "Goodbye."[7]

There's no time for Hazel to ask where to send the flowers; she has to hurry outside to meet her motor trip friend, Martha (Marjorie Gateson). The final draft of the screenplay describes Martha as a "large, handsome Amazon ... the lesbian who occupies Hazel's time."[8] The shooting script (written a month later) is a bit less sharp, calling Martha handsome and athletic with a "rich voice and closely shingled hair."[9] Of course, with Hazel and Martha's lesbianism strewn all over the cutting room floor, Martha's only real value to the plot now is to make it seem that Hazel is a proper girl on a respectable trip with a suitable escort.

As the usual timbre of circus takes place around them, Hazel and Martha lock arms and exchange knowing glances—the censors didn't get *everything*. The lovers find their seats and soon the Raskob sisters are airborne, earning gasps and applause from their memorized audience. (In Thayer's book, June and May are gluttonous, obese twins in a sideshow, not lithe, flexible daredevils of the air.)

This scene captures a fine range of emotion on Peg's face as she watches the trapeze act. She has no dialogue here, but it's easy to see why theater welcomed her. She first exudes joy and pride as the sisters complete their first stunt; then in gradual, smooth, natural-looking increments, Peg transits to concern when she sees June becoming more and more nervous and unsure as her sister prepares to attempt their world-famous double flip.

June is so convinced that her horoscope predicted May's death she cannot stop herself from causing it. May somersaults toward her, and just as she's about to grab June's outstretched arms, June tucks them in. With a dizzying fall and a tormented scream May's life ends almost as fast as the career of the actress who played her. Before coming to RKO, Harriet Hagman was a chorine in *Earl Carroll's Vanities*, a popular Broadway music revue.

After filming *Thirteen Women,* she secretly wed a West Point cadet named Henry Sebastian. Cadets were prohibited by Army rules to marry. Sebastian was discharged with no small fervor. Hagman had her named dragged through the press also. They both quietly faded away.

After May's demise the story takes us to the home of Swami Yogadachi. Here we learn that his secretary, Ursula (Myrna Loy), is the half-caste outcast out to get the girls. She's been intercepting the swami's happy horoscopes and sending the women counterfeits filled with horrid prophesies. Upon marking an X over the yearbook photos of June and May, Ursula sets the pen tip on Hazel's. With a loud crescendo of doom-around-the-corner music, we fade to a newspaper headline: "Young Wife Kills Husband with Knife."[10] And now a clever superimposed effect of the headline and crime as Hazel pulls the knife from his heart. "Hazel!"[11] he cries with his last breath and falls to the floor. The camera zooms in on her face—a crazed, murderous look as the newspaper remains superimposed to the end of the scene.

This is where Peg Entwistle shined. Her interpretation is expertly done. Hazel's slowly widening eyes and increasingly rapid breathing as she comes out of a trance, realizes she's just committed murder, then spins into madness, are more than nice touches; they are the marks of a finely tuned professional actress who knew how to climax drama. The performance here lasts only 14 seconds but is unquestionably superb and would do students well if shown in acting classes, specifically during the moment it takes for Hazel's mind to shatter. Peg brings her hands to the sides of her head and lets fly with three high-pitched shrills so uniquely anguished they deserve their own category in the Academy Awards. She reaches deep into Hazel and emerges not with screams of fright, but with screams of unimaginable psychological trauma.

A girl being carried by King Kong to the top of the Empire State Building screams one way; a girl who awakens from a hypnotic state and discovers she unwittingly committed murder screams another. The former is heart-stopping fear; the latter a mind destroyed beyond hope. It is in the latter vein that Peg distinguished herself. We witness Hazel's escalating agony through the fury of her animation; with increasing intensity she squeezes, rattles, shakes and tilts back her head more and more—we see the bend before the break.

Peg did a first-rate job here, but given the trauma of her childhood and marriage, one might wonder if she had not simply been acting. Could she have unconsciously given voice to her own repressed agonies? Peg was an exceptional actress but this performance seems to have more than talent behind it. Howard Fine, the respected acting coach who has worked with the likes of Brad Pitt, Salma Hayek, and Oscar winner Jennifer Connelly, insists that the best actors can cry on demand using mental techniques such as remembering a childhood tragedy. If this can be done by design for tears, could it similarly work for screams—even subconsciously?

It will never be known if Hazel Cousins' screams were really Peg Entwistle's pain, but she had certainly been traumatized enough to employ the technique, purposely or not.

* * *

With the end of Hazel Cousins' sanity came the end of Peg's appearance in the film. Even if her deleted scenes had remained, her role is over at this point.

Top billing went to Irene Dunne who played Laura, the primary target of Ursula's revenge, and Ricardo Cortez as Sergeant Barry Clive, the handsome sleuth who saves the day. However, it is Myrna Loy who steals the show. Prior to her role as Ursula, Loy had made 70 films going back to 1925. She is probably best remembered for the *Thin Man* films with William Powell. The original *Thin Man* story was by Dashiell Hammett, but all six screen adaptations were written by Frances Goodrich and Albert Hackett, close friends of Peg and her Aunt Jane and Uncle Charles.

Dunne got her start on Broadway in 1921. Her rise to stardom actually began with a pretty blue hat in 1928, the day after she returned to New York from a honeymoon in Europe. She was riding an elevator when Florenz Ziegfeld stepped in. He admired the hat and before she knew it, Dunne had the role of Magnolia Hawks in *Show Boat*. She was spotted by a talent scout during the musical's Chicago run and soon found herself at RKO. Dunne was nominated for a Best Actress Oscar five times and was known as the First Lady of Hollywood.

Cortez was a popular leading man in 1930s Hollywood. There was talk that he would become the next Rudolph Valentino. But he wasn't even *Ricardo Cortez*, never mind Valentino. He was Jacob Krantz; and he was from Austria, not Spain, as studio myth-makers and fan magazines claimed.

Perhaps the most enjoyable character in *Thirteen Women* is the super-spiritual Grace, an oddball swayed to no small extent by the horoscopes. She's harmless, really, but of the type one wouldn't be surprised to see parading downtown with aluminum foil on her head while holding a sign declaring THE END IS NEAR. Florence Eldridge did a fine job as Grace. The role could have easily been played over the top, but she gave Grace just enough peculiarity to keep an oddball from becoming a screwball. The results show why she would one day be nominated for a Tony Award with real-life husband Fredric March in *Long Day's Journey into Night*.

And then there's Jo. A marvelous invention, this Jo. She has a delightfully reserved British accent (think, "Rah-thuh"). She is very pretty, but tomboyish. Jo slouches in her chair, chain smokes like Frank Sinatra, tosses matches to the floor, and expounds a unique philosophy: "To me, life is just an ashtray full of cigarette butts."[12]

Jill Esmond's role as Jo came to her after a dispute with RKO. Selznick wanted her to play Sydney Fairfield in *A Bill of Divorcement*, but at half her usual salary. Esmond's husband, Laurence Olivier, convinced her to turn it down, so, to *Thirteen Women* she did go.

Kay Johnson was also a very good actress. She proved as much in her role as the extremely depressed (and depressing) Helen, a girl who carries a revolver despite the horoscope predicting she will end her life by her own hand. Johnson didn't leave behind a vast résumé just 24 films and ten Broadway plays; however, she did work with the biggest stars of the era, including Bette Davis and Clark Gable. She was also the mother of the Oscar-nominated actor James Cromwell.

C. Henry Gordon played the swami rather stiffly, but it probably wasn't his idea to cake on so much makeup as to resemble a mannequin. Gordon acted in 80 or so films but is most remembered for his 1936 role as Surat Khan, murderer of women and children in Warner Brothers' *The Charge of the Light Brigade* with Errol Flynn.

Laura's son Bobby was played by Wally Albright, a future *Our Gang* standout.

Ed Pawley's film debut was as the chauffeu who falls under Ursula's spell. He had relative success until butting heads with powerful Hollywood types who did not appreciate his protests against actors who were Communist sympathizers. Pawley did some radio and returned to Broadway where he got his start. When he retired, he divided his time between writing poetry and breeding champion goats.

There were three actresses whose roles as sorority sisters in *Thirteen Women* were completely deleted. Their images are seen briefly when Ursula opens the St. Albans yearbook: Phyllis Cerf made less than 20 films. For 30 years she was the wife of Bennett Cerf, co-founder of Random House and long-time panelist on TV's *What's My Line?* She started Beginner Books, a Random House imprint for children. Her business partner was Ted Geisel (Dr. Seuss).

Betty Furness was a popular actress, author, spokesperson, consumer advocate and *Today Show* anchor. She got her start as a teen model for the prestigious John Powers Agency.

Furness starred in nearly 50 films and appeared in dozens of television and radio programs.

Julie Haydon was of the Theater Guild. In 1940 she originated the role of Kitty Duval in Saroyan's *The Time of Your Life*, that year's winner of the Pulitzer Prize for Drama. While most of Haydon's stage, film, and television roles were minor, she set the Broadway bar for excellence with her role as Laura Wingfield in the original production of Tennessee Williams' *The Glass Menagerie* opposite Peg's *Alice Sit-by-the-Fire* co-star, Laurette Taylor.

Like many films of that time, *Thirteen Women* has a few gaffes and bloopers: When Irene Dunne's Laura becomes suspicious of candy sent to her son, she brings it to Detective Clive to have it tested. "Well, the candy's okay," says a top-notch police chemist, "but it's been tampered with ... if anybody had eaten it, he'd have strangled to death in 30 seconds."[13] *Hmmm....* The candy's "okay" but will kill you if you eat it?

When Grace receives a letter she thinks is from the swami, she unfolds it and begins reading it aloud to Laura and Jo. Watch as a large, unscripted housefly lands discreetly on the letter and starts crawling along the paper without the actresses noticing ... *very* creepy.

And speaking of letters, after Ursula destroys the swami's letter to Hazel, she substitutes her counterfeit and forges the swami's signature. We get a good look at this letter's last sentence: "Life imprisonment will be the judgment of karma."[14] After Hazel murders her husband, the camera pans to the letter and zooms in, but it now ends, "You will end your life in prison."[15]

When Laura opens her son's closet door to place a birthday gift on the top shelf, we see about a dozen other gifts already there. But they are haphazardly piled, as if they had been tossed up to the shelf. Laura shuts the closet door and tells her son he can't open any of them until his party. Moments after she leaves the room, the boy is off to the closet. When he opens the door, we see that all the gifts are neatly, *perfectly* stacked.

But there is more to this closet. Take a look near the bottom for a quick glimpse of a clever novelty involving a toy pooch and doggie door. It's a marvelous bit of imaginative craftsmanship fabricated by Carroll Clark, a seven-time Oscar nominated set designer.

Helen has shot herself in her train compartment. Detective Clive is kneeling over the body. "Suicide," says the coroner to another detective with him in the doorway. "Clive says the restrictive angles of the compartment prove as much."[16] *Hmmm* ... did the coroner mean that Clive had suggested the compartment was too small to simultaneously accommodate a killer *and* a victim? Indeed he did, and so agreed the three other men *inside the compartment* with Clive.

When Clive is informed by his investigators that Ursula recently purchased dynamite ... from a *hardware store,* one might wonder how such a purchase would occur: *Okay, let's see if I've got everything: weed killer, garden rake, toilet plunger, floor polish ... I think that's it ... oops, almost forgot! Excuse me, where do you keep the blasting caps?*

If you've seen the film, you may have wondered why there are only eight women in *Thirteen Women.* Well, actually there are 13 women, but only in the one scene where Ursula opens the college yearbook to cross out photos of her victims. Notice the 12 photos of the Kappa sorority women on the page (the photo at the top right — above the grouped 12 — is a teacher). Ursula is not among the girls because in the story she had run away, and so would not have her photo there. Nevertheless, as she sits with the book, she is the "thirteenth" woman.

But here's the rub: RKO never intended to tell the tales of all 13; that would take too long. Only 11 actresses were cast, and even that was too many. So, as stated earlier, three of them were deleted from the film. And that's why there are eight women in *Thirteen Women*.

But there's more ... RKO's adaptation presents 13 women as having gone to college together, however, in the book, only ten girls were in the sorority, three were not, including Martha, Hazel's lover. And speaking of Hazel's lover, the book was nationally promoted in major newspapers with various quarter-page ads. These ads often mentioned a "baker's dozen" of women,[17] and, "some of them ladies ... one almost a man!"[18]

As mentioned earlier, the production values in *Thirteen Women* were excellent for 1932. This is no doubt due in part to the top-notch music and photography. The score was composed by the legendary Max Steiner. The Austrian-born Steiner is said to have been taught his craft by Gustav Mahler (other sources include Johannes Brahms). Steiner composed the music for hundreds of films and received 19 Oscar nominations. His three wins were for *The Informer* (1935), *Now, Voyager* (1942), and *Since You Went Away* (1944). Included in his phenomenal résumé are *Gone with the Wind* (1939) and *Casablanca* (1942).

Thirteen Women's director of photography was Leo Tover, one of only 302 members (as of this writing) of the prestigious American Society of Cinematography. Tover, who was twice nominated for an Academy Award, shot more than 140 films, including the sci-fi classics *The Day the Earth Stood Still* (1951) and *Journey to the Center of the Earth* (1959).

Steiner and Tover were RKO's very best. Their participation in *Thirteen Women* is strong evidence that David O. Selznick had immense confidence in the film's success.

As with every production, there are stories behind the story. *Thirteen Women* was an unusual film and from its handful of real-life stories comes what might be the most unusual behind-the-scenes story of any film ever made: the actual horoscope and astrologers reportedly used by director George Archainbaud to determine the film's shooting schedule.

Here is what Jessie Henderson wrote (in part) for his August 22, 1932, syndicated column *Keeping Pace with Hollywood*: "In the [astrology] chart ... it was found Mars happened to be close to the mid-heaven, a favorable indication of success. The sun, Uranus and Jupiter also were in a position to promise success for the picture ... the position of the moon indicated that there would be appreciation of the film and another indication was that young women would be greatly pleased with it...."[19]

Interesting, isn't it? RKO's astrologers could see the future of *Thirteen Women*, yet they had no visions of one sad, lonely Aquarian atop Hollywood's Sign just a few weeks later.

18

Cameras and Clapboards, Take One

To survive in Hollywood, you need the ambition of a Latin American revolutionary, the ego of a grand opera tenor, and the physical stamina of a cow pony. — Billie Burke[1]

In late May, while Peg was still performing in *The Mad Hopes,* Hollywood's major studios announced their projects for the coming year. The eight heavyweights planned on producing 360 films. United Artists hoped for a conservative 12. The ambitious brothers at Warner aimed for 70, while RKO would shoot for 62, three less than Paramount. In addition, because of a current revival of the "indie" market, independent studios planned to bring together about 300 more groups of cast and crew between May 1932 and May 1933.

Of the 62 from RKO, the studio named six as their most important productions. Two of these were *A Bill of Divorcement* and *Thirteen Women.*

As mentioned earlier, the role of Sydney Fairfield in *Bill of Divorcement* was offered to *Thirteen Women* co-star Jill Esmond, who turned it down. In her biography *Katharine Hepburn: A Remarkable Woman,* author Anne Edwards adds Norma Shearer, Irene Dunne, and Anita Louise to the Sydney Fairfield list. As most film history buffs can tell you, the role went to Katharine Hepburn; it was her screen debut and it made her a star.

However, Peg Entwistle should now be included as one of those considered to play Sydney Fairfield. For alongside Selznick's memo mentioning Peg for *A Bill of Divorcement,* a related event was recalled by her cousin, Helen Reid. "Mother told us how she was with [Aunt] Jane and our Grandmother [Matilda] when Babs came tearing in [the Beachwood Drive house] like a tornado, hopping up and down, holding [Aunt Jane's] hands and going on and on about playing Billie Burke's daughter in a movie."[2]

Rudy Behlmer's *Memo from David O. Selznick* says that the role of Sydney Fairfield went to Hepburn after Selznick and Cukor viewed a series of screen tests. Other sources say Cukor persuaded Selznick to use Hepburn. At any rate, even though Peg didn't get the part, she had been on a short list with a very prestigious group of actresses.

Selznick's memo to Cukor regarding Peg and *A Bill of Divorcement* is not mentioned in Behlmer's book; there's no need for it there, really, but it's mentioned here, and that's important to her story. It's important because it speaks to the notice she was getting. To be mentioned and talked about by two of the biggest names in Hollywood (and now in Hollywood history) is no insignificant aspect to Peg Entwistle, the so-called failed actress.

The memo from Selznick telling George Cukor to call Peg for *Bill of Divorcement* sat

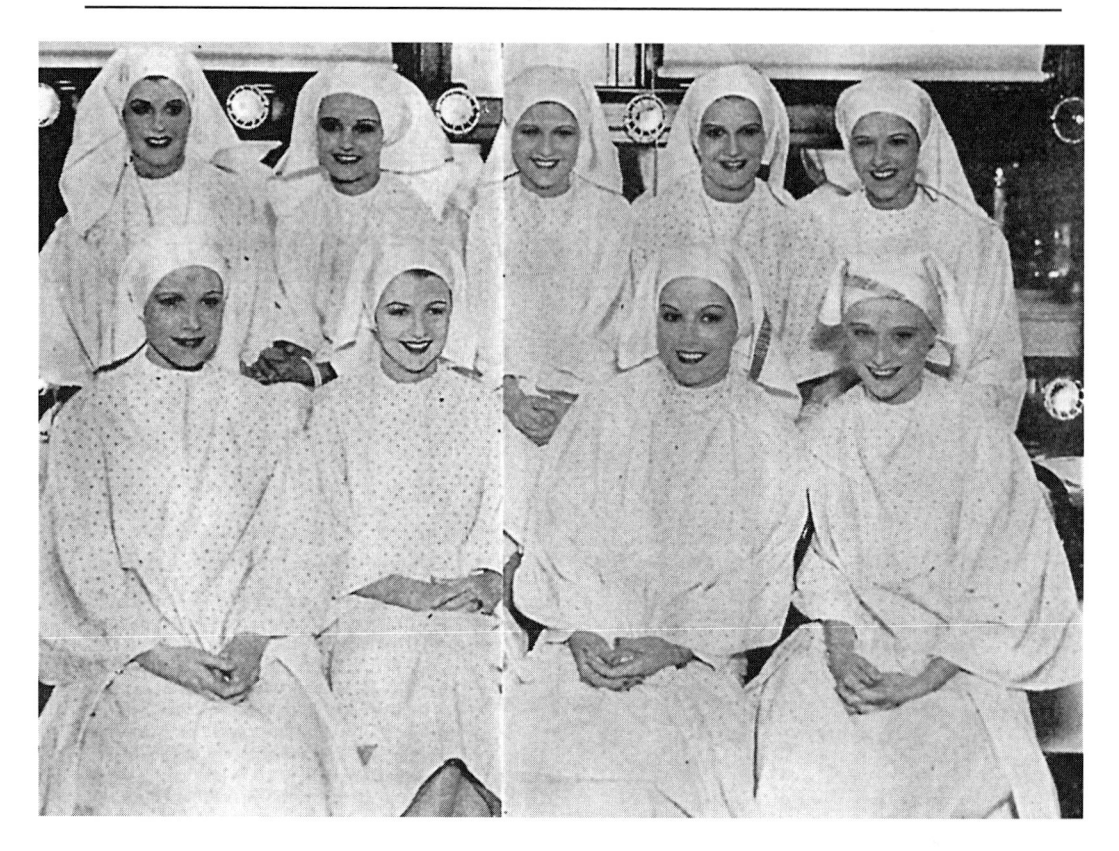

After signing with Selznick, Peg reported to the studio with these other starlets. For one week the girls learned to do everything the RKO way. This photograph shows Peg and the other "Radio Pictures starlets" during a cosmetics class. Top row (left to right): Sandra Shaw, Rochelle Hudson, Phyllis Fraser, Harriet Hagman and Dorothy Wilson. Front row (left to right): Julie Haydon, Betty Furness, Eleanor Post and Peg (author's collection).

in a vault at the Margaret Herrick Library of the Academy of Motion Picture Arts and Sciences, tucked in a folder, overlooked, forgotten, or ignored for nearly 80 years.

There's no question that Peg could have held her own as Sydney Fairfield. She might even have done a better job than Katharine Hepburn, for she was far more experienced and accomplished. In fact, five days before Selznick told Cukor of his interest in Peg, Selznick's story editor, Katharine Brown, sent a memo to Cukor advising him not to screen test Hepburn. Apart from agreeing with RKO's New York office that Hepburn's salary of $1,000 was excessive, Brown thought she was too inexperienced: "As far as I can recall, she has done only three plays."[3] Peg had been on stage for most of seven years. But in the end, Katie won the day and the calla lilies bloomed for her.

If Peg had played Sydney Fairfield, it would have been the first time two prominent Broadway actresses played back-to-back mother-daughter roles on stage and in a talking picture.

When Peg signed her *Thirteen Women* contract she was grouped together with eight other attractive young women, "The Radio Pictures Starlets."[4] (Four of them — Betty Furness, Julie Haydon, Harriet Hagman and Phyllis Cerf — were discussed earlier.) The others were Sandra Shaw, Rochelle Hudson, Dorothy Wilson, and Eleanor Post. With Peg, these girls were RKO's promising freshman class. However, before any of them got to hear a director yell *action!* they first had to be trained and groomed. They had to learn to fly before they could soar. These girls were getting paid to learn how to become movie stars; to be the faces of RKO in whichever projects the studio bosses saw fit to send them. They were recruited to become famous, to make millions for the studio's moguls. And they made quite an interesting bunch...

Sandra Shaw was Veronica "Rocky" Balfe before taking her stage name. She'll marry Gary Cooper in 1933. Her father was the governor of the New York Stock Exchange; her uncle was Cedric Gibbons, the most famous art director in Hollywood history, and a founder of the Academy of Motion Pictures Arts and Sciences. Her aunt, by marriage to Gibbons, was actress Dolores Del Rio. Despite these connections, she made just several films and is remembered best as the blonde tossed away by the hairy title character of *King Kong*. Shaw picked up a shotgun in her spare time and became the skeet-shooting champion of California.

Rochelle Hudson was a champion in her own right during World War II. In 1939 she will marry Harold Thompson, head of the story department at Disney. But that was his day job — he was also a spy doing espionage work as a civilian for the United States government. Hudson became a sort of true-life "Bond Girl" when she teamed up with her husband. Together they posed as a vacationing couple in Mexico, but in reality they were scouring that country in search of German activity. Just prior to the December 7, 1941, attack on Pearl Harbor, they discovered a huge supply of aviation gasoline which had been hidden by German agents in Baja, California. When not hunting Nazis, Hudson made over 100 films, but is remembered mostly as Natalie Wood's mother in *Rebel Without a Cause*.

Dorothy Wilson wasn't "discovered" in legendary fashion *a la* Lana Turner at the soda fountain of Schwabs on Hollywood and Vine (Turner was actually discovered at the Top Hat Café on Sunset). Wilson was already "in the biz," working as a secretary for RKO. She was noticed on the lot one day and offered a screen test. They liked her, and thus began a sudden wave of coast-to-coast publicity. She was dubbed the Secretary to the Stars. The truth is she simply typed or ran errands for lesser known directors. She was given one of 13 spots in a 1932 promotional campaign of the Western Association of Motion Picture Advertisers (WAMPAS). Young starlets who received this recognition were known as WAMPAS Baby Stars, and pampered accordingly. (Clara Bow, Joan Crawford, and Loretta Young were WAMPAS girls.) Wilson's husband was Lewis Foster, a prolific writer and composer who won an Oscar for *Mr. Smith Goes to Washington* (1939).

Eleanor Post made just one film at RKO. *No Other Woman* was another one of the studio's many Irene Dunne vehicles. This film also featured fellow starlet Betty Furness (in yet another "scenes deleted" effort), and the beautiful but tragic Gwili Andre, who died in a fire (purported by some to be suicide) in her Los Angeles oceanfront home in 1959.

*　*　*

Although her contract stated she was to report to the studio on or about July 2, Peg wasn't called in until July 6. RKO payroll records show her salary of $350 per week was bumped to $500 (equal to about $7,800 today). It isn't known what led to this sudden raise; perhaps it was an apologetic compensation for losing the role in *Bill of Divorcement*. It's unlikely this was a clerical error, for the payroll index cards were approved by the same person who approved her Payroll Advice records. At any rate, her work in the film didn't actually begin on the day she arrived. Her first week was spent learning the RKO ropes.

She would have been very busy during this week. There would be introductions and meetings with directors and cast members, fittings with the wardrobe department, test shots on "cold" sets to determine lighting and camera angles. The publicity department would want some of her time, too: Fan magazines were always hungry for fresh, pretty faces.

Peg enjoyed the attention and her new friends, but there had been a bump. Helen Reid remembered her mother and Aunt Jane talking about a "row" with a girl at RKO.[5] Peg had been accused of conceit. Mrs. Reid was unable to provide more detail, but it sounds like Peg may have been innocently talking about her stage experiences in such a way that the other girl thought she was showing off. Such confrontations weren't unheard of, particularly between Broadway thoroughbreds and Hollywood purebreds. Stage people were coming to Hollywood in droves, and there was occasional resentment between them and film players who had never walked the boards. It probably didn't help that many of these Broadway thespians were British. It was one thing to be condescending (even innocently), and quite another to be so when your accent was a slave to the King's English. Actor Conrad Nagel alluded to these rifts in the documentary *Stardust: The Bette Davis Story*. Nagel was referring to stage actors having the higher brow over screen actors, but there's no question the studios were favoring stage veterans over those who never saw the back of an asbestos curtain.

Rufus LeMaire, who was head of the Warner–First National casting bureau while Peg was at RKO, gives convincing evidence that film players who lacked stage experience had fair reason to hold a grudge. While visiting Broadway to scout recruits, LeMaire told the *New York Times* that the stage players were better than film players, and that it was the young actors with stage experience that his studio wanted. He pointed out to the *Times* reporter that the preponderance of players under contract with Warner–First National were from the stage. To further prove his point, LeMaire pulled a random card from a stack containing the studio's production schedules. The card was for the film *Life Begins.* Of the 21 actors in the cast, all but two had previous stage experience, and one of those was that anomaly Loretta Young, arguably the most talented and successful stage virgin in film and television history. "We haven't the time to train them the way they did in the old silent days," said LeMaire, "they must now have the poise, the grace, the speaking voice to begin with. Either our players know their business or out they go before they ruin the picture."[6]

And that's just the point: Peg wasn't discovered wearing a tight sweater at a Hollywood soda fountain, or walking across a studio lot with a typewriter in her arms and a wiggle in her dress. It was *stage* talent that took her name to the desk of David O. Selznick. An RKO exec had come to *The Mad Hopes* to see Billie Burke in the spotlight, and found Peg in the footlights.

But Peg had to jump through the same hoops as any of them. One of the first involved reciting a dramatic scene in a test director's office. No cameras here. This scene would have been one of her own choosing, something with which she was already familiar; perhaps from a Guild play. Then she would be weighed and measured and have her hair and eye color noted. If she'd been too heavy they would have told her to reduce and come back another time. If she stood taller than five and a half feet she probably would never feel the heat of a Klieg lamp. If her face was too round or fleshy, her shoulders too broad, or her bust too large, she might be groomed as a character actress, but more than likely turned away.

Peg would next have her screen test. In keeping with the norm for screen tests as described in a December 1932 *Photoplay* article, Peg would have no makeup, no special hairstyle, and the light of a thousand suns bringing every blemish, wrinkle, and nose hair to life. She would be asked to walk across the set to see how she traveled; how she carried her spine, swung her arms, tossed her head and worked her eyes. There would be long shots and close-ups from every angle.

When viewing the unedited results, many of the girls were often horrified: *My heavens, do I really walk like that?! Just look at that pimple; the Rock of Gibraltar! Ugh! Why hadn't anyone told me the inside of my nose was a forest?!* All the girls went through it.

Next came a rehearsal with two or three other players being tested. A director would group together those whom he thought could work best with each other. He'd choose a short sketch of several continuous scenes with which they were all familiar, usually from a play. They would be given every opportunity to perform in a natural, intelligent manner. When sketch day arrived, each actor was given a turn at center stage. Peg would be the "star" as the others fed her lines. Then another became the "star," and then the third, and so on. During the sketch, the directors would also study the others while the "star" was in action. Body language and emotion would be noted because even when an actor hasn't a line to recite, they are still part of the scene. Given her stage training, Peg would do extremely well here. This part of the test would take an entire day and be divided into morning and late afternoon sessions. The sessions were treated as actual film productions and used the same equipment and manpower. When it was over, the players were dismissed, the film studied, and the actors called back ... or maybe not.

* * *

One day Peg was in an RKO class learning makeup techniques. *Photoplay* came by to photograph the Radio Pictures Starlets. They wore barbershop smocks over their dresses and towels wrapped upon their heads. Far from glamorous, the gals are beautiful nonetheless, smiling brightly, radiant and glowing. Peg is beaming, absolutely thrilled in the moment. She's seated in the front row, young and pretty. Her face says it all.

Peg Entwistle's life has taken a fantastic, unexpected turn, offering new and promising opportunities. Her life was becoming enriched with wonderful experiences at the Dream Factory. Her life was good. Her life was exciting. *Photoplay* published the snapshot in October.

Her life had ended two weeks earlier.

19

Cameras and Clapboards, Take Two

The stage is a true and trusted friend. The motion picture industry is an acquaintance!—Helen Hayes[1]

Thirteen Women started production on June 9, 1932, with the actual photography beginning six days later. Peg's first day in front of the camera was July 11, when she shot part of the scene of Hazel killing her husband. Movies are rarely, if ever, filmed in the chronological sequence of the story's events, so it wasn't unusual that Peg's first takes were of her final scene.

On July 12, she arrived at nine o'clock with Marjorie Gateson, the actress playing Martha, Hazel's lover. Mary Duncan and Harriet Hagman (the Raskob sisters) reported to the set an hour later. After a short rehearsal, the scenes in the circus tent were filmed: Hazel comes into the dressing room with May to see June. Later they filmed Hazel coming through the tent's passageway to meet May (this entire shot was deleted). Then Hazel is filmed coming out of the dressing room to meet up with Martha. Most of this was deleted, including Peg's lines to Martha and a close-up of Martha smiling lovingly at her. According to production reports, everything looks to have gone smoothly. Peg was dismissed at 5:45 P.M.

More than 80 extras were used that day. Someone playing a non-speaking role, such as "Man," "Woman," or "Child," received $5 a day. Others made between $7.50 and $15. Stuntmen were used to double for Duncan and Hagman during the actual trapeze act. The Flyer got $200, the Catcher, $50—not a bad day's work during the Great Depression.

The next day, Peg reported at ten o'clock. Duncan and Hagman had been on the set since nine o'clock, shooting some of the trapeze action. Gateson was also on the set, but only in case a retake or added scene was needed.

Peg spent most of her second day getting filmed in closeup as she watches the trapeze performance. There was no one on the swings during these takes. She is actually only reacting to the director's instructions as he describes what her character would be seeing in the air (much in the same way silent pictures were directed). During this sequence, Peg brings her hands to the sides of her head. In the released version of the film it seems anxiety alone has prompted this action, as if Peg's Hazel is thinking *Oh, heavens!* as the Raskob sisters get set to attempt their "breath-taking, death-defying" double flip.[2] However, if the entire film had survived the cutting room, one would have soon learned that she was trying to block out an increasingly loud drum roll. Hazel isn't holding her head in fear and worry—she is covering her ears.

This was a recurring stage direction of Peg's original role. In this particular scene, a snare drummer in the circus orchestra begins a timpani roll to affect the circus audience with heightened suspense as the sisters get ready for their double flip. This is still in the film, but because of editing, viewers of *Thirteen Women* cannot realize the drum's cadence is hypnotically torturing Hazel. This plot device was deleted in four other scenes where the timpani roll, and its association with seeing May die, haunts Hazel. It manifests when she least expects it, and rises to exaggerated volume inside her mind, helping to push her over the edge of sanity and into murder. Had this device remained in the film, one would have seen Peg grasping her head to cover her ears numerous times.

This second day of shooting for Peg also completed filming of Duncan and Hagman. Peg was dismissed at seven o'clock that evening. She didn't have to report until one o'clock the next day, but she would work until 1:10 A.M. the following morning. This was her longest day because she was shooting her longest — and most important — sequence of scenes with Marjorie Gateson and Ken Thompson, who played Hazel's husband Tom.

Over the course of the next twelve hours, Peg will interpret the last, most controversial role of her life. It is in these scenes that the lesbian relationship between Hazel and Martha becomes blatant. This part of the story received the harshest scrutiny and the sharpest knife. Ironically, according to her cousin Helen, Peg thought her work here was some of the best she had ever done. It crushed her to see it destroyed.

Fortunately, memos, production notes, scripts, synopses and other documents regarding *Thirteen Women* were found in the special collections departments at UCLA, and the Margaret Herrick Library of the Academy of Motion Picture Arts and Sciences. When carefully studied, these items help tell a fascinating behind-the-deleted-scenes tale of a most risqué character in a highly unusual film. And so, because this looks to be the only film she ever made, and so closely tied to her suicide just six weeks after her final day of filming, here's an examination of Peg Entwistle's deleted scenes playing man-killing adulteress Hazel Clay Cousins, RKO's original lesbian psycho...

During the chitchat in the circus dressing room, before discussions of horoscopes enter the dialogue, May and June hurl questions at Hazel after she tells them she is on a motor trip with a friend. The sisters pry a bit and ask about her husband and her childlessness, but Hazel avoids being direct. After May leaves the room and June croons despairingly regarding her horoscope, Hazel says she also got a dire horoscope from the swami. But Hazel doesn't believe in such nonsense; besides, according to the final script, "She is too happy right now to be bothered."[3] Before leaving, Hazel says she'll be back after the trapeze act so they can talk about old times. As she leaves, Hazel asks, "Which one of you is which so I can tell when I watch?"[4] May says, "I do the tailspin ... June catches!"[5]

Had all of the above remained in Peg's opening scene, her "goodbye" to June would not have appeared so stilted or as abrupt as the final print of the film makes it seem.

And now Hazel, her skirt whipped up by a bucking wind, comes running from the dressing room to find Martha, "the lesbian who occupies Hazel's time," standing alone near the center ring.[6] Hazel apologizes for taking so long and asks why she hadn't gone in to the seats. Martha doesn't answer, she only smiles affectionately, links her arm around Hazel's, and "pats her hand protectively."[7] Had the entire shot remained unedited clear through to where they walk arm in arm to their seats, one would have noticed the overt affection and then recalled Hazel's slightly aloof, indirect responses to the sisters' questions about marriage and children. One would now suspect that Hazel wasn't thinking of her husband when she said she was "too happy right now to be bothered,"[8] and that her motor trip friend was probably not *just* a friend.

In the next shot, as tension builds in the early part of the trapeze act, Hazel's body gets rigid and Martha "presses more closely to her, patting her."[9] The drum roll intensifies; Hazel covers her ears. After May falls to her death, the shot cuts to Hazel and Martha. Hazel stands, in shock. A close-up shows her dreadfully mouthing the words "The swami."[10] Here we would have seen that she is now a believer—the horoscopes aren't nonsense after all.

At this point the scene dissolves to the swami's office where he and Ursula are introduced. Minutes later, when Ursula puts the tip of her pen on Hazel's yearbook photo to indicate she is her next victim, this scene in the final print cuts to Hazel murdering her husband, but originally it faded to Hazel's boudoir, where...

... It is late afternoon. The room is quaint: a bed in an alcove, a writing desk, a chaise lounge by an open French window. A slight breeze stirs the hangings. Hazel paces feverishly as the long roll of drums echo in her head. She covers her ears. The drums stop. She removes her hands and the drums beat on. She moans; hurries to the desk. After a bit of rummaging she finds her horoscope letter and reads it with shaking hands. A knock at the door sends Hazel running to it. She was hoping to see Martha on the other side, but it's only her husband, Tom. He has a suitcase. He's going to a business meeting out of town and has come to kiss his wife goodbye ... actually; it's not *just* a kiss Tom is after...

    Hazel
        Oh, I thought it was...
        (Hastily)
        Why should *you* knock?[11]
    Tom
        I thought I was being a nice husband to knock
        before I barged in. (Eyeing her) Still upset?[12]
    Hazel
        No. Are you leaving?[13]
    Tom
        Yeah.
        (He regards her as she turns away, then impulsively goes to her and grips her arms—pleadingly)
        Please, dear![14]
    Hazel
        (Freeing herself—wearily)
        Don't let's start that again.
        (She gets away from him, as if stung. He turns in startled surprise.)
        I ... don't like to be ... pawed, that's all.[15]
    Tom
        You used to.[16]
    Hazel
        (Tiredly)
        No. I didn't. I never liked it. I just let you because I thought I had to.
        (Abstractedly)
        Have a good time.[17]

They argue like this a bit longer ... Tom wanting her ... Hazel wanting Martha. Tom presses her for a reason as to why she's so bothered. "Seeing an old friend go like that," she says of May's death.[18] Tom counters, "But something has been on your mind for months."[19] Suddenly the drums return. Hazel covers her ears and sobs, "I can't sleep! Or eat! I hate you!"[20] Tom offers to cancel his trip so he can look after her. He holds her and begins kissing her brow and her neck, but Hazel recoils at his touch. After a tight silence, Tom gives up and says goodbye to his apologetic mess of a wife. The moment he's gone, Hazel gets dizzy. Her head is pounding. She hurries to the desk to finish reading her horoscope. Martha quietly comes in to surprise her little captive. Hazel knows she's there without even looking...

> Hazel
> (Without turning)
> Martha!
> (Turning, dropping the letter on the desk.)
> I'm so glad. I've been miserable.[21]
> Martha
> I eased into (Nodding back) the breakfast room
> to wait until your husband left.[22]
> Hazel
> (Hands to head again)
> I'll be sour company for dinner. My head's splitting.
> (She drops tiredly to the chaise lounge)[23]
> Martha
> Let's stay in then. We can have sandwiches here. And just talk.[24]

The stage direction now has Martha soothing Hazel on the chaise lounge with plenty of touching ... hands around her forehead, gently rubbing. Hazel relaxes completely and leans back against her with a sigh. But suddenly Hazel loses it again and is crying almost uncontrollably. Martha asks what's wrong and we learn she is having visual hallucinations to accompany the audio of the drums: She tells Martha about her troubling dreams and how she awakens at night and sees her own horoscope on the wall. Hazel says she's fine when she's away from her husband. Martha tells her the problem is Tom, not the swami's horoscopes. But Hazel is convinced the predictions are true: "But he wrote me I'd go to jail. P-prophesied it! *Why*? Why should I go to jail?"[25] And again the drums come loudly. When she tries to rise from the lounge, Martha restrains her and tells her to relax. Hazel complies. The drums quiet slowly and the scene dissolves on what will probably not become a bible study or game of gin rummy...

Fade in a moment later ... night ... still in Hazel's boudoir. The women are no longer on the chaise lounge; light from street lamps shining through the window illuminate its solitude, telling us the women are in Hazel's bed. Tom comes quietly through the door. Off screen, Hazel laughs: "a rippling, restorative peal."[26] Tom hears this and abruptly turns on the light. As he throws his hat to the chair, Hazel enters from the alcove. (She wears the negligee seen in the final print.) Hazel recoils in fear when she sees him. He explains he couldn't go through with his business meeting because he was worried about her. But he senses something. The moment he asks what's wrong, Martha enters from the alcove. She is dressed in a hat and coat, drawing on her gloves as she goes to Hazel while avoiding Tom's startled look. Hazel is petrified. Tom is aghast. "I thought I told you to stay away from *her*," he growls to Martha while nodding toward his wife.[27] Martha pales and hurries to the door. Hazel is blazing mad now. She tells Martha she will go with her. Tom orders that she will stay. Hazel runs into the alcove to get her things. Tom follows behind. Martha stands near the door and listens with fascination as they argue.

> Hazel
> (Almost hysterical)
> I won't. I won't do anything you say. I'm going to leave you.
> I can't stand you...
> (Going to alcove)

Hazel [cont'd]
   I'm getting dressed ... so *you* get out.
   (Sobbing brokenly)[28]
Tom [off screen]
   (From the alcove; pleading)
   Hazel! Please! You're sick! Let me...[29]
Hazel [off screen]
   (Interrupting)
   Keep away from me![30]
Tom [off screen]
   ... Let me hold you...[31]
   [on Hazel and Tom]
   (He tries to take her in his arms)

There were several close-ups of Martha listening to the argument. Tom seems to be working himself up to the point of raping Hazel, almost as if to punish her for her tryst with Martha—this is not *specifically* written in the script, but the context strongly hints of it...

Hazel [off screen]
   Don't! I told you not to touch me again! Leave me alone![32]
Tom
   (Rising angrily)
   I'll touch you, and you'll like it![33]
Hazel
   [off screen, angle on Tom]
   (With a pitiful cry)
   Don't![34]

The camera closes on Martha as she continues to listen. She hears a blow, then a gasp from Tom, the thump of his body falling to the floor. Cut to Hazel crying "Oh! Oh!" as she moves in the semi-dark.[35] The stage direction calls for the flowing negligee to give Peg a ghostly appearance. She goes to the bedside and struggles to turn on a lamp. When the room is lighted, a tray on the bed table shows remains of the women's snack—cold cuts, cheese, bread, sandwich items sliced with a kitchen knife. Tom is on the floor, kneeling against the bed as his blood spreads over the covers, the big knife buried to the hilt under his shoulder blade.

As Hazel realizes what she has done and screams away her sanity, the camera closes on her desk and zooms in on the horoscope letter. As she continues screaming, the camera pans down to the swami's signature, which now floats up off the paper, grows huge, and is coming at us on the screen. Dissolve...

* * *

The production report for July 14 has the notation, "Picture Closed, 1:10 A.M., July 15, 1932."[36] It also notes that Peg, Gateson, and Ken Thompson had finished playing their roles in the film.

Thirteen Women was thought to be completed, "in the can" as they say. But on August 12, Myrna Loy, C. Henry Gordon, and Ed Pawley will have to spend a long night doing retakes involving scenes in Ursula's room, her canyon house, and the swami's office. None of this had any direct relevance to Peg's work, but two weeks earlier, on July 29, she and Thompson were called back for a full day to film the rewrite of Tom's murder. The result is what you see in the current version of the picture.

Hazel did not kill her husband as ruthlessly as RKO's murder of Peg's screen debut.

Except for very early in the film now, Martha is non-existent, so there is no lesbian love. No sensual lesbian massage of Hazel's head. No post-coital lesbian snack of ham and cheese on rye. No jealousy between the horny husband and the mannish lesbian Amazon. No ghostly, flowing-negligee–clad Peg wandering wraith-like in the dark. Tom dies quick while standing, not bleeding to death against a bed still warm from the forbidden love between his wife and her woman. The only dialogue in the scene now is Tom's death shout of his wife's name and Hazel's screams. The cheesy flying signature of the swami is gone, too, thank goodness. (Although one still must endure his cheesy disembodied head floating toward Ursula later on.)

Peg was paid $350 for the retake. RKO optioned her to a term contract the next day. The *Los Angeles Times* announced the signing on July 31.

Three hundred fifty dollars for a day's work, along with a term contract, wasn't bad compensation for having most of her screen debut deleted. Of course, Peg would rather have had all her scenes left intact. David O. Selznick also would have preferred leaving the scenes intact; that's why he had the director film the lesbian storyline ... even after Will Hays, czar of the Motion Picture Production Code, was told it would not be filmed.

The next chapter will examine correspondence, production reports, and other dated documents proving the lesbian sequence was filmed contrary to assurances made. RKO had every intention of featuring the saucy Peg Entwistle as the lusty object of mannish Amazon desire. But then Hays announced he was coming to Hollywood the first week of August. The *New York Times* described the trip as a sort of missionary journey: Like an apostle, Hays was going to check on his saints and lead side-slipping producers back into the righteous paths.

Was this announcement by the influential overseer of film decency a blanket statement covering all the producers in Hollywood, or just a certain few? Or had he just one producer in mind? Did his representatives in Los Angeles get wind of a covert operation taking place at RKO? It's unclear, really; but the July 29 filming of the rewrite of Peg's final scene, shot more than two weeks after she had done the original takes, and the suddenness of it amid the announcement of Hays' arrival to Hollywood was too convenient to be coincidence.

20

The Love That Dared Not Speak Peg's Name

I believe in censorship. I made a fortune out of it. — Mae West[1]

To begin with, RKO should have listened to Miriam Meredith. She was, after all, one of their best scenario agents. In January 1932, Meredith sat in the New York City office of Claude Kendall Publishing and read a synopsis of Tiffany Thayer's manuscript for the *Thirteen Women* novel. In her report to Hollywood, she said the story "Doesn't pretend to be realistic" and that it had an extremely complicated plot.[2] "Nothing for pictures," she added, and advised against acquiring the rights for adaptation.[3] RKO executives ignored her advice and paid $12,500 ($195,000 today) for the film rights to a novel none of them had read and which was still six weeks away from hitting its first book store.

Fortunately for Thayer, the book became a bestseller. But for RKO the film was a bomb. Critics panned it unmercifully, one calling it an utterly implausible and dreadful mess. Another reviewer thought *Thirteen Women* had more defects and deficiencies than *Chandu the Magician* (Fox Films' magician-yogi-secret agent man out to destroy Bela Lugosi's death ray!). Even the women's clothing hadn't escaped the poison pen. Norbert Lusk at the *Los Angeles Times* did little to hide his feelings in a diatribe attacking the costume designs as grotesque. Lusk even went so far as to accuse the designers of showing the piquantly interesting Jill Esmond a very special kind of spite.

One can almost imagine Miriam Meredith choking back an I-told-you-so.

* * *

Many say the trouble began in the 1920s.

The *Roaring* Twenties.

In 1921 the Hollywood colony already had a reputation for loose living and immorality when Roscoe "Fatty" Arbuckle, one of the era's most popular movie stars, was accused of raping actress Virginia Rappe during a party at the St. Francis Hotel in San Francisco. She died a few days after the alleged assault of complications resulting from a ruptured bladder. Arbuckle was indicted and tried for manslaughter (police claimed that during the rape, his weight caused her internal injuries, thus her death). The hefty star would be acquitted after three sensational trials, but civic and religious groups had already declared war on the movie industry. Movies and movie stars were blamed for much of society's ills; moviemakers were seen as purveyors of vice and sin most miserable. (Vice and sin apparently never occurred before the invention of the motion picture camera.)

Women's clubs, church organizations, and various reform groups demonstrated across the country. Banks cut off lines of credit to producers. There was a national call for censorship of Hollywood films. The federal government and three dozen states considered passing laws against the industry. Studio moguls needed to act fast to stop the fanning flames. Producers Lewis J. Selznick and Saul Rogers approached Will Hays, a Presbyterian teetotaler, respected Republican conservative, and recent dark-horse candidate for U.S. president. He was the postmaster general of the United States when Selznick and Rogers met him to present an idea: They needed a spokesman to represent the interests of the film industry and to rebuild its image. Hays liked what he heard. In January 1922, after resigning his cabinet position, he became head of the newly formed Motion Picture Producers and Distributors of America (MPPDA). Its purpose was to oversee every film production. Each studio would (more or less) volunteer to adhere to a morality code. Before a production could begin, the screenplay would first be sent to the MPPDA for review. It was understood by all the studios that voluntary cooperation with Hays was essential if they wished to avoid enactment of state and federal censorship laws.

In three short months, Hays had smoothed things over with the pro-censorship groups. Banks began loaning money to the studios again. By 1926 President Calvin Coolidge put aside federal efforts aimed at regulation of Hollywood. Hays had become so influential that the MPPDA came to be known as the Hays Office.

Hays had compiled a list of subjects he thought film studios would be wise to avoid. He called this "the formula," but it was popularly known as the "don'ts and be carefuls."[4] In 1930 the Studio Relations Committee (SRC) was created to implement this formula. Hays appointed Colonel Jason S. Joy, a former American Red Cross executive, to head the Committee. His job was to supervise productions and to advise studios where script changes or cuts were required.

Also in 1930, several studio heads, including Irving Thalberg of MGM, met with Martin Quigley, editor of the prominent trade paper *Motion Picture Herald*, to discuss a code of standards which Quigley and several concerned Catholic priests had sent to every film studio a year earlier. Out of adjustments and revising of the Hays formula and the Catholic-based code of standards, the so-called Production Code was born. From now on, sin and wickedness in a movie could not go unpunished. Gangsters and murderers must die or go to prison. Clergy, police, judges, and politicians must not be seen to be corrupt unless the story made it clear such villainy was the exception to the rule. Abortion, interracial love, and profanity were forbidden. Homosexuality was not specifically mentioned in the Code, but it was clearly understood that such a thing must *never* be spoken of, implied, or shown. (It is sometimes argued that the Code's fourth prohibition — "Any inference of sex perversion"[5] — was meant to include homosexuality.)

But for all its barking, the Code lacked any real teeth. Moreover, Jason Joy and his small staff at the SRC were overwhelmed with the 500 scripts coming to their office each year. Producers began complaining loudly as they fell behind schedule while waiting for a green light. Colonel Joy began to sympathize with Hollywood and from time to time looked the other way, which wasn't hard to do, for even Hays understood that his Production Code was really only a guide for producers; at the end of the day, it was up to the studios to police themselves.

Then in July 1934 the Production Code Administration was created. Heavy fines could now be levied for violations. Films made in Hollywood from 1930 until July 1934 are known as pre–Code films. Some argue that all films made before 1934 can be considered as such.

RKO's *Thirteen Women* is pre–Code, but once upon a time it had been *very* pre–Code.

This takes us to Dorothy Cormack, a script supervisor in the RKO Story Department (and likely related to *Thirteen Women* screenwriter Bartlett Cormack). On June 2, 1932, she sent a copy of the *Thirteen Women* script to Colonel Jason Joy, whose office was about two miles away on Hollywood Boulevard. With the script was a letter: "Dear Sir, I am sending you herewith a copy of the estimating script of our production, *Thirteen Women.* We are very anxious to get your reaction on this at the earliest possible moment."[6]

On June 4, Joy sent his reply, but not to the Story Department: "Dear Mr. Selznick, I got a great kick out of reading [the script of] *Thirteen Women* and I look forward to seeing an even better picture. Of course I know you will want to get rid of *The Captive* element which is now apparent in the relationship between Hazel and Martha, for even a hint of this sort of thing is impossible under the Code. No one now could fail to catch the taint of lesbianism in the various scenes between the two women, and my advice is to kick it right out of the picture...."[7]

Joy did a very interesting thing here: "The Captive," as he termed the relational element between Hazel and Martha, is the title of the play about lesbians that was raided by police on Broadway in 1927. (The reader will remember this event from an earlier chapter.) Colonel Joy could just as easily have gotten his message across to Selznick without referring to a play whose cast had been jailed under the Padlock Law. Like Joy, Selznick knew the play and its history, therefore he would know that Joy's comparison of *Thirteen Women* to *The Captive* was not simply a clever way of expressing advice, it was a shot across the bow.

On June 7, Joy's associate, Lamar Trotti, sent this to Hays: "We have discussed the script of *Thirteen Women* with Mr. Tamar Lane [story editor] of RKO Studios to make certain that all suggestions of lesbianism were eliminated."[8] A day later, Miss Cormack wrote to Joy: "I am sending you herewith by special delivery, two copies of the Final Script of *Thirteen Women.* This picture goes into production June 9, 1932."[9] This final script was virtually identical to the first one she had sent on June 2, so now things are going to get a bit snippy between RKO and representatives of the Hays Office...

On June 9, Selznick received a terse reply from Joy. (The "Mr. Montagne" to whom he refers is Edward J. Montagne, an RKO executive and ally of the Selznicks who had been with them since the early 1920s when he was the top writer at Selznick Pictures.)

"Dear Mr. Selznick: We have again discussed with Mr. Montagne the opening sequences in *Thirteen Women,* and he has asked us to write you further regarding our opinion of those sequences which involve the two women, Hazel and Martha. It seems incredible to me that it is possible to play these scenes without getting into them the feeling of lesbianism which is apparent from the opening lines through the murder of Hazel's husband. This, of course, is a Code matter and any suggestion of that subject would run afoul of the Code. It seems to me you had better find some other excuse for Hazel's quarrel with her husband, which results in his murder."[10] Then he adds another one of his head-scratchers into the mix: "The above thought is not influenced in any way with what the book may have contained because I have never read the book."[11] (If he had, he would have found a sensuous illustration showing Hazel and Martha in bed together. It's hard to determine which woman is which, for neither looks "mannish," but one is sitting up, dressed in a slip, gazing adoringly upon her naked, obviously spent lover ... the caption reads, "Hazel thought it was very beautiful."[12])

Joy closes this letter with a bit of kissing up: He reminds Selznick about the previous letter in which he said he liked the story, and adds, "In fact, we here [at the Studio Relations Committee] thought it one of the most interesting stories we have run across in a long time."[13]

Our score at halftime: Per rules of the Hays Office, RKO submits the original *Thirteen Women* script to Joy, who says the lesbians have to go. RKO sends a final draft, but little has changed — Hazel and Martha are still breathing heavy. Then came discussions between Joy and Montagne, who tried to persuade Joy that Hazel's affair was important to the film. Joy pushed back, invoking the Code. Montagne stood his ground and countered that the Code mentions nothing about lesbians, was not law, and that this entire hullabaloo was akin to telling Selznick he didn't know beans about being an executive producer. Montagne refuses to discuss it any further, and tells him to talk to Selznick, which he does in the June 9 letter, and throws in a "You had better,"[14] which everyone knew included an unsaid "or else."

After reading Joy's letter, Selznick called in Montagne and Archainbaud to discuss the matter. On June 10, Montagne sent this: "Dear Colonel: We have discussed at length the episode you are worrying about in *Thirteen Women*. We have confidence in Mr. Archainbaud's ability to treat it in a way that will be neither offensive nor objectionable. However, just as soon as Mr. Archainbaud completes the shooting of this episode, and before the picture is completed, I will have it assembled for you to look at. You may rest assured that we will depend upon your good judgment in anything you suggest in the handling of this sequence. It is perhaps superfluous to say that this episode has been entirely rewritten, both as to dialogue and business."[15]

Montagne (and RKO) would have him believe most of the lesbian sequences are now gone, and what does remain will be tastefully shot under the direction of Archainbaud. Indeed, this was Joy's understanding, for the next day he wrote to Hays (dutifully addressing him by his former cabinet title):

> Dear General: In *Thirteen Women* RKO has a very exciting and interesting story and while a little of the lesbianism was left in the script sequence, we have told the studio that, of course, this cannot even be hinted at and I am sure that in the finished picture it won't be there at all. The fact that it is a good story without that phase is all to the good because Selznick won't want to take a chance on spoiling it with that unusable material.[16]

But RKO records show otherwise ... Selznick *did* want to take a chance.

Keep in mind the June 10 letter to Joy, when Montagne told him, "This episode has been entirely rewritten, both as to dialogue and business."[17] Now, either Montagne was incompetent and had no clue as to what was taking place in *his* department, or he was flat-out lying, because Marjorie Dudley, one of *his* writers in *his* scenario department, drafted a synopsis of the script's June 8 final draft. This synopsis is dated June 10, and includes a rather detailed outline of the love affair between Hazel and Martha, all of it coinciding with the lesbianism found in the stage direction and dialogue of that final draft...

... And the details in Peg's *July* production reports note the scene numbers she filmed. These are the same scene numbers of the lesbian sequences found in the shooting script, which matches exactly the content of the June 8 final draft. None of this involved a clerical error or an oversight on the part of RKO's scenario department; there were no other drafts of a final script or synopsis containing rewrites of *less* lesbianism — there never would be. This is evidenced in an October 1952 synopsis by Lewis Clay, who notes it was based on the June 8 final draft. Clay's synopsis is very brief and makes no mention of Martha or lesbianism; however, it does include details about Hazel's marriage which are found only within the lesbian storyline.

The June 8 final draft and June 10 synopsis are evidence enough that RKO intended to film the *entire* lesbian storyline, not a "little of the lesbianism" as Joy was led to believe and so related to Hays on June 11.[18] The mid–July shooting script and production reports show that the filming of this storyline took place *a month* after Montagne's assurance to Joy that the episode had been entirely rewritten.

So, why did Selznick try to put one past the censors?

Well, no RKO memos stating his reason were found; however, one might suppose a number of reasons all rolled into one. Selznick obviously thought the affair between Hazel and Martha was important to the story, otherwise he would have ordered a rewrite long before the first draft hit Joy's desk. And while lesbianism was not a new plot line in Hollywood, a lesbian adulteress turned hypnotic killer who goes insane would have made for one hell of an edgy, sexy horror flick, and quite possibly a very profitable one.

Given these factors (and others), and the mounting pressure from Joy, Selznick decided to keep secret the filming of the lesbian sequences. He probably grew weary of hearing it from the morality police, so he lied (by having others lie for him) to get the censors off the

Only eight gals made the final cut of **Thirteen Women**. Clockwise from Peg (front right): Harriet Hagman, Florence Eldridge (a brunette in the film), Mary Duncan, Irene Dunne, Myrna Loy, Kay Johnson and Marjorie Gateson. What makes this photograph interesting is Gateson, who played Peg's lover in the original version. Gateson's lines were deleted when the lesbian plotline was cut. Her presence in this image is evidence that RKO intended to release the motion picture with the lesbian story intact, for the photograph was taken *after* filming was completed, when Gateson's role still had significance. Her part then was cut to less than twenty seconds (courtesy Jacqui Lewis Mittleman).

studio's back. He was a film producer; not a Boy Scout leader, and no doubt believed he should be able to produce *Thirteen Women* as he saw fit, especially given the censorship inconsistencies on Colonel Joy's résumé. One glaring example of hypocrisy to which Selznick could have pointed was Josef von Sternberg's *The Blue Angel*, which violated a good number of Code precepts. This film, which starred Marlene Dietrich and Emil Jannings, was made in Germany. Before making its way into U.S. distribution in 1930, it was screened by Joy. Despite its numerous transgressions, he cleared the film for release without requesting a single elimination, and in complete contradiction of a fellow censor who had called *The Blue Angel* indecent.

There were other examples of Joy hypocrisies, and so it would be okay to bet the farm that Selznick was counting on *Thirteen Women* to be included among them.

Of course, there is still the little problem with regard to Montagne telling Joy he would assemble the new sequence for his review. The evidence suggests this was done, but that Joy had only seen a specially edited version of the sequence, one with a little of the lesbianism intact (a memo below indicates as much). After the film's release, Joy would of course be livid upon discovering that the wool had been pulled over his eyes, but he would powerless. He and the rest of the Hays Office would simply move on to the hundreds of scripts yet to be scrutinized.

The original print of *Thirteen Women* might very well have made it to the public, but then Hays made his announcement about coming to Hollywood to lead side-slipping producers back into righteousness. With Hays arriving in the first week of August, Selznick scrambled. RKO called Peg and Ken Thompson to come in on July 29 to retake their murder scene.

At some point during this time, RKO also discarded that special sequence Montagne had prepared for Jason Joy.

So Selznick blinked, but why?

Either before or upon his arrival to Hollywood, Hays may have discovered or suspected RKO's ruse, or, blind to it still, had just gone about his business reminding Selznick and all the other Hollywood moguls that there was reaping to be had with the sowing of Code violations. Boycotts were a legitimate concern of the studios. If provoked, conservative reformers (such as those within the National Conference of Catholic Churches) could marshal millions of pitchforks and torches in short order. Hays need only have indirectly suggested that boycotts could make the Depression all the more depressing for studios and the thousands of good, hard-working people and their families who depended on their income.

Or Hays might have pointed out that while studios may indeed legally release films with blatant Code violations, he would see to it that the coveted "Passed by the National Board of Review" legend would be absent from the main titles. This term is found in films which the Board recognized as having merit and had endorsed as a form of art. At any rate, out went the forbidden love in *Thirteen Women*, and in went the National Board of Review stamp of approval.

However it all may have occurred, it's unlikely the meetings adjourned with group hugs.

It doesn't matter when Hays completed his missionary journey to Hollywood, or how many souls he saved while there, but it is interesting that for more than three weeks there was no correspondence between his representatives and RKO in relation to *Thirteen Women*. Then on August 24, Selznick received the following from Joy: "Dear Mr. Selznick: We have just seen your picture, *Thirteen Women*, and are glad to find that the note of lesbianism which appeared in the script and in the first version of the picture has been discarded by you. The picture is now wholly satisfactory under the Code."[19]

Joy may have thought it was satisfactory, but he wasn't satisfied. He goes on with his concern for the scene where Helen shoots herself. A day later he sent a letter to the Hays Office outlining this concern regarding Helen's suicide. It all just never seemed to end...

When previewing a film yet to be released, audiences would record their comments and suggestions on Applause Cards, small index cards that were given to them by the studio; only a few of these cards were found for *Thirteen Women,* and none of them mention Peg or Hazel Cousins.

Less than two weeks after Peg's suicide, the film had a limited debut release. Some sources, including the American Film Institute and the Internet Movie Database (IMDb), say *Thirteen Women* was released on September 16, 1932, the date of Peg's suicide, but this could not be confirmed. The earliest release was found to be September 26, within a syndicated Hollywood wire in a Maryland newspaper discussing her death. No ads or reviews for the film were found in any of the largest cities' newspapers until late September and early October. It is the opinion of the author that respected sources such as AFI and the IMDb are incorrect in saying that the film was released on September 16, 1932; that this purported release date was accepted over the years after having been grafted onto Hollywood lore by the oft-reported myth that Peg Entwistle killed herself on the night her only film had its Hollywood premiere.

It is a romantically tragic notion, to be sure, but one that has never been confirmed.

Except for those who had known her best, Peg was all but forgotten by the time RKO gave *Thirteen Women* a limited re-release in September of 1935.

Nearly every reviewer in 1932 had panned it. Interestingly, while the picture was released in the wake of Peg's well publicized death, critics didn't mention her suicide, despite having mentioned a suicide depicted in the film.

One would be hard-pressed to find such blatant disregard for tabloid etiquette today.

RKO's *Thirteen Women* has become a sort of cult classic over the years — more so because of Peg Entwistle's unusual death than of Myrna Loy or Irene Dunne's star power.

In 1932 the film was considered awful by audiences and critics who would never come to know of the lesbianism disputed between RKO and the Hays Office, or that the delicate ingénue Entwistle had lost 75 percent of her film debut because of prudish, hypocritical cads who hadn't a creative bone in their bodies.

It is anyone's guess as to how the film would have been received had the love between Hazel and Martha remained, but given Peg's proven track record of talent there seems little doubt that while the film may still have been dismissed, she would have been warmly embraced.

And not just by mannish, Amazon women...

21

24 Years 7 Months 12 Days

*My castle shall stand on a height ... on a very great height ...
with a clear outlook on all sides, so that I can see far, far around.*
— Hilda in *The Master Builder*[1]

Dateline: Hollywood, California, 1932.
Los Angeles Examiner
September 14: "Three of Radio's eleven starlets have been dropped already. Harriet Hagman, Phyllis Fraser, and Peg Entwistle are the three who don't think eleven's such a lucky number anymore."[2]
September 15: "I muffed that one about three of Radio's eleven baby stars being off the list. Phyllis Fraser, mentioned as one of the three, wires: 'Don't know about eleven being an unlucky number, but thirteen's alright. Radio took up my option on the 13th. Harriet, is that nice — to blight a budding starlet?'"[3]
September 16: "E. J. Montagne, Scenario Chief at R-K-O Dies...."[4]
It isn't known if Peg learned of the death of the man who had tried to keep her *Thirteen Women* work off the cutting room floor. She wouldn't have much cared ... a 47-year-old stroke victim would mean little to a dead girl walking.
On Friday evening, September 16, 1932, Peg stood at the door of her family's Beachwood Drive home and told her uncle and aunt that she was going to get a book from a drugstore in Hollywoodland, and then see some friends
They never saw her alive again.
There hadn't been much concern when she didn't return home that night. She was, after all, an adult, an actress fond of mingling with other actresses into the wee hours. Peg stayed out overnight before, so it wasn't like she just suddenly *vanished*. And she specifically mentioned a "rendezvous," which always meant she was off to see her girlfriends[5] ... Miss Entwistle would never just simply *meet* her friends, you see; she would *rendezvous*. Helen Reid remembered Uncle Charles teaching Peg a phrase in French: "Monsieur Entwistle, je suis loin au rendez-vous avec l'amour, au vin, et au fromage!"[6]
Mr. Entwistle, I am off to rendezvous with love, wine, and cheese!
"Enty was fluent, of course," recalled Helen.[7] "Babs would sometimes sing this as she was leaving the house. It was charming. Her voice was lovely."[8]
Because Peg's farewell had all the usual tones, Charles presumed his niece had gone to one of her usual haunts, such as the nearby Hollywood Studio Club, a women-only apartment complex and activity center which at the time was run by the YWCA and supported

by Constance DeMille, wife of legendary producer Cecil B. DeMille. Hundreds of actresses lived at the Studio Club, a safe environment for young, struggling girls who had tried, or were still trying, to "make it big" in Hollywood. (Marilyn Monroe would later live there.) Men were not allowed to stay overnight, and burly matrons "manned" the desk and patrolled the property. Rules were strictly enforced. No booze, no drugs, no smoking. But it was clean and pretty and rents were low and past-dues often forgiven, and for a young, attractive girl whose film aspirations were going bust, it sure beat the casting couch, and worse.

Contrary to what has often been claimed, Peg Entwistle never lived at the Hollywood Studio Club. She rented a room in an apartment building very near her family home. Milton Entwistle recalled that the building could be seen from his back yard.

When Saturday became Saturday night, Aunt Jane became worried. She went to the Studio Club and asked about Peg, but none of the girls remembered seeing her. Jane returned home, more worried, but not in a panic. Peg's brothers were young teenagers, but there was no need to complicate their lives. Charles and Jane kept up appearances; the lads were none the wiser as their aunt and uncle made calls and queried neighbors and shop owners in Beachwood Village, the community's town square just inside the gates of Hollywoodland.

On Sunday, the family's calls and queries continued, but still no word had come.

At 9 P.M. on Sunday evening, September 18, 1932, Officer Crum was manning the complaint desk at LAPD's Central Station in downtown Los Angeles when his telephone rang. The woman on the line was concise, but cryptic: She told Crum she had been hiking near the Hollywoodland Sign, and near the bottom found a woman's shoes and jacket. A little further on she noticed a purse. In it was a suicide note. She looked down the mountain and saw a body. Although she told Crum that she didn't want any publicity in the matter, she had nonetheless wrapped up the jacket, shoes, and purse in a bundle and laid them on the steps outside the Hollywood Police Station.

When Crum asked the caller her name, a moment's silence was followed by the "click" of a hang-up. He immediately called Captain Fred Trosper at the Hollywood Station and relayed the information. Trosper hurried outside. There, he found the bundle on the steps, just as the woman had said. Trosper brought the bundle into the station and a minute later the items were being examined: The shoes, though showing signs of considerable wear, had been expensive, purchased from an exclusive Pasadena boutique, according to a logo inside. The coat was lightweight, full-length, and luxurious, a wavy mix of tan suede and soft black leather; a label from a Beverly Hills clothier was sewn into the lining, a jeweled breast pin (similar in design to the crest on Peg's stationery) was fastened to the lapel. The purse matched the coat, and was empty except for the note:

"I am afraid I'm a coward. I am sorry for everything.

If I had done this a long time ago it would have saved a lot of pain."[9]

Trosper sent homicide detective Lieutenant Paul Stevens and two patrolmen to investigate the Hollywoodland Sign. It took nearly an hour for them to find Peg's body. Stevens quickly surmised that she had climbed a ladder behind the massive 50-foot-tall H. She had either climbed to the very top and leapt, or near the top came off the ladder and made her way onto one of several horizontal pipes used to brace the two vertical sections of the H. She would had to have clung to one of the vertical edges in order to maintain her balance before jumping.

In typical Hollywood fashion, her fall will sometimes be described as "spectacular,"[10] but it was more grotesque than anything else...

She hadn't impacted head-first. Death had not come in a merciful instant; it was cruel, ugly, bloody and clumsy. She *smashed* to the ground at freeway speeds, awkwardly at a horizontal angle. Her pelvis shattered like a china plate thrown violently to the floor.

The trauma was massive; the pain, unbearable.

But it had only just begun.

The kinetic energy of the impact and the steep angle of the slope leading away from the structure propelled her helpless, flailing body nearly 100 feet downward ... she tumbled and rolled and agonized through chaparral until the grotesque journey ended in a shallow ravine. Fractures to her limbs were numerous, but the dismantled pelvis ruptured her blood vessels, which in turn caused fatal internal bleeding. Peg could not have lived more than four minutes; if she hadn't been knocked out by a concussion, she could have been conscious for as long as two minutes, or until her heart could no longer feed blood to her brain.

Her screams and sufferings would have been heard only by a few scurrying animals and Peg Entwistle died in the glow of the magnificent flashing Sign which she had seen born.

HOLLY ... WOOD ... LAND ... HOLLYWOODLAND...

* * *

By the time her body got to the morgue, it was ten minutes to midnight of September 19, 1932 (Monday). Her personal effects were documented. The note was examined, of course, but did little to shed light on an identity, for it was signed using only the initials "P.E."[11] The investigators had no idea who she was, but with just those two letters Peg may have been telling them who *she* thought she was ... *nobody*.

One could argue that by not signing the note with any of her names, Peg was separating herself from herself, and used "P.E." as a kind of disassociation. "Peg" would have personified her existence, reminding her that she was a fan and child of the theater, for that was where she had taken the name and found her calling. Signing the note "Peg Entwistle" would have reminded Peg that she was an actress of note, a woman young and pretty. And you can just forget about signing a suicide note with "Babs." Using her nearly lifelong pet name would only have evoked fond memories of family and friends—she would then have to confront the fact that people loved Babs ... *cared* for her. No, one mustn't have such things tagging along with a *nobody* on a damn mountain ... up a damn ladder ... off a damn sign...

P.E.

She knew the press would publish the note and that Aunt Jane and Uncle Charles read the papers every day—they would know immediately that this "P.E." was her. The initials served Peg's disassociation and would also tell her family where her body could be found.

"Girl Ends Life In Hollywood Mountain Leap: Pretty Young Woman Jumps to Death from Top of Letter 'H' of Huge Sign; Initials 'P.E.'"[12]

On Monday, September 19, 1932, the *Los Angeles Examiner* told the city about her; all the city's sheets had told it, and all in similar, dramatic fashion. Bold headlines towered over articles that couldn't seem to decide whether to be sympathetic or sensational.

At the request of police, newspapers described her features and published the sad note with its only real clue to the tragic girl's identity. Surely someone had to be missing this P.E., whom many news outlets described somewhat affectionately as a pretty, blue-eyed blonde.

Peg's Cousin Helen recalled Aunt Jane's sorrowful wail from within the house, and how she and her mother, Marguerite, hurried next door to Peg's. Charles was on the phone to police when Helen arrived. Jane had collapsed to her knees on the floor, the headline-streaked newspaper clutched to her chest as Marguerite stooped to help. (Milton Entwistle could not recall this event, and believes he and his brother were out of the house.)

It is not likely that anyone in the home that day had turned to the theatrical section of the *Los Angeles Examiner,* where Florence Lawrence, the drama critic who had written so glowingly of Peg on numerous occasions, had an item in her column announcing a new play at the El Capitan Theater starring Billie Burke and Alan Mowbray...

The ironic twists in Peg Entwistle's life — and death — seem to never end.

Uncle Charles went alone to the Hollywood Police Station. He was taken to the county morgue; there he was met by the autopsy surgeon. Dr. Wagner took him to the body. Peg was positively identified. Charles had to stay until the afternoon, when an inquest was conducted and a few questions asked of him. A "No Jury" verdict of suicide caused by despondency was soon rendered by Wagner and Coroner Frank Nance.[13] Peg's body was released, meaning Charles was now free to make burial arrangements. A funeral director came to collect her. The clothing she had worn that night was also taken to Hollywood Cemetery. Charles was allowed to keep the note. (The breast pin from Peg's coat was misplaced during shuffles between agencies, but was eventually found and returned in late January 1933.)

Charles was taken back to the Hollywood Station to complete some paperwork and answer a few more routine questions for detectives. He was met by reporters, too. They were allowed to sit in on the police questions and toss a few of their own his way. *The Los Angeles Times* remembered some of it like this: "The bereaved uncle ... fumbled the brief note she had left and between the lines read for the authorities a tragic story of his niece's bitter and unbearable disappointment over her failure to 'click' in the studios."[14]

Charles also gave them a very brief synopsis of her career. However, because he was either not thinking clearly in his grief, or because he just couldn't remember certain details of events, or a little of both, the well-intentioned, good-hearted man inadvertently corrupted Peg's résumé to the press. In so doing, he helped establish the "failed actress" tag which has followed her name for decades. (Charles also conveyed some inaccuracies regarding her vital statistics for the coroner; these are discussed later.)

"Although she never confided her grief to me," said Charles, "I was somehow aware that she was suffering intense mental anguish. She was only 24. It is a great shock to me that she gave up the fight as she did."[15] When pressed by reporters' queries of a broken love affair, or feelings toward her ex-husband as a motive for the suicide, Charles brushed all that aside, characterizing it as absurd. He concluded with, "The Sign always exercised a fascination for her ... she often rode [horses] in its vicinity."[16]

The weary gentleman was given his leave by the police. And by the time he was home a few minutes later, comforting his distraught wife, the newspapers were already turning out the evening editions...

"Defeated In Her Film Career, Peg Entwistle Leaps Off Giant Sign"[17]

"Suicide Beauty Identified as Hollywood Actress"[18]

"New York Actress Leaps to Death from Giant Sign"[19]

"Actress' Death Leap Laid to Film Defeat"[20]

"Suicide Laid to Film Jinx"[21]

Death Leap Actress. Beauty and the Leap. Leaping Beauty ... on and on it went.

No one considered the possibility she might have changed her mind while teetering up there, and may have been the "Accidently-fell-while-trying-to-get-back-on-the-ladder Actress."

On Tuesday, September 20, 1932, a traditional Episcopal service was held in a chapel at Hollywood Cemetery. Peg's brothers were kept away on their uncle's orders, but joining other family members were some gals from the Hollywood Studio Club, and a number of Broadway friends and players she had worked with on stage. Grace Hampton, Frances Goodrich, Sidney Toler, Hardie Albright, Arthur Byron and the distinguished English actor Wyndham Standing were there. Alan Mowbray had driven Charles and Jane to the service. Helen Reid recalled, "Aunt Jane and Enty told me [years later] how warm Alan was and [he] said Billie [Burke] was so sorry to hear about Babs, but she couldn't go through another [funeral] so soon."[22]

Burke had buried her husband, Florenz Ziegfeld, just two months earlier. (The play she was about to open with Mowbray a few days hence was no sign that she had gotten over his death—it was a necessity created by the vast debt Ziegfeld had left behind.) With no reason to doubt the sincerity of her message to Charles and Jane, there remains the possibility that the world-famous Billie Burke also did not desire to have the press see her attend the funeral of a girl, an *actress,* who killed herself, or who killed herself in such a sensationalized manner.

It looks as though none of the starlets from Peg's RKO freshmen class attended the service, and RKO executives, mourning their own loss of Edward Montagne, completely ignored the Entwistle family. Of course, Peg had no longer been on the RKO payroll, so the studio's slight makes sense, but it would have been a sweet show of solidarity if the starlets had come.

Robert Keith, who at the time was working in San Francisco with his wife Dorothy Tierney, had to have known what happened, for Peg's death made headlines in all the Bay Area papers, too. Nonetheless, neither his condolences nor a dime of the thousands of dollars he owed Peg would ever grace the Entwistle household.

Walter Hampden and his wife were in New York, but they called the house and sent flowers. They were sickened by it all, for they had deep affection for Peg and her family.

Peg's body, inside a simple pine coffin draped with a pall, was pushed into a furnace and cremated shortly after the service. There was no viewing, of course, and with her went the clothing she had with her the night she died, including the blue floral dress made by Aunt Jane.

It had been a gift to celebrate her signing with RKO. Peg wore it the day she first reported to the studio.

She left no last will and testament—but how many 24-year-old people do? Still, even if she had drafted a will, there was virtually nothing of value to add. The actress who once upon a time lived in Valentino's Natacha Rambova–designed penthouse overlooking Central Park had lived her last days in a tiny room above a garage and died penniless.

So Peg was cremated. Charles intended to bring her remains to Ohio, where they would be interred with her father, but money for a family trip east was tight. Finally, on January 5, 1933, Charles and Jane were joined by a few Ross family members and friends for a small, private burial service at the Oak Hill Cemetery in Glendale, Ohio.

22

Why?

There is every reason why I should say good-bye and farewell!
There is every reason... — Sherlock Holmes[1]

The first thing that should be addressed is why RKO fired her.

Following her part in *Thirteen Women*, while Peg was under her term contract waiting for the studio to put her in something, David O. Selznick decided it was time to trim the fat. Everyone — including Selznick — would have to sacrifice in order to keep the studio afloat. RKO stars and execs received significant reductions in pay, and many term contract players like Peg were let go. She was released in the third week in August, just days after the *Reno Gazette* had done a special feature on her regarding the new contract.

Like so many whose companies had to cut costs through reductions in personnel, even talented personnel, Peg was simply an unfortunate employee positioned at the bottom of the totem pole. Of course, not all of the bottom of the totem was let go (i.e., Phyllis Fraser), for there was naturally a certain favoritism based on what type of girls the studio thought were better suited for coming productions.

That's it in a nutshell — no conspiracy, no vendetta for refusing rides on casting couches.

* * *

The general consensus handed down through more than three quarters of a century is that Peg Entwistle killed herself because she hadn't "clicked" with the studios. As previously stated, this is a misconception, brought to life by the less-than-accurate public comments made by her Uncle Charles. It didn't help that the news hounds of that time snapped up that irresistible bone of a storyline, namely that of a young, beautiful actress who was brought to the depths of despair by the rejection of Tinsel Town. Moreover, this myth was helped along through the decades as books, articles, and television specials featuring Peg in topics about "tragic" starlets and celebrity deaths and suicides were presented without any in-depth research into her life or career.

It was simply easier for an author, journalist, filmmaker, or Hollywood historian to peruse indexes of the era's newspapers to find articles about her death; then, after lunch, spend another hour in the city library rolling through a spool of microfilm. A few scribbles on a notepad later, and voilà, one was now an expert on the Hollywood Sign Girl. No one seemed to notice or care that there were almost as many contradictions in the reported details of Peg's life, death, and career as there were authors, journalists, filmmakers, and Hollywood historians "detailing" her.

Peg was certainly no "failed actress." Her role as originally filmed in RKO's *Thirteen Women* was hardly a "bit" part. You know, too, that she had survived dry spells between stage productions, and had sometimes been rejected and broke. And it bothered her, too. Remember that one letter to her Aunt Jane, from January 1928, when Peg had been off the boards for several months? "It looks as though this business has retired me," she demurred.[2] But soon after that, she got a nearly year-long tour with the Theater Guild, and rave notices from sea to shining sea. Being broke and out of work was not strange to Peg. She knew well that being an actress meant crackers one day and caviar the next. Getting let go by RKO was no more devastating to her than having the curtain lowered on a Broadway flop a week after opening night (*She Means Business*), or losing a hoped-for cherished role to Ruth Gordon (*Serena Blandish*), or having extremely popular productions suddenly go dark because of a heat wave (*Tommy*) or an alcoholic star (*Alice Sit-by-the-Fire*).

If Peg had slogged through flop after Broadway flop, endured one bad review after another, month after month, year in and year out, and then came to Hollywood and trudged from studio lot to studio lot with nothing to show for her efforts but uncredited bit parts, then yes, it could be argued that she would have fit the bill of a "failed actress."

But it is simply not true that Peg killed herself because RKO fired her. Yes, she was hurt and angry that her screen debut had been butchered, but she had no intention of committing suicide because of it. Upon being let go by the studio, she had immediately set about getting on with her life and began making plans for a Broadway comeback. Peg Entwistle was disappointed, but she was looking forward to another caviar day.

So, if Peg didn't kill herself because she got fired from RKO, then *why* did she?

It's no mystery. She told us why in her suicide note ... *I am sorry for everything.*

But to rightly piece it all together, to know what it was that Peg had been sorry for, and what she meant by *I am afraid I'm a coward* and *If I had done this a long time ago it would have saved a lot of pain,* one first had to know a good deal more about the "mental anguish" Charles Entwistle mentioned to the press.[3] One also had to know a great deal more about her career and personal life than that which has been presented over the years. Of particular importance are the events preceding her *Thirteen Women* contract with David O. Selznick, and a heartbreaking moment of realization that will occur in the driveway of her family's home.

You see, Peg Entwistle did not kill herself because she was *fired* from RKO.

Peg Entwistle killed herself because she allowed herself to be *hired* by RKO.

* * *

The first rungs of the tragic ladder are Broadway producer Bela Blau, Peg's New York roommate Mari, and an old friend of Aunt Jane's who was living with Peg's family.

We begin with Peg and Mari's Tudor City tower apartment in New York. Their colorful neighbors included A-list actresses Alice Brady and Gertrude Lawrence, aviator Bernt Balchen (Admiral Byrd's flight engineer), and Snoopie, an aged cat dubbed "The Mayor of Tudor City,"[4] whose charm earned him plenty of attention from the likes of Peg and Mari. Snoopie was well known to socialites and cat shows, and the mishap that severed half his tail was comically publicized in society pages as a revolving door misunderstanding.

The "City" was comprised of several skyscrapers grouped together and contained restaurants, shopping malls, theaters, swimming pools and spas—even a golf course. Tudor City rents could get pricey, but not Park Avenue crazy and it was safe ... unless you were a cat's tail.

In a letter from Mari to Peg dated June 6, 1932, Mari gossips about their other roommate, Marta. There is friction between Mari and Marta, and it is clear from part of the letter's context that Peg had control of their apartment. She was expected to decide which of the two roommates should go. Mari writes, "Her attitude about this apartment has got under my skin too often. She was going to write you, as she thought something should be done ... well, dear, so do I ... I do WISH you would let me know, I am terribly at sea about it all."[5]

Of the two roommates, Mari was the closer friend of Peg's. After having opened with "Dearest Babs," she closed: "I hope you are not overworking, Babs, dear, and that this picture thing will lead to something in the way of a permanent contract for you ... I hope Enty is well [and] also Jane ... give her my love and tell her I have never forgotten her kindness to me when I visited her and that I hope she is happy. Love to the boys whom I am sure have forgotten me. AND to you madam, well you know how I feel about you. As ever and with very fondest love and waiting for instructions [signed] Mari."[6]

Mari is a close friend, not simply a roommate trying to win the day. Her affection for Peg's family is deep and genuine. This could only have come about if Peg had the same feelings for Mari. This is important to keep in mind, for if Peg ever had a sister, it would have been Mari. It's also important to note Mari's comments about "this picture thing."[7] She wrote this letter two days after *The Mad Hopes* closed and in the same week Selznick told Cukor to call Peg ... but even before the play closed, Peg was exuding RKO-related excitement to her family ... and now through Mari we see Peg had also spread the news immediately to her people in New York ... for she was giddy and chatty at having been called by George Cukor at the behest of Selznick ... and she was all aflutter at the mention of a co-starring role in a film with Billie Burke ... and so she shared this good fortune in a very animated manner with everyone ... her family, her friends back east, and the cast and crew of *The Mad Hopes*.

And *that* did not sit well with Bela Blau, the play's New York producer.

Blau lost both his stars for the planned 1932-33 Broadway production of *The Mad Hopes*. He was angry at both women, particularly with Peg. But he had to be careful how he reacted, especially to Billie Burke, for she was a megastar — a household name. During the last few performances of *The Mad Hopes* Blau could only grit his teeth and smile at Billie, for to treat an actress of her caliber with bitterness would come back to kick him in his stage door. Moreover, she was married to Florenz Ziegfeld, one of the most influential theatrical producers alive. Sure, the Great Ziegfeld was scheduled to appear at the Pearly Gates Theater in about six weeks, but Blau didn't know the man's heart was on its last pumps, so handling Billie with kid gloves even while wanting to wring her neck would serve his best interests. Billie would want to return to Broadway one day, and that was a bridge Blau did not want to see burned.

But Peg had no such protection. And as Blau watched her on stage, confident, skillful, and carefree while earning energetic laughter and applause with Burke, he had to have wondered about his coming Broadway season and the people he had made assurances to regarding Peg and *The Mad Hopes*. And this had to have angered him, for Blau was from the old school — a handshake was a *promise,* a promise was a *commitment,* and unless your name was Billie Burke, that, my friend, was *a contract.*

The Mad Hopes closed and Blau immediately returned to New York. Broadway news items tell us he began making plans for several other plays while continuing to work out details for a fall production of Romney Brent's comedy ... and evidence strongly suggests that Blau was also spreading the word of Peg's unholy theatrical sin. Her cousin Helen recalled the regret: "Babs was in rough shape over that. No one had come right out and said she was banned or anything, but a few times she mentioned not being back on Broadway for a time."[8] Helen also recalled Peg's angst concerning "theater people" in New York "talking [negatively] about her."[9] All of this is in the context of Peg's dropping out of her *Mad Hopes* agreement with Blau.

This brings us back to Mari, who was out of a job and so broke that she could not afford to send a traditional opening night telegram to her and Peg's mutual friend, Alvin Kerr, an actor and playwright whose new play, *Sad Words to Gay Music,* was being tested in Milbrook, Connecticut. Peg knew Mari's plight but she wasn't too concerned, for her original intention was to return to New York soon after *The Mad Hopes* closed. And regardless of the outcome of the situation with the troublesome Marta, Peg planned to cover Mari's portion of the rent and bills until Mari could get some work. But everything changed when George Cukor called. Peg told Mari that her new intention was to remain in Hollywood only long enough to add some screen roles to her résumé. She hoped to do two or three films before returning to New York and estimated her stay would last no more than six months. Mari understood all of this, and in spite of her hope that Peg would get a permanent studio contract, Peg wanted no such thing, for Broadway still held the center stage of her heart. She still considered New York her home and intended to keep the Tudor City flat and send money to Mari for rent and living expenses. But her schedule and social life became increasingly busy because of her new associations at RKO. She became preoccupied, so much so that she neglected to follow up with Mari. And then she was let go by the studio. And by the time Peg had come to her senses, her money had been swallowed up and she was too broke to help Mari.

Mari's days in Tudor City were numbered. Unable to carry the rent alone (Marta had moved out), she vacated the luxury apartment that August and moved to a tenement in Brooklyn with a mutual friend named Connie Kent.

Peg had let down her best friend in a most selfish, humiliating way.

I am sorry for everything...

Most of Peg's possessions, including furniture, dozens of dresses and gowns, jewelry, boxes of shoes and hats and many other items were held against the back rent she owed to the Tudor City management — she would never recover them. Losing her apartment and belongings and Broadway reputation was bad enough, but when Peg realized what she had done to her dearest friend, she became quite despondent.

I am sorry for everything...

And as the Tudor City drama had unfolded, there was Lucretia.

Peg could no longer afford the apartment she rented near her family's houses: Uncle Charles and Aunt Jane were renting her old room to family friend Harry Haven, a silent era screenwriter. Harry was a gent in his sixties, and no one (especially Peg) wished him to leave just so she could sleep in her old room. So she moved into the small room over her family's garage. But this came at the sacrifice of Lucretia Craig, a bygone actress everyone knew as "Crete." She was one of Aunt Jane's closest friends going back to 1919 when they met while Crete was in a Broadway musical with Beatriz Michelena's sister, Vera. Milton Entwistle remembered Crete as a "heavy smoker and drinker," but not unkindly.[10]

Cousin Helen recalled helping Crete move out so Peg could move in: "I don't remember exactly, but [it was when] Enty was in a picture with Alan [Mowbray]."[11] (*Two Against the World,* with Mowbray and Constance Bennett, premiered that August 23.) "Babs was by the car, talking to Aunt Jane. I came down with Crete; I had her cat and then I don't know what happened ... Babs looked at [Crete] and hurried into the house. She felt horrible about pushing Crete out like that."[12]

I am sorry for everything...

When asked why Peg didn't sleep on the couch, Helen replied, "I suppose she could have, but such things weren't really done. [It] gave the impression of a flop house, I imagine. I don't really know. Maybe she was embarrassed to sleep on a sofa. I don't know. Aunt Helen [Jane's sister] might have invited her to stay with us, but we had a houseful."[13] (Cousin Helen and her parents had been living with Aunt Helen since 1931.)

Helen Reid was familiar with the Hollywood Studio Club, where out-of-work actresses could stay, but she didn't know why Peg had not gone to live there. (Perhaps there were no vacancies.)

"Harry [Haven] was a very sweet man, and had no family but us. It would have broken our hearts to see him go; Babs would never have allowed it ... it wasn't even an option. Crete was sad too, I think for Babs, too. [Peg] was very troubled by it ... [Crete] went to live with her family ... up north, I think."[14] (Milton Entwistle remembers her moving to San Francisco.)

Peg's regrets suddenly, overwhelmingly, began coming upon her like a flood.

She was not wrong to be bitter and disappointed at RKO, for there's no question they had handled her terribly, but Peg's focus in those days immediately after being released by the studio had been (quite naturally) on herself... *her* loss of the role in *Bill of Divorcement*; *her* screen debut butchered in *Thirteen Women*; *her* second contract quickly voided; *her* embarrassment at having *her* firing cavalierly printed in the press and trades.

But then it hit her that day in the driveway with Crete ... *her* decisions had come with consequences, and others had suffered because of them ... because of *her*. If she had stayed true to her commitment with Bela Blau (or Herbert L. Swett and Lakewood) and returned to New York (or Maine) as she had promised, Crete and Mari would not have had to leave their homes, and the broke, out-of-work Peg would not have become an added financial burden to her family. A roast chicken, quart of milk, and loaf of bread only went so far in a house whose population of six included very little income and two growing, always hungry teenage boys.

I am sorry for everything...

* * *

"Dear Miss Entwistle, Thank you for your note. It is nice to hear from you again, and I am glad to know that you are not going to live in Hollywood. Kindest regards."[15]

The above reply, dated August 31, 1932, is from Broadway producer and director Guthrie McClintic. He mailed it from his office in New York to Peg at her Hollywood home. It probably arrived a week or so later, about a week before her death. The words are few and details are lacking; nevertheless, it sheds no small bit of light into what was going on in that pretty blonde head in the days following her release from RKO: McClintic was running the Belasco Theater on Broadway when he wrote to Peg. It isn't certain how they came to know each other, for Peg never worked with him. But in 1916 McClintic had been married to Estelle Winwood, the noted stage actress whose career began that year when she appeared with Peg's father in *Hush!* So perhaps Peg and McClintic had been acquainted through her father. Also, the Belasco Theater in New York, like the Belasco in Los Angeles, was founded by the late actor and producer David Belasco, and was owned by David's brother Edward and his partner, Homer Curran. It was Edward Belasco and Curran, the reader will recall, who brought Peg west for *The Mad Hopes*. So it is just as possible that she was introduced to McClintic by Belasco, either during *The Mad Hopes*, or shortly after RKO let her go ... probably the latter if Belasco was indeed the bridge to McClintic.

And still a third possibility exists, for in 1932 McClintic was married to the popular stage actress Katharine Cornell, who appeared in Los Angeles that May and June in *The Barretts of Wimpole Street*. Peg could quite easily have met her (and thus her husband) through Billie Burke or visiting backstage on her own if she went to see Cornell's play, or perhaps if Cornell had come to *The Mad Hopes*.

Regardless of how Peg came to know McClintic, it is really his marriage to Katharine Cornell that makes Peg's communication with him so interesting. For Cornell was on the board of directors of the Rehearsal Club, a place where young stage actresses could stay while looking for work. It was Broadway's version of the Hollywood Studio Club. Peg was not just trolling Broadway producers for work, she was flat broke, and so while trying to find a way to return to New York, she was feeling out job prospects *and* living arrangements that might be had once she arrived. But the key here is "feeling out."

Cornell was somewhere in the Swiss Alps at this time, which would explain why Peg received a reply from McClintic instead of his wife. But even if Cornell had still been in New York or Los Angeles it wouldn't have mattered much, for Peg's ego would not allow her to brave the humility required to come right out and say that she had made a mess of things; that she had broken promises to people and let them down — important people and very dear friends. Peg enjoyed being attractive and considered sharp and to her there just wasn't anything flattering about admitting wrongs while pleading for help. She desperately wanted to return to New York and Broadway, but she didn't have it in her to come right out and ask McClintic (or Cornell) for a loan of a train ticket, meal money, or a bed in the Rehearsal Club. In the context of it all, it would seem that Peg had been ambiguous in her initial contact with McClintic and that she probably had hoped he would prod a bit more, offer a part, or perhaps invite her to see him.

If Peg had meekly approached the right people, she might have found measures of grace from the Broadway or Lakewood set. But she just could not grovel. To become humble at the feet of powerful theatrical bosses in this situation demanded more courage than she could muster. The humility she needed here was a fear she could never embrace.

I am afraid I'm a coward...

Everyone has defects of character ... people would be boring without them. Peg's impulsiveness was her most glaring defect, but she had an ego problem, too—the kind of ego familiar to many actresses and actors. In her documentary *Under the Hollywood Sign*, filmmaker Hope Anderson noted that Peg was "an actress through and through."[16] It simply never occurred to her to look for another line of work. Peg would never, could never, work as a typist, waitress, salesgirl, or any other job even if just long enough to save the money she needed for a return to New York. For Peg Entwistle, acting was all or *nothing*.

So, in mid–September 1932, she found herself stuck. A shot at a fabulous Broadway run with Billie Burke had lured Peg away from her promise to Lakewood Theater's cast and company, then Hollywood had beckoned and she responded by turning her back on *The Mad Hopes* and its well-known Broadway producer. And then Hollywood had no more use for her. She desperately needed help — a return to the stage, but such was her transgression in the eyes of the moguls of the Great White Way that she could not even bring herself to ask Walter Hampden for help. He was a dear family friend and had helped pave her way to the Boston Repertory, but he had also been there when she made her "handshake" deal with Henry Jewett and received admonishment from her uncle about the importance of keeping one's word to a producer. Under such circumstances, it would be immensely humiliating to ask him for such a huge favor — and then what if he turned her away?

On the subject of why Peg had not gotten help from Hampden or his wife, Helen Reid said, "There were complicated things about old stage people like Uncle Enty and Walter. It's hard to explain ... hard to understand. Walter had money. I'm sure they would have helped Babs ... she must never have asked [them]."[17]

It is important to try to understand the severity of Peg's "sin" in the minds of the people who controlled Broadway during her era: In breaking her promises by bowing out as she did, Peg had brought dishonor and embarrassment to respected producers who had put themselves out front with her name on their lips. This caused her to become *completely* ostracized. In essence, Peg Entwistle had been blacklisted by the theatrical colony. Guthrie McClintic's reply had been polite, but distant and carefully worded. He offered no help or advice and with a gentlemen's courtesy had simply dismissed her — it was a brush-off that ended with "Kindest regards."[18]

At least he had written back.

* * *

So now one comes to better understand what had driven Peg Entwistle to such horrific, wasteful action at the Hollywood Sign. What happened to her at RKO had indeed played a part, but it had not been the last straw, or by any means the heaviest.

I am afraid I'm a coward...

A *coward* because she just didn't have the courage to humble herself and ask for another chance. And even if she had managed to find her way back to New York, and groveled and pleaded, Peg knew that she might not have gotten a measure of grace anyway. And even if she had, there would have been an unspoken probation — small parts; no starring or supporting roles. She just didn't have the courage to be seen on stage in such humiliating footlights after having become so accustomed to scene-ending applause and the "Bravo!s" of curtain-calls.

I am afraid I'm a coward ... because she just could not

While she was working at RKO, Peg had a portfolio done by theatrical photographer Anthony Bruno, known among the New York and Hollywood stage and screen set as "Bruno of Hollywood." For more than half a century it had been rumored that Peg's financial desperation during the last weeks of her life drove her to pose nude for Bruno, but she did not (author's collection).

stomach the thought of becoming that Girl at Table actress after having accomplished so much.

I am sorry for everything...

Sorry because of the disappointment and embarrassment she had caused others; sorry for losing the trust and respect of wonderful people who had supported her, befriended her ... loved her; sorry because her misguided, impulsive choices had forced Aunt Jane and Uncle Charles to evict an old friend so she could have a bed.

I am sorry for everything ... because ambition had become more important than people and promises.

* * *

If I had done this long ago I could have saved a lot of pain.

Peg's extreme despondency and excruciating mental anguish was not solely owed to what she had done ... Robert Keith's success with his new wife and re-energized acting career had also caused her much pain: As she perused the trade papers in hopes of a gig, Peg could not have missed reading about her ex-husband's good fortunes. On the same day that Guthrie McClintic sent her his dismissive note, the press announced that Keith's new play, *Original Sinning,* had been bought and was being tested by Brock Pemberton, the famous writer and director.

Newspapers in Oakland and San Francisco (where Keith had been steadily working on stage since Peg divorced him) published stories of his wonderful marriage to actress Dorothy Tierney; of their peaceful, loving relationship, and of their fun in leisure and work together on the stage. In the last two weeks of her life, dissolved of finances, empty of love, saddened in heart and broken in spirit, Peg had seen that Keith's new marriage had become everything theirs was supposed to have been.

"And he was so sweet and lovely and patient about everything....

No matter what ever might happen, I would always love him."[19]

In her last days, Peg remembered how much she had once loved the man, and how that love, that hope of *happily ever after,* was destroyed by lies and by drink; by abusive tirades and beatings, by his arrests and the shame and public humiliation that followed her across the country and then back to New York — to the office of Theresa Helburn and the Theater Guild.

And now just days before her fateful climb up the sign she sees he sold a play to one of the most noted men in New York City ... Robert Keith is working, and his wife is working, and he is selling plays and making money and Peg is penniless; her mind filled with the images of the small fortune she had given or loaned him to pay his child support, his bail, his booze...

If I had done this a long time ago it would have saved a lot of pain.

23

Setting Some Things Straight

I don't care what you say about me, as long as you say something about me, and as long as you spell my name right.—George M. Cohan[1]

Peg's "lot of pain"[2] was likely not limited to the events just previously described. The trauma of her childhood may very well have come into play. It will be recalled that she never really came to terms with the experiences of watching her precious stepmom and loving father die slow, miserable deaths. If Peg suffered from post-traumatic stress disorder (PTSD), the memories of that awful time would only have added to her emotionally unstable state of mind during her last days. This is only speculation, of course, but it is reasonable. The author believes Peg's childhood trauma contributed to her depression, and that today she would have been clinically diagnosed with PTSD and perhaps a bipolar disorder or other similar malady.

When one reads articles or other books discussing Peg, one will become familiar with what has become one of the most famous myths attached to her death. It is said that the day after Peg died, or the day after her body was found, or the day after her funeral (it all depends who is writing), a letter came to her Hollywood home. This letter—goes the story—was from the Beverly Hills Community Playhouse (or, again, depending on the writer, the Beverly Hills Community Players, or the Pasadena Playhouse, or the Pasadena Community Players). The letter—goes the story—was sent to inform Peg that she had won the leading female role in a stage production; that she was to play a young woman who kills herself in the final act.

This event never happened, but something like it did occur. According to Milton Entwistle, a letter did arrive shortly after Peg's death, and although he could not recall if it was the day after, he remembered it as having come from RKO Studios, *not* a theatrical company. "Enty was very angry [at RKO] because the letter was sent just before she died," said Milton.[3] "It was [an offer] for a picture role."[4] Milton didn't remember the film or role she was to play, but he was clear in his memory of how livid Uncle Charles and Aunt Jane had been about it all, for the studio had the phone number to their house and could have called. "Enty was very mad that they didn't call. He was mad for a long time after that."[5]

This letter has since disappeared, perhaps trashed by livid Uncle Charles.

If RKO's letter or a phone call had arrived in time, would this have saved Peg Entwistle's life? Perhaps, but no one can say for certain.

* * *

Peg's cousin Helen said Peg auditioned for a stage role shortly after RKO released her, but she did not remember where. Given Peg's timeline and opening dates of plays in the Los Angeles area at the time, there looks to have been just one production in which she could have auditioned. It was at the Beverly Hills Playhouse. The play was *Insult,* a drama in which a young woman kills herself. It opened October 2, but director Wilfred North had been holding auditions and rehearsals since early September. Peg may have tried for the starring role but the part was awarded to Nola Luxford, an actress from New Zealand who had come to Los Angeles to cheer on her country's team during the 1932 Summer Olympics taking place at the Los Angeles Coliseum. Nola had become a celebrity and was making the rounds in Hollywood (luncheons, teas, etc.), and eventually found her way into the hearts of the local producers and directors of stage and the screen. Luxford was about seven years older than Peg, but the two women resembled each other and it is not out of the question that Peg had been on the short list for the female lead until Luxford's media-doll status peaked.

Interestingly, the tryout of *Insult* allowed audiences to choose the story's final scene. For several weeks, two entirely different endings were presented at each performance: happy and tragic. When all the votes were tabulated at the close of the tryout, Mr. North used the more popular ending for the run of the play: Suicide had won the day.

So, while no letter regarding *Insult* (or any other play) had come to Peg's house, a letter from RKO had. And there was another letter, so tragic, so ironic, that without its existence one might have thought the following to be simply another myth attached to the life of Peg Entwistle.

It had been no secret to her family that Peg was troubled ... Aunt Jane's mother, Matilda Ross, sent Jane a letter. It didn't arrive until a few days after Peg's death, and reads in part: "I am so sorry for Babs, I hope ere this [letter arrives] she has a contract [and] is all set. Tell her not to give up, there is always a better time coming."[6]

The letter is dated September 16, 1932 ... mailed the day Peg killed herself...

Tell her not to give up. There is always a better time coming

But as sensitive to Peg's predicament as she had been, Matilda made no bones about her feelings a few days later. Upon hearing of Peg's suicide, Matilda sent another letter — this one dated September 22, 1932, two days after Peg's remains were cremated: "My Dearest Daughter, you will never know Dear how very sorry we all feel for you [and] Enty [and] the boys. Bless their hearts it seems Babs should have thought of them in her going as she did. She has always had her own way, even in leaving this world. It is a lesson that we should profit by. I hope our dear boys will seek all that is good. What did ail the dear child? Something more than the disappointment in her work. It was to [sic] bad the picture was a failure, if it had been good she would have gone over big, because she was good. But all that is past now. To [sic] late to make amends. Try Dear and look up [and] do the best you can, teach the boys not to be selfish. Think of others first."[7]

* * *

There has been a bit of confusion over the years about the date of Peg's death, for there are *two* dates given on her death certificate and on the coroner's register. The two dates in question (September 16 and 18) seem in conflict with each other, but they are not. The confusion is caused when one does not carefully read or understand what the authorities were saying, and how such things were said, done, and interpreted in 1932.

The "Date of Death" line on Peg's death certificate was recorded as September 18[8] (Sunday) because this was the date she was *declared* dead by the medical examiner. On the coroner's register (which was completed following an inquest), a similar line is worded "Date of Death or When Found Dead."[9] The coroner first recorded "September 16," and then wrote an "8" over the "6."[10] He seems conflicted here, but he had simply made a clerical error and then corrected himself using the 8. Again, September 18 is the date Peg was *declared* dead, and so the context of the coroner's correction is simply to clarify September 18 as "When [she was] Found [and declared] Dead."[11]

Peg's death certificate and coroner's register each has a line asking if the manner of death was from an accident, homicide, or suicide. Both documents of course record a suicide. Now the coroner must record the date of the suicide—he wrote clearly and concisely on both documents: "September 16, 1932."[12] Even in 1932 a medical examiner could determine how long a person had been deceased, and so when one carefully deciphers the information in these documents it becomes clear and unmistakable: Peg medically died on September 16, 1932, the night she jumped, but was officially declared dead on September 18, the night her body was found.

Other discrepancies regarding Peg's death certificate include the order and spelling of her first and middle name: she is listed as Lillian Millicent but was actually born Millicent Lilian. The latter is confirmed by her birth certificate, Ellis Island records, several census registers, news articles of her father's death, and her father's last will and testament.

Another pair of inaccuracies on the death certificate include the date and place of her birth, which is recorded as February 6, 1908, in London, England. This entry should have read February 5, 1908, and Port Talbot, Wales. Interestingly, in light of these errors, the coroner accurately recorded Peg's time on earth as 24 years, 7 months, and 12 days, which reflects her true lifespan from February 5, 1908, to September 16, 1932.

Because Uncle Charles could not recall the first name of Peg's mother (Emily), it is omitted from the document, and then probably due to clerical error Peg is recorded as having lived in America ten years—it was actually about 19. Ten years is also recorded as the length of time she had been a California resident. Nine years is legally accurate for she was brought to Hollywood to live in 1923, but maintained her California residency even as she lived in Boston and New York as an actress.

These are relatively minor errors, of course, and might be indicative of the distress Peg's uncle was feeling and the result of a very busy, understaffed coroner's office.

Some have claimed Peg had been drunk the night she died. This is completely unfounded. The coroner would have found evidence of intoxication, but nothing of the sort is mentioned in the death certificate or the coroner's register which was completed after a public inquest.

* * *

An interesting question is raised with regard the contents—or lack of them—in Peg's purse. Where were the items one would usually find in a woman's purse—lipstick, handkerchief, makeup, perfume, house keys, identification, etc.? She hadn't left them at her house—her cousin was quite sure of that during an interview for this book. The author believes Peg discarded the purse's usual contents into a trash can in Hollywoodland. But why would she do that? Perhaps for the same reason she had signed the suicide note using "P.E." instead of her name or nickname ... dissociation. Of course, there is the possibility that the anonymous woman who found Peg had stolen the purse's contents, but this is unlikely given the honesty she exhibited with regard to bringing the pricey handbag, coat, and breastpin to the police station.

And just who was this anonymous woman? She needs to be discussed, for her actions were very mysterious indeed:
- She is hiking at the Hollywoodland Sign.
- She finds Peg's coat, shoes, and the purse containing the suicide note.
- She sees Peg's body.
- She stealthily deposits the found items on the steps of the Hollywood police station.
- She anonymously reports her discovery to police in downtown Los Angeles.

Her call came in to Los Angeles Police Headquarters at 9:00 P.M. Headquarters was in downtown Los Angeles, about nine miles from the Hollywood Sign. The Hollywood police station—where one would normally (and logically) report finding a dead body near the sign—was less than a mile from Peg's house. So, what kind of fear or trepidation would prompt the average Jane Q. Citizen to quietly place Peg's items at the entrance of the Hollywood station, and then leave without a word only to call a station *nine miles* away? Why not simply walk into the Hollywood station with them and report the body to the desk sergeant?

"I don't want any publicity in this matter," she told Headquarters over the phone.[13] Okay, that makes sense as far as not walking into the Hollywood station with the items, but again, why did she call the downtown station *instead* of the Hollywood station? Well, in 1932 there was really only one group of people who would have used the word "publicity," and who also would not want any in this circumstance—celebrities ... people who very often have distinctive, easily recognizable voices to go with their faces. Realistically, would an average, non-famous person have taken such pains to avoid public or official attention in the matter? It may very well have been that this anonymous woman was a movie star or the wife or other relation of a movie star or industry insider; someone who was a "Hollywoodlander," or "Beachwooder," and who thought their face—and voice—would have been easily recognized at the Hollywood station.

Or maybe it wasn't a woman who found Peg ... one may also ponder a scenario in which a famous actor (or other well-known man) found Peg, and then, wishing no "publicity" in the matter, had his wife (or some other woman close to him) deposit the items and make the call.

A dozen or more questions and points on the matter could be entertained, but such monotony would only create a larger and larger circle of wonder with no solid answers.

Whatever the actualities may have been, it is all very mysterious, to say the least.

* * *

Murder most foul?

In 2010, Leo Braudy, a professor at USC in Los Angeles, published *The Hollywood Sign: Fantasy and Reality of an American Icon*. In his book Braudy wonders if Peg Entwistle could have been killed elsewhere and her suicide staged. His narrative presents a number of points to this end, yet not a single one of them can be supported by solid evidence or common sense.

Within his reasoning is speculation that Peg could not have made it up the steep slopes to the sign; he notes her lack of athletic clothing. But according to Peg's brother Milton and her cousin Helen, she sometimes climbed the massive letters for fun and adventure (as did many of the locals). Peg was a strong, athletic 24-year-old who was as familiar with the footpaths and trails near the sign as she was with the structure itself: she hiked and rode horses there many times. She was conditioned and practiced; she knew the shortcuts ... a dress and evening shoes could *slow* but not *stop* her.

Let us explore Braudy's question a bit deeper and pretend Peg was murdered elsewhere, let's say somewhere near the Hollywoodland village, for this was where she told her family she was going: Instead of fleeing the initial crime scene, the killer (let's say a very strong man acting alone) gets the brilliant idea of covering up the murder by staging a suicide leap from that big electric sign on Mt. Lee. Now, assuming he wore athletic clothing (or was it just Peg who needed running shoes to get up there?), imagine how incredibly difficult this rugged, steep-sloped journey would still have been while carrying 100-plus pounds of dead weight.

One could argue that the killer drove as close to the sign as possible and then carried her from the car. This would certainly make the burden of dead weight less arduous, but why did he place her body in a ravine *100 feet below the H*? That was where the police found her. If our killer wanted the murder to look like a suicide leap, why didn't he place her at the structure, directly, or almost directly underneath it? Isn't that where a "jumper" would normally end up? Common sense dictates that her body's close proximity to the base of the sign would lessen any suspicion of foul play. Besides, the killer had to go up to the sign to deposit Peg's coat, shoes, and purse, for that is where the anonymous woman had found them.

(This woman, by the way, can be ruled out as a suspect or accomplice. If she was involved, she would definitely have avoided the risk of *any* contact whatsoever with the authorities. The fact that she abandoned these items on the steps of one police station and then reported her actions to another station is odd, but it is also strong evidence of her innocence.)

Back to the ravine: How could the killer have guessed the police would surmise that upon impact to the ground the inertia of Peg's body had caused it to tumble that far down the incline? Perhaps the killer had gone that extra mile (so to speak) and actually carried Peg up the H, tossed her over, and the body's tumble to the ravine had been an unintentional event. Please consider the superhuman effort this would entail, for every one of the permanently affixed ladders were 50 feet tall, very narrow, and *vertical.*

But who would want to murder Peg? What motive would there be? If she was killed during a crime of opportunity (such as robbery), why would our killer have risked capture while going through such elaborate and laborious time-consuming staging of her suicide? And why (if one is to trust the coroner's findings with regard to Peg's physical cause of death) did he shatter her pelvis as opposed to fracturing her skull or ribs? Wouldn't vicious blows to the head or upper body be more reliable to a killer in need of wielding blunt force?

Leo Braudy seems to want to strengthen a murder scenario by suggesting that if Peg wanted to kill herself from a height, she could (or would) have used one of the tall buildings in Hollywood (he names several). He reasoned these were closer to her home than her home was to the sign, but this is not accurate; the sign is about two miles from Peg's former house (not his estimate of three to four miles), and the buildings he mentioned were about three miles away.

And what about her suicide note? Was Peg forced to write it, and forced to allude in it to the heart-rending mental anguish which only her family and closest friends knew about? Could her killer have been so clever? Perhaps this note was forged, and her family — who was given the note by police — hadn't noticed the handwriting didn't match Peg's familiar style of penmanship.

Nonsense most foul.

In a similar vein, a well-meaning acquaintance of this author put forth the theory that

Robert Keith killed Peg out of jealousy. However, Keith was in San Francisco and very much in love with his wife Dorothy Tierney at the time Peg died. Still another person wondered if Peg had been struck by a car while walking along one of the roads in Hollywoodland, and that the panicked driver staged a suicide to cover vehicular manslaughter. While a car-vs-pedestrian event would not be impossible, the driver would still have had to put her in the car, drive as close to the sign as the area would allow (logically, somewhere near the maintenance shed on the plateau above the sign), and then carry her body from the car, down the very steep slope, and then up the 50-foot vertical ladder. There would also be that business about the note...

All these interesting plot twists may work nice on television and in novels (or poorly researched biographies about Hollywood), but in real life they are all just dead ends.

Peg was a suicide, pure and simple.

* * *

According to a press release given by Los Angeles Chief Coroner Frank A. Nance (the man who performed Peg's autopsy), there were 13 suicides in Los Angeles during the weekend that Peg took her own life. Her death certificate, coroner's register, and subsequent inquest note the time she had been officially ruled by Nance to be a suicide. At 11:50 P.M., Sunday, September 18, Peg Entwistle, dead since the previous Friday, had officially become the thirteenth recorded victim to die by their own hand.

Peg may have been the most notable suicide of those 13 unfortunates, but the most ironic was Robert Leroy Watson, who, before he was found dead in his car of a self-inflicted gunshot, was president of the Pasadena Optimists Club.

* * *

In the syndicated column "Hollywood Notebook," writer Robbin Coons had this to say on September 30, 1932: "Peg Entwistle took Hollywood too seriously. A few months ago she appeared here with Billie Burke in *The Mad Hopes* and did a credible job. She had then one of those trial contracts with a film company. She apparently didn't measure up and was released. A few days ago her body was found at the foot of one of the giant letters in the sign 'Hollywoodland' which shines day and night from the hills ... she had chosen a spectacular exit from heartbreak town, standing far above it in her leap to death."[14]

And Peg — or rather her method of death — was still making news five years later...

On July 24, 1937, screen legend Edward G. Robinson was filling in as a guest columnist for famed writer Walter Winchell. He wrote the following: "Hollywood, they would have you believe, is Heartbreak Town, the Land of Lost Hopes, the City of Sorrow, and all the other ponderous appellations. But it isn't, really. It's a pretty healthy community with a suicide rating a great deal less than hundreds of other American small towns. In New York, if a girl doesn't click on the stage, too tragically often she leaps from her hotel room or goes out on the street to join the foot-sore and heart-weary Manhattan players of the Oldest Trade. But in Hollywood, a Peg Entwhistle [sic] episode is a rarity...."[15]

Robinson went on to note that most girls who found disappointment in Hollywood headed home a little discouraged, but had not tired of life. They became waitresses, secretaries, schoolteachers, etc., and had long, pleasant lives. But, as stated earlier, Peg was an actress ... an actress through and through. She could never dream of waiting on real tables for nickels and dimes when she could pretend to do so while earning ovations and dollars by the thousands.

The home of Mr. and Mrs. Roff Heald in a photograph taken on September 22, 1932, two days after Peg Entwistle's funeral. In the near background is the path which she had likely taken on her approach to the Sign. Just to the left of the path is the 35-foot electric dot which punctuated the Hollywoodland Sign after all three sections were illuminated (courtesy Bruce Torrence Hollywood Collection).

Robinson was not privy to all the facts of Peg's case; if he had known of all the disappointments and indignities she had suffered during her marriage and stage career, he may have actually been amazed that she had not gone out a New York window years before coming to RKO. Like Robbin Coons (and many other writers), Robinson was close to the truth of it all ... Peg Entwistle had killed herself and Hollywood disappointment had indeed played a role; however, as you now know, this disappointment was just a supporting player in the drama — a single rung of the ladder...

Perhaps the strangest thing ever mentioned about Peg in a newspaper was an item by Nelson Bell of the *Washington Post*. In his 1933 article titled "The Dead That Live," Bell pays tribute to a number of people from stage and screen who had recently died.[16] Among them: "Peg Entwistle, English character actress, more recently of the films, who may be remembered best for her performance with Gary Cooper and Beryl Mercer in the film version of Sir James M. Barrie's *The Old Lady Shows Her Medals*."[17] Peg is not known to have appeared with Cooper or Mercer on stage or in films, and none of them were in a film version of this Barrie play. And if Peg had been in this film, she would most certainly have been "remembered best for her performance,"[18] and easily would have earned the biggest Academy Award ever, perhaps in a category called "The Dead That Act," for there was indeed a film called

23. Setting Some Things Straight

The Old Lady Shows Her Medals, but it was released in 1937, five full years after Peg Entwistle's death...

* * *

Peg's story — her death, mostly — has been bandied about in films, television, books, articles, and so on. The results are sometimes appalling. In his notorious *Hollywood Babylon,* Kenneth Anger included a photograph of a beautiful, semi-nude model. The caption says this is Peg Entwistle. It is not her. As a result of this infamous photograph, there came rumors that Peg had become so desperate for money in her last days that she posed nude for the photographer "Bruno of Hollywood." (Anthony Bruno is sometimes mistaken for the more famous Bruno "Bernard of Hollywood.") Although Anger did not actually claim Peg had posed nude, his photo of the topless model almost always can be found wherever the rumor is reported and whenever Peg Entwistle images are searched for on the Internet.

It has plagued Peg's family for decades.

Side-by-side comparisons of close-up images of Peg and the bare-breasted model in *Hollywood Babylon* clearly prove this is *not* Peg Entwistle ... Peg's features are as different from Anger's model as Joan Crawford's are from Broderick Crawford.

Anthony "Bruno of Hollywood" had taken glamour shots of Peg in 1932, but he had also done portraits of Charles and Jane Entwistle. He had been the Entwistle family photographer for a number of years. There is no evidence that he — or anyone else — photographed Peg in the nude.

* * *

Over the years a number of writers claimed that Peg jumped from the 13th letter ... the last D in HOLLYWOODLAND. This, of course, is ridiculous, for the police found her about 100 feet below the H. One would have to imagine Peg first placed her coat, shoes, and purse at the base of the H, walked to the last D, climbed to the top, jumped, and then somehow scrambled (with massive injuries) nearly 500 feet across rugged terrain to where police found her. The reason attributed to a leap from the 13th letter is often linked to her film, *Thirteen Women.*

There is no question that Peg fell from the H. And many believe she chose it as a symbol for "*Hollywood.*" While it's not impossible that she might have had a symbolic thought as she climbed the ladder, her likely path to the sign made the H more of a convenience than a symbol.

It is worth noting here that some have postured the HOLLYWOODLAND Sign had not become a symbol of Hollywood filmdom, stardom, etc., until many years after Peg's death, when the last four letters had been removed. But at least one Los Angeles newspaper saw more in the sign than just remnants of a billboard. The *Evening Herald and Express* opened its September 19, 1932, article about Peg's suicide thus: "High in the Hollywood hills, glittering down on the glamorous sight that is Hollywood, stands a giant 50-foot sign, spelling out in electric lights the magic name of the world's film capital. To many that name signifies the highest hopes— the ultimate attainment ... but to Peg Entwistle it spelled only shattered hopes— defeat — despair."[19]

To many people the sign was becoming more and more symbolic of Tinsel Town. And upon her death, Peg had in a very real way completed the transformation ... no one would ever again think of it as a billboard ... "Broken and crushed by bitter defeat, she climbed to the top of the glittering 'H' that had grimly mocked her for months, and jumped to the ground...."[20]

Her climb up the H may or may not have been more about convenience, but whether she meant to do so or not; Peg's fall did indeed make a powerful, tragically symbolic statement.

A number of writers have stated that other starlets began using the Hollywood Sign as a suicide tool. (Kenneth Anger said Peg had set a trend.) This is simply not true. The Los Angeles Police Department records have *only* Peg Entwistle committing suicide by jumping from the Hollywood Sign. From 1932 until the time of this writing, there has *never* been another such incident. Moreover, there are no reports of any suicide leaps from the sign prior to 1932.

This brings us to David Wallace, who says in his book *Lost Hollywood* that Peg came to Hollywood in 1929 and was determined to break into films. As the reader will recall, Peg was indeed in Los Angeles in 1929, but she was on tour with the Theater Guild, not shopping herself to the studios. Such inaccuracies are bound to occur from time to time as dates and names and places can sometimes fall out of line during the course of writing a history book. However, Wallace included a major head-scratcher in his *Lost Hollywood*. Of Peg's death he writes: "But like her career, even her suicide was not a success, at least not immediately. Instead of hitting the stony ground more than five stories below and dying instantly, Entwistle landed on a cactus. Despite a number of operations, she died a painful death several days later."[21]

A cactus? A number of operations? Why was there no mention of this in any of the Los Angeles newspapers or coroner's documents? Needless to say, Peg was never taken to a hospital. She was found *dead* in front of the sign. And from there she was taken directly to the morgue, so said the police, the coroner, Peg's family, thousands of news articles ... and this book.

And just when you think it cannot possibly get any odder than Wallace's cactus fabrication, we find Australian film critic Clark Forbes writing a passing mention in his review of *Mulholland Drive*, "the famed Hollywood sign from which young actor Peg Entwistle hanged herself in 1932."[22] And then there is Stephen Banham, author of a biography about typeface. In an interview for an Australian newspaper in which he discusses his book *Fancy*, Banham says Peg's death was "especially fascinating from a typographical point of view ... if you look at all the letters, the H is clearly the best letter to jump off because of the height from the middle stroke. She's the only person we know of who has killed herself using type."[23]

Banham is hardly the first to think of such a thing about Peg and the H. Years before his book was published, author Eve Golden wrote an article about Peg and had lightened the mood by comparing the sign's letters. Ms. Golden noted the L was too steep, a D would just have a girl sliding down the side, but the H was an ingenious choice, for a girl could take a rest halfway up to the top. One has to wonder if Mr. Banham had read Ms. Golden's article...

* * *

Ever since Edward G. Robinson cited Peg's suicide in print in 1935, her influence has crept into a variety of pop culture mediums. She is mentioned in films such as *Stand-ins* (1997), *After I'm Gone* (2006), and *Hollywood Sign Girls* (2007); on TV in *This Is Your Life* (1957), *Ripley's Believe It or Not!* (1983), *E! Mysteries and Scandals* (1998), *Jeopardy!* (2002), the BBC series *Burn Hollywood Burn* (2007) and, of course, several Bette Davis documentaries, including *Stardust: The Bette Davis Story* (2006).

In music, there is Dory Previn's popular 1972 folk ballad "Mary C. Brown and the Hollywood Sign," rock 'n' roll surf guitarist Ralph Senese's 2009 song "Hollywood Suicide," Lagoon's 2005 song "Peg Entwistle, Are You Listening?" and Holy Ghost Revival's 2007 song "Catching Peg Entwistle." Research for this book discovered a dozen more songs from all genres in which Peg's influence was found.

Peg has influenced artists as well. One can find a horrid caricature of her in front of a blood-spattered Hollywood Sign, or more sensitive works such as a stunning 2012 watercolor portrait by professional artist Brian Forrest, and a surprisingly subdued 2006 watercolor by bass guitarist Bradley Stewart (aka "Gidget Gein" of the alternative metal band Marilyn Manson), who displayed his Peg in a Los Angeles exhibit called "Gollywood." Dexter Dalwood, a former member of the British punk band The Cortinas, had his "Peg Entwistle" painting exhibited at the Gagosian Gallery in Beverly Hills during the summer of 2010. In 2007, sculptor Bill Mack purchased the original Hollywood Sign. He paints portraits of screen legends on sections of the panels. Mack told this author that he might consider featuring Peg on one of the panels.

In novels one can find Peg in James McCourt's 2002 *Wayfaring at Waverly in Silver Lake*. Here, the memory of Peg Entwistle haunts movie star Kaye Wayfaring, who finds it surprising that after the Hollywood Sign was repaired they didn't install a mechanical Peg Entwistle that would jump off the H every day at noon, accompanied by civil defense sirens.

In *The Truth Be Told* (2010), author H.P. Oliver has Peg murdered by a drug dealer, and a modern-day screenwriter investigates said crime with the help of her ghost.

Newspapers and magazines near and far find Peg fascinating as well. Pat Morrison of the *Los Angeles Times* wrote the 1994 article "Dial M for Madness," and suggested that Hollywood be assigned the area code "ENtwistle."[24] The British tabloid *The Sun* once featured Peg in a macabre article about cursed B-movie actresses including Tura Satana (*Faster, Pussycat! Kill! Kill!*), Susan Cabot (*The Wasp Woman*), and Maila Nurmi (Vampira of *Plan 9 from Outer Space*). In September 2011, entertainment writer Juliette Michaud wrote about Peg in *Studio Cine Live*, a French magazine similar to *Rolling Stone* and *Entertainment Weekly*.

There has even been stage inspiration: In *Sweet FA*, which was produced in England, the woes of silent era comedian Roscoe "Fatty" Arbuckle are combined with Peg Entwistle's pathos. And another musical about Peg, this one called *Goodnight September*, was expected to have a London opening in late 2012.

* * *

There is no ignoring the fact that Peg Entwistle and her "Hollywood Sign Girl" moniker have touched the hearts of a great many individuals from all over the world. She has become the Hollywood Sign's mistress, its patron saint. She had seen it born, and by it died, and even all these years later Peg and the Hollywood Sign are a haunting, inseparable part of each other.

There have been numerous reports of sightings of an apparition walking toward the sign. Tourists, locals, and even a park ranger have given similar accounts of an overpowering aroma of gardenia blossom (Peg's favorite perfume) filling the air. A beautiful young blonde woman is noticed walking sadly toward the H. She wears 1930s clothing ... sometimes a dress and sometimes a negligee, like the one she wore in *Thirteen Women*. As this alleged "spirit" nears the sign, she and the gardenia scent slowly vanish, fading out in dramatic fashion.

Peg Entwistle — an actress even in death?

Who can say for sure if it is her ghost that appears there, but one thing is certain: She would have been quite pleased at all the attention.

* * *

In 1945, the grounds and Hollywood Sign were acquired by Los Angeles as an adjunct parcel to Griffith Park. In 1949 the H fell down, leaving the city with "OLLYWOODLAND."

How this came about depends on which of two versions to believe. While the Hollywood Chamber of Commerce and the Los Angeles media blamed a windstorm, a local legend insists Albert Kothe, the original caretaker, was the culprit. The story has him losing control of his car while driving drunk on the road above the sign; he careened down the hill and smashed into the H, demolishing both it and his 1928 Ford. But a lack of police reports, photographs, and news articles of the event, mingled with the claim that he crawled out of the wreckage unscathed, does little to give the story merit. But even if this adventure is true, Kothe wouldn't have had to worry about losing his job as the sign's caretaker, for the Hollywoodland company had been bankrupt and maintenance of the sign abandoned since 1939.

Over the years, Kothe remained a familiar Hollywoodland character. After the sign and its company both went dark, he moved into a small apartment above the village market. He got a job taxiing residents around in one of Beachwood Canyon's jitneys (an interesting line of work for a résumé said to include driving drunk and crashing into tons of steel and wood). Photographs of Kothe clearly disprove another Hollywoodland legend: He did not suffer from dwarfism. But he was as much a part of Hollywoodland's color as was Peter the Hermit, the movie stars, the sign, and its sadly famous mistress. Albert Kothe died in 1974.

Also in 1949, the Hollywood Chamber of Commerce entered into an agreement with the Department of Recreation and Parks to take over control of the sign. The Chamber repaired the damaged H and then, in order to disassociate the structure from its Hollywoodland forefathers and promote the town itself, they removed the last four letters (LAND). To save money, they turned off the electricity. Thus came the second generation of the Hollywood Sign.

For the next 20 years or so there had been fierce bickering among citizens' groups regarding the importance of the Hollywood Sign. To some it was an eyesore, nothing but expensive litter strewn across a pleasant vista, while others saw the sign as a beacon of the industry, a symbol of Tinsel Town's chief export. In the end, the pro–Sign folks ruled the day and in 1973 the Los Angeles Cultural Heritage Board designated the sign as a monument. However, by 1978 the structure had become so deteriorated it could no longer be rehabilitated. The Chamber formed a "Save the sign" committee, recruiting such A-list names as singing cowboy Gene Autry, *Playboy* founder Hugh Hefner, crooner Andy Williams and rocker Alice Cooper. They raised nearly $250,000 to build an entirely new Sign. The Pacific Outdoor Advertising Company was contracted for the project. Raiden Peterson, Pacific's on-site supervisor in charge of the project, provided some interesting trivia while interviewed for this book: Although the sign is often said to have been 50 feet tall, the letters themselves were actually four to five feet off the ground because of the vertical supports; thus, the top of the structure was about 55 feet high. Peterson (who rattled off the project's statistics as if he worked on it yesterday) also noted that the letters are not 45 feet tall as claimed by the Hollywood Sign Trust, the organization in charge of upkeep and history of the landmark. Peterson and his architects used the sign's original blueprints as their guides;

if anyone knows that Sign, it is he. Also according to Raiden Peterson, the new letters were placed in the *exact* spots held by their predecessors.

During his work, Peterson found several of the original 1923 HOLLYWOODLAND light bulbs. He tested them in a lamp and to his amazement discovered they still worked. They were made by General Electric and he insists they are 15-watt bulbs, not the 40-watt or 20-watt bulbs traditionally ascribed by various sources detailing the lighting system. Peterson explained that General Electric did not make 40-watt and 20-watt bulbs in 1923.

The demolition of what remained of Peg Entwistle's HOLLYWOODLAND Sign began on August 8, 1978. On November 11 the new Hollywood Sign had its star-studded premiere in typical fashion. And why not, for this was the 75th anniversary of filmdom's capitol and the city had been enjoying a week-long party to celebrate. CBS broadcast a two-hour prime time event, *Hollywood's Diamond Jubilee*, hosted by bombshell actress Raquel Welch and 1930s leading man Douglas Fairbanks, Jr. Special guests included screen luminaries Bette Davis, Fred Astaire, Gregory Peck and John Wayne. The show was seen by an estimated 60 million people. However, what was not supposed to have been seen — not until the broadcast began, anyway — was the sign itself. A shroud had been placed over the face of the structure so a dramatic unveiling could take place. On the director's cue the shroud would drop to the ground, revealing Hollywood's shiny new tiara in a glorious ovation of awe and wonder. But just before the live television event aired, a windstorm blew through the hills. The Sign withstood the assault but the shroud did not. Event organizers were dismayed to see the covering torn away before the scripted cue.

The last known photograph of Peg Entwistle, taken a few days before her suicide. She looks to be wearing a ring on her right pinky, and clutches her fingers just the way she did in a number of childhood photographs (courtesy Entwistle Family).

Had this sudden ill-timed wind been simply a blow from Mother Nature paying a visit on the landmark, or had there been something more to it? Purveyors of the alleged ghostly sightings of Peg might imagine a passing thought in the mind of guest star Bette Davis as the howling-mad wind blasted the shroud away: *Had someone forgotten to invite the Hollywood Sign Girl?*

Yes, it takes quite a stretch of the imagination to envision that Peg Entwistle was somehow reminding the *Diamond Jubilee* about an "uninvited guest," but after all, isn't it with imagination such as this that Hollywood has always thrived?

24

The Curtain Lowers

You have now seen that in spite of the previous claims about the ingénue Peg Entwistle, she was neither an aspiring stage actress, nor a failed movie starlet; that she was in fact an extremely talented and well-trained professional thespian.

Unfortunate, any backward look she may have had regarding her successes did not help her deal with the depression and emotional pain that overwhelmed her in the days leading up to the fall from the Hollywood Sign.

In her suicide note Peg said she was a coward, but she wasn't, really. Indeed, her ability to continue working so gracefully and skillfully during her Theater Guild tour, while suffering for months on end the onslaught thrown at her by Robert Keith, proved she could muster a good measure of strength and courage when she wanted to.

There were a number of contributing factors to Peg's last walk, and in the end it was mostly all about her not being able to face the people she had so dramatically disappointed during those final weeks of 1932's summer. No, Peg was not truly a coward; she was ashamed, and it was this shame that had ultimately uprooted her desire for life.

Many have given up the fight over lesser pains, and many have seen even greater torments through to another, often better day. It is all relative. It is never easy.

Peg's suicide didn't make her a bad girl, just a girl who suffered more than she cared to endure. However, as is so common with most suicides, her final act left behind a wake of hurt and confusion among the survivors—her family, her friends... those who knew her as "Babs."

* * *

Peg Entwistle killed herself, and the world continued spinning without her...

When *The Mad Hopes* opened on Broadway in December of 1932, Billie Burke and Humphrey Bogart were not in the cast and Peg was of course no longer alive. Producer-director Bela Blau had been casting the play even as he spread the word on Broadway that she could not be trusted. As late as a few days before she died, Peg had read in the theatrical notices that Blau was desperately seeking to fill the role of Geneva Hope, the character she had so marvelously played opposite Burke. Blau eventually cast 22-year-old Jane Wyatt, now best remembered as Robert Young's wife in television's *Father Knows Best* (1954–60). Peg had had no hope of reviving her role in *Hopes*, the damage had been done; forgiveness was not an option. Blau's stubbornness had won the day... or so he thought. *The Mad Hopes* received poor reviews during its run in New York. It lasted a mere 12 performances; a Boston run fared no better. In fact, the east coast production had fewer performances than the West Coast pre–Broadway tryout had enjoyed with Peg, Burke, and Bogart.

On August 7, 1933, nearly a year after her death, a Broadway revival of *Tommy* opened at the Forrest Theater. It was directed by Alan Bunce, who had also cast himself as Bernard, the role he played as Peg's second suitor during the successful 1926-27 season. Bunce was the only member of the original cast present for the 1933 production.

It lasted a dismal 24 performances.

Peg's Uncle Charles never returned to Broadway. As a bit player and character actor he appeared in over 50 films before his death in 1944. And while his performances are hardly memorable in the annals of film history, he did get to share screen credits with many A-listers of the era, including Bette Davis, James Cagney, Mae West, Charles Laughton, Norma Shearer, Clark Gable, Katharine Hepburn, Errol Flynn, the Barrymore siblings and Bob Hope. His silent films are for the most part obscure, but his talkies include some notables which still hold up well today: *Little Women* (1933), *Treasure Island* (1934), *Mutiny on the Bounty* (1935), *The Adventures of Robin Hood* (1938), *Wuthering Heights* (1939) and *Kitty Foyle* (1940) are among the 50 or so titles on his résumé.

Except for one film in which she played a dancer (1947's *Fiesta*, with Esther Williams), Peg's Aunt Jane stayed away from acting. After Peg's brothers grew up, she went to work as a secretary and script copyist at a number of Hollywood studios, including MGM and Paramount. She never remarried after Charles died and joined her Enty forever in 1957.

Peg's younger brother Bobby enjoyed a career as a carpenter and set builder for film studios in Hollywood. He passed away in 2003 at the age of 84, before research for this book began. Dozens of anecdotes about Peg are lost forever, for, according to Milton Entwistle, Peg and Bobby were very close and shared a great deal of time together. Later, when Peg became an adult, she and Bobby often went horseback riding together in the hills of Hollywood whenever she was in town.

There is a somewhat puzzling aspect of Peg's story from Bobby Entwistle's recollections, however. In 1998 he and his brother Milton were interviewed for the E! Network's popular television series *Mysteries and Scandals*. Bobby says on-camera that Peg had been in other plays with Billie Burke, but this is inaccurate. Burke's career on stage and in films and television is without question completely accounted for. After a meticulous search of Billie's résumé during the period when Peg was alive, she is found in just one production with Burke: *The Mad Hopes*' West Coast tryout in 1932 is the only time that they worked together. Bobby Entwistle went on to say that Billie had a difficult time remembering her lines, and that Peg often had to whisper them to her. Such a scenario—even in the one production—is unlikely. And while the author cannot fully explain Bobby's mention of his sister having been in numerous productions with Burke, it stands to reason that if Peg had to whisper lines to any actress of note during her career, it would have been Laurette Taylor, who had a reputation for drinking before curtain rise during her engagement with Peg in the revival of *Alice Sit-by-the-Fire*.

As of this writing Milton Entwistle has enjoyed 93 birthdays; 64 of those were shared with his wife Geraldine prior to her death in 2003. Before tying the knot in 1939, Milton was a Marine Reservist while working at Lockheed Aircraft in Burbank, California. Shortly after his honorable discharge in 1942, the Marine Company to which he had been attached was sent to the Philippines. During the infamous war crime known as the Bataan Death March, every one of Milton's Marine buddies was slaughtered during a week-long 60-mile trek to a Japanese POW camp. With the Pacific Fleet dangerously crippled from the attack at Pearl Harbor, the call went out for sailors. Milton heeded that call. He enlisted in the Navy and went to war in the Pacific, serving as a Corpsman aboard the aircraft carrier USS

Shipley Bay. After the war, he went back to Lockheed and years later retired to the sleepy beachfront community of Santa Cruz, California. As kind and gentle a man one could ever hope to meet, Milt spends many hours of his days with his best friend Bruno, a retired Army major who had been one of Patton's senior medical officers during the Battle of the Bulge. (Bruno and Milton were entertaining hosts and friends to the author.)

Peg's cousin, Helen Reid, who was so remarkable and gracious during interviews with the author, is about 100 years old as this is written (she never volunteered her age and the author didn't dare to ask). A joy to engage, with a mind and wit sharp as a razor, Helen sometimes cut short the interviews in order to meet friends for "Martini Bingo."

The "Greatest Generation" might also be called the most charming.

Peg's first and only husband, Robert Keith, remained devoted to Dorothy Tierney, the woman he married after Peg divorced him. He was able to tuck a good number of Broadway outings under his belt, including the magnificent production of *Mister Roberts* (1948–51, in which he originated the role of Doc. Also in the cast of this play, which starred Henry Fonda in the title role, was Keith's son Brian. Robert also became a respected character actor in over 50 films and television programs, including some memorable performances in episodes of *The Twilight Zone*. He died in 1966 at the age of 68.

Brian Keith went on to enjoy an acting career spanning eight decades. Interestingly, his first film role had occurred some three years before he became Peg's stepson: In 1924 he played a toddler in *Pied Piper Malone*, which starred Emma Dunn, Peg's old drill sergeant at the Boston Repertory. His birth mother, with whom he was living when Peg saw his photo on that piano in Rudolph Valentino's former home in 1927, was Helena Shipman, a minor player who is often mistaken for Helen Shipman, an actress of more notable success and the wife of actor Edward Pawley, whom the reader will remember as Irene Dunne's chauffeur in *Thirteen Women*. According to a Keith family website (which makes no mention of Peg), Brian was raised by Shipman in Long Island, New York. It isn't known how well Peg and her stepson had gotten along ... there is nothing in her family archives noting much interaction, and the Keith family did not reply to the author's queries.

Despite all his success, Brian Keith's life ended with almost unfathomable tragedy. His 26-year-old daughter, Daisy, a beautiful but troubled soul who once acted with him in a TV show called *Heartland*, was unable to conquer her demons. She killed herself with a gunshot on April 16, 1997. Two months later, on June 24, while suffering from emphysema and a broken heart over his daughter's suicide, Brian Keith sat in his Malibu Colony home and used the same gun on himself. It was two days before Daisy would have turned 27. Brian Keith was 75.

* * *

Peg was only 24 when her death made national headlines, but at only 17 her reputation as a theatrical prodigy had also gotten national attention. Critics and co-players loved her, and despite a few snippy comments by her step-grandmother, Ross family matriarch Matilda, there is a profound lack of accounts bespeaking a difficult or headstrong actress.

Her résumé is not lengthy, for her life was short, yet she performed many hundreds of times in cities that took theater seriously, and she seems to have always come away a winner even if the show was not.

Charles Dickens wrote, "It is a hopeless endeavor to attract people to a theater unless they can be first brought to believe that they will never get in."[1] No truer were the words of this philosophy than with Peg's plays at the Boston Repertory, the Theater Guild national tour, her co-starring role with William Gillette's farewell tour of *Sherlock Holmes*, and the final two plays of her life, Broadway's revival of *Alice Sit-by-the-Fire* and the California tryout of *The Mad Hopes*. These productions were sold-out weeks and sometimes months in advance.

Was she the best actress to ever grace the stage? No. But she hadn't lived long enough to attain such status—if such status can even be had. However, she was certainly very, *very* good. And as to her surviving moments on film, Peg Entwistle's screams during her murder scene in RKO's *Thirteen Women* are among the best ever done. But it was the stage, not film, which had always really been her true love. This is evidenced by the simple fact that she had left Hollywood when she was 17 years old. As stated in a previous chapter, if Peg had wanted to be a movie star she could have pitched herself to the many film studios and agents just down the street from her Hollywood home. But the play was her thing, and so she had gone east to pursue theater. As stated earlier, Peg had a dream ... she wanted to be like Maude Adams, who at that time had been the most successful woman in the history of the stage.

Later, in 1930, Peg again showed her preference for stage over film when she turned down a chance to portray her originating Broadway role as Marie Thurber in RKO's screen adaptation of *Tommy*. (This film, called *She's My Weakness,* featured *Tommy*'s Alan Bunce as Bernard. Bunce seems to have never tired of this role.)

So, to the boards and footlights went Peg, and there she learned her craft and received the finest training and worked with some of the best that the drama world had to offer. Given her abilities and large number of positive, upward-trending reviews, Peg might very well have been recognized for a number of Tony Awards, had she chosen to live.

There is little doubt that she would have found her way into theater's forgiveness after the falling-out with Herbert L. Swett and Bela Blau. How long this would have taken is anyone's guess, but Peg would have easily picked up right where she had left off, for she was a brilliant stage actress, and she delighted in pleasing audiences in the tradition of the light heart, in the style of the comedic genius of the era's Laurette Taylors and Billie Burkes. Peg was tailor-made for this, but her dramatic expression was no less important or impressive, and of this, Bette Davis's own words and witness is all the validation Peg Entwistle needs.

Reflect for a moment on some of the greatest actresses to ever appear during the era of Bette Davis ... Crawford, Hepburn, Garbo, de Havilland, Dietrich, Bergman, Stanwyck.... And yet in all the Bette Davis books, articles, documentaries and interviews researched and sifted for Peg Entwistle's biography, there was not found any other person to whom Bette had pointed as having so profound an effect on her.

If any of the abovementioned screen legends had made Bette reach for a hankie during any of their performances throughout the years, she hadn't said much about it. But whenever the question of how she became an actress had come to her, Bette never forgot Peg, or that night of Ibsen in 1926 when Peg's tragic Hedvig seared into Bette's soul.

* * *

Peg's humanity made her both fragile and strong, and she sometimes found herself in a sort of "no man's land," wandering amid the trenches in a war between doubt and confidence. When she was unsure of herself she would sometimes crumble and tuck away in the dark behind window blinds, locked doors, and unanswered rings of the phone. But when she was confident and on top of her game, she was one of the best.

With regard to her craft we find a sort of "duality" in Peg Entwistle—two natures, separate but complementary to one and other ... the reserved "thespian" on one side, and the light-hearted "actress" on the other. The thespian in Peg was the mature, learned adult who studied with intensity her dramatic lines, plots, and character arcs. In this, the thespian held her own with grace, politeness, and restraint alongside Broadway's A-list. But the actress in her was the fun-loving inner child; the little one who found a playground in the world of theater, and whose rehearsals and comedic performances were as carefree and enjoyable to behold as a squealing girl soaring to and fro from a tree swing.

Every record indicates that Peg's theatrical family — her fans and fellows — loved watching the girl Entwistle at play ... soaring and squealing. And in this, Peg "Babs" Entwistle was more herself when she was not herself, when, like all happy little girls, she could "pretend" and play "dress-up" and "make believe" with her friends.

The Tony Award had not been invented by 1932, but perhaps it should have been.

Better yet, the little girl should have stayed soaring in her swing.

Peg Entwistle Career Résumé

Broadway

Hamlet

A Tragedy Revival in Five Acts by William Shakespeare
Starring Walter Hampden and Ethel Barrymore
Hampden's Theater

Peg Entwistle's first stint on a professional stage took place between October 10 and 24, 1925. She was given an uncredited non-speaking walk-on role by Walter Hampden. Peg carried the king's train and brought in the poison cup. She appeared in approximately 14 performances.

The Repertory Theater of Boston

Henry Jewett, Proprietor

Opening dates reflect only the debut of a play at the Boston Repertory. Most plays ran six days per week for one or two weeks, and then closed for a week or several weeks (or more) before being revived. The "Performances" number reflects the approximate total of all performances for each play during Peg Entwistle's engagement at the Repertory.

The Rivals

A Comedy of Manners by Richard Brinsley Sheridan
Staged in Nine Curtailed Scenes by Francis Wilson
Opened: November 10, 1925. Performances: 12
This inaugural production of the new Boston
Repertory was simulcast live on WBZ radio.

Lucy— Peg Entwistle (as "Margaret Entwistle")
Lydia Languish— Olive Tell
Julie— Carolyn Ferriday
Mrs. Malaprop— Emma Dunn
Sir Anthony Absolute— George Riddell
Sir Lucius O'Trigger— Henry Jewett
Fag— Horace Pollock
Capt. Jack Absolute— William Kershaw
Faulkland— Eric Stanley Kalkhurst
Bob Acres— Francis Wilson
David— Lawrence Sterner
Footman— Robert T. Hambleton

Rip Van Winkle

A Comedy in Four Acts by Dion Boucicault
From the Washington Irving story
Staged by Francis Wilson
Opened: November 23, 1925. Performances: 24

Hendrick — Peg Entwistle (as "Margaret Entwistle")
Gretchen — Emma Dunn
Von Beekman — George Riddell
Nick Vedder — Lawrence Sterner
Cockles — William Kershaw
Rip Van Winkle — Francis Wilson
Little Meenie — Dora Cramer
Jacob Stein — Arthur Stone
Dwarf — Lawrence Sterner
Hendrick Hudson — Henry Jewett
Meenie — Olive Tell
Katchen — Carolyn Ferriday
Seth — Robert Hambleton
Brom Dutcher — William Ghere
Vedder — Eric Stanley Kalkhurst

The Wild Duck

A Comedy-Drama in Five Acts by Henrik Ibsen
Directed by Henry Jewett
Opened: December 7, 1925. Performances: 54–60

Hedvig — Peg Entwistle
Petterson — Agnes Scott
Jensen — Carolyn Ferriday
Man Servant — Richard Capran
Ekdal — Horace Pollock
Mrs. Sorby — Lenore Chippendale
Flabby Gentleman — William Mason
Thin-haired Gentleman — William Ghere
Short-sighted Gentleman — Arthur Stone
Werle — Arthur Bebrens
Gregers Werle — William Kershaw
Hjalmar Ekdal — Dallas Anderson
Graaberg — Robert Hambleton
Gina Ekdal — Blanche Yurka
Relling — John Thorn
Molvik — Eric Kalkhurst

Enter Madame

A Comedy in Three Acts by Gilda Veresi and Dolly Byrne
Directed by Henry Jewett
Opened: December 14, 1925. Performances: 18

Aline Chalmers — Peg Entwistle
Flora Preston — Lenora Chippendale
Gerald Fitzgerald — Arthur Behrens
John Fitzgerald — Ross Alexander
Bice — Agnes Scott
Tamamoto — William Kershaw
Archimede — John Thorn
Miss Smith — Carolyn Ferriday
The Doctor — Horace Pollock
Madame Liza Della Robbin — Blanche Yurka

WBZ Radio Special Solo Broadcasts

Peg Entwistle in the character of Snow White reading and singing children's stories
Opened: December 14–24, 1925. Nightly 6 P.M. Performances: 10–11
Opened: Christmas Eve Show Live from Boston Common. 9:30 P.M.
Special Christmas Eve Production at Boston Common
Peg Entwistle in the character of Snow White as Hostess of Beacon Hill Holiday Event
Opened: December 24, 1925. 5 P.M. to Midnight.
(Included Live 9:30 P.M. WBZ Radio Broadcast by Peg Entwistle)

Snow White and the Seven Dwarfs

A Fairy Tale Play in Six Acts by Jessie Braham
Directed by Henry Jewett
Opened: December 21, 1925. Performances: 12

Princess Snow White— Peg Entwistle
Sir Dandiprat Bombas— William Mason
Rosalys— Ethelyne Hoizman
Astolane— Elizabeth Leavitt
Christabel— Helen Wallace
Ermengarde— Willa Griffin
Amelotte— Susan Shenfane
Ursula— Pauline Connoly
Lynette— Adelaide Connoly
Guinivere— Martha Dunder
Prince Florimond— Ross Alexander
Valentine— Arthur Menadier
Vivian— William Dunne
Victor— Richard Capran
Queen Brangomar— Lenore Chippendale
Witch Hex— Agnes Scott
Berthold— Robert Hambleton
Blick— Esther Keefe
Flick— Arthur Stone
Glick— Hilda Goldthwaite
Snick— Lucile Wright
Plick— Imogene Garner
Whick— Frances L. Fagan
Quee— Betty White
Long Tall— William Dunne
Peddler Woman— Helen Wallace

Mrs. Partridge Presents

A Comedy in Three Acts by Mary Kennedy and Ruth Hawthorne
Directed by Blanche Yurka
Opened: December 28, 1925. Performances: 16

Delight— Peg Entwistle
Ellen— Agnes Scott
Phillip— Ross Alexander
Stephen Applegate— Dallas Anderson
Maisie Partridge— Blanche Yurka
Katherine Everett— Carlotta Irwin
Charles Ludlow— John Thorn
Agnes Hamilton— Helen Wallace
Clementine— Elizabeth Leavitt
La Fleur— Ethelyne Hoizman

Much Ado About Nothing

A Comedy in Five Acts by William Shakespeare
Directed in Five Scenes by Henry Jewett
Opened: January 11, 1926. Performances: 12

Hero— Peg Entwistle
Leonato— William Mason
Conrade— Ross Alexander
Beatrice— Eve Walsh Hall
Don Pedro— Dallas Anderson
Benedick— Henry Jewett
Don John— William Kershaw
Claudio— Charles Meredith
Borachio— Charles Stillwell
Antonio— Horace Pollock
A Boy— Elizabeth Leavitt
Balthazar— Ethelyne Hoizman
Margaret— Helen Wallace
Ursula— Agnes Scott
Dogberry— John Thorn
Verges— George Hare
Beacoal— Arthur Stone
Oatcake— Robert Hambleton
Friar Francis— Horace Pollock
A Sexton— James H. Bell
A Messenger— Richard Capran

Loyalties

A Drama in Three Acts by John Galsworthy
Directed in Seven Scenes by Henry Jewett
Opened: February 8, 1926. Performances: 12

Mabel Daney—Peg Entwistle
Charles Winsor—George Stillwell
Lady Adela Winsor—Agnes Scott
Ferdinand de Lewis—John Davidson
Treisure—Louis Leon Hall
General Canynge—William Kershaw
Margaret Orme—Mary Servos
Capt. Ronald Daney—Charles Quartermaine
Inspector Dede—Ralph Roberts
Robert—Richard Capran

A Constable—Myles Nuttall
Augustus Borring—George Hare
Lord St. Erth—Horace Pollock
A Footman—Arthur Stone
Major Colford—William Mason
A Clerk—Robert Hambleton
Edward Graviter—Ross Alexander
Gilman—Ralph Roberts
Jacob Twisden—Horace Pollock
Ricardos—Louis Leon Hall

Caesar and Cleopatra

A Historical Comedy in Five Acts by George Bernard Shaw
Staged in Nine Scenes by Henry Jewett and James H. Bell
Opened: February 22, 1926. Performances: 12

Charmian—Peg Entwistle
Belzanor—William C. Mason
The Persian—Frank Thomas
Nubian Sentinel—Richard Capran
Bel Affris—George A. Stillwell
A Woman—Helen M. Wallace
Ftatateeta—Agnes Scott
Caesar—Charles Quartermaine
Cleopatra—Mary Servos
Pothinus—Horace Pollock
Theodotus—George Hare
Ptolemy—Arthur Stone
Achilles—R. Henry Handon

Rufio—Louis Leon Hall
Britannus—Ralph Roberts
Lucius Septimus—William Kershaw
Apollodorus—Ross Alexander
Roman Sentinel—Frank Thomas
Centurion—George Stillwell
First Auxiliary Soldier—Myles Nuttall
Second Auxiliary Soldier—Paul Kimball
Musician—George Hare
Iris—Helen Wallace
Palace Official—Robert Hambleton
Major Domo—William Mason
A Priest—William Dunne

Heartbreak House

A Satirical Comedy in Three Acts by George Bernard Shaw
Directed by Henry Jewett
Opened: March 8, 1926. Performances: 12

Ellie Dunn—Peg Entwistle
Nurse Guinness—Agnes Scott
Capt. Shotover—Louis Leon Hall
Lady Utterwood—Mary Servos
Hesione Hushabye—Ruth Taylor

Mazzini Dunn—Horace Pollock
Hector Hushabye—Charles Quartermaine
Boss Mangan—William Kershaw
Randall Utterwood—George Stillwell
The Burglar—Ralph Roberts

Minick

A Comedy in Three Acts by George S. Kaufman and Edna Ferber
Directed by Henry Jewett
Opened: March 15, 1926. Performances: 12

Lil Corey—Peg Entwistle
Nettie Minick—Mary Servos
Annie—Helen Wallace
Jim Corey—George Stillwell
Fred Minick—Ross Alexander
Old Man Minick—Frank Thomas
Al Diamond—Ralph Roberts
Marge Diamond—Ruth Taylor

Lula—Alicia B. Crawford
Mr. Dietenhofer—Louis Leon Hall
Mr. Price—George Hare
Mrs. Smallridge—Ethel Frances Roberts
Miss Crackenwald—Valentine Sidney
Mr. Lippinscott—Agnes Scott
Miss Stack—Elizabeth Leavitt

The Circle

A Satirical Comedy in Three Acts by W. Somerset Maugham
Directed by Henry Jewett
Opened: March 29, 1926. Performances: 12

Elizabeth Champion-Cheney— Peg Entwistle
Arnold Champion-Cheney— William Kershaw
The Footman— Robert Hambleton
Mrs. Shenstone— Agnes Scott
Edward Luton— Ross Alexander

Clive Champion-Cheney— Charles Quartermaine
The Butler— Ralph Roberts
Lady Catherine Champion-Cheney— Ruth Taylor
Lord Porteous— Horace Pollock

Little Minister

A Drama by Sir James M. Barrie
Directed by Dallas Anderson and Maude Adams
Opened: May 3, 1926. Performances: 12

Lady Babbie— Peg Entwistle
Rob Dow— Horace Pollock
Joe Cruickshanks— R. Henry Handon
Thomas Whamond— Louis Leon Hall
Snecky Hobart— Ralph Roberts
Micah Dow— Marie Handon
Gavin Dishart— Dallas Anderson
Lord Rintoul— Charles Quartermaine
Captain Halliwell— George Stillwell
Nannie Webster— Agnes Scott
Sergeant Davidson— Ross Alexander
Jean, a maid servant— Ruth Taylor

Andrew Mealmaker— William Kershaw
Silva Tosh— George Hare
Bell McQuhatty— Sarah R. Keigwin
Felice, Lady Babbie's maid— Mercedes Raynor
Thwaites, a butler— William Mason
Townspeople-Soldiers— John Brown, Ruth Auld, Dorothy Carr, Frances Eder, Rebecca Field, Mary Hawes, Marjorie Soderlund, William Dunne, Paul Kimball, Myles Nuttall, David Pickett, Hambleton Stone, Lorrie Duplex, Marion Matthews, Mary Moschhilli, Louise Smith, Helen Toner, George Zorn

The Swan

A Comedy in Three Acts by Ferenc Molnar
Directed by Henry Jewett
Opened: May 10, 1926. Performances: 12

Arsene— Peg Entwistle
Dr. Nicholas Agl— Dallas Anderson
George— David Pickett
Princess Beatrice— Ethel Morrison
Alexandra— Ruth Taylor
Father Hyacinth— Horace Pollock
Symphorosa— Mercedes Raynor
Prince Albert— Charles Quartermaine

Colonel Wunderlich— William Kershaw
Count Luzen— Robert Hambleton
Alfred— Louis Leon Hall
Husser— Ralph Roberts
Maid— Helen Toner
Princess Maria— Agnes Scott
Countess Erdely— France Eder

Broadway

Opening dates reflect the date of a production's first Broadway performance. "Performances" total are the approximate number of the Broadway run *and* any pre–Broadway tryouts.

The Man from Toronto

A Comedy in Three Acts by Douglas Murray
Produced by Bannister and Powell
Directed by Albert Bannister
Opened at Selwyn Theater: June 17, 1926. Performances: 31

Martha— Peg Entwistle
Fergis Wimbush— Curtis Cooksey
Mr. Priestly— George Graham
Mrs. Calthorpe— Beatrice Hendricks
Minnie— Mona Hungerford

Ruth Wimbush— Ethel Martin
Robert— Gavin Muir
Ada— Lota Sanders
Mrs. Hubbard— Marion Stephenson

The Home Towners

A Comedy Farce in Three Acts by George M. Cohan
Directed by John Meehan under Supervision of George M. Cohan
Opened at Hudson Theater: August 23, 1926. Performances: 64

Beth Calhoon— Peg Entwistle
Bell Boy— Spencer Bentley
Lottie Bancroft— Georgia Caine
Stone— Walter Calligan
Nellie Calhoon— Florence Earle
Vic Arnold— William Elliot

Maid— Doris Freeman
Mort Calhoon— Ben Johnson
P.H. Bancroft— Robert McWade
Wally Calhoon— Chester Morris
Joe Roberts— Walter Plimmer
Casey— William Walcott

Tommy

An Original Comedy in Three Acts by
Howard Lindsay and Bertrand Robinson
Produced by George C. Tyler.
Directed by Howard Lindsay and Bertrand Robinson
Opened at the Gaiety Theater: January 10, 1927.
Performances: 265–270

Marie Thurber— Peg Entwistle
Bernard— Alan Bunce
Tommy Mills— William Janney
Judge Wilson— Ben Johnson

Mr. Thurber— Lloyd Neal
David Tuttle— Sidney Toler
Mrs. Thurber— Maidel Turner
Mrs. Wilson— Florence Walcott

The Uninvited Guest

An Original Drama in Three Acts by Bernard J. McOwen
Produced by L.M. Simmons. Staged by Russell Mack
Opened at the Belmont Theater September 27, 1927. Performances: 23

Johanna Jackson— Peg Entwistle
T. Jefferson White— John Carmody
Hanna White— Mabel Colcord
Horace Bascom— Robert Conness

James Malcolm— Walter Davis
Alfred Jackson— Elmer Grandin
Matty Jackson— Helen Strickland

Theater Guild Anniversary Tour

This tour was done in the repertory style, with all the players constantly changing roles in the four productions presented.

A number of players were removed or added for various reasons during the span of the tour. Peg Entwistle's roles and the roles of other principals are detailed in the narrative. Below are the members of the Guild Repertory Company's starting lineup.

Physical limitations coupled with a lack of extant documents and articles during research prevented a precise accounting of all the cities and towns in which the Guild Repertory Company appeared. The numbers of performances were estimated based upon a *New York Times* article declaring that *The Doctor's Dilemma* had been booked for 100 performances. This is explained more fully within the narrative of this book.

The Guild Repertory Company Productions

The Doctor's Dilemma — A Comedy in Five Acts by George Bernard Shaw
The Second Man — A Comedy in Three Acts by S.N. Berman
Ned McCobb's Daughter — A Drama in Three Acts by Sidney Howard
John Ferguson — A Drama in Four Acts by St. John Ervine
Tour Produced by the New York Theater Guild
Productions and Rehearsals Directed by Edwin Maxwell and Philip Moeller
Costumes and Settings by Raymond Sovey and Lee Simonson
Theresa Helburn, Executive Director of the Theater Guild

The Players

Peg Entwistle, Robert Keith, Elisabeth Risdon, Alan Mowbray, Warburton Gamble, Edwin Maxwell, Brandon Evans, P.J. Kelly, Lawrence Leslie, Beatrice Hendricks, Lowden Adams, Payson Edwards, Jack Quigley, Neal Caldwell, Richard Stevenson, Douglas Montgomery, Paul McGrath.

Opened: October 1928, Montclair, New Jersey
Closed: June 1929, San Diego, California
Performances of all four productions: 380 to 400

William Gillette Farewell Tour

Sherlock Holmes

Revival of a Four-Act Drama by Arthur Conan Doyle and William Gillette
Produced by George C. Tyler and A.L. Erlanger.
Staged by William Postance
Tour Opened: November 15, 1929. Tour Closed: May 12, 1930
Performances: 125 (approximate)

Alice Faulkner— Peg Entwistle
Sherlock Holmes— William Gillette
Count Von Stahlburg— Alfred Ansel
Jim Craigin— William H. Barwald
Madge Larrabee— Roberta Beatty
Thérèse— Kate Byron
Parsons— Donald Campbell
Dr. Watson— Wallis Clark
Billy— Burford Hampden
Alfred Bassick— J. Augustus Keough
Mrs. Smeedley— Rose Kingston
"Lightfoot" McTague— Henry Lambert
Professor Moriarty— John Miltern
Mrs. Faulkner— Dorothy Peabody Russell
Sidney Prince— William Postance
Sir Edward Leighton— Byron Russell
John Forman— Brinsley Shaw
James Larrabee— Montague Shaw
John— Fred Tasker
Thomas Leary— Herbert Wilson

The Lakewood Players 1930

Lakewood Theater, Skowhegan, Maine
Willard H. Cummings, President Herbert L. Swett, Gen. Mgr.
Howard Lindsay, Director

Little Accident

An American Comedy in Three Acts by Floyd Dell and Thomas Mitchell
Staged by Samuel T. Godfrey
Opened: June 23, 1930. Six Performances

Isabel Drury— Peg Entwistle
Mrs. Overbeck— Kathryn Keys
Doris Overbeck— Eileen Byron
John— Donald J. McGinnis
J.J. Overbeck— Thurston Hall
Norman Overbeck— Hugh O'Connell
Gilbert Rand— Robert Hudson
Lucinda Overbeck— Virginia Godfrey
Janet Park— Ann Merrill
Emily Crane— Kathleen Robinson
Madge Ferris— Kate Byron
Reverend Doctor Gifford— A.G. Andrews
Miss Clark— Winona Shannon
Hicks— Samuel T. Godfrey
Rudolpho Amendelaro— William R. Barry
Miss Hemingway— Frances Goodrich
Doctor Zerneke— Beatrice Terry
Monica Case— Robin Simpson
Mrs. Case— Beatrice Terry

Holiday

A Comedy in Three Acts by Philip Barry
Staged by Samuel T. Godfrey
Opened: July 7, 1931. Six Performances

Linda Seton— Peg Entwistle
Johnny Case— Hardie Albright
Julia Seton— Kate Byron
Laura Cram— Kathryn Keyes
Seton Cram— Thurston Hall
Edward Seton— Wallis Clark
Ned Seton— William Carey
Nick Potter— Hugh O'Connell
Susan Potter— Dorothy Stickney
Henry— Samuel T. Godfrey
Charles— Donald J. McGinnis
Delia— Marjorie North

A Butterfly on the Wheel

A Play in Four Acts by Edward G. Hemmerde and Francis Neilson
Staged by Samuel T. Godfrey
Opened: July 14, 1930. Six Performances

Peggy Admaston—Peg Entwistle
Jacques, a waiter—William E. Barry
Pauline—Kathryn Keyes
A Detective—Robert Hudson
Roderick Collingwood—Frank Wilcox
Lady Atwill—Frances Goodrich
Lord Ellerdine—Hugh O'Connell
Right Hon. George Admaston—Wallis Clark

Sir John Burroughs—Arthur Byron
Sir Robert Fyffe—Samuel T. Godfrey
Gervaise McArthur—Thurston Hall
Stuart Menzies—Robert Hudson
Mr. Parks—Hardie Albright
Stevens, the Railroad Porter—Albert Rights
Court Usher—Donald J. McGinnis
(Solicitors, Barristers, Associate Judges, etc.)

The Plutocrat

A Play in Three Acts by Arthur Goodrich
Based on the Booth Tarkington Novel of the Same Name
Staged by Charles Coburn
Opened: July 28, 1930. Six Performances

Olivia Tinker—Peg Entwistle
Smoking Room Steward—John Daly Murphy
Albert Jones—William Carey
Lawrence Cole—Hardie Albright
Mrs. Tinker—Ivah Coburn
Mme. Momoro—Peggy Allenby
Hyacinthe Momoro—Willard Cummins, Jr.
Earl Tinker—Charles Coburn
Wackstle—Frank Wilcox

Weatheright—Thurston Hall
Doc. Taylor—William E. Barry
Sir William Broadfeather—Wallis Clark
Lady Broadfeather—Kathryn Keyes
Cayzac—Samuel T. Godfrey
Waiter at Hotel Bindar—William E. Barry
Prince Karno—Robert Hudson
Native Officer—Donald J. McGinnis

Let Us Be Gay

A Comedy by Rachel Crothers
Staged by Samuel T. Godfrey
Opened: August 4, 1930. Six Performances

Dierdre Lessing—Peg Entwistle
Kitty Brown—Peggy Allenby
Bob Brown—Samuel T. Godfrey
Mrs. Bouccicault—Kathryn Keyes
Townley Town—Thurston Hall
Bruce Keen—William Carey

Madge Livingstone—Susanne Willa
Wallace Grainger—J. Colvil Dunn
Whiteman—Wallis Clark
Struthers—Donald J. McGinnis
Perkins—Gladys Webster
Williams—William E. Barry

Escape

A Play in Nine Episodes by John Galsworthy
Opened: August 11, 1930. Six Performances

The Girl of the Town—Peg Entwistle
Matt Dennant—Hardie Albright
The Plain Clothes Man—J. Colvil Dunn
The Policeman—Thomas Tempest
The Other Policeman—Donald J. McGinnis
The Fellow Convict—John Daly Murphy

The Warder—Thurston Hall
The Other Warder—Morton L. Stevens
The Shingled Lady—Peggy Allenby
The Maid—Susan Willa
The Old Gentleman—Wallis Clark

Broken Dishes

A Comedy in Three Acts by Martin Flavin
Staged by Samuel T. Godfrey
Opened: August 18, 1930. Six Performances

Elaine, the Youngest Daughter— Peg Entwistle
Ma Bumpstead— Jean Adair
Myra Bumpstead, a Daughter— Gladys Webster
Mabel Bumpstead, a Daughter— Susanne Willa
Cyrus, "Pa" Bumpstead— Donald Meek

Billy Clark, the Delivery Boy— Hardie Albright
Sam Green, just a Crownie— Morton L. Stevens
Dr. Stump— Wallis Clark
A Stranger— Thurston Hall
Mr. Quinn— William E. Barry

Western Union, Please

A Comedy by Albert Hackett and Frances Goodrich
Staged by Samuel T. Godfrey
Opened: August 27, 1930. Four Performances

Alice Daley— Peg Entwistle
Jennie Daley— Jean Adair
Aurora Neusbickle— Jessie Crumette
Danny Daley— Donald Meek
Joe Graybell— William Carey

Hal Stoddard— Samuel T. Godfrey
Thaddeus Taylor— Thurston Hall
J.M. Gillespie— Morton L. Stevens
A Messenger Boy— Philip Godfrey

Broadway

She Means Business

An Original Comedy by Samuel Shipman
Produced by James Elliott Staged by Frederick Stanhope
Opened at the Ritz Theater, January 26, 1931. Performances: 8

Charlotte B. Evans— Peg Entwistle
Mary— Kate Byron
Allen T. Evans— Wallis Clark
Ware— Robert Cummings
Doris Roberts— Ann Davis
Jane Barton— Ruth Donnelly
Margie— Desiree Foster
John Roberts— Ernest Glendinning

Reubens— Lee Kohlmar
Edgar Lawson— Ivan Miller
William Brighton— Herbert Rawlinson
George Forbes— Houston Richards
Holbrook— Bennett Southard
Aiken— Tom Tempest
Groff— Edwin Walter
Walter Norman— Douglas Wood

Getting Married

A Comedy Revival by George Bernard Shaw
Produced by the Theater Guild
Staged by Philip Moeller
Opened at the Guild Theater March 30, 1931. Performances: 48

Edith Bridgenorth— Peg Entwistle
Leo— Dorothy Gish
Mrs. Bridgeport— Margaret Wycherly
William Collins— Henry Travers
Cecil Sykes— Romney Brent
The General— Ernest Cossart
Lesbia Grantham— Irby Marshall

Reginald Bridgenorth— Hugh Buckler
The Bishop— Reginald Mason
St. John Hotchkiss— Hugh Sinclair
Oliver Cromwell Soames— Ralph Roeder
Mrs. George Collins— Helen Westley
The Beadle— Oscar Stirling

The Lakewood Players 1931

Lakewood Theater, Skowhegan, Maine
Willard H. Cummings, President Herbert L. Swett, General Manager
Melville Burke, Director

Whispering Friends

A Comedic Farce in Two Acts by George M. Cohan
Opened: June 1, 1931. Six Performances

Emily Sanford— Peg Entwistle
Joe Sanford— William Harrigan
Al Wheeler— Owen Davis, Jr.

The Butler— Thurston Hall
Nathalie— Kate Byron
Doris— Gladys Hurlbut

Craig's Wife

A Drama in Three Acts by George Kelly
Staged by Melville Burke
Opened: June 8, 1931. Six Performances

Ethel Landreth— Peg Entwistle
Miss Austin— Jessamine Newcombe
Mrs. Harold— Suzanne Willa
Mazie— Gladys Webster
Mrs. Craig— Gladys Hurlbut
Walter Craig— William Harrigan

Mrs. Frazier— Kathryn Keyes
Billy Birkmire— Wallis Clark
Joseph Catelle— Thurston Hall
Harry— Paul Anglin
Eugene Fredericks— Owen Davis, Jr.

Rebound

A Comedy in Three Acts by Donald Ogden Stewart
Staged by Melville Burke
Opened: June 14, 1931. Six Performances

Evie Lawrence— Peg Entwistle
Liz Crawford— Gladys Hurlbut
Lyman Patterson— William Harrigan
Les Crawford— Wallis Clark
Marta— Kate Byron
Sara Jaffrey— Sylvia Field

Bill Truesdale— Harland Tucker
Johnnie Coles— Owen Davis, Jr.
Mrs. Jaffrey— Jessamine Newcombe
Pierre— Harold Moffet
Jules— Houston Richards
Henry Jaffrey— Thurston Hall

The Thirteenth Chair

A Mystery Play in Three Acts by Bayard Veiller
Staged by Melville Burke
Opened: June 22, 1931. Six Performances

Helen Trent— Peg Entwistle
Rosalie La Grange— Margaret Wycherly
Helen O'Neill— Sylvia Field
Will Crosby— Owen Davis, Jr.
Mrs. Crosby— Jessamine Newcombe
Roscoe Crosby— Thurston Hall
Edward Wales— Wallis Clark
Mary Eastwood— Gladys Hurlbut
Grace Standish— Kate Byron

Braddish Trent— William Carey
Howard Standish— William Barry
Philip Mason— Houston Richards
Elizabeth Erskine— Suzanne Willa
Pollock— Tom Tempest
Tim Donahue— Harland Tucker
Sergeant Dunn— Harold Moffet
Doolan— Frank McDonald

Love 'Em and Leave 'Em

A Comedy in Three Acts by John Weaver and George Abbott
Staged by Melville Burke
Opened: June 29, 1931. Six Performances

Pearl— Peg Entwistle
Lem Woodruff— Wallis Clark
Ma Woodruff— Jessamine Newcombe
Kenyon— Harold Moffett
Jim Somers— Owen Davis, Jr.
Bill Billingsly— Harland Tucker
Janie Walsh— Sylvia Field
Mame Walsh— Gladys Hurlbut

Miss Streeter— Gladys Webster
Sam— William Carey
Agnes— Suzanne Willa
Mr. McGonigle— Thurston Hall
Mr. Aiken— Houston Richards
Jack— Frank McDonald
Hazel— Kate Byron

Just to Remind You

A Drama in Three Acts by Owen Davis
Staged by Melville Burke
Opened: July 6, 1931. Six Performances

Nettie Pierce— Peg Entwistle
Ben Fairchild— Humphrey Bogart
Dick Tanner— William Carey
Irma Tanner— Mary Phillips
Mrs. Robins— Jessamine Newcombe
Jimmie Alden— Paul Kelly
Doris Sabin— Sylvia Field
John, a Chinaman— Houston Richards
Miss Fallen— Suzanne Willa
Jennie— Gladys Hurlbut

Judge Higgins— Thurston Hall
Austin Jones— Wallis Clark
Dave Morris— Harland Tucker
Eddie Mason— Owen Davis, Jr.
Dan Costigan— Harold Moffett
Tony— Frank McDonald
Jake— Paul Anglim
Nolan— Robert Hudson
Mack— Tom Tempest
Bill— William Barry

So This Is London

A Comedy in Three Acts by Arthur Goodrich
Staged by Melville Burke
Opened: July 13, 1931. Six Performances

Eleanor Beauchamp— Peg Entwistle
Hiram Draper— Charles Coburn
Hiram Draper (Junior)— Owen Davis, Jr.
Lady Amy Ducksworth— Ivah Coburn
Mrs. Hiram Draper— Kathryn Keyes
A Flunky at the Ritz— Frank McDonald

Sir Percy Beauchamp— Wallis Clark
Lady Beauchamp— Jessamine Newcombe
Alfred Honeycutt— Harland Tucker
Thomas— Tom Tempest
Hornsby— Houston Richards

Broadway

Just to Remind You

A Drama in Three Acts by Owen Davis
Produced by Sam H. Harris
Staged by Melville Burke
Opened at the Broadhurst Theater September 7, 1931. Performances: 16

Nettie Pierce — Peg Entwistle	Judge Higgins — Edward H. Robins
Ben Fairchild — Jerome Cowan	Austin Jones — Harold Healy
Dick Tanner — Tom Fadden	Dave Morris — Calvin Thomas
Irma Tanner — Isabel Baring	Eddie Mason — Owen Davis, Jr.
Mrs. Robins — Jessie Graham	Dan Costigan — Frank Shannon
Jimmie Alden — Paul Kelly	Tony — Frank McDonald
Doris Sabin — Sylvia Field	Jake — Charles Richards
John, a Chinaman — Charlie Fang	Nolan — Charles Slattery
Miss Fallen — Genevieve Bowman	Mack — Henry Shelver
Jennie — Gladys Hurlbut	Bill — Charles McNaughton

Little Women

A Drama in Four Acts by Marian De Forest
Adapted from the Story by Louisa May Alcott
Produced and Staged by William A. Brady
Opened at the Playhouse Theater December 7, 1931. Performances: 17

Amy — Peg Entwistle	Aunt March — Jane Corcoran
Meg — Lee Patrick	Mr. Laurence — Carson Davenport
Jo — Jessie Royce Landis	Laurie — Lee Crowe
Beth — Joanna Roos	Professor Frederick Bhaer — Arthur Donaldson
Mrs. March — Marie Curtis	John Brooks — Harry Worth
Mr. March — Burr Carruth	Hannah Mullet — Caroline Newcombe

Alice Sit-by-the-Fire

A Page from a Daughter's Diary in Three Acts by James M. Barrie
Revival Produced by William A. Brady
Staged by Stanley Logan
Opened at the Playhouse Theater March 7, 1932. Performances: 37

This play was the front piece of a double bill of what was popularly known as "The Barrie Revivals" or "A Night of Barrie." Details of the second bill, called *The Old Lady Shows Her Medals,* are here omitted as Peg Entwistle did not appear in it.

Amy Gray — Peg Entwistle	Leonora Dunbar — Lucille Lisle
Mrs. Gray — Laurette Taylor	Nurse — Jane Corcoran
Colonel Gray — Charles Dalton	Fanny — Alice May Tuck
Cosmo Gray — Maurey Tuckerman	Richardson — Nan Sheldon
Stephen Rolle — Robert Harrigan	

San Diego, Santa Barbara, Los Angeles

The Mad Hopes

A pre-Broadway Tryout Comedy in Three Acts by Romney Brent
Produced by Edward Belasco, Homer Curran, Romney Brent, Bela Blau
Directed by Bela Blau and Edgar MacGregor
Stage Settings by Joseph Urban
Miss Burke's and Miss Entwistle's Gowns Designed by Adrian

Opened: May 15, 1932, San Diego. Performances: 5
Opened: May 20, 1932, Santa Barbara. Performances: 3
Opened: May 23, 1932. Los Angeles. Performances: 16

Geneva Hope— Peg Entwistle
Clytie Hope— Billie Burke
Henry Frost— Humphrey Bogart
Lady Ingleby— Grayce Hampton
Croesus— Claude King
Claude Hope— Rex O'Malley

Maurice Klein— Pierre De Ramey
Hilton Hope— Alex Courtney
Comte Rene D'Entain— Marcelle Corday
Sheriff— Emile Bistagne
Charlemagne— Karl De la Motte

Radio-Keith-Orpheum — RKO Radio Pictures, Inc.

Thirteen Women

Produced by David O. Selznick
Directed by George Archainbaud
Screenplay by Bartlett Cormack and Samuel Ornitz
From the Novel *Thirteen Women* by Tiffany Thayer
Cinematography: Leo Tover
Music Score: Max Steiner
Art Director: Carroll Clark
Released: September 1932.

Hazel Clay Cousins— Peg Entwistle
Laura Stanhope— Irene Dunne
Police Sgt. Clive— Ricardo Cortez
Jo Turner— Jill Esmond
Ursula Georgi— Myrna Loy
June Raskob— Mary Duncan
Helen Frye— Kay Johnson
Grace Coombs— Florence Eldridge
Swami Yogadachi— C. Henry Gordon
May Raskob— Harriet Hagman
Burns— Edward Pawley
Miss Kirsten— Blanche Friderici
Bobby Stanhope— Wally Albright
Tom Cousins— Ken Thompson
Martha Viborg— Marjorie Gateson
Trapeze Artist— Buster Bartell
Trapeze Artist— Clayton Behee

Trapeze Artist— Eddie DeComa
Trapeze Artist— Eddie Viera
Wire Walker— Teddy Mangean
Chief of Detectives— Edward LeSaint
Detective— Mitchell Harris
Inspector— Lloyd Ingraham
Mike, the Detective— James Donlan
Policeman— Lew Meehan
Policeman— Bob Reeves
Police Chemist— Louis Natheaux
Train Conductor— Lee Phelps
Equestrienne— Aloha Porter
Equestrienne— Audrey Scott
Nan, Bobby's Nanny— Elsie Prescott
Porter— Oscar Smith
Henry, a Butler— Eric Wilton

In bit roles or deleted scenes: Alan Pomeroy, Betty Furness, Phyllis Fraser, Julie Haydon, Violet Seaton, Leon Ames, Cliff Herbert

Chapter Notes

Prologue

1. William Shakespeare, *The Tempest,* Act II, Scene 1, 1610–11.
2. Bette Davis, *The Lonely Life: An Autobiography* (New York: G.P. Putnam's Sons, 1962), 59.
3. Ibid.
4. Ibid.
5. Henrik Ibsen, *The Wild Duck,* Act IV, 1884.
6. Ibid.
7. Davis, *The Lonely Life*, 59.
8. Ibid., 58.
9. Ibid.
10. Ibid., 59.

Act I

1. Sir William Schwenck Gilbert, *An English Girl,* from the opera *Utopia Limited*, 1893.

Chapter 1

1. Entwistle Family History Association, Lancashire, England.
2. Interview with Milton Entwistle, 2008.
3. Ibid.
4. Ibid.
5. Jane Ross Entwistle, diary, January 4, 1913.
6. Jane Ross Entwistle, diary, January 8, 1913.
7. Ibid.
8. Jane Ross Entwistle, diary, April 1913.
9. Interview with Milton Entwistle, 2008.
10. Jane Ross Entwistle, diary, September 6, 1913.
11. Jane Ross Entwistle, diary, September 9, 1913.
12. *New York Times,* September 7, 1914, 12.
13. Lionel Ashcroft, *Movie Studios & Movie Theaters in Marin: A History Since 1898* (San Raphael, CA: Marin County Historical Society, 1998), 21.
14. Frederick D. Ellis, *The Tragedy of the Lusitania* (New York: George W. Berton, 1915), 38–39.
15. Ibid.
16. Entwistle Family Archive, Restaurant Frascati menu, February 26, 1916.
17. James M. Barrie, *The Little Minister* (New York: Grosset and Dunlap, 1898).
18. Jane Ross Entwistle, Diary, March 5, 1916.
19. "An Irish Tragedy at the Garrick," *New York Times,* April 9, 1917, 11.
20. "Stately Jane Ross is Lover of Horses: Beautiful Actress to be Seen in *Hobson's Choice* is Remarkable Horsewoman," *Toronto Sunday World,* October 29, 1916.
21. Ibid.
22. "Otis Skinner Acts in Polite Comedy," *New York Times,* September 17, 1918, 11.
23. Entwistle Family Archive, birthday card for Milton Entwistle, September 27, 1918.

Chapter 2

1. Jane Ross Entwistle, diary, March 20, 1916.
2. Robert Entwistle, Last Will and Testament, December 15, 1922.
3. Interview with Helen Reid, 2008.
4. Interview with Milton Entwistle, 2008.
5. Robert Entwistle, Last Will and Testament, December 15, 1922.
6. Milton Entwistle, Entwistle Family Archive, Easter card, April 1944.
7. Molly McClain, *The Bishop's School: 1909–2000* (San Diego: Journal of San Diego History, 2009), 3.
8. Ibid., 22.
9. Ibid., 18.
10. Interview with Helen Reid, 2008.
11. Ibid.
12. Ibid.
13. Ibid.
14. Matilda Ross, letter to Jane Ross Entwistle, September 20, 1932.
15. Interview with Helen Reid, 2008.

Chapter 3

1. Hope Anderson, *Under the Hollywood Sign,* Hope Anderson Productions, 2009.
2. Hollywoodland pamphlet, S. H. Woodruff & Tracy E. Shultz Co., 1923.
3. Ibid.
4. Ibid.
5. Lynn Simross, "Man Behind the Hollywood Sign," *Los Angeles Times,* January 18, 1977, IV 6.
6. Ibid.
7. Ibid.
8. Interview with Helen Reid, 2008.
9. Hollywood Theater Community School print advertisement, clipping found in Entwistle Family Archive, periodical and date unknown.
10. Charles Entwistle, letter to Jane Entwistle, February 1924.
11. Ibid.
12. Ibid.
13. Ibid.
14. Ibid.
15. Ibid.
16. Ibid.
17. Ibid.
18. Ibid.
19. Ibid.
20. Ibid.
21. Ibid.
22. Ibid.

Act II

1. Walt Whitman, *A Broadway Pageant*, 1860.

Chapter 4

1. Winthrop Ames, *Snow White*, Scene I, 1912.
2. R.K.I., "The Crimson Playgoer: A Home Town Comedy to Remind the City Hicks of Arlstook — Miss Entwistle Crashes the Big Time," *Harvard Crimson*, December 1, 1926, 1.
3. Ibid.
4. Carter Irving, "Boston to Launch Repertory Theater: Common Wealth Encourages New Enterprise by Exempting it from Taxation," *New York Times*, May 17, 1925, SM12.
5. "New Theater to be Civic Affair," *Boston Globe*, May 30, 1925, 11.
6. Winifred Lenihan, "The Novice Gets His Choice," *New York Times*, September 6, 1925, X2.
7. Ibid.
8. Ibid.
9. Ibid.
10. Ibid.
11. William Shakespeare, *Romeo and Juliet*, Act 2, Scene 2, 1591.
12. Interview with Helen Reid, 2008.
13. Ibid.
14. Ibid

Chapter 5

1. Bette Davis, *The Lonely Life: An Autobiography* (New York: G. P. Putnam's Sons, 1962), 59.
2. Richard Brinsley Sheridan, *The Rivals*, Act II, 1775.
3. Winifred Lenihan, "The Novice Gets His Choice," *New York Times*, September 6, 1925, X2.
4. "*The Rivals* Opens Repertory Theater: Gov. and Mrs. Fuller, Duchess of Rutland, In Box — Francis Wilson in role of 'Bob Acres,'" *Boston Globe*, November 11, 1925, 17.
5. "Special Armistice Eve Program and Repertory Theater Play Tonight," *Boston Globe*, November 11, 1925, A12.
6. "Will Sacrifice All For Career: Peg Entwistle Will Give Up Even Love And Marriage to Gain Stage Fame," *Boston Globe*, December 5, 1926, C20.
7. "Miss Yurka Believes in Repertory: An Interview with Miss Blanche Yurka Star of *The Wild Duck* and *Enter Madame*," *Harvard Crimson*, December 16, 1925, 1.
8. "Blanche Yurka Stars in Housewifely Role," *Oxnard Daily Courier*, January 12, 1926, page number unknown.
9. Ibid.
10. Hendrik Ibsen, *The Wild Duck: A Play In Five Acts* (London: Walter Scott, 1905) Act III, 119.
11. Davis, *The Lonely Life*, 58.
12. Ibid., 59.
13. Ibid.
14. Ibid.
15. *This Is Your Life*, NBC Television Network, May 13, 1957.
16. Davis, *The Lonely Life*, 100.
17. Ibid., 108.
18. Al Cohn, "Bette Davis: 'I'm Liberated Because Of Belief in Myself,'" *Newsday* article reprinted in *Salt Lake Tribune*, November 11, 1976, 12E.
19. Ibid.

Chapter 6

1. "Popular Weekly Radio Features Have New Offerings for Fans," *Boston Globe*, December 21, 1925, A6.
2. "Madam Yurka Enters to Applause," *Harvard Crimson*, December 16, 1925, page number unknown.
3. "Fairy Play at Repertory Matinees: *Snow White* for Children Afternoons and *Enter Madam* for Grown-ups Evenings," *Boston Globe*, December 22, 1925, A15.
4. Ibid.
5. "What the Boston Critics Said About Our Production for Children of *Snow White and the 7 Dwarfs*," Boston Repertory playbill published in *Boston Herald*, December 12, 1925, 9.
6. Ibid.
7. "Popular Weekly Radio Features Have New Offerings for Fans," *Boston Globe*, December 21, 1925, A6.
8. "Carol Singers Out Tonight: Elaborate Celebration of Christmas Eve," *Boston Globe*, December 24, 1925, 18.
9. "Peg Entwistle as Snow White," *The Billboard*, January 2, 1926, 7.
10. "Two Plays at the Repertory Theater: Blanche Yurka in *Mrs. Partridge Presents*, *Snow White* at Children's Matinees," *Boston Globe*, December 29, 1925, 17.
11. Ibid.
12. Ibid.
13. Ibid.
14. Ibid.
15. "Miss Yurka Praises Laboratory Theater: Actress Speaks at Meeting of Repertory Club," *Boston Globe*, December 31, 1925, 4.
16. Ibid.
17. Ibid.
18. Interview with Helen Reid, 2009.
19. William Shakespeare, *Much Ado About Nothing*, Act III.
20. "Classic Comedy at the Repertory: Interesting Revival of *Much Ado About Nothing* by Mr. Jewett and His Players," *Boston Globe*, January 1, 1926, 8.
21. Ibid.
22. Ibid.
23. "Will Sacrifice All for Career: Peg Entwistle Will Give up Even Love and Marriage to Gain Stage Fame," *Boston Globe*, December 5, 1926, C20.
24. Ibid.
25. "Loyalties At The Repertory: Galsworthy's Trenchant Drama of Class Prejudice Given Welcome Revival," *Boston Globe*, February 9, 1926, 17.
26. "Will Sacrifice All for Career: Peg Entwistle Will Give up Even Love and Marriage to Gain Stage Fame," *Boston Globe*, December 5, 1926, C20.
27. "The Repertory Muddles Through in a Typically English Fashion, But Shaw and the Audience Suffer," *Harvard Crimson*, March 11, 1926, page number unknown.
28. "*The Circle* at the Repertory: Somerset Maugham's Brightly Told Play Well Acted by the Resident Company," *Boston Globe*, March 30, 1926, A21.
29. "Plays and Films Current and Coming," *Boston Globe*, May 5, 1926, 10.
30. "*The Swan* on Repertory Stage: Molnar's Charming Satirical Romance Given Interesting Revival by Resident Company," *Boston Globe*, May 11, 1926, A25.
31. Ibid.
32. "Ibsen's *Wild Duck* at Repertory: Interesting Revival by Mr. Jewett's Players With Blanche Yurka the Guest Star," *Boston Globe*, December 8, 1925, 9.
33. R.K.I., "The Crimson Playgoer: A Home Town Comedy to Remind the City Hicks of Arlstook — Miss Entwistle Crashes the Big Time," *Harvard Crimson*, December 1, 1926, 1.
34. "Will Sacrifice All For Career: Peg Entwistle Will Give Up Even Love And Marriage to Gain Stage Fame," *Boston Globe*, December 5, 1926, C20.

Chapter 7

1. "Will Sacrifice All For Career: Peg Entwistle Will Give Up Even Love And Marriage to Gain Stage Fame," *Boston Globe*, December 5, 1926, C20.

2. J. Brooks Atkinson, "The Play: Smart Comedy in June," *New York Times*, June 18, 1926, 27.
3. Ibid.
4. Clarence Taylor, "The New Plays on Broadway: *The Man from Toronto*," *The Billboard*, June 26, 1926, 10.
5. Lucy Jeanne Price, "New York Letter," *Fayetteville Democrat*, July 2, 1926, 3.
6. Wood Soanes, "Curtain Calls: Exits and Entrances," *Oakland Tribune*, June 16, 1926, 12.
7. "And Who Is Peg Entwistle," *New York Times*, February 20, 1927, VII4.
8. J. Brooks Atkinson, "Mr. Cohan Fashions a Play," *New York Times*, August 24, 1926, 19.
9. Ibid.
10. Ibid.
11. Ibid.
12. J. Brooks Atkinson, "Mr. Cohan Fashions a Play," *New York Times*, August 24, 1926, 19.
13. Ibid.

Chapter 8

1. R.K.I., "The Crimson Playgoer: A Home Town Comedy to Remind the City Hicks of Arlstook — Miss Entwistle Crashes the Big Time," *Harvard Crimson*, December 1, 1926, 1.
2. "Mr. Tyler Practically Makes a Statement," *New York Times*, August 21, 1927, VII 1.
3. Ibid.
4. "News and Gossip of the Rialto," *New York Times*, November 21, 1926, Section 8, 1.
5. R.K.I., "The Crimson Playgoer: A Home Town Comedy to Remind the City Hicks of Arlstook — Miss Entwistle Crashes the Big Time," *Harvard Crimson*, December 1, 1926, 1.
6. "Will Sacrifice All for Career: Peg Entwistle Will Give up Even Love and Marriage to Gain Stage Fame," *Boston Globe*, December 5, 1926, C20.
7. "An American Comedy," *New York Times*, January 9, 1927, Section 7, 5.
8. Percy Hammond, "A Dexterous, Wholesome and Amusing American Comedy, Well Played at the Gaiety," *New York Herald Tribune*, 11, 1927, 22.
9. "THEATER: New Plays," *Time*, January 24, 1927, 28.
10. Robert Benchley, "Drama: A Big Relief," *Life*, February 17, 1927, 19.
11. "Tommy is Exponent of the Clean Drama: A Wholesome Comedy of American Life Aided by Performance of Sidney Toler as its Hero," *New York Times*, January 11, 1927, 36.
12. Robert Benchley, "Drama: A Big Relief," *Life*, February 17, 1927, 19.
13. "And Who Is Peg Entwistle," *New York Times*, February 20, 1927, VII4.
14. Ibid.
15. "*Tommy* on Redpath Program," *The Gazette*, June 8, 1928, 2.
16. "New Plays Out of Town," *Boston Transcript*, as reprinted in *New York Times*, December 5, 1926, X6.
17. Ibid.
18. Ibid.

Chapter 9

1. "We get along splendidly..." Peg Entwistle, letter to Jane Entwistle, 1927.
2. Peg Entwistle, Divorce Action, Los Angeles Superior Court, April 18, 1929, 2.
3. Peg Entwistle, letter to Jane Entwistle, 1927.
4. "Peg Entwistle Marries After Four Days' Wooing: Actress and Robert Keith Meet on Thursday, Engaged Friday and Wed on Monday," *New York Herald Tribune*, April 19, 1927, 10.
5. Ibid.
6. Peg Entwistle, letter to Jane Entwistle, 1927.
7. Ibid.
8. Ibid.
9. Ibid.
10. Ibid.
11. Ibid.
12. Ibid.
13. Ibid.
14. Ibid.
15. Ibid.
16. Ibid.
17. Ibid.
18. Ibid.
19. Ibid.
20. Ibid.
21. Ibid.
22. J. Brooks Atkinson, "The Play: Chiefly About Money," *New York Times*, April 18, 1927, 18.
23. Peg Entwistle, letter to Jane Entwistle, 1927.
24. Ibid.
25. Ibid.
26. Ibid.
27. Ibid.
28. Ibid.
29. Ibid.
30. Ibid.
31. Ibid.
32. John J. Daly, "In the Playhouse," *Washington Post*, January 6, 1930, 8.
33. Peg Entwistle, letter to Jane Entwistle, 1927.
34. Peg Entwistle, Robert Keith, New York State Marriage Certificate Number 126874, April 18, 1927, 2.
35. Ibid.
36. Ibid.
37. Peg Entwistle, letter to Jane Entwistle, 1927.
38. "Will Sacrifice All For Career: Peg Entwistle Will Give Up Even Love And Marriage to Gain Stage Fame," *Boston Globe*, December 5, 1926, C20.
39. Peg Entwistle, Divorce Action, Los Angeles Superior Court, April 18, 1929, 2.
40. Peg Entwistle, letter to Jane Entwistle, 1927.
41. "Will Sacrifice All For Career: Peg Entwistle Will Give Up Even Love and Marriage to Gain Stage Fame," *Boston Globe*, December 5, 1926, C20.
42. Richard Watts Jr., "*Uninvited Guest* Aims at Comedy, Finds Tragedy," *New York Herald Tribune*, September 28, 1927, 15.
43. "Uninvited Guest Falters: New Play at the Belmont Suffers From Inexpert Writing," *New York Times*, September 28, 1927, 28.
44. Richard Watts Jr., "*Uninvited Guest* Aims at Comedy, Finds Tragedy," *New York Herald Tribune*, September 28, 1927, 15.
45. "*Uninvited Guest* Falters: New Play at the Belmont Suffers From Inexpert Writing," *New York Times*, September 28, 1927, 28.
46. Peg Entwistle, letter to Jane Entwistle, 1927.
47. Ibid.
48. Ibid.
49. Ibid.
50. "*Uninvited Guest* Falters: New Play at the Belmont Suffers From Inexpert Writing," *New York Times*, September 28, 1927, 28.
51. Peg Entwistle, letter to Jane Entwistle, 1927.
52. Ibid.
53. Ibid.
54. Ibid.
55. Ibid.
56. Ibid.

Chapter 10

1. Peg Entwistle letter to Jane Entwistle, 1928.
2. Peg Entwistle, letter to Jane Entwistle, 1927.
3. Peg Entwistle, letter to Jane Entwistle, 1928.
4. Peg Entwistle, letter to Jane Entwistle, 1927.

5. Ibid.
6. Ibid.
7. Ibid.
8. Ibid.
9. Ibid.
10. Ibid.
11. Ibid.
12. Ibid.
13. Ibid.
14. Ibid.
15. Ibid.
16. Ibid.
17. Ibid.
18. Peg Entwistle letter to Jane Entwistle, 1928.
19. Ibid.
20. Ibid
21. Ibid.
22. Ibid.
23. Ibid.
24. Ibid.
25. "Perhaps even somebody else..." "More Christmas Prospects: A Week With Twenty Openings—That Ol' Davil Road," *New York Times*, December 11, 1927, X1.
26. Peg Entwistle letter to Jane Entwistle, 1928.

Chapter 11

1. "Theatrical Notes," *New York Times*, April 19, 1928, 23.
2. Norman Nadel, *A Pictorial History of the Theatre Guild* (New York: Crown, 1969), 5.
3. "Mowbray Noted as Playwright," *Los Angeles Times*, April 25, 1929, A11.
4. Peg Entwistle, letter to Jane Entwistle, 1927.
5. Peg Entwistle, Divorce Action, Los Angeles Superior Court, April 18, 1929, 3.
6. Ibid.
7. Ibid.
8. Alma Whitaker, "Road Not Dead Proves Guild: Colleges Used as Theater on Recent Tour," *Los Angeles Times*, April 21, 1929, C13.
9. Ibid.
10. Ibid.
11. William Kane, "Theater Guild Actress Learns 90 Thousand Words," *Santa Monica Outlook*, April 28, 1929, Section Three, 5.
12. Ibid.
13. "Brooke Judge Gives Lecture: Postponement of Case on Tuesday Brings Fire from Sommerville," *Steubenville Herald-Star*, November 14, 1928, 16.
14. Ibid.
15. Peg Entwistle, Divorce Action, Los Angeles Superior Court, April 18, 1929, 4.
16. Peg Entwistle, Divorce Action, Los Angeles Superior Court, April 18, 1929, 4.
17. Peg Entwistle, Divorce Action, Los Angeles Superior Court, April 18, 1929, 3.
18. "First Time in Albuquerque," *Albuquerque Journal*, March 11, 1929, 12.
19. Marquis Busby, "Shaw at Best in Keen Satire: *Doctor's Dilemma* Stands Test of Time," *Los Angeles Times*, April 16, 1929, Part I, 11.
20. Robert Hutton, "New York Guild Scores Success: Shaw Satire Given Brilliant Performance in Los Angeles," *Santa Monica Outlook*, April 16, 1929, 16.
21. Robert Hutton, "Footlights and Gaslights," *Santa Monica Outlook*, April 21, 1929, Section Three, 3.
22. Florence Lawrence, "Gotham Guild Players Open Here in Shaw Comedy: Performance by Repertory Cast Proves Capable," *Los Angeles Examiner*, April 17, Section III, 6.
23. Ibid.
24. Peg Entwistle, Divorce Action, Los Angeles Superior Court, April 18, 1929, 2.
25. Peg Entwistle, Divorce Action, Los Angeles Superior Court, April 18, 1929, 4.
26. "Stage Folk Air Discord in Romance: Peg Entwistle Say Actor Mate Was Cruel to Her, and Wins Divorce," *Los Angeles Times*, May 3, 1929, A8.
27. "He had No Prompter: Actor Forgets Lines and Marriage Secret Is Out," *Oakland Tribune*, June 4, 1930, 6.
28. Ibid.
29. Ibid.
30. Ibid.

Chapter 12

1. "Will Sacrifice All For Career: Peg Entwistle Will Give Up Even Love And Marriage to Gain Stage Fame," *Boston Globe*, December 5, 1926, C20.
2. Interview with Helen Reid, 2009.
3. Robert Hutton, "*The Second Man* Is Quite Ironical: The New York Theater Guild in New Play at Repertory Is Oscar Wildish," *Santa Monica Outlook*, April 23, 1929, 16.
4. Ibid.
5. Edwin Schallert, "*Second Man* Smart Comedy: Behrman Play Both Human and Ironic," *Los Angeles Times*, April 23, 1929, A11.
6. Florence Lawrence, "Ned McCobb's Daughter Drama of Vivid Contrasts: Sidney Howard Play Ably Given by Gotham Cast," *Los Angeles Examiner*, April 30, 1929, Section III, 6.
7. Ibid.
8. Edwin Schallert, "Guild Company Again Lauded: Excellent Work Distinguishes Ned McCobb's Daughter," *Los Angeles Times*, April 30, 1929, A11.
9. Peg Entwistle, "L. A. Wins Praise as Show Center," *Los Angeles Examiner*, May 6, 1929, Section III, 6.
10. "N. Y. Theater Guild to Play Season in S. F.: English Actress New to Bay Area to Appear in Productions," *Oakland Tribune*, May 5, 1929, A12.
11. Ibid.
12. Marquis Busby, "Drama of Soil at Playhouse: Ervine's *John Ferguson* Staged by Guild," *Los Angeles Times*, May 7, 1929, Part II, 13.
13. St. John G. Ervine, *John Ferguson, A Play in Four Acts*, Act IV, 1915.
14. Marquis Busby, "Drama of Soil at Playhouse: Ervine's *John Ferguson* Staged by Guild," *Los Angeles Times*, May 7, 1929, Part II, 13.
15. Robert Hutton, "Theater Guild's Last Play Given: Declare *John Ferguson* Performance to Be Remarkable," *Santa Monica Outlook*, May 7, 1929, 3.
16. Florence Lawrence, "New York Guild Artists Score in *John Ferguson*: Ervine's Drama Presented with Marked Realism," *Los Angeles Examiner*, May 7, 1929, Section III, 6.
17. Interview with Helen Reid, 2008.
18. Ibid.
19. Peg Entwistle to Mabel Webb, Guest Book page, Heritage Galleries, July 8, 1929.
20. "Pentwistle," Ibid.
21. Ibid.
22. Ibid.
23. Ibid.

Chapter 13

1. Henry Zecher, *William Gillette, America's Sherlock Holmes* (Bloomington, IN: Xlibris, 2011), 16.
2. Charles Higham, *The Adventures of Conan Doyle: The Life of the Creator of Sherlock Holmes* (New York: Norton, 1976), 153, 154.
3. Vincent Starrett, *The Private Life of Sherlock Holmes* (Chicago: University of Chicago Press, 1960), 139.
4. Ibid.
5. *The Return of Sherlock Holmes*, Paramount Pictures, 1929.
6. William Gillette, Sir Arthur Conan Doyle, *Sherlock Holmes*, Act II, Scene II, 1899.

7. "Elementary, My Dear Watson," *New York Times,* November 23, 1929, 20.
8. John J. Daly, "In the Playhouse," *Washington Post,* January 7, 1930, 11.
9. "Lakewood, Maine's Theatrical Center Where Greater and Lesser Lights of Broadway Work and Play During the Summer Months," *Lewiston Daily Sun,* July 18, 1931, 3.
10. "Silence: Tense Melodrama Presented as Second Play of Lakewood Season," *Lewiston Daily Sun,* June 3, 1930, 13.
11. Lakewood Theater playbill, June 23, 1930.
12. Ibid.
13. Ibid.
14. "*Holiday* at Lakewood is Scintillating Comedy," *Lewiston Evening Journal,* July 8, 1930, 6.
15. Ibid.
16. "Lakewood Activities," *Lakewood Theater Magazine,* July 7, 1930, 4.
17. "Famous Drama Stirringly Produced at Lakewood," *Lewiston Evening Journal,* July 15, 1930, 6.
18. E. B. W., "Plutocrat Is Notable Production at Lakewood: Stage Version of Maine Written Novel by Tarkington," *Lewiston Evening Journal,* July 29, 1930, 2.
19. "Let Us Be Gay Smart Comedy, Smartly Played," *Lewiston Evening Journal,* August 5, 1930, 2.

Chapter 14

1. "Will Sacrifice All For Career: Peg Entwistle Will Give Up Even Love and Marriage to Gain Stage Fame," *Boston Globe,* December 5, 1926, C20.
2. Ward Chase, "The New Plays on Broadway: Ritz," *The Billboard,* February 7, 1931, 32.
3. Howard Barnes, "*She Means Business*: Samuel Shipman Play Opens at the Ritz Theater," *New York Herald Tribune,* January 27, 1929, 12.
4. J. Brooks Atkinson, "The Play: Shaw and the Guild," *New York Times,* March 31, 1931, 33.
5. "The Players: No. 4, Peg Entwistle," *Lakewood Theatre Magazine,* June 29, 1931, 5.
6. "Comedy of Bluffs Opens Lakewood: Whispering Friends Pleased the Season's First Night Spectators," *Lewiston Daily Sun,* June 2, 1931, 16.
7. "Can You Guess These?" *Lakewood Theater Magazine,* June 8, 1931, 4.
8. "At Lakewood," *Lewiston Daily Sun,* June 16, 1931, 28.
9. "At Lakewood," *Lewiston Daily Sun,* July 9, 1931, 3.
10. "At Lakewood," *Lewiston Daily Sun,* July 2, 1931, 18.
11. Brooks Atkinson, "Debunking the Gangsters," *New York Times,* September 8, 1931, 39.
12. "Theater: New Plays in Manhattan," *Time,* September 21, 1931, 29.
13. J. Brooks Atkinson, "Little Women Revived," *New York Times,* December 8, 1931, 36.
14. "Theatrical Notes," *New York Times,* January 9, 1932, 21.

Act III

1. Anne Caparn, note to Peg Entwistle, July 1929.

Chapter 15

1. Tennessee Williams, "An Appreciation: Creator of *The Glass Menagerie* Pays Tribute to Laurette Taylor," *New York Times,* December 15, 1946, X4.
2. J. Brooks Atkinson, "The Play: Laurette Taylor Returning to the Stage in Revivals of Two Barrie Plays," *New York Times,* March 8, 1932, 19.
3. Ibid.
4. Ibid.
5. "Drama: Mr. Barrie's New Plays," *New York Tribune,* December 26, 1905, 7.
6. Richard Watts Jr., "A Barrie Revival: Laurette Taylor Appears in Two Plays at the Playhouse," *New York Tribune,* March 8, 1932, 14.
7. J. Brooks Atkinson, "The Play: Laurette Taylor Returning to the Stage in Revivals of Two Barrie Plays," *New York Times,* March 8, 1932, 19.
8. "Two Barrie Revivals Suddenly Canceled: Audience for Laurette Taylor Has Money Refunded, W. A. Brady Declines to Explain," *New York Times,* March 15, 1932, 17.
9. "Barrie Revivals Abruptly Ended: W. A. Brady Says Inability of Laurette Taylor to Appear Terminated Engagement," *New York Times,* April 7, 1932, 29.

Chapter 16

1. Billie Burke, quote attributed on Burke's Internet Movie Database biography.
2. "Happy Outlook Brings Youth, Star Asserts," *Los Angeles Times,* May 29, 1932, B11.
3. Robert Garland, "Cast and Miscast," *New Theater,* May 24, 1932, 6.
4. Florence Lawrence, "Mad Hopes New Triumph for Miss Burke Here," *Los Angeles Examiner,* May 24, 1932, Section I, 9.
5. Edwin Schallert, "Billie Burke Stars in *Mad Hopes* at Belasco," *Los Angeles Times,* May 25, 1932, A9.
6. Interview with Milton Entwistle, 2008.
7. Ibid.
8. Ibid.
9. Interview with Helen Reid, 2008.
10. Alma Whitaker, "Passage of Time Fails to Bother Billie Burke," *Los Angeles Times,* May 22, 1932, B7.
11. Ibid.
12. Charles Richards, RKO Studio memo, May 31, 1932, George Cukor Papers, Academy of Motion Picture Arts and Sciences.
13. Ibid.
14. David O. Selznick, notation on Charles Richards's RKO Studio memo, May 31, 1932, George Cukor Papers, Academy of Motion Picture Arts and Sciences.
15. Billie Burke, *With a Feather on My Nose* (New York: Appleton-Century-Crofts, 1949), 234.
16. David O. Selznick, RKO Studio memo, May 31, 1932, George Cukor Papers, Academy of Motion Picture Arts and Sciences.
17. Interview with Helen Reid, 2008.
18. Ibid.
19. Ibid.

Chapter 17

1. Elizabeth Yeaman, "Guild Asks Consent of II Dulce for Film," *Hollywood Citizen News,* June 7, 1932, Section I, 6.
2. *Thirteen Women,* RKO Radio Pictures, 1932.
3. Ibid.
4. Ibid.
5. Ibid.
6. Ibid.
7. Ibid.
8. *Thirteen Women,* RKO Radio Pictures, Final Script, June 8, 1932, 2, University of California Los Angeles, Performing Arts Special Collections.
9. *Thirteen Women,* RKO Radio Pictures, Shooting Script, July 1932, 7, University of California Los Angeles, Performing Arts Special Collections.
10. *Thirteen Women,* RKO Radio Pictures, 1932.
11. Ibid.
12. Ibid.
13. Ibid.

14. Ibid.
15. Ibid.
16. Ibid.
17. "Book Review Section," *New York Times,* February 28, 1932, 15.
18. Ibid.
19. Jesse Henderson, "Keeping Pace With Hollywood," *Santa Monica Outlook,* August 8, 1932, 7.

Chapter 18

1. Billie Burke, quote attributed by Dictionary.com.
2. Interview with Helen Reid, 2008.
3. Katherine Brown, RKO Studio memo, May 26, 1932, George Cukor Papers, Academy of Motion Picture Arts and Sciences.
4. Cal York, "Cal York's Monthly Broadcast From Hollywood," *Photoplay,* October 1932, 38–39.
5. Interview with Helen Reid, 2008.
6. "Casting Films," *New York Times,* June 12, 1932, X3.

Chapter 19

1. Helen Hayes, quote attributed by HelenHayes.com.
2. *Thirteen Women,* RKO Radio Pictures, 1932.
3. *Thirteen Women,* RKO Radio Pictures, Final Script, June 8, 1932, 2, University of California Los Angeles, Performing Arts Special Collections.
4. Ibid.
5. Ibid.
6. Ibid.
7. Ibid.
8. Ibid.
9. *Thirteen Women,* RKO Radio Pictures, Shooting Script, July 1932, 9, University of California Los Angeles, Performing Arts Special Collections.
10. Ibid.
11. Ibid.
12. Ibid.
13. Ibid.
14. Ibid.
15. Ibid.
16. Ibid.
17. Ibid.
18. Ibid.
19. Ibid.
20. "I can't sleep! Or eat! I hate you!" Ibid.
21. *Thirteen Women,* RKO Radio Pictures, Shooting Script, July 1932, 12, University of California Los Angeles, Performing Arts Special Collections.
22. Ibid.
23. Ibid.
24. Ibid.
25. Ibid.
26. Ibid.
27. Ibid.
28. *Thirteen Women,* RKO Radio Pictures, Shooting Script, July 1932, 17, University of California Los Angeles, Performing Arts Special Collections.
29. Ibid.
30. Ibid.
31. Ibid.
32. Ibid.
33. Ibid.
34. Ibid.
35. Ibid.
36. *Thirteen Women,* RKO Radio Pictures, Daily Production Report, July 14, 1932, University of California Los Angeles, Performing Arts Special Collections.

Chapter 20

1. Mae West, quote Attributed by ThinkExsist.com.
2. Miriam Meredith, *Thirteen Women* Manuscript Synopsis, RKO Scenario Department, January 12, 1932, University of California Los Angeles, Performing Arts Special Collections.
3. Ibid.
4. Gerald Mast, *The Movies in Our Midst: Documents in the Cultural History of Film in America* (Chicago: University of Chicago Press, 1982), 213–214.
5. Ibid.
6. Dorothy B. Cormack, RKO Studios letter to Colonel Jason S. Joy, June 2, 1932, George Cukor Papers, Academy of Motion Picture Arts and Sciences.
7. Colonel Jason S. Joy, letter to David O. Selznick, June 4, 1932, George Cukor Papers, Academy of Motion Picture Arts and Sciences.
8. Lamar Trotti, letter to Will Hays, June 7, 1932, George Cukor Papers, Academy of Motion Picture Arts and Sciences.
9. Dorothy B. Cormack, RKO Studios letter to Colonel Jason S. Joy, June 8, 1932, George Cukor Papers, Academy of Motion Picture Arts and Sciences.
10. Jason S. Joy, letter to David O. Selznick, June 9, 1932, George Cukor Papers, Academy of Motion Picture Arts and Sciences.
11. Ibid.
12. Tiffany Thayer, *Thirteen Women* (New York: C. Kendall, 1932), 179.
13. Jason S. Joy, letter to David O. Selznick, June 9, 1932, George Cukor Papers, Academy of Motion Picture Arts and Sciences.
14. Ibid.
15. Edward J. Montague, letter to Colonel Jason S. Joy, June 10, 1932, George Cukor Papers, Academy of Motion Picture Arts and Sciences.
16. Colonel Jason S. Joy, letter to Will Hays, June 11, 1932, George Cukor Papers, Academy of Motion Picture Arts and Sciences.
17. Edward J. Montague, letter to Colonel Jason S. Joy, June 10, 1932, George Cukor Papers, Academy of Motion Picture Arts and Sciences.
18. Ibid.
19. Colonel Jason S. Joy, letter to David O. Selznick, August 24, 1932, George Cukor Papers, Academy of Motion Picture Arts and Sciences.

Chapter 21

1. Henrik Ibsen, *The Master Builder,* Act III, 1892.
2. Harriet Parsons, "Fan Demand Puts Charlie Farrell into *Tess of Storm Country* with Janet Gaynor: Barbara Stanwyck Given Top Role for Warners Film, *Women in Prison,*" *Los Angeles Examiner,* September 14, 1932, Section I, 9.
3. Harriet Parsons, "Warner Baxter and Bebe Daniels May Get Leads in *42nd Street*: Entire Thatcher Colt Series Mystery Tales Taken Up by Columbia," *Los Angeles Examiner,* September 15, 1932, Section I, 9.
4. "E. J. Montague, Scenario Chief at R-K-O, Dies: Veteran Writer Succumbs After Stroke While Conferring With Officials," *Los Angeles Examiner,* September 16, 1932, Section I, 1.
5. Interview with Helen Reid, 2008.
6. Ibid.
7. Ibid.
8. Ibid.
9. "GIRL LEAPS TO DEATH FROM SIGN: Electric Letter 'H' Scene of Dramatic Suicide," *Los Angeles Times,* September 19, 1932, A1.
10. "Friends Fear Her Role In 'Thirteen Women' Led To Spectacular Coast Suicide of 'Peg' Entwistle: Young Actress Played Murder Victim in Tale of Neuroticism," *Syracuse Herald,* September 25, 1932, Section Three, 10.
11. "GIRL LEAPS TO DEATH FROM SIGN: Electric Letter 'H' Scene of Dramatic Suicide," *Los Angeles Times,* September 19, 1932, A1.
12. "Girl Ends Life in Hollywood Mountain Leap: Pretty Young Woman Jumps to Death From Top

of Letter 'H' of Huge Sign; Initials 'P. E.,'" *Los Angeles Examiner,* September 19, 1932, Section I, 3.
13. Dr. A. F. Wagner, Los Angeles County Coroner's Register, File Number 42884, September 19, 1932.
14. "Suicide Laid to Film Jinx: Uncle Identifies Body of Peg Entwistle," *Los Angeles Times,* September 20, 1932, A1.
15. Ibid., A2.
16 Ibid.
17. "Suicide Beauty Identified as Hollywood Actress: Defeated in Her Film Career, Peg Entwistle Leaps Off Giant Sign," *Los Angeles Evening Herald and Express,* September 19, 1932, A1.
18. Ibid., A4.
19. "Girl Ends Life After Failure in Hollywood: New York Actress Leaps to Death From Electric Sign," *Syracuse Herald,* September 20, 1932, 5.
20. "Actress Death leap Laid to Film Defeat: Spectacular Suicide Comes As Work Fails," *Daily Illustrated News,* September 20, 1932, A1.
21. "Suicide Laid to Film Jinx: Uncle Identifies Body of Peg Entwistle," *Los Angeles Times,* September 20, 1932, A1.
22. Interview with Helen Reid, 2008.

Chapter 22

1. William Gillette, Sir Arthur Conan Doyle, *Sherlock Holmes,* Act IV, 1899.
2. Peg Entwistle, letter to Jane Entwistle, 1928.
3. "Suicide Laid to Film Jinx: Uncle Identifies Body of Peg Entwistle," *Los Angeles Times,* September 20, 1932, A2.
4. "CITY PETS WILL VIE IN CONTEST SUNDAY: Nine Classes of Animals to Be Judged in Speyer Hospital's Annual Convention," *New York Times,* April 26, 1931, 23.

5. Mari, letter to Peg Entwistle, June 6, 1932.
6. Ibid.
7. Ibid.
8. Interview with Helen Reid, 2008.
9. Ibid.
10. Interview with Milton Entwistle, 2008.
11. Interview with Helen Reid, 2008.
12. Ibid.
13. Interview with Helen Reid, 2008.
14. Ibid.
15. Guthrie McClintic, note to Peg Entwistle, August 31, 1932.
16. Hope Anderson, *Under the Hollywood Sign,* Hope Anderson Productions, 2008.
17. Interview with Helen Reid, 2008.
18. Guthrie McClintic, note to Peg Entwistle, August 31, 1932.
19. Peg Entwistle, letter to Jane Entwistle, 1927.

Chapter 23

1. George M. Cohan, quote attributed by ThinkExsist.com.
2. Peg Entwistle, suicide note, September 16, 1932.
3. Interview with Milton Entwistle, 2008
4. Ibid.
5. Ibid.
6. Matilda Ross, letter to Jane Entwistle, September 16, 1932.
7. Matilda Ross, letter to Jane Entwistle, September 22, 1932.
8. State of California Department of Public Health, Standard Death Certificate No. 10501, September 18, 1932.
9. Dr. A. F. Wagner, Los Angeles County Coroner's Register, File Number 42884, September 19, 1932.
10. Ibid.
11. Ibid.
12. State of California Department of Public Health, Standard Death Certificate No. 10501, September 18, 1932; Dr. A. F. Wagner, Los Angeles County Coroner's Register, File No. 42884, September 19, 1932.
13. "Girl Leaps to Death from Sign: Electric Letter 'H' of Hollywoodland Scene of Dramatic Suicide," *Los Angeles Times,* September 19, 1932, A1.
14. Robin Coons, "Hollywood Notebook," *Emporia Daily Gazette,* September 30, 1932, 6.
15. Edward G. Robinson, "Walter Winchell on Broadway," *Logansport Pharos-Tribune,* July 24, 1937, 6.
16. Nelson B. Bell, "The Upswing Begins—Summer Weapons—The Dead That Live," *Washington Post,* July 9, 1933, S4.
17. Ibid.
18. Ibid.
19. "Suicide Beauty Identified as Hollywood Actress: Defeated in Her Film Career, 'Peg' Entwistle Leaps Off Giant Sign," *Los Angeles Evening Herald and Express,* September 19, 1932, A1.
20. Ibid.
21. David Wallace, *Lost Hollywood* (New York: St. Martin's, 2001), 109.
22. Clarke Forbes, "Going La-La With Lynch," *Sunday Herald Sun,* February 3, 2002, 84.
23. Thompton McCamish, "A Bold Type of Guy; On the Spot," *The Age,* May, 19, 2004, Section A3, 2.
24. Pat Morrison, "On the Town: Dial M for Madness," *Los Angeles Times Magazine,* November 13, 1994, 6.

Chapter 24

1. "It is a hopeless..." Charles Dickens, *The Life and Adventures of Nicholas Nickleby* (London: Chapman and Hall, Hablot Knight Browne, and Edward Francis Finden, 1839), Chapter 30.

Bibliography

AFI Catalogue of Feature Films.
The Age.
Albuquerque Journal.
Alton Evening Telegraph.
Anger, Kenneth. *Hollywood Babylon*. San Francisco: Straight Arrow, 1975.
_____. *Hollywood Babylon II*. New York, New York: Penguin Group, 1984.
Anniston Star.
Arcadia Tribune.
Ashcroft, Lionel. *Movie Studios & Movie Theaters in Marin: A History Since 1898*. San Raphael, CA: Marin County Historical Society, 1998.
The Bakersfield Californian.
Banham, Stephen. *Fancy: Typographic Embellishments*. Melbourne, Australia: Letterbox, 2004.
Barrymore, Ethel. *Memories: An Autobiography by Ethel Barrymore*. London, England: Hulton, 1956.
Beachwood Voice.
Behlmer, Rudy. *Memo from David O. Selznick*. New York, New York: Viking, 1972.
Beinecke Playbill Collection, University of Florida.
Beinecke Rare Book and Manuscript Library, Yale University.
Bell, Geoffrey. *The Golden Gate and the Silver Screen*. Cranbury, New Jersey: Associated University Press, 1984.
The Billboard.
Blythville (Arkansas) *Courier News.*
Boston Daily Globe.
Boston Herald.
Boston Tribune.
Braudy, Leo. *The Hollywood Sign: Fantasy and Reality of an American Icon*. New Haven, CT: Yale University Press, 2011.
Bruce Torrance Hollywood Historical Photograph Collection.
Bunson, Matthew. *Encyclopedia Sherlockiana*. New York: Macmillan, 1994.
Burke, Billie. *With a Feather on My Nose*. New York: Appleton-Century-Crofts, 1949.
California Motion Picture Corp Payroll Ledger, October 1914.
The Call Bulletin.
Census of United Kingdom, Bath Row, Birmingham, England, 1891.
Census of United Kingdom, Glamorganshire, Wales, 1901.
Census of United States, New York, NY, 1920.
Certificate of Death, #10501, Peg Entwistle, Los Angeles County Registrar-Recorder
Certificate of Entry of 1908 Birth, Neath, Wales, WCN 062974.
Certificate of Marriage, Peg Entwistle, Robert Keith, #12687, City of New York Department Of Health, April 18, 1927.
Certificate of Marriage, Robert Entwistle, Emily Stevenson, #COL 811405, Warwick County, Birmingham, England, November 3, 1904.
Certificate of Naturalization, Charles Harold Entwistle, #2135098, U.S. District Court, New York, NY, July 25, 1925.
Certificate of Naturalization, Jane Ross Entwistle, #2074157, U.S. District Court, Los Angeles County, July 18, 1924.
Certificate of Record of Marriage, Robert Entwistle, Lauretta Ross, All Saints Episcopal Church.
Charles Young Research Library, University California Los Angeles.
Charleston Daily Mail.
Chillicothe Tribune.
Cook, Doris E. *Catalogue of the William Gillette Exhibit*. Stowe-Day Foundation, 1970.
Corpus Christi Times.
Courtney, Marguerite. *Laurette*. New York: Rinehart, 1955.
Crimson Playgoer.
Davis, Bette. *The Lonely Life: An Autobiography*. New York: G.P. Putnam's Sons, 1962.
_____, and Michael Herskowitz. *This 'n That: Bette Davis*. New York, New York: G.P. Putnam's Sons, 1987.
Eaton, Walter Prichard. *The Theatre Guild the First Ten Years*. New York: Brentano's, 1929.
Edwards, Anne. *Katharine Hepburn: A Remarkable Woman*. New York: St. Martin's Griffin, 1985.
Ellis, Frederick D. *The Tragedy of the Lusitania*. London: George W. Berton, 1915.
Ellis Island Foundation.
Emporia Weekly Gazette.
Evening Tribune.
Fitchburg Sentinel.

Fresno Bee.
The Gazette.
George Cukor Papers, Margaret Herrick Library, Academy of Motion Picture Arts and Sciences.
Gillette, William. *Sherlock Holmes.* New York: E. O. Skelton, 1901 (Playbill).
Grave Registration Index #1481, Peg Entwistle, Oak Hill Cemetery, Cincinnati, Ohio.
Green, Roger Lancelyn. *Fifty Years of Peter Pan.* London: P. Davies, 1954.
Guild Magazine.
Hamilton Daily News.
Hartford Courant.
Harvard Crimson.
Higham, Charles. *The Adventures of Conan Doyle: The Life of the Creator of Sherlock Holmes.* New York: W.W. Norton, 1976.
Hollywood Citizen News.
Hollywood Reporter.
Internet Broadway Database.
Internet Movie Database.
Jefferson City Post-Tribune.
Journal of San Diego History.
Kabatchnik, Amnon. *Sherlock Holmes on the Stage: A Chronological Encyclopedia of Plays Featuring the Great Detective.* Lanham, MD: Scarecrow Press, 2008.
Keith, Gaelyn Whitley. *The Father of Hollywood: The True Story.* El Dorado Hills, CA: BookSurge, 2006.
Kingsport Times.
Lakewood Theater Archives and Playbill Collection.
Leader-Times.
Lewiston Daily Sun.
Lewiston Evening Journal.
Life Magazine.
Logansport Pharos-Tribune.
London Times.
Long Beach Independent.
Long Beach Press Telegram.
Los Angeles County Tax Assessor.
Los Angeles County Coroner.
Los Angeles County Coroner Registration #42884, September 20, 1932.
Los Angeles Examiner.
Los Angeles Police Department.
Los Angeles Police Historical Association.
Los Angeles Public Library Newspaper Archives Database.
Los Angeles Times.
Lowell Sun.
Lowell Sun Radiographs.
Manifest of Passengers, SS *Philadelphia*, 1916.
Mansfield News-Journal.
Mast, Gerald. *The Movies in Our Midst: Documents in the Cultural History of Film in America.* Chicago: University of Chicago Press, 1982.
McClain, Molly. *The Bishop's School: 1909–2000.* San Diego: Journal of San Diego History, 2009.
Mid-week Pictorial.
Milwaukee Journal.
Monitor Index and Democrat.

The Morning Herald.
Nadel, Norman. *A Pictorial History of the Theatre Guild.* New York: Crown, 1969.
New Theater.
New York American.
New York Herald Tribune.
New York Penal Code Sections 80, 82, 1050, 1051, 1142 (Enacted 1909).
New York Public Library, Billy Rose Theater Collection.
New York Times.
New York World.
Newsday.
Oakland Tribune.
Oakland Tribune Daily Magazine.
Oelwein Daily Register.
Ogden Standard Examiner.
Photoplay.
Pictorial Weekly.
Pitt, Leonard, and Dale Pitt. *Los Angeles A to Z: An Encyclopedia of the City and County.* Berkeley: University of California Press, 1997.
Proquest Historical Newspapers Archives.
Reno Gazette.
The Register (Sandusky, Ohio).
RKO Production Reports, *Thirteen Women*, 1932, Charles Young Special Collections, UCLA.
RKO Screen Play, *Thirteen Women*, 1932, Charles Young Special Collections, UCLA.
RKO Shooting Scripts, *Thirteen Women*, 1932, Charles Young Special Collections, UCLA.
RKO Synopsis, *Thirteen Women*, 1932, Charles Young Special Collections, UCLA.
Robert Birchard Collection.
Salt Lake Tribune.
Samuel French Publications.
San Antonio Light.
San Francisco Chronicle.
San Mateo Times.
Sandusky Star-Journal.
Santa Monica Main Library Micro Film Archives.
Santa Monica Outlook.
Saturday Night.
Screen and Radio Weekly.
SilentEra.com.
Stardust: The Bette Davis Story, Turner Home Video, 2006.
Starrett, Vincent. *The Private Life of Sherlock Holmes.* Chicago: University of Chicago Press, 1960.
Sunday Herald Sun.
Sunday Times-Signal.
Superior Court, Los Angeles County, Affidavit of Plaintiff, June 30, 1929.
Superior Court, Los Angeles County, Complaint of Divorce, April 18, 1929.
Superior Court, Los Angeles County, Final Judgment of Divorce, May 6, 1930.
Syracuse Herald.
Thayer, Tiffany. *Thirteen Women.* New York: C. Kendall, 1932.
Theatre Arts Monthly.
Theresa Helburn Theatre Collection.
ThinkExsist.com.

This Is Your Life, NBC Television Network, May 13, 1957.
Thompson, David, *Showman: The Life of David O. Selznick.* New York: Alfred A. Knopf, Inc., 1992.
Time Magazine.
The Times (Chicago).
Titusville Herald.
Toledo News-Bee.
The Toronto Star.
Toronto Sunday World.
Tracy, Jack. *Sherlock Holmes, the Published Apocrypha.* Boston: Houghton Mifflin, 1980.
Under the Hollywood Sign, Hope Anderson Productions, 2009.
Variety.
Vogue.
Wall Street Journal.
Wallace, David. *Lost Hollywood.* New York: St. Martin's Press, 2001.
Washington Post.
WBZ Radio Logs.
Woodland Daily Democrat.
Yurka, Blanche. *Bohemian Girl; Blanche Yurka's Theatrical Life.* Athens: Ohio University Press, 1970.
Zanesville Signal.
Zecher, Henry. *William Gillette, America's Sherlock Holmes.* Bloomington, IN: Xlibris, 2011.

Index

Numbers in ***bold italics*** indicate pages with photographs.

Abbott, George 139, 224
Abbott and Costello 47
Abie's Irish Rose 132
abortion 100–103, 121–122, 124, 135–136, 177
Academy Award 133, 161, 164, 202; *see also* Oscar
Academy of Motion Picture Arts and Sciences 3, 166, 171, 231–232, 236
Actors' Equity 17, 28, 30, 56, 115, 128, 134, 137–138, 149
Adair, Jean 133, 222
Adams, Lowden 110, 219
Adams, Maude 4, 22, 30, 56, 59, 77, 79, 109, 143, 211, 217
Adler, Felix 47
The Adventures of Robin Hood 209
AFI 182, 235; *see also* American Film Institute
After I'm Gone 204
Ah! Sweet Mystery of Life 13
Albright, Hardie 220–222, 133, 187
Albright, Wally 162, 226
Alcott, Louisa 141
Alexander, Ross 71, 73, 214–217
Alibi 82
Alice Sit-by-the-Fire 147–***148***, 153, 163, 189, 209, 211, 225
Allen, Frank G. 133
Allen, Viola 57
Allworth, Frank 94, 96
Ambassador Theater 142
American Film Institute 22, 182; *see also* AFI
American Theater (venue) 24
An American Tragedy 81
Ames, Winthrop 56, 61, 67, 71, 228; *see also* White, Jessie Braham
Anastasia 56
Anderson, Hope 8, 43, 45, 193, 227, 233, 237
Andre, Gwili 167
Andrews, Julie 14
Anger, Kenneth 203–204, 235
Anything Goes 57
Arbuckle, Roscoe "Fatty" 176, 205
Archainbaud, George 164, 226

Arliss, George 30
Arms and the Man 109
Arsenic and Old Lace 133
Arthur, Robert 13
As the World Turns 142
Ashcroft, Lionel 22, 227
Astaire, Fred 207
Atkinson, Brooks 82, 86, 95, 135, 141–142, 147–148, 229, 231
Auld Lang Syne 36
Autry, Gene 206

Baer, Arthur 87
Bagnold, Enid Algerine 106
Bainter, Fay 106–107
Baker, Helen 49
Balchen, Bernt 189
Banham, Stephen 204, 235
Bannister, Albert 80, 218
Barker, Granville 15, 61
The Barretts of Wimpole Street 193
Barrie, James 20, 22, 24, 77, 79, 109, 147, ***148***, 202, 217, 225, 227
Barrie Revivals 147, 148–149, 151–153, 225, 231
Barry, Philip 132, 220
Barrymore, Ethel 17, 22, 28, 31, 37, 40, 64–65, 110, 143, 147, 213, 235
Barrymore, John 14, 22, 67, 152, 157
Barrymore, Lionel 131, 152
Baumann, Charles O. 25
Beach, Albert 44
Beachwood Canyon 13, 38, 43–45, 46–47, 126, 155, 206
Beachwood Drive 40–41, 42–45, 47–48, 50, 106, 158, 165, 183
Beacon Hill 62, 72–73, 214
The Beautiful Adventure (film) 26
The Beautiful Adventure (play) 20–21, 22
Beery, Wallace 152
Beetle Juice 62
The Beggar of Cawnpore 25
Behlmer, Rudy 165, 235
Behrman, S.N. 109, 120, 230
Belasco, David 28, 51, 56, 80, 110, 192
Belasco, Edward 151–153, 155, 225

Belasco Theater (Broadway) 28, 192
Belasco Theater (Los Angeles) 152–154, 156, 158, 192, 231
Bel Geddes, Norman 138
Bell, Nelson 202
Belmont Theater 99, 218
Benchley, Robert 86–87, 139, 229
Ben-Hur 43
Bennett, Belle 22
Bennett, Constance 191
Benton, Captain James 122
Benton, Jay 58
Bergman, Ingrid 211
Berkeley, Busby 47
Bernard, Bruno 203
Bernhardt, Sarah 49, 110
Best Supporting Actress 27, 62
The Better Half 27
Beverly Hills Community Players 196
Beverly Hills Community Playhouse 196
Beverly Hills Playhouse 197
Bickford, Charles 28
A Bill of Divorcement 156–157, 162, 165, 167, 192
The Billboard 31, 73, 80–81, 114, 134, 228–229, 231, 235
Biltmore Theater 51, 115
Birchard, Robert 22, 236
The Black Bird 142
Blau, Bela 151, 154–157, 189, 190–192, 208, 211, 225
Blondell, Joan 156
The Blue Angel 181
The Bob Cummings Show 134
Bogart, Humphrey 4, 87, 93, 137, 139–141, 151–156, 208, 224, 226
La Bohème 57
Bolton, Guy 56
Booth, Edwin 14
Booth, John Wilkes 14
Booth, Shirley 138
Boston Blackie 82
Boston Globe 25, 66, 71–73, 75–77, 134, 228–231, 235
Boston Herald 72, 228, 235
Boston Opera House 57
Boston Repertory 4, 9, 56–59, 62–64, 66–68, 69, 71–74, 76–

239

240 Index

78, 81, 83–84, 86, 89, 93, 157, 194, 210, 213, 228
Bow, Clara 126, 167
Brady, Alice 27–28, 189
Brady, William A. 27, 141–143, 146–147, 148–149, 153, 225, 231
Brady, William, Jr. 141
Brahms, Johannes 164
Braudy, Leo 199–200, 235
Brent, Romney 67, 134–*136*, 151–152, 154–157, 190, 222, 225
Broken Dishes 133, 222
Brook, Clive 128
Brothers 115
Brothers Grimm 71
Brown, Katherine 166, 232
Browning, Robert 49
Browning, Tod 139
Bruning, Albert 40
Bruno, Anthony 194, 203
Bryn Mawr 3, 38, 108
Buckler, Hugh 135–*136*, 222
Bunce, Alan 86, 209, 211, 218
Burke, Billie 4, 14, 22, 30–31, 143, 151–158, 165, 168, 186–187, 190, 193, 201, 208–209, 211, 225–226, 231–232, 235
Burn Hollywood Burn 204
Burnett, Carol 160
Busby, Marquis 117, 123, 230
Butler, William 56
A Butterfly on the Wheel 17–19, 132, 220
Byrne, Dolly 71, 214
Byron, Arthur 138, 187, 221
Byron, Walter 152

Cabot, Susan 205
Caesar and Cleopatra 76, 216
Cagney, James 81, 134, 209
Caldwell, Neal 110, 120–121, 124, 219
Calhern, Louis 59
California Motion Picture Corporation (CMPC) 21
Campbell, Kane 86
Campbell, Mrs. Patrick 14, 59
Caparn, Anne 125–126, 145, 231
Capone, Al 141
Capra, Frank 19, 133
Captain Brassbound's Conversion 76
The Captive 87, 178
Carmen 57
Carrillo, Leo 87
Carter-Waddell, Joan 126
Casablanca 164
Castle, Irene 1
Castle, Vernon 1
Catching Peg Entwistle 205
censorship 176–177, 160, 180–181; *see also* Padlock Law
Cerf, Bennett 163
Cerf, Phyllis 163, 166
Chan, Charlie 86
Chandler, Harry 45, 48
Chandler, Helen 67
Chandu the Magician 176
Chaplin, Charlie 47–48, 129

The Charge of the Light Brigade 162
Chase, Ward 134, 231
Chatterton, Ruth 30, 79–80
Child of Manhattan 149
The Chrysler Hour 156
The Circle 76, 217, 228
Cisco Kid 87
Claire, Ina 30
Clark, Carroll 163, 226
Clark, E.P. 45
Clark, Marguerite 72
Clay, Lewis 179
Coburn, Charles 133, 140, 221, 224
Coburn, Ivah 133, 140, 221, 224
Code 177–179, 181–182; *see also* Motion Picture Production Code; Pre-Code; Production Code
Cohan, George M. 59, 81–83, 85, 89, 106, 137–138, 140, 196, 218, 223, 229, 233
Cohn, Al 70, 228
Command Decision 140
Conan Doyle, Arthur 127–128, 219, 230, 233, 236
Connelly, Jennifer 161
The Constant Nymph 85
Conti, Giulia 71
Coogan, Jackie 139
Cooksey, Curtiss 80, 218
Coolidge, Pres. Calvin 56–57, 59, 128, 177
Coolidge, Grace 57
Coons, Robbin 201–202, 233
Cooper, Alice 206
Cooper, Gary 167, 202
Copley Theater (Toy Theater) 57
The Copperhead 131
Coquelin, Benoit Constant 49
Cormack, Bartlett 159, 178, 226
Cormack, Dorothy 178, 232
Cornell, Constance 52, 54
Cornell, Katharine 193
Cortez, Ricardo 159, 161–162, 226
The Cortinas 205
Cortis, Ernest 142
Cortis, Louise 142
Cossart, Ernest 135, 222
The Count of Monte Cristo 24
Courtney, Marguerite 146, 235
Craig, Lucretia 191; *see also* Crete
Craig's Wife 138, 223
Crawford, Broderick 203
Crawford, Cheryl 108
Crawford, Joan 167, 203, 211
Crescent Sign Company 48
Crete 191–192; *see also* Craig, Lucretia
Crews, Laura Hope 61–62
Cromwell, James 162
Crothers, Rachel 133, 221
Crouse, Russell 85
Cukor, George 3, 156–157, 165–166, 190–191, 231–232, 236
Cummings, Bob 134, 222
Curran, Homer 151–156, 193, 225
Cyrano de Bergerac 49, 59

Dalton, Charles **148**
Dalwood, Dexter 205
Daly, John J. 130, 229, 231
Dark Rosaleen 28, 110
Davies, Marion 27
Davis, Bette 4, 9–10, 59, 64, 67–68, 69–70, 74, 133, 152, 156, 162, 168, 204, 207, 209, 211, 227–228, 235
Davis, Police Chief James E. 122
Davis, Owen 138–140, 141, 224
Davis, Owen, Jr. 138, 223–225
Davis, Ruthie 9, 69
The Day the Earth Stood Still 164
Dead End 62
de Forest, Marian 225, 141
de Havilland, Olivia 211
Delario, Jon 46
Dell, Floyd 132, 220
Del Rio, Dolores 167
DeMille, Cecil B. 43, 184
DeMille, Constance 184
Dennis the Menace 137
The Devil and Miss Jones 133
Devol, Dr. Ed 149
Diaz, Raphaelo 57
Dickens, Charles 210, 233
Dietrich, Marlene 181, 211
Dinner at Eight 14, 131, 152
Dinner Is Served 124, 153
Disney, Walt 72, 96, 167
The Divorcée 28, 37
The Doctor 132
The Doctor's Dilemma 109, 112–113, 115, 117, 219
A Doll's House 67
Dracula 67
Dreiser, Theodore 81
Dressler, Marie 152
Drew, John 14, 22, 30, 40, 74
Duchess of Rutland 65, 228
Dudley, Marjorie 179
Duncan, Mary 159–160, 170–171, **180**, 226
Dunn, Emma 62, 65–66, 77, 89, 157, 210, 213–214
Dunne, Irene 159, 161–163, 165, 167, **180**, 182, 210, 226
Durante, Jimmy 159
Duse, Eleanora 110, 151

E! Mysteries and Scandals 204
Earl Carroll's Vanities 160
An Early Frost 62
Edge of Night 142
The Education of Elizabeth 31
Edward VII (His Majesty) 15, 129
Edwards, Anne 165
Edwards, Payson 110, 219
Edwards, Ralph 69
El Capitan Theater 186
Eldridge, Florence 162, **180**, 226
Electra 59
Elizabeth Sleeps Out 131
Elliott, William 82, 218
Ellis Island 20, 198, 235
Eltinge, Julian 89
Eltinge Theater 89–90
Empire All Star Corporation 26

Index

The Enchanted April 86
Enders, Loretta 101
An Enemy of the People 67
Enter Madam 67, 71–73, 214, 228
Entertainment Weekly 205
Entwistle, Bobby 4, 30, *36*, *125*, 209
Entwistle, Charles (Enty; Harold; Uncle Charlie; Uncle Charles) 13–14, *15*–18, 22–26, 27–28, 30–31, 34–35, *36*, 38, 40, 41–42, 43, 49, 52–53, 54, 56, 59, 62–63, 74, 81–82, 94–95, 97, 102, 105, *125*–126, 135, 155, 158, 162, 183, 185–187, 188–191, 194–198, 209, 227, 235
Entwistle, Emily 12, 14–15, 32, 35, 198; *see also* Stevenson, Emily
Entwistle, Ernest 23
Entwistle, Geraldine 209
Entwistle, Henry 23–24
Entwistle, Jane (Aunt Jane; Jane Ross) 4, *19*, 28, 30, 34–35, *36*, *125*, 155, 203, 227, 229–230, 233
Entwistle, Lauretta Ross 18, *21*–22, 24–26, 28–30, 32–35, 37–38, 52, 60, 102, 235
Entwistle, Lillian 23
Entwistle, Milton 4, 8, 13–14, 16, 26, 30, 32, 34–35, *36*–38, 41, 43, 45, 49, 52, 53, 60, *125*, 155, 184, 186, 191–192, 196, 199, 209–210, 227, 231, 233
Entwistle, Peg 4, *27*, *39*, *51*, *53*, *60*, *69*, *88*, *109*, *116*, *121*, *125*, *130*, *136*, *141*, *148*, *166*, *180*, *194*, *207*
Entwistle, Robert *13*
Entwistle, Rosina 15, 23
Entwistle, Vivienne 23–24
Erlanger, A.L. 51, 89, 219
Ervine, St. John 109, 123, 219, 230
Escape 133, 221
Esmond, Jill 162, 165, 176, 226
Esquire Theater 59
Evans, Brandon 110, 121, 124, 219
Evening Herald and Express 203, 233

Fairbanks, Doug, Jr. 47, 207
Fairbanks, Douglas 47
Family Affair 96
Fancy 204, 235
Farmer, Michael 126
Faster, Pussycat! Kill! Kill! 205
Father Knows Best 208
Faust 57, 109
Ferber, Edna 76, 216
Field, Sylvia 73, 137, 139–140, 141, 223–225
Fields, W.C. 48
Fiesta 209
Figueroa Playhouse 115, 120–121, 122
Fine, Howard 161
Fiske, Minnie Maddern 30, 56
Fitzgerald, F. Scott 139
The Five Frankfurters 19, 20, 134
Flavin, Martin 133, 222
Flynn, Errol 162, 209
The Fog 93
Fonda, Henry 210

Fontanne, Lynn 98, 109, 113
Forbes, Clark 204, 233
Ford, John 132
Forrest, Brian 205
The Forsyte Saga 133
Forty-Ninth Street Theater 95
Foster, Lewis 167
Fox Films (studios) 176
Fraser, Phyllis *166*, 183, 188, 226
Fraser, Winifred 25, 87
Frazee, Harry Herbert 29
Freel, Aleta 71
Frohman, Charles 14–15, 16, 18–19, 20, 22, 24, 26–27, 31, 133, 147
Frohman, Daniel 133
Fuller, Mrs. Alvan 56, 65, 74, 228
Furness, Betty 163, *166*–167, 226

Gable, Clark 162, 209
Gaiety Theater 86, 89, 218, 229
Gallagher, Skeets 138
Galsworthy, John 76, 133, 215, 221, 228
Gamble, Warburton 67, 110, 115, 117, 124, 219
Garbo, Greta 211
Gardiner, William T. 133, 137
Garland, Robert 154, 231
Garrick Theater 24, 61, 227
Gateson, Marjorie 160, 170–171, 174, *180*, 226
Geisel, Ted 163
Gentlemen Prefer Blondes 81
George V, King 15
Gershwin, George 57, 87
Getting Married 67, 134–135, *136*–137, 139, 222
Ghosts 67
Gibbons, Cedric 167
Gilbert, John 1
Gilbert, W.S. 11
Gillette, Francis 127
Gillette, William 22, 56, 59, 126–129, *130*, 132, 146, 148, 211, 219–220, 230, 233, 235–237
Gilmore, Frank 56, 149
Girl Crazy 57
Gish, Dorothy 59, 135–*136*, 222
Gish, Lillian 135
Glass, Carter 146
The Glass Menagerie 146, 163, 231
Gleason, James 115
Goff, Thomas 48
Golden, Eve 1, 132, 204
Gone with the Wind 132, 160, 164
Goodnight September 205
Goodrich, Arthur 140, 221, 224
Goodrich, Frances 80, 84, 131–133, 137, 162, 187, 220–222
Gordon, C. Henry 160, 162, 174, 226
Gordon, Ruth 73, 106–107, 189
Graham, Rendell 23
Grand Theater and Opera House 13
Grant, Cary 132–133, 142
Grasshopper 24
Grauman, Sid 43
The Great Gatsby 139
The Great God Brown 92, 138

Great White Way 51, 59, 79, 90, 92–103, 156, 193
Green Grow the Lilacs (*Oklahoma!*) 108
The Green Hat 132
The Green Years 133
Greenberg, Adrian Adolph 151, 154, 225
Gressing, Marion 27, 33–35
Grounds for Divorce 56
The Guardsman 109
Guild (periodical) 31, 236

Hackett, Albert 80, 84, 131–133, 137, 162, 222
Hagman, Harriet 160–161, *166*, 170–171, *180*, 183, 226
Half an Hour 20
Hamlet 14, 49, 67, 213
Hammett, Dashiell 162
Hammond, Percy 86, 229
Hampden, Burford 129, 220
Hampden, Walter 14, 22, 30, 34, 36–37, 40, 49, 52, 59–60, 62–63, 74, 89, 95, 105, 111, 126, 128, 138, 187, 194, 213
Hampden's Theater 65, 79, 213
Hampton, Grayce 187, 226
Hanna, Betty 130
Harlow, Jean 7, 152
Harrigan, William 138, 223
Harris, Julie 146
Harte, Bret 21
The Harvard Crimson 57, 71, 76, 78, 84, 86, 228–229, 235–236
Have a Heart 57
Haven, Harry *125*
Hawthorne, Ruth 71, 215
Haydon, Julie 163, *166*, 226
Hayek, Salma 161
Hayes, Helen 170, 232
Hays, Will 175, 177–179, *180*–182, 232
Hays Office 177–179, 181–182; *see also* Motion Picture Producers and Distributors of America (MPPDA)
Hazel Flagg 132
Heald, Roff *202*
Hearst, William Randolph 27, 87
Heartbreak House 76, 216
Heartland 210
Hedda Gabler 67
Hefner, Hugh 206
Helburn, Theresa 3, 98, 101, 108, 109–111, 114, 124, 135, 136, 195, 219, 236
Hemingway, Ernest 139
Henderson, Jessie 164, 232
Hendricks, Beatrice 110, 112–113, 117, 124, 218–219
Henry Jewett Players 57, 62, 70–71, 77–78, 228
Henry V 59
Hepburn, Audrey 14
Hepburn, Katharine 132, 151, 157, 165–166, 209, 235
Herbert, Victor 13
Heston, Charlton 43

Hicks, Seymour 13
His Majesty's Theater, London 15
Hitchcock, Alfred 142
Hobson's Choice 16–17, 25, 227
Holiday 132, 220, 231
Hollywood Babylon 203, 235
Hollywood Babylon II 235
Hollywood Citizen News 153, 156, 231, 236
Hollywood Playhouse 153
Hollywood Reporter 236
Hollywood sign 1, 3, 7–8, 10, 42–43, 45–**46**, 164, 185, 193–194, 199–202, 203–206, 207–208, 227, 233, 237
The Hollywood Sign: Fantasy and Reality of an American Icon 199, 235
Hollywood Sign Girl 3, 5, 7, 188, 205, 207
Hollywood Sign Girls 204
Hollywood Studio Club 183–184, 187, 192–193
"Hollywood Suicide" (song) 205
Hollywood Theater Community School (HTCS) 52–53, 60, 227
Hollywoodland (company) 45, 47–48, 206, 227
Hollywoodland (sign) 7, 44–**46**, 47–49, 125, 184–186, 195, 199–**202**, 203–207, 233
Hollywoodland (town) 8, 43–44, 47, 126, 183–184, 198, 200–201, 206, 208
Hollywood's Diamond Jubilee 207
"Holy Ghost Revival" (song) 205
The Home Towners 81–86, 106, 218
Hooker, Elisabeth Daggett 127
Hooker, Reverend Thomas 127
Hoover, Herbert 129–130
Hoover, Lou Henry 129
Hope, Bob 209
Hopkins, Miriam 81–83, 106–107
Houghton, Stanley 20
Houseman, Laurence 61
Howard, J.B. 13
Howard, Leslie 131
Howard, Sidney 109, 121, 219, 230
Hudson, Rochelle **166**–167
Hudson Theater 82, 218
Humpty Dumpty 26
Hurlbut, Gladys 137, 139–140, 223–225
Hush! 25, 192
Hutchens, John 31, 148
Hutton, Robert 117, 120, 123, 230

Ibsen, Henrik 9, 51, 67–68, 69, 77, 98, 214, 227–228, 232
Icebound 139
In Old Chicago 27
In the Hollow of Her Hand 27
The Informer 164
Insult 197
Internet Movie Database (IMDb) 3, 182, 231, 236
Irving, Carter 58, 228
Irving, Henry 13

Irwinn, Carlotta 73, 215
It's a Wonderful Life 19, 132, 134

Janney, William 86, **88**, 90, 218
Jannings, Emil 181
Jeopardy! 204
Jewett, Frances 56–58, 65, 74
Jewett, Henry 9, 56–59, 60, 62–65, 67–68, 70–71, 73–78, 89, 157, 194, 213–217, 228
John Ferguson 109, 112, 123, 219, 230
John Gilbert: The Last of the Silent Film Stars 1
Johnson, Ben 86, 218
Johnson, Bishop Joseph 38
Johnson, Kay 162, **180**, 226
Jolivet, Rita 22
Jorulesco, Jonel 72
The Journal of San Diego History 38, 227, 236
Journey in the Dark 133
Journey to the Center of the Earth 164
Joy, Jason 177–**180**, 181, 232
Judy 93
Julius Caesar 15
Just Married 132
Just to Remind You 7, 139–**141**, 224

Katharine Hepburn: A Remarkable Woman 165, 235
Kaufman, George S. 76, 139, 216
Kay-Bee Pictures 25
Keith, Brian 96, 111, 210
Keith, Daisy 210
Keith, Ian 67
Keith, Robert 4, 8, 91, 93–99, 101, 103–104, 108–109, 111, 113, **116**, **121**–122, 124, 129, 135, 137–138, 140, 187, 195, 201, 208, 210, 219, 229, 235
Kelly, George 138, 223
Kelly, Grace 138
Kelly, Paul 139–140, 141, 224–225
Kelly, P.J. 110, 124, 219
Kennedy, Madge 30
Kennedy, Margaret 85
Kennedy, Mary 71, 215
Kenton, Edna 108
Kern, Jerome 57
Kerr, Alvin 191
The Killers 139
King Kong 161, 167
Kitty Foyle 209
Klaw, Marcus 89
Kothe, Albert 206, 44

La Bohème 57
Lady Be Good 57
Lady Frederick 28
Lagoon 205
Lakewood Players 84, 131, 137–138, 140, 152, 155, 220, 223
Lakewood Theater 3, 131, 133, 137–138, 193, 220, 223, 231, 236
Landis, Jessie Royce 141–142, 225
Lane, Tamar 178
Lang, Fritz 93

Langer, Lawrence 108
Larimore, Earl 109
The Laugh Parade 155
Laughton, Charles 209
Laurel and Hardy 47
Laurette 146, 235
Lawrence, Florence 117, 123, 154, 186, 230–231
Lawrence, Gertrude 189
Lawrence, T.E. 12
LeMaire, Rufus 168
Lenihan, Winifred 61–64, 66, 228
Leslie, Lawrence 110, **121**, 124, 219
Let Us Be Gay 133, 221, 231
Let's Get Married 132
Lewiston Daily Sun 131, 139, 231, 236
Life Begins 168
Life Magazine 86–87, 229, 236
Life with Father 59
Lillie, Beatrice 7
Lincoln, Abraham 14, 90
Lindsay, Howard 84–85, 131, 133, 138, 218, 220
Little Accident 132, 138, 220
The Little Minister 24, 77, 217, 227
Little Theater 25
Little Women (film) 209
Little Women (play) 141–142, 147, 225, 231
Lloyd, Harold 47
Lobero Theater 153
Lombard, Carole 27, 122
Long Day's Journey into Night 162
Loos, Anita 81
Los Angeles Herald Examiner 117, 122, 183, 185–186, 230–233, 236
Los Angeles Herald-Express 152
Los Angeles Times 45, 48, 112, 117, 120, 122–124, 153–154, 156, 175–176, 186, 205, 227, 230–233, 236
Lost Hollywood 204, 233, 237
Louise, Anita 165
Love 'Em and Leave 'Em 139, 224
Love of Life 142
Loy, Myrna 159, 161, 174, **180**, 182, 226
Lugosi, Bela 176
Lunt, Alfred 98, 109
Lusitania 22–24, 227, 235
Lusk, Norbert 176
Luxford, Nola 197
Lyceum Theater 19–20, 22, 26
Lyric Theater 22

Macbeth 30, 49
MacGregor, Edgar 151–152, 154, 225
The Machine-wreckers 57
Mack, Bill 205
Mackaye, Dorothy 140
The Mad Hopes 151–158, 165, 168, 190–191, 193, 201, 208–209, 211, 225, 231
The Mad Hopes (*No Money to Guide Her*) 151–158, 165, 168,

Index

190–191, 193, 201, 208–209, 211, 225, 231
Mahler, Gustav 164
The Maltese Falcon 141
The Man from Toronto (Perkins) 79–81, 83, 110, 218, 229
Mann, Louis 74
Mannering, Mary 56
Manners, John Hartley 31, 146
March, Fredric 162
Marco Millions 109
Marilyn Manson (band) 205
Mario, Queena 57
Marion, Francis 25
Marlowe, Julia 59, 74
Mars Attacks! 62
Marsh, Daniel 56
Marshall, Irby 135–**136**, 222
"Mary C. Brown and the Hollywood Sign" (song) 205
Mason, Bill 75
Mason, Reginald 135–**136**, 222
Masquers Club 36, 115
Massinger, Philip 49
The Master Builder 67, 183, 232
Mathis, June 28
Maude, Cyril 74
Maugham, W. Somerset 28, 76, 217, 228
Maxwell, Edwin 110, 113, 219
Mayer, Louis B. 43
McClain, Dr. Molly 38, 227, 236
McClintic, Guthrie 192–194, 195, 233
McComb, Marshall 118
McCourt, James 205
McCrea, Joel 62
McFadden Construction Company 41–42
McGillicuddy, Harold 99
McGrath, Paul 110, 219
McGuire, P.J. 114
McOwen, Bernard 99, 218
McWade, Robert 82, 218
Meehan, John 82, 218
Meek, Donald 133, 222
Meeker, Eleanor 93
Meeker, George 93
MEMO from David O. Selznick 165, 235
Memorial Open Air Theater 51
Menken, Helen 87, 93
Mercer, Beryl 202
The Merchant of Venice 49
Meredith, Miriam 176, 232
Merrill, E.B. 138
Metro Pictures 28
Metropolis 93
Metropolitan Opera House 151
Meyer, Josephine A. 108
MGM 21, 151, 177, 209
Michelena, Beatriz 21–22, 191
Michelena, Fernando 21
Michelena, Vera 191
A Midsummer Night's Dream 51
Millay, Edna St. Vincent 149
Milne, A.A. 132
Minick 76, 216
Mister Roberts 210

Mr. Smith Goes to Washington 167
Mitchell, Thomas 132, 220
Moeller, Philip 61, 108–109, 110, 112–113, 117, 134, 219, 222
Molnar, Ferenez 77, 217, 228
Monmouth, Geoffrey 12
Monroe, Marilyn 81, 184
Monsieur Beaucaire 25
Montagne, Edward J. 178–180, 181, 183, 187
Moore, Mabel 14, 22, 59, 64, 74
The More the Merrier 133
Morgan, Claudia 142
Morgan, Frank 21, 93, 141
Morosco Theater 51, 151
Morris, Chester 82, 218
Morrison, Pat 205, 233
Mother Mary of the Eucharist 48
Motion Picture Herald 177
Motion Picture Producers and Distributors of America (MPPDA) 177; see also Hays Office
Motion Picture Production Code 175; see also Code; Pre-Code; Production Code
Mt. Lee 200
Mowbray, Alan 100, 110, **116**, 120–121, 124, 153, 186–187, 191, 219, 230
Mrs. Partridge Presents 71, 73, 215, 228
Mrs. Wiggs of the Cabbage Patch 22
Much Ado About Nothing 74, 77, 215, 228
Muir, Gavin 71, 79, 218
Mulholland Drive 204
Mulvaney, Joseph 100
Murray, Douglas 79, 218
Mutiny on the Bounty 209
My Lady Friends (*No, No, Nanette*) 29
My Man Godfrey 27

Nagel, Conrad 168
Nagel, Terese Rose 98
Nance, Frank A. 186, 201
The Nation 108
National Theater, New York City 49, 95
National Theater, Washington, D.C. 129
National Velvet 106
Nebraska Film Company 23
Ned McCobb's Daughter 109, 112–113, 115, 121–122, 219, 230
Negri, Pola 47
New Amsterdam Theater 85, 128
New Theater 228, 231, 236
A New Way to Pay Old Debts 49
New York American 100, 236
New York Herald Tribune (*Herald Tribune*) 86, 93–94, 99, 134, 229, 231, 236
New York Newsday 236
New York Telegraph 99
New York Theater Guild 4, 7, 26, 31, 37, 59–60, 61–64, 98, 101,

104, 108–109, 110–116, 117, 119–121, 122–125, 129, 134–136, 137, 148, 152, 163, 168, 189, 195, 204, 208, 210, 219, 222, 230–231, 235
New York Times 7, 19–20, 22, 24, 26–27, 30–31, 58, 61, 80, 82, 85–87, 89, 90, 95, 100, 113, 141–142, 147, 153, 155, 168, 175, 219, 227–233, 236
Nichols, Ann 132
Nichols, Malcolm 56
North, Wilfred 197
North by Northwest 142
Novarro, Ramon 43
Now, Voyager 164
Nurmi, Maila 205

Oakie, Jack 13
O'Connell, William Henry 56
Of Human Bondage 70
The Old Lady Shows Her Medals 147, 202–203, 225
Oliver, H.P. 205
Olivier, Laurence 59, 162
One for All 142
One Man's Woman 80
101-Bison 23
O'Neill, Eugene 51, 59, 92, 109, 124, 138
Original Sinning 195
Ornitz, Samuel 159, 226
Orpheum Theater 51
Oscar 27, 62, 70, 80–82, 131–134, 139, 159, 161–164, 167; see also Academy Award
Othello 49
The Other Kind of Love 93
Our Gang 162
"Over There" (song) 81

Padlock Law 87, 178; see also censorship
Pantages Theater 52
Paramount Pictures (Studios) 27, 156, 230
The Parent Trap 96
Park Theater 86
Parker, Dorothy 139
Pasadena Community Players 196
Pasadena Playhouse 196
Patrick, Lee 141, 225
Pavlova, Anna 32
Pawley, Ed 162, 174, 210, 226
Payne, Iden 24
Peck, Gregory 207
"Peg Entwistle, Are You Listening?" (song) 205
Pemberton, Brock 195
The Perfect Alibi 132
Perils of Pauline 16
Peter Pan (*The Great White Father*) 20, 22–23, 29, 147, 236
Peter the Hermit 43, 47, 206
Peters, Charles Rollo 108
Peters, Rollo 108
Peterson, Raiden 206–207
The Petrified Forest 152
Philadelphia (ship) 19, 23–24, 236
The Philadelphia Story 132, 139

Phillips, Mary 137, 139–140, 155, 224
Photoplay 60, 168–169, 232, 236
Pied Piper Malone 210
Pitt, Brad 161
Plan 9 from Outer Space 205
Playboy 206
Playhouse Theater 141, 147, 225
The Plutocrat 132, 221, 231
Pocahontas 86
Police Gazette 139
Porgy 109
Porter, Cole 57
Post, Eleanor **166**–167
Powell, William 27, 162
Pre-Code 159, 178; *see also* Code; Motion Picture Production Code; Production Code
Previn, Dory 205
Price, Jeanne 80, 229
Price, Lucy 175, 177
Production Code 175, 177; *see also* Code; Motion Picture Production Code; Pre-Code
Prunella 61–62, 64
Pulcinella 32
Pygmalion (*My Fair Lady*) 14

Queen Mary 15–16
Quigley, Jack 110, 219
Quigley, Martin 177
Quinn, Jeff 131

Radio-Keith-Orpheum Studios (RKO) 3–4, 20, 139, 156–160, 162, 164–168, 169, 171, 174–176, 178–179, 180–182, 187–194, 196–197, 202, 211, 226, 231–232, 236
Rains, Claude 109
Rambova, Natacha 94, 105, 187
Rappe, Virginia 176
Rathbone, Basil 87
Rayae, Leonard 13
Raymond, Ray 139–141
Rebel Without a Cause 167
Rebound 139, 223
Reed, Florence 28, 37
Rees, Charlie 36–37, 50, **125**
Reid, Helen 4, 8, 35, 40, 42, 63, 74, 106, **125**, 157, 165, 168, 171, 183, 185, 187, 191–192, 194, 197, 199, 210, 227–228, 230–233
Rennie, Hugh 110
Rice, Alice Hegan 22
Rich, Irene 122
Richards, Charles 156, 225, 231
Riggs, Lynn 108
The Ring and the Book 49
The Ring of Truth 49
Rip Van Winkle 66–67, 71, 214
Ripley's Believe it or Not! 204
Risdon, Elisabeth 26, 109–110, 112, 115–**116**, 117, 120–**121**, 124–125, 219
The Rivals 57, 65–66, 77, 213, 228
Robertson, Forbes 30
Robinson, Bert 84–85, 218
Robinson, Corrine Roosevelt 128

Robinson, Edward G. 201–202, 204, 223
Robinson, Mary 96
Robson, May 52
Roche, John 48
Rockefeller, John D. 35, 56, 59
Rockstrom, Carl 72
Rockwell, Norman 33
Roeder, Ralph 135, 222
Rogers, Saul 177
Rolling Stone 205
Romeo and Juliet 49, 61, 228
Rongetti, Amenti 101
Roos, Joanna 141–142, 225
Roosevelt, Franklin Delano 82, 114
Roosevelt, Teddy 96, 128
Roseleigh, Jack 80
Ross, Betsy 20
Ross, Charles 18
Ross, Harold 126
Ross, Helen 18
Ross, John 16
Ross, Lois 18
Ross, Marguerite 18
Ross, Matilda 16, 32, 37–38, 40, 49–50, 53–54, 60, 97, 102, 105, 111, **125**, 165, 197, 210, 227, 233
Ross, Milton H. 50, **125**
Rostand, Edmond 49
Rothschilds 19
Rowley, Billie 23
Royal Alexandra Theater 25
Royle, Selena 138
Russell, Lillian 30
Ruth, Babe 29, 87

Sad Words to Gay Music 191
St. Agnes Academy 26, 28
St. Francis Hotel 22, 176
Salomy Jane 21–22
Salomy Jane's Kiss 21
Sands, Dorothy 31
Saroyan, William 163
Satana, Tura 205
Schaefer, Matthew T. 129
Schallert, Edwin 120, 122, 154, 230–231
Schmitt, George 20
The School for Scandal 40, 65
Scott, Agnes 75, 214–217
Scripps, Ellen Browning 38
Seabrook, Gay 90, 99
Seaton, Laura 15, 18, 23
Sebastian, Henry 161
The Second Man 109, 112–113, 120–**121**, 219, 230
Segal, George 142
Select Pictures Corporation 27
Selwyn, Arch 80
Selwyn, Edgar 80
Selwyn Theater 79–80, 218
Selznick, David O. 4, 27, 156–157, 162, 164–166, 168, 175, 178–180, 181, 188–190, 226, 231–232, 235, 237
Selznick, Lewis J. 177
Senese, Ralph 205
Sennett, Mack 47

Serena Blandish 106, 189
The Servant in the House 49
Shakespeare, William 9, 13–14, 15, 32, 50, 56–57, 61, 64–65, 74–75, 98, 142, 213, 215, 227–228
Shaw, George Bernard 14, 51, 59, 67, 75–76, 98, 109, 113, 115, 134–136, 137, 216, 219, 222, 228, 230–231
Shaw, Montague **130**
Shaw, Sandra **166**–167
She Means Business 134, 189, 222, 231
Shearer, Norma 165, 209
Sheridan, Richard Brinsley 40, 57, 64–65, 98, 213, 228
Sherlock Holmes 126–130, 131, 134, 143, 148, 188, 211, 219–220, 230, 233, 236–237
Sherman, Moses Hazeltine 45
She's My Weakness 211
Shipman, Helen 210
Shipman, Helena 96–97, 210
Shipman, Samuel 134, 222, 231
Shoults, Tracey E. 45
Show Boat 162
Shubert, J.J. 17, 19, 25, 95, 132
Shubert, Lee 17–19, 25, 82, 95, 132
Sidney, Sylvia 61–62, 64
Siegel, Bugsy 47
Simmons, L.M. 100, 218
Simonson, Lee 108, 219
Since You Went Away 164
Sinclair, Hugh 135–**136**, 222
Sisk, Robert 113
Skinner, Otis 26, 128, 227
Slike, Lauretta 41, 106
Smith, Alfred 33, 87
Smith, Queenie 93
Snow White (character) 56, 72–74, 77, 142, 214–215, 228
Snow White (play) 56, 63, 67, 71–72, 215–228
So This Is London 140, 224
"Some Day My Prince Will Come" (song) 72
Somerville, Judge J.B. 114
Son of Satan 85
Sothern, E.H. 59, 74
The Sound of Music 85
Sousa, John Phillip 128
Soutter, Edward 118
Sovey, Raymond 113, 219
The Stage 82
Stage Door 139
Stagecoach 132
Stahl, John M. 28
Standing, Wyndham 187
Stand-ins 204
Stanwyck, Barbara 211, 232
Stapleton, Maureen 146
Stardust: The Bette Davis Story 168, 204, 236
State of the Union 85
Steiner, Max 164, 226
Steubenville Herald 114, 230
Stevenson, Caroline 12

Index

Stevenson, Emily 12, 14–16, 32, 35, 198, 235; *see also* Entwistle, Emily
Stevenson, John 12
Stewart, Bradley 205
Stewart, Donald Ogden 139, 223
Stewart, Jimmy 88, 132, 134
Stirling, Oscar 135, 222
Stone, Lucy 95–96
Strange Interlude 109, 113, 124–125
Stravinsky, Igor 32
Studio Relations Committee (SRC) 177, 179
Sturges, Preston 149
suicide 1, 3, 4, 7, 138, 163, 167, 171, 182, 184–186, 188–189, 197–201, 203–205, 207–208, 210, 232–233
The Summer Girl 25
Summer Wishes, Winter Dreams 62
The Sun 205
The Surrender 23
The Swan 77, 217, 228
Swanson, Gloria 47–48, 126
Sweet FA 205
Swett, Herbert L. 155, 192, 211, 220, 223

Talmadge, Constance 27
Talmadge, Norma 47
The Taming of the Shrew 49
Tandy, Jessica 146
Tarkington, Booth 25, 128, 133, 221
Taylor, Clarence 80, 229
Taylor, Laurette 31–32, 76, 110, 138, 143, 146–*148*, 149–150, 152, 211, 225, 231
Taylor, Ruth 76, 216–217
Templeton, Fay 30
The Ten Commandments 43
Terry, Ellen 22, 30, 147
Thalberg, Irving 177
Theatre Arts Monthly 31, 148, 236
Theatre Magazine 31, 231
Theatre World 31
The Thin Man 162
Thirteen Women (book) 158–160, 176, 226, 232, 236
Thirteen Women (film) 4, 157–159, 161–166, 170–171, 174, 176, 178–*180*, 181–183, 188–189, 192, 203, 205, 210–211, 226, 231–232, 236
The Thirteenth Chair 139, 223
This Is Your Life 69, 204, 228, 237
Thomas, Augustus 131
Thomas, Dylan 12
Thompson, Harold 167
Thompson, Ken 171, 174, 181, 226
Three on a Match 151
Tierney, Dorothy 118–119, 187, 195, 201, 210
The Tightwad 93, 95
Tilden, Bill 138

The Time of Your Life 163
Toler, Sidney 86, *88*–90, 187, 218, 229
Toller, Ernst 57
Tommy (*Tommy Helps Himself*) 78, 84, *88*–91, 93, 95–96, 98–99, 101, 110, 125, 127, 131, 148, 189, 209, 211, 218, 229
Too Fat to Fight 26
Tover, Leo 164, 226
Toy Theater 57
Travers, Henry 19, 109, 134–135, *136*, 222
Treasure Island 209
Tree, Henry 15
The Triumph of X 93
Trosper, Fred 184
The Truth Be Told 205
Turner, Lana 167
Twain, Mark 127
Twilight Zone 210
Two Against the World 191
Tyler, George C. 85–86, 89–90, 99, 127–128, 218–219, 229

Under the Hollywood Sign 8, 45–46, 193, 227, 233, 237
The Uninvited Guest 99–100, 104, 218, 229
Universal Pictures (Studios) 23, 70
Urban, Joseph 151, 225

Valentino, Rudolph 48, 69, 94–95, 105, 162, 187, 210
Varesi, Elena 71
Varesi, Gilda 67, 71
Variety 90, 237
Vaudeville 25, 51, 110, 112, 143
Veiller, Anthony 139
Veiller, Bayard 139, 223
Vincent, George 56
Vitagraph Studios 139
Vogue 31, 60, 237
Volpone 109

Walcamp, Marie 138
Wald, Jerry 126
Walker, June 81
Wallace, David 204, 233, 237
Warfield, David 51, 56
Warner, H.B. 25
Warner Brothers (Warner-First National) 152, 156, 161, 165, 168, 232
Warren, James 87
The Warrior's Husband 151
Washington Post 96, 130, 202, 229, 231, 233, 237
The Wasp Woman 205
Watson, Robert Leroy 201
Watts, Richard 99, 229, 231
Wayfaring at Waverly in Silver Lake 205
Wayne, John 207
WBZ Radio 66, 71–72, 213–214, 237

Weaver, John 139, 224
Webb, Clifton 126
Webb, Mabel "Ma" 126, 230
Welch, Raquel 207
Welles, Orson 127
Wertheim, Maurice 108
West, Mae 31, 87, 176, 209, 232
Western Union Please 133, 222
Westley, Helen 108, 134–*136*, 222
Weyerman, W.F. 122
Whispering Friends 137–138, 223, 231
Whitaker, Alama 112, 230–231
White, Jessie Braham 72; *see also* Ames, Winthrop
White Heat 134
Whitley, Hobart 48, 236
Whitman, Slim 62
Whitman, Walt 55, 227
The Wild Duck 9–10, 67–69, 71–72, 74–75, 77, 214, 227–228
Wilhelm, Kaiser 23
Williams, Andy 206
Williams, Esther 209
Williams, Gesner 117–118
Williams, Tennessee 146, 163, 231
Wilson, Dorothy *166*–167
Wilson, Francis 65, 213–214, 228
Wilson, Woodrow 23
Winchell, Walter 201, 233
The Wind and the Lion 96
Winter, Dale 118–119
Winwood, Estelle 25, 192
The Witching Hour 131
With a Feather on My Nose 156, 231, 235
The Wizard of Oz 14, 21, 151, 154
The Woman Under Oath 28, 37
Wood, Natalie 167
Woodruff, Sidney H. 45, 227
World Telegram 154
Wupperman, Carlos 93
Wuthering Heights 209
Wyatt, Jane 208
Wycherly, Margaret 134, *136*, 139, 222–223
Wyndham, Frederick 13
Wynn, Ed 155

Yankee Doodle Dandy 81
You Won't Be So Pretty 141
Young, Brigham 18
Young, Loretta 167–168
Young, Rida 13
Young, Robert 208
The Younger Generation 19–21
Yurka, Blanche 9–10, 59, 62, 65, 67–68, 70–71, 73–74, 76–78, 89, 214–215, 228, 237

Zecher, Henry 127–128, 230, 237
Ziegfeld, Florenz 31, 139, 141, 152, 156, 162, 187, 190
Ziegfeld Theater 151
Zimbalist, Efrem 32
Zukor, Adolph 27